CHILTON'S
REPAIR & TUNE-UP GUIDE
DATSUN/NISSAN F10, 310, STANZA, PULSAR 1976-86

All U.S. and Canadian models of F10 • 310 • Stanza • Pulsar

President LAWRENCE A. FORNASIERI
Vice President and General Manager JOHN P. KUSHNERICK
Editor-in-Chief KERRY A. FREEMAN, S.A.E.
Senior Editor RICHARD J. RIVELE, S.A.E.
Editor RICHARD T. SMITH

CHILTON BOOK COMPANY
Radnor, Pennsylvania
19089

SAFETY NOTICE

Proper service and repair procedures are vital to the safe, reliable operation of all motor vehicles, as well as the personal safety of those performing repairs. This book outlines procedures for servicing and repairing vehicles using safe, effective methods. The procedures contain many NOTES, CAUTIONS and WARNINGS which should be followed along with standard safety procedures to eliminate the possibility of personal injury or improper service which could damage the vehicle or compromise its safety.

It is important to note that repair procedures and techniques, tools and parts for servicing motor vehicles, as well as the skill and experience of the individual performing the work vary widely. It is not possible to anticipate all of the conceivable ways or conditions under which vehicles may be serviced, or to provide cautions as to all of the possible hazards that may result. Standard and accepted safety precautions and equipment should be used when handling toxic or flammable fluids, safety goggles or other protection should be used during cutting, grinding, chiseling, prying, or any other process that can cause material removal or projectiles.

Some procedures require the use of tools specially designed for a specific purpose. Before substituting another tool or procedure, you must be completely satisfied that neither your personal safety, nor the performance of the vehicle will be endangered.

Although information in this guide is based on industry sources and is as complete as possible at the time of publication, the possibility exists that the manufacturer made later changes which could not be included here. While striving for total accuracy. Chilton Book Company cannot assume responsibility for any errors, changes, or omissions that may occur in the compilation of this data.

PART NUMBERS

Part numbers listed in this reference are not recommendations by Chilton for any product by brand name. They are references that can be used with interchange manuals and aftermarket supplier catalogs to locate each brand supplier's discrete part number.

SPECIAL TOOLS

Special tools are recommended by the vehicle manufacturer to perform their specific job. Use has been kept to a miminum, but where absolutely necessary, they are referred to in the text by the part number of the tool manufacturer. Datsun special tools referred to in this guide are available through Kent-Moore Corporation, 29784 Little Mack, Roseville, Michigan 48066. For Canada, contact Kent-Moore of Canada, LTD., 2395 Cawthra Mississauga, Ontario, Canada L5A 3Ps., or an equivalent tool can be purchased locally from a tool supplier or parts outlet.

ACKNOWLEDGMENTS

The Chilton Book Company Epresses its appreciation to the Nissan Motor Corporation in the U.S.A., Carson, California 90248 for their generous assistance.

Copyright © 1986 by Chilton Book Company
All Rights Reserved
Published in Radnor, Pennsylvania 19089 by Chilton Book Company

Manufactured in the United States of America
   567890   543210987

Chilton's Repair & Tune-Up Guide: Datsun/Nissan F-10, 310, Stanza, Pulsar 1976–86
ISBN 0-8019-7660-X pbk.
Library of Congress Catalog Card No. 85-47961

7.50

CONTENTS

Quick Reference Specifications For Your Vehicle

Fill in this chart with the most commonly used specifications for your vehicle. Specifications can be found in Chapters 1 through 3 or on the tune-up decal under the hood of the vehicle.

Tune-Up

Firing Order_____

Spark Plugs:

    Type_____

    Gap (in.)_____

Torque (ft. lbs.)_____

Idle Speed (rpm)_____

Ignition Timing (°)_____

    Vacuum or Electronic Advance (Connected/Disconnected)_____

Valve Clearance (in.)

    Intake_____   Exhaust_____

Capacities

Engine Oil Type (API Rating)_____

    With Filter Change (qts)_____

    Without Filter Change (qts)_____

Cooling System (qts)_____

Manual Transmission (pts)_____

    Type_____

Automatic Transmission (pts)_____

    Type_____

Front Differential (pts)_____

    Type_____

Rear Differential (pts)_____

    Type_____

Transfer Case (pts)_____

    Type_____

FREQUENTLY REPLACED PARTS

Use these spaces to record the part numbers of frequently replaced parts.

PCV VALVE	OIL FILTER	AIR FILTER	FUEL FILTER
Type_____	Type_____	Type_____	Type_____
Part No._____	Part No._____	Part No._____	Part No._____

General Information and Maintenance

1

HOW TO USE THIS BOOK

This book is structured in ten easy to follow chapters, using as little mechanic's jargon as possible and highlighting important procedures with scores of illustrations. Everything from engine rebuilding to replacing your radiator cap is covered. Of course, even the best mechanic won't attempt a repair without the proper tools. That's why an operation like rebuilding your transaxle is not included here–they require a range of special tools which are too expensive to be useful to the average shadetree mechanic.

Before tangling with any repairs, read through the entire section and make sure you have the time, tools and replacement parts necessary. This will save you the frustration of running down to the bus stop Monday morning because you forgot a widget or a what-cha-ma-call-it while making repairs on a Sunday afternoon.

Each section begins with a brief description of the particular system and a smattering of the theory behind it. When repairs involve a high level of technical know-how, we tell you how to remove the part and replace it with a new or overhauled unit. In this way you can shave dollars off your regular labor costs.

A few basic mechanic's rules should be mentioned here. First, whenever the left side of the vehicle is referred to, it means the driver's side of the car. The right side is the passenger's side. Second, most screws, nuts and bolts are removed by turning them counterclockwise or tightened by turning clockwise. Never crawl under a car supported only by a floor or bumper jack–use support stands! Never smoke or position an exposed flame near a battery or any part of the fuel system. Common sense is your best safeguard against injury.

TOOLS AND EQUIPMENT

The following list contains the basic tools needed to perform most of the procedures described in this guide. Your vehicle is built with metric screws and bolts; if you don't have a set of metric wrenches–buy them. Standard wrenches are either too loose or too tight a fit on metric fasteners.

1. Metric sockets, also a $^{13}/_{16}$ in. spark plug socket. If possible, buy various length socket drive extensions. One break in this department is that the metric sockets, available in the US, will all fit the ratchet handles and extensions you may already have ($^{1}/_{4}$, $^{3}/_{8}$ and $^{1}/_{2}$ in. drive).

2. Set of metric combination (one end open and one box) wrenches.

3. Spark plug wire gauge.

4. Flat feeler gauge for breaker points and valve lash checking.

5. Slot and phillips heads screwdrivers.

6. Timing light, preferably a DC battery hook-up type.

7. Dwell/tachometer.

8. Oil can with a filler spout.

9. Oil filter strap wrench; makes removal of a tight filter much simpler. Never use to install filter.

10. Pair of channel lock pliers (always handy to have).

11. Two sturdy jackstands–cinder blocks, bricks and other makeshift supports are just not safe.

In addition to these basic tools, there are several other tools and gauges you may find useful. These include:

1. A compression gauge. The screw-in type is slower to use but eliminates the possibility of a faulty reading due to escaping pressure.

2. A manifold vacuum gauge.

3. A test light.

4. An induction meter. This is used for determining whether or not there is current in a wire. These are handy for use if a wire is broken somewhere in a wiring harness.

As a final note, you will probably find a torque wrench necessary for all but the most basic work. The beam type models are perfectly adequate, although the newer click type are more precise.

NOTE: *Special tools referred to in this guide are available through Kent-Moore Corporation, 29784 Little Mack, Roseville, Michigan 48066. For Canada, contact Kent-Moore of Canada, Ltd., 2395 Cawthra Mississauga, Ontario, Canada L5A 3P2.*

SERVICING YOUR CAR SAFELY

It is virtually impossible to anticipate all of the hazards involved with automotive maintenance and service, but care and common sense will prevent most accidents.

The rules of safety for mechanics range from "don't smoke around gasoline," to "use the proper tool(s) for the job." The trick to avoiding injuries is to develop safe work habits and take every possible precaution.

Do's

• Do keep a fire extinguisher and first aid kit within easy reach.

• Do wear safety glasses or goggles when cutting, drilling, grinding or prying, even if you have 20-20 vision. If you wear glasses for the sake of vision, they should be made of hardened glass that can serve also as safety glasses or wear safety goggles over your regular glasses.

• Do shield your eyes whenever you work around the battery. Batteries contain sulphuric acid. In case of contact with the eyes or skin, flush the area with water or a mixture of water/baking soda and get medical attention immediately.

• Do use safety stands for any undercar service. Jacks are for raising vehicles; safety stands are for making sure the vehicle stays raised until you want to come down. Whenever the car is raised, block the wheels remaining on the ground and set the parking brake.

• Do use adequate ventilation when working with any chemicals or hazardous materials. Like carbon monoxide, the asbestos dust resulting from break lining wear can be poisonous in sufficient quantities.

• Do disconnect the negative battery cable when working on the electrical system. The

Always use jackstands or ramps when working under your car

secondary ignition system can contain up to 40,000 volts.

• Do follow manufacturer's directions whenever working with potentially hazardous materials. Both brake fluid and antifreeze are poisonous if taken internally.

• Do properly maintain your tools. Loose hammerheads, mushroomed punches and chisels, frayed or poorly grounded electrical cords, excessively worn screwdrivers, spread wrenches (open end), cracked sockets, slipping ratchets or faulty droplight sockets can cause accidents.

• Do use the proper size and type of tool for the job being done.

• Do, when possible, pull on a wrench handle rather than push on it and adjust your stance to prevent a fall.

• Do be sure the adjustable wrenches are tightly closed on the nut or bolt and pulled so that the face is on the side of the fixed jaw.

• Do select a wrench or socket that fits the nut or bolt. The wrench or socket should sit straight, not cocked.

• Do strike squarely with a hammer; avoid glancing blows.

• Do set the parking brake and block the drive wheels if the work requires the engine running.

Don'ts

• Don't run an engine in a garage or anywhere else without proper ventilation—EVER! Carbon monoxide is poisonous; it takes a long time to leave the human body and you can build up a deadly supply of it in your system by simply breathing in a little every day. You may not realize you are slowly poisoning yourself. Always use power vents, windows, fans or open the garage doors.

• Don't work around moving parts while wearing a necktie or other loose clothing. Short sleeves are much safer than long, loose sleeves; hard-toed shoes with neoprene soles protect your toes and give a better grip on slippery surfaces. Jewelry such as watches, fancy belt buckles, beads or body adornment of any kind is not safe working around a car. Long hair should be hidden under a hat or cap.

• Don't use pockets for toolboxes. A fall or bump can drive a screwdriver deep into your body. Even a wiping cloth hanging from the back pocket can wrap around a spinning shaft or fan.

• Don't smoke when working around gasoline, cleaning solvent or other flammable material.

• Don't smoke when working around the battery. When the battery is being charged, it gives off explosive hydrogen gas.

• Don't use gasoline to wash your hands; there are excellent soaps available. Gasoline may contain lead, which can enter the body through a cut, accumulating in the body until you are very ill. Gasoline also removes all the natural oils from the skin so that bone dry hands will suck up oil and grease.

• Don't service the air conditioning system unless you are equipped with the necessary tools and training. The refrigerant (R-12) is under pressure; when released into the air, it will instantly freeze any surface it contacts, including your eyes. Although the refrigerant is normally non-toxic, R-12 becomes a deadly poisonous gas in the presence of an open flame. One good whiff of the vapors from burning refrigerant can be fatal.

HISTORY

In 1976, Datsun introduced the F10 model, equipped with an A14 engine. In 1979, the vehicle was changed to a 310 model, still equipped with the A14 engine. In 1981, the 310 model became equipped with an A15 engine, which is 5.0 cu. in., larger than the A14 engine. In 1982, the 310 model A15 engine was converted from the conventional point-type distributor to an electronic design; the newly converted engine is known as the E15 engine.

In 1982, Datsun Corporation merged with Nissan Corporation to become known as the Datsun/Nissan Corporation; in 1984, the Datsun name was dropped and the new company emerged as Nissan Corporation. The newly formed 1982 company dropped the 310 model and emerged with a newly designed Stanza model, which is equipped with a much larger CA20 engine. In 1984, the Stanza engine was redesigned into the CA20E (Electronic Fuel Injection) engine; the Canadian version is known as the CA20S engine and is still carbureted.

In 1983, a new sport model was introduced; known as the Pulsar, it uses an E16 carbureted engine, which is larger than the E15 engine. Only during 1984, did Nissan introduce into Canada the E15ET (EFI) engine, which is the Turbo-charged version of the E15 engine.

SERIAL NUMBER IDENTIFICATION

Chassis

The chassis serial number is stamped into the right-side of the firewall. The model designation, such as 310, precedes the serial number. The chassis number is also located on a dashboard plate which is visible through the left-side of the windshield.

Vehicle Identification Plate

The vehicle identification plate is attached to the right-side of the firewall. This plate gives the vehicle type, identification number, model, body color code, trim color code, engine model

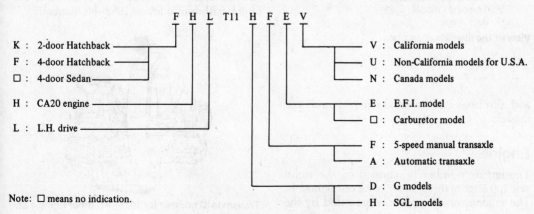

```
              F  H  L  T11  H  F  E  V
```

K : 2-door Hatchback
F : 4-door Hatchback
☐ : 4-door Sedan

H : CA20 engine

L : L.H. drive

V : California models
U : Non-California models for U.S.A.
N : Canada models

E : E.F.I. model
☐ : Carburetor model

F : 5-speed manual transaxle
A : Automatic transaxle

D : G models
H : SGL models

Note: ☐ means no indication.

Description of the vehicle identification number

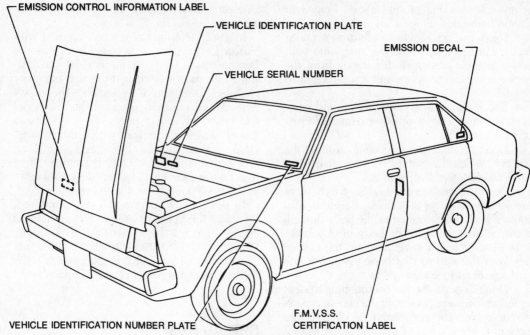

EMISSION CONTROL INFORMATION LABEL

VEHICLE IDENTIFICATION PLATE

EMISSION DECAL

VEHICLE SERIAL NUMBER

VEHICLE IDENTIFICATION NUMBER PLATE

F.M.V.S.S.
CERTIFICATION LABEL

Locations of various identification plates

View of the identification plate

1. Type
2. Vehicle identification number
   (chassis number)
3. Model
4. Body color code
5. Trim color code
6. Engine model
7. Engine displacement
8. Transaxle model
9. Axle model

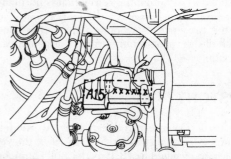

Engine ID number for 1976–81, other models are similar

Transaxle

The transaxle number is stamped on the front upper face of the transaxle case (1976–81 manual and 1982–86 automatic) or attached to the clutch withdrawal lever (1982–86 manual).

Transaxle ID number for 1976–81, other models are similar

and displacement, transaxle model and axle model.

Engine

The engine number is stamped on the right-side top edge of the cylinder block on all models. The engine serial number is preceded by the engine model code.

ROUTINE MAINTENANCE

Air Cleaner

All vehicles covered in this guide are equipped with a disposable paper cartridge air cleaner element. At every tune–up or sooner, if the car is operated in a dusty area, remove the housing cover and withdraw the element. Check the element. Replace the filter if it is extremely dirty. Loose dust can sometimes be removed by striking the filter against a hard surface several times or by blowing through it with compressed air. The filter should be replaced every 30,000 miles or 24 months. Before installing either the original or a replacement filter, wipe out the inside of the air cleaner housing with a clean rag or paper towel. Install the paper air cleaner filter, seat the top cover on the bottom housing and tighten the cover.

NOTE: *The Stanza (1984 and later) and the Pulsar (1984 Turbo), use flat-rectangular cartridge type air cleaner elements, which have the word "UP" printed on them; be sure the side with "UP" on it, faces upward.*

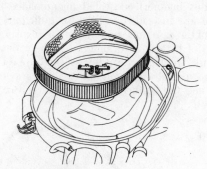

Air filter replacement

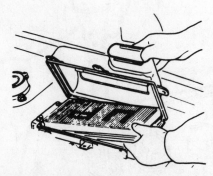

Replacing the air filter; Stanza (1984 and later) and Pulsar (1984 Turbo)

Air Induction Valve Filter

This filter is located in the air cleaner, both fuel injected and carburetor models. To replace it, remove the screws and the valve filter case.

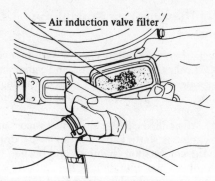

Air induction valve filter replacement

Install the new filter, paying attention to which direction the valve is facing so that exhaust gases will not flow backwards through the system.

Positive Crankcase Ventilation (PCV) Valve

This valve feeds crankcase blow-by gases into the intake manifold to be burned with the normal air/fuel mixture. The PCV valve should be replaced every 24,000 miles. Make sure that all PCV connections are tight. Check that the connecting hoses are clear and not clogged. Replace any brittle or broken hoses.

To replace the valve, which is located in the intake manifold directly below the carburetor:

1. Squeeze the hose clamp with pliers and remove the hose.

2. Using a wrench, unscrew the PCV valve and remove the valve.

3. Disconnect the ventilation hoses and flush with solvent.

4. Install the new PCV valve, then replace the hoses and clamp.

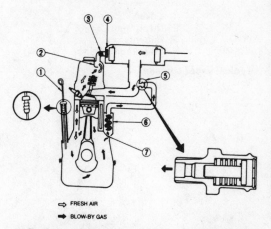

⇨ FRESH AIR
➡ BLOW-BY GAS

1. Seal type oil level gauge
2. Baffle plate
3. Flame arrester
4. Filter
5. P.C.V. valve
6. Steel net
7. Baffle plate

Typical PCV system

Fuel Evaporative Emissions System

Check the evaporation control system every 12,000 miles. Check the fuel and vapor lines for proper connections and correct routing as well as condition. Replace damaged or deteriorated parts as necessary.

A carbon filled canister stores fuel vapors until the engine is started and the vapors are drawn into the combustion chambers and burned.

To check the operation of the carbon canister purge control valve, disconnect the rubber hose between the canister control valve and the T-fitting, at the T-fitting. Apply vacuum to the hose leading to the control valve. The vacuum condition should be maintained indefinitely. If the control valve leaks, remove the top cover of the valve and check for a dislocated or cracked diaphragm. If the diaphragm is damaged, a repair kit containing a new diaphragm, retainer and spring is available and should be installed.

The carbon canister has an air filter in the bottom of the canister. The filter element should be checked once a year or every 12,000 miles; more frequently if the car is operated in dust areas. Replace the filter by pulling it out of the bottom of the canister and installing a new one.

Battery

SPECIFIC GRAVITY (EXCEPT "MAINTENANCE FREE" BATTERIES)

At least once a year, check the specific gravity of the battery. It should be between 1.20–1.26 at room temperature.

The specific gravity can be checked with an hydrometer, an inexpensive instrument available from many sources, including auto parts stores. The hydrometer has a squeeze bulb at one end and a nozzle at the other. Battery electrolyte is sucked into the hydrometer until the float is lifted from its seat. The specific gravity is then read by noting the position of the float. Generally, if after charging, the specific gravity between any two cells varies more than 50 points (0.050), the battery is bad and should be replaced.

It is not possible to check the specific gravity (in this manner) on sealed maintenance free batteries. Instead, the indicator built into the top of the case must be relied on to display any signs of battery deterioration. If the indicator is dark, the battery can be assumed to be OK. If the indicator is light, the specific gravity is low and the battery should be charged or replaced.

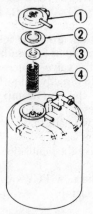

1. Cover
2. Diaphragm
3. Retainer
4. Diaphragm spring

Typical vapor canister

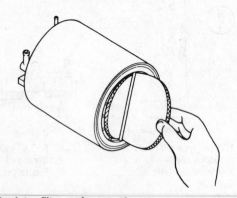

Canister filter replacement

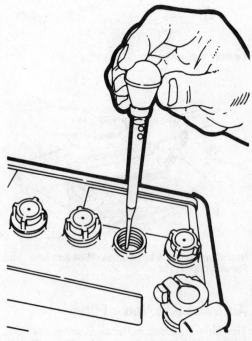

Specific gravity can be checked with an hydrometer

INDICATOR

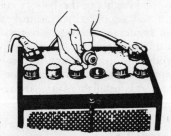

Make sure the battery electrolite is at the bottom of the filler holes

CABLES AND CLAMPS

Once a year the battery terminals and the cable clamps should be cleaned. Loosen the clamps and remove the cables, the negative cable first. On top post batteries, a special puller is used to remove the cable clamps; these are inexpensive and are available from the auto parts stores. The side terminal battery cables are secured with a bolt.

Clean the cable clamps and the battery terminal with wire brush, until corrosion, grease and etc. are removed and the metal is shiny. It is especially important to clean the inside of the clamp thoroughly, since a small deposit of foreign material or oxidation will prevent electrical flow. Special tools are available for cleaning these parts, one type for conventional batteries and another type for side terminal batteries.

Before installing the cables, loosen the bat-

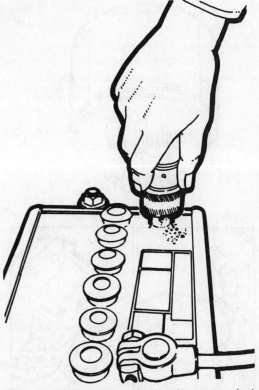

Clean the posts with a wire brush or a terminal cleaner made for the purpose (shown)

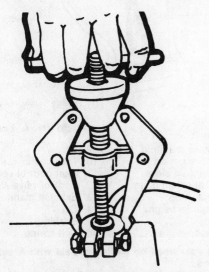

Removing the cable clamp with a special puller

Clean the inside of the clamps with wire brush or the special tool

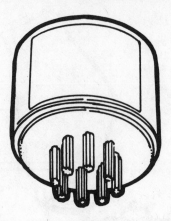

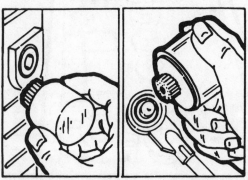

Special tools are also available for cleaning the posts and clamps on side terminal batteries

REPLACEMENT

When it becomes necessary to replace the battery, select one with a rating equal to or greater than the original. Deterioration, embrittlement or just plain aging of the battery cables, starter motor and associated wiring makes the batteries job harder in successive years. The slow increase in electrical resistance over time makes it prudent to install a new battery with a greater capacity than the old. Details on battery removal and installation are covered in Chapter 3.

Heat Control Valve

The heat control valve or Early Fuel Evaporative (EFE) System, is a thermostatically operated valve in the exhaust manifold. It closes when the engine is warming up to direct hot exhaust gases to the intake manifold, in order to pre-heat the incoming air/fuel mixture. If it sticks shut, the result will be frequent stalling

tery hold-down clamp or strap, remove the battery and check the battery tray. Clear it of any debris and check it for soundness. Rust should be wire brushed away and the metal given a coat of anti-rust paint. Replace the battery and tighten the hold-down clamp or strap securely, but be careful not to overtighten, which will crack the battery case.

After the clamps and the terminals are clean, reinstall the cables, negative cable last; do not hammer on the clamps to install. Tighten the clamps securely but do not distort them. Give the clamps and terminals a thin coat of petroleum jelly after installation, to retard corrosion.

Check the cables at the same time that the terminals are cleaned. If the cable insulation is cracked, broken or if the ends are frayed, the cable should be replaced with a new cable of the same length and gauge.

NOTE: *Keep flames or sparks away from the battery; it gives off explosive hydrogen gas. The electrolyte contains sulphuric acid. If you should splash any on your skin or in your eyes, flush the affected area with plenty of fresh water; if it gets into your eyes, get medical help immediately.*

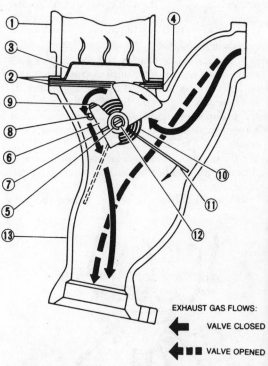

EXHAUST GAS FLOWS:

◀ VALVE CLOSED

◀■■ VALVE OPENED

1. Intake manifold	9. Screw
2. Stove gasket	10. Thermostat spring
3. Manifold stove	11. Heat control valve
4. Heat shield plate	12. Control valve shaft
5. Snap ring	13. Exhaust manifold
6. Counterweight	14. Cap
7. Key	15. Bushing
8. Stopper pin	16. Coil spring

Heat riser used on earlier models with A series engines

HOW TO SPOT WORN V-BELTS

V-Belts are vital to efficient engine operation—they drive the fan, water pump and other accessories. They require little maintenance (occasional tightening) but they will not last forever. Slipping or failure of the V-belt will lead to overheating. If your V-belt looks like any of these, it should be replaced.

This belt has deep cracks, which cause it to flex. Too much flexing leads to heat build-up and premature failure. These cracks can be caused by using the belt on a pulley that is too small. Notched belts are available for small diameter pulleys.

Cracking or weathering

Oil and grease on a belt can cause the belt's rubber compounds to soften and separate from the reinforcing cords that hold the belt together. The belt will first slip, then finally fail altogether.

Softening (grease and oil)

Glazing is caused by a belt that is slipping. A slipping belt can cause a run-down battery, erratic power steering, overheating or poor accessory performance. The more the belt slips, the more glazing will be built up on the surface of the belt. The more the belt is glazed, the more it will slip. If the glazing is light, tighten the belt.

Glazing

The cover of this belt is worn off and is peeling away. The reinforcing cords will begin to wear and the belt will shortly break. When the belt cover wears in spots or has a rough jagged appearance, check the pulley grooves for roughness.

Worn cover

This belt is on the verge of breaking and leaving you stranded. The layers of the belt are separating and the reinforcing cords are exposed. It's just a matter of time before it breaks completely.

Separation

during warm–up, especially in cold or damp weather. If it sticks open, the result will be a rough idle after the engine is warm.

The heat control valve should be checked for free operation every six months or 6,000 miles. Simply give the counterweight a twirl (engine cold) to make sure that no binding exists. If the valve sticks, apply a heat control solvent to the ends of the shaft. This type of solvent is available in auto parts stores. Sometimes lightly rapping the end of the shaft with a hammer (engine hot) will break it loose. If this fails, the components will have to be removed from the car for repair.

NOTE: *The 1980 and later engines do not use the heat control valve. Instead, these engines warm the fuel mixture by a coolant passage under the carburetor. No maintenance is required.*

Belts

TENSION CHECKING, ADJUSTING AND REPLACEMENT

Check the belts driving the fan, air pump, air conditioning compressor and the alternator for cracks, fraying, wear and tension every 6,000 miles. It is recommended that the belts be replaced every 24 months or 24,000 miles. Belt deflection at the midpoint of the longest span between pulleys should not be more than 7/16 of an inch with 22 lbs. of pressure applied to the belt.

To adjust the tension on all components except the air conditioning compressor, power steering pump and some late model air pumps, loosen the pivot and mounting bolts of the component which the belt is driving, then, using a wooden lever, pry the component toward or away from the engine until the proper tension is achieved.

CAUTION: *An overtight belt will wear out the pulley bearings on the assorted components.*

Tighten the component mounting bolts securely. If a new belt is installed, recheck the tension after driving about 1,000 miles.

NOTE: *The replacement of the inner belt on multi-belted engines may require the removal of the outer belts.*

Belt tension adjustments for the factory installed air conditioning compressor and power steering pump are made at the idler pulley. The idler pulley is the smallest of the three pulleys. At the top of the slotted bracket holding the idler pulley there is a bolt which is used to either raise or lower the pulley. To free the bolt for adjustment, it is necessary to loosen the lock nut in the face of the idler pulley. After

adjusting the belt tension, tighten the lock nut in the face of the idler pulley.

NOTE: *1980 and later California models come equipped with special fan belts which, if loose, generate friction heat by slipping and shrink, taking up the slack.*

The optional air conditioning drive belt is adjusted in a similiar fashion.

Hoses

HOSE REPLACEMENT

Remove the radiator cap and drain the radiator into a clean pan if you are going to reuse the old coolant. Remove the hose clamps and remove the hose by either cutting it off or twisting it to break its seal on the radiator and engine coolant inlets. When installing the new hose, do not overtighten the hose clamps or you might cut the hose. Refill the radiator with coolant, run the engine with the radiator cap on and then recheck the coolant level.

Air Conditioning

This book contains no repair or maintenance procedures for the air conditioning system. It is recommended that any such repairs be left to the experts, whose personnel are well aware of the hazards and who have the proper equipment.

CAUTION: *The compressed refrigerant used in the air conditioning system expands into the atmosphere at a temperature of $(-)2°F$ or lower. This will freeze any surface, including your eyes, that it contacts. In addition, the refrigerant decomposes into a poisonous gas in the presence of a flame. Do not open or disconnect any part of the air conditioning system.*

SIGHT GLASS CHECK

You can safely make a few simple checks to determine if your air conditioning system needs service. The tests work best if the temperature is warm (about 70°F).

NOTE: *If your vehicle is equipped with an after-market air conditioner, the following system check may not apply. You should contact the manufacturer of the unit for instructions on systems checks.*

1. Place the automatic transmission in Park or the manual transaxle in Neutral. Set the parking brake.

2. Run the engine at a fast idle (about 1,500 rpm) either with the help of a friend or by temporarily readjusting the idle speed screw.

3. Set the controls for maximum cold with the blower on High.

HOW TO SPOT BAD HOSES

Both the upper and lower radiator hoses are called upon to perform difficult jobs in an inhospitable environment. They are subject to nearly 18 psi at under hood temperatures often over 280°F., and must circulate nearly 7500 gallons of coolant an hour—3 good reasons to have good hoses.

A good test for any hose is to feel it for soft or spongy spots. Frequently these will appear as swollen areas of the hose. The most likely cause is oil soaking. This hose could burst at any time, when hot or under pressure.

Swollen hose

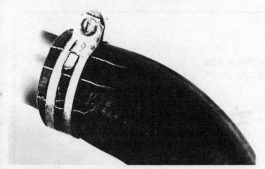

Cracked hoses can usually be seen but feel the hoses to be sure they have not hardened; a prime cause of cracking. This hose has cracked down to the reinforcing cords and could split at any of the cracks.

Cracked hose

Weakened clamps frequently are the cause of hose and cooling system failure. The connection between the pipe and hose has deteriorated enough to allow coolant to escape when the engine is hot.

Frayed hose end (due to weak clamp)

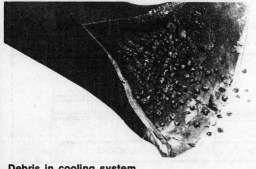

Debris, rust and scale in the cooling system can cause the inside of a hose to weaken. This can usually be felt on the outside of the hose as soft or thinner areas.

Debris in cooling system

4. Locate the sight glass in one of the system lines. Usually it is on the left alongside the top of the radiator.

5. If you see bubbles, the system must be recharged. Very likely there is a leak at some point.

6. If there are no bubbles, there is either no refrigerant at all or the system is fully charged. Feel the two hoses going to the belt-driven compressor. If they are both at the same temperature, the system is empty and must be recharged.

7. If one hose (high-pressure) is warm and the other (low-pressure) is cold, the system may be all right. However, you are probably making these tests because you think there is something wrong, so proceed to the next step.

8. Have an assistant in the car, turn the fan control on and off to operate the compressor clutch. Watch the sight glass.

9. If bubbles appear when the clutch is disengaged and disappear when it is engaged, the system is properly charged.

10. If the refrigerant takes more than 45 seconds to bubble when the clutch is disengaged, the system is overcharged. This usually causes poor cooling at low speeds.

CAUTION: *If it is determined that the system has a leak, it should be corrected as soon as possible. Leaks may allow moisture to enter and cause a very expensive rust problem.*

NOTE: *Exercise the air conditioner for a few minutes, every two weeks or so, during the cold months. This avoids the possibility of the compressor seals drying out from lack of lubrication.*

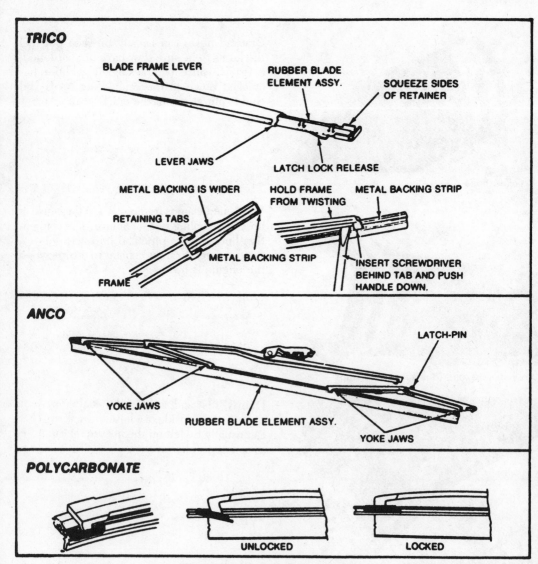

Three types of wiper blade retention

Windshield Wipers

For maximum effectiveness and longest element life, the windshield and wiper blades should be kept clean. Dirt, tree sap, road tar and so on will cause streaking, smearing and blade deterioration if left on the windshield. It is advisable to wash the windshield carefully with a commercial glass cleaner at least once a month. Wipe off the rubber blades with a wet rag afterwards. Do not attempt to move the wipers back and forth by hand; damage to the motor and drive mechanism will result.

If the blades are found to be cracked, broken or torn they should be replaced immediately. Replacement intervals will vary with usage, although ozone deterioration usually limits blade life to about one year. If the wiper pattern is smeared or streaked, or if the blade chatters across the glass, the blades should be replaced. It is easiest and most sensible to replace them in pairs.

There are basically three different types of wiper blade refills, which differ in their method of replacement. One type has two release buttons, approximately ⅓ of the way up from the ends of the blade frame. Pushing the buttons down releases a lock and allows the rubber blade to be removed from the frame. The new blade slides back into the frame and locks in place.

The second type of refill has two metal tabs which are unlocked by squeezing them together. The rubber blade can then be withdrawn from the frame jaws. A new one is installed by inserting it into the front frame jaws and sliding it rearward to engage the remaining frame jaws. There are usually four jaws; be certain when installing that the refill is en-

gaged in all of them. At the end of its travel, the tabs will lock into place on the front jaws of the wiper blade frame.

The third type is a refill made from polycarbonate. The refill has a simple locking device at one end which flexes downward out of the groove into which the jaws of the holder fit, allowing easy release. By sliding the new refill through all the jaws and pushing through the slight resistance when it reaches the end of its travel, the refill will lock into position.

Regardless of the type of refill used, make sure that all of the frame jaws are engaged as the refill is pushed into place and locked. The metal blade holder and frame will scratch the glass if allowed to touch it.

Tires

Check the air pressure in your tires every few weeks. Make sure that the tires are cool, as you will get a false reading when the tires are heated because air pressure increases with temperature. A decal tells you the proper tire pressure for the standard equipment tires. Naturally, when you replace tires you will want to get the correct tire pressures for the new ones from the dealer or manufacturer. It pays to buy a tire pressure gauge to keep in the car, since those at service stations are usually inaccurate or broken.

While you are checking the tire pressure, take a look at the tread. The tread should be wearing evenly across the tire. Excessive wear in the center of the tread could indicate over-inflation. Excessive wear on the outer edges could indicate underinflation. An irregular wear pat-

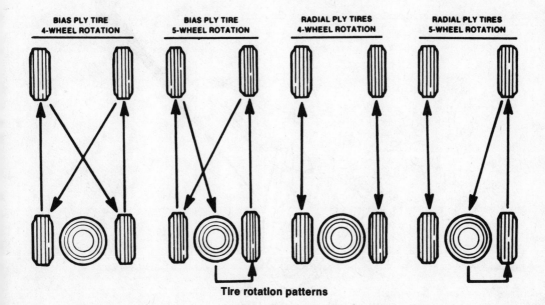

Tire rotation patterns

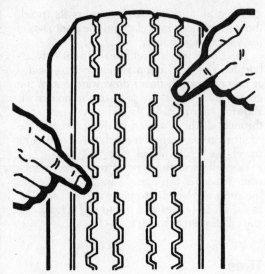

Tread wear indicators will appear when the tire is worn out

tern is usually a sign of incorrect front wheel alignment or wheel balance. A front end that is out of alignment will usually pull the car to one side of a flat road when the steering wheel is released. Incorrect wheel balance will produce

vibration in the steering wheel, while unbalanced rear wheels will result in floor or trunk vibration.

Rotating the tires every 6,000 miles or so will result in increased tread life. Use the correct pattern for your tire switching. Most automotive experts agree that radial tires are better all around performers, giving longer wear and better handling. An added benefit which you should consider when purchasing tires is that radials have less rolling resistance and can give up to a 10% increase in fuel economy over a bias-ply tire.

Tires of different construction should never be mixed. Always replace tires in sets of four or five when switching tire types and never substitute a belted tire for a bias-ply, a radial for a belted tire or etc. An occasional pressure check and periodic rotation could make your tires last much longer than a neglected set and maintain the safety margin which was designed into them.

Fuel Filter

The fuel filter on all models is a disposable plastic unit; located at the rear of the engine compartment. The filter should be replaced at least

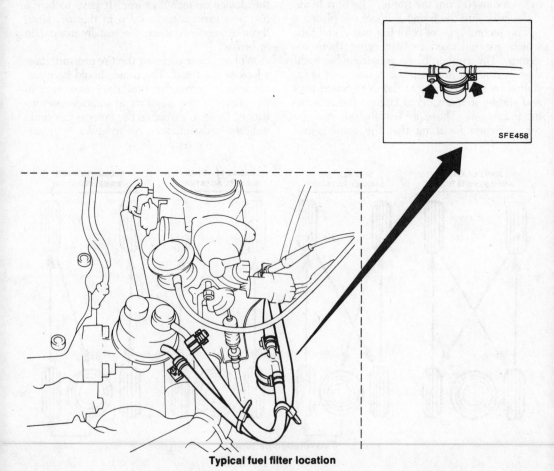

SFE458

Typical fuel filter location

every 24,000 miles. A dirty filter will starve the engine and cause poor running.

REPLACEMENT

CAUTION: *If equipped with an EFI engine, refer to the Fuel Pressure Release Procedure in this section and release the fuel pressure.*

1. Locate fuel filter on right-side or the rear of the engine compartment and place a container under the filter to catch the excess fuel.

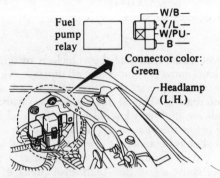

Location of the turbo fuel pump relay

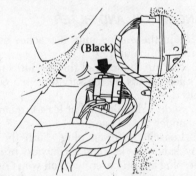

Location of the nonturbo fuel pump electrical connector

2. Disconnect the inlet and outlet hoses from the fuel filter. Make certain that the inlet hose (bottom) doesn't fall below the fuel tank level or the gasoline will drain out.

3. Pry the fuel filter from its clip and replace the assembly.

4. Replace the inlet and outlet lines. Secure the hose clamps to prevent leaks.

5. Start the engine and check for leaks.

FUEL PRESSURE RELEASE PROCEDURE

1. Start the engine.

2. On non-turbocharged engines, disconnect the (black) electrical harness connector, located under the passenger seat. On the turbocharged engines, disconnect the (green) electrical connector from the fuel pump relay, located on the fender at the front-left of the engine compartment.

3. After the engine has stalled, crank it over 2–3 times.

4. Turn OFF the ignition switch and reconnect the electrical connector.

FLUIDS AND LUBRICANTS

Fuel

All engines covered in this book have been designed to run on unleaded fuel. The minimum octane requirement is 91 RON (Research Octane Nunber) or 87 AKI (Anti-Knock Index); all unleaded fuels sold in the U.S. are required to meet this minimum octane rating.

The use of a fuel too low in octane (a measurement of anti-knock quality) will result in spark knock. Since many factors such as altitude, terrain, air temperature and humidity affect the operating efficiency, knocking may re-

Capacities

Year	Model	Engine Crankcase (qts)		Transaxle (pts)			Fuel Tank (gal)	Cooling System (qts)	
		with Filter	w/o Filter	4-sp	5-sp	Auto.		with Heater	w/o Heater
1976–78	F10	3.5	3.0	4.9	4.9	—	10.6①	7.0	6.4
1979–81	310	3.4	2.8	4.9	4.9	—	13.25	6.2	5.6
1982	310	4.1	3.6	4.9	5.75	12.75	13.25	6.5	5.5
1982–83	Stanza	4.1	3.75	—	5.75	12.75	14.25	7.75	6.9
1984	Stanza	4.0	3.75	—	5.75	12.75	14.25	7.1②	6.1②
1985–86	Stanza	3.6	3.25	—	5.75	12.75	14.25	7.1②	6.1②
1983–84	Pulsar	4.1	3.6	—	5.75	12.75	13.25	5.0③	4.4③
1985–86	Pulsar	3.5	3.1	—	5.75	12.75	13.25	5.0③	4.4③

① Wagon 9.1 gal.
② For A/T, add ⅜ qts.
③ For A/T, add ⅝ qts.

sult even though the recommended fuel is being used. If persistent knocking occurs, it may be necessary to switch to a higher grade of fuel. Continuous or heavy knocking may result in engine damage.

NOTE: *Your engine's fuel requirement can change with time, mainly due to carbon buildup, which will in turn change the compression ratio. If your engine pings, knocks or runs on, switch to a higher grade of fuel. Sometimes just changing brands will cure the problem. If it becomes necessary to retard the timing from the specifications, don't change it more than a few degrees. Retarded timing will reduce power output and fuel mileage, in addition to increasing the engine temperature.*

Engine

OIL RECOMMENDATION

Oil must be selected with regard to the anticipated temperatures during the period before the next oil change. Using the chart, select the oil viscosity for the lowest expected temperature and you will be assured of easy cold starting and sufficient engine protection. The oil you pour into your engine should have the designation "SE or SE/SF" marked on the top of its container.

Oil Viscosity Selection Chart

	Anticipated Temperature Range	SAE Viscosity
Multi-grade	Above 32°F	10W—40 10W—50 20W—40 20W—50 10W—30
	May be used as low as −10°F	10W—30 10W—40
	Consistently below 10°F	5W—20 5W—30
Single-grade	Above 32°F	30
	Temperature between +32°F and −10°F	10W

FLUID LEVEL CHECK

The best time to check the engine oil is before operating the engine or after it has been sitting for at least 10 minutes in order to gain an accurate reading. This will allow the oil to drain back in the crankcase. To check the engine oil

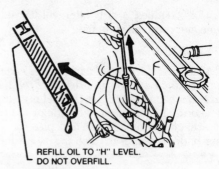

REFILL OIL TO "H" LEVEL.
DO NOT OVERFILL.
Oil dipstick markings

level, make sure that the vehicle is resting on a level surface, remove the oil dipstick, wipe it clean and reinsert the stick firmly for an accurate reading. The oil dipstick has two marks to indicate high and low oil level. If the oil is at or below the "low level" mark on the dipstick, oil should be added as necessary. The oil level should be maintained in the safety margin, neither going above the "high level" mark or below the "low level" mark.

CHANGING OIL AND FILTER

1. Run the engine until it reaches normal operating temperature.

2. Jack up the front of the car and support it on safety stands if necessary to gain access to the filter.

3. Slide a drain pan of at least 6 quarts capacity under the oil pan.

4. Loosen the drain plug. Turn the plug out by hand. By keeping an inward pressure on the plug as you unscrew it, oil won't escape past the threads and you can remove it without being burned by hot oil.

5. Allow the oil to drain completely and then install the drain plug. Don't overtighten the plug or you'll be buying a new pan or a trick replacement plug for damaged threads.

6. Using a strap wrench, remove the oil filter. Keep in mind that it's holding about one quart of dirty, hot oil.

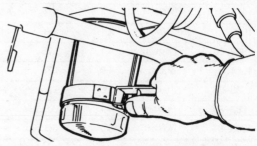

Removing the oil filter with a strap wrench

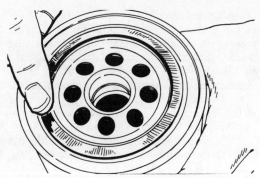

Apply a light coat of oil to the filter gasket before installation

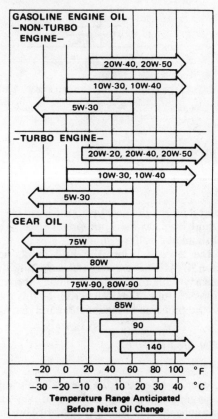

Manual transaxle and engine oil recommendations; automatic transaxle uses Dexron automatic transmission fluid.

7. Empty the old filter into the drain pan and dispose of the filter.

8. Using a clean rag, wipe off the filter adapter on the engine block. Be sure that the rag doesn't leave any lint which could clog an oil passage.

9. Coat the rubber gasket on the filter with fresh oil. Spin it onto the engine *by hand*; when the gasket touches the adapter surface give it another ½–¾ turn. No more or you'll squash the gasket and it will leak.

10. Refill the engine with the correct amount of fresh oil. See the Capacities chart.

11. Crank the engine over several times and then start it. If the oil pressure indicator light doesn't go out or the pressure gauge shows zero, shut the engine down and find out what's wrong.

12. If the oil pressure is OK and there are no leaks, shut the engine off and lower the car.

Transaxle

FLUID RECOMMENDATION

For manual transaxles, there are a variety of fluids available (depending upon the outside temperature); be sure to use fluid with an API GL-4 rating.

For automatic transaxles, use Dexron® AFT (automatic transaxle fluid).

FLUID LEVEL CHECK

Manual

Check the level of the lubricant in the transaxle every 3,000 miles. The lubricant level should be even with the bottom of the filler hole. Hold in on the filler plug when unscrewing it. When you are sure that all of the threads of the plug are free of the transaxle case, move the plug away from the case slightly. If lubricant begins to flow out of the transaxle, then you know it is full. If not, add gear oil as necessary.

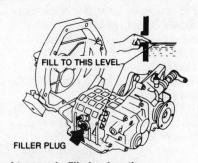

Manual transaxle fill plug location

Automatic

Check the level of the automatic transaxle fluid every 2,000 miles. There is a dipstick at the right rear of the engine. It has a scale on each side, one for COLD and the other for HOT. The transmisssion is considered hot after 15 miles of highway driving.

Park the car on a level surface with the engine running. If the transaxle is not hot, shift into Drive, Low, then Park. Set the handbrake and block the wheels.

Remove the dipstick, wipe it clean, then

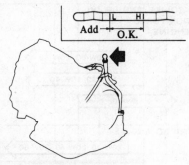

Automatic transaxle dipstick

reinsert it firmly. Remove the dipstick and check the fluid level on the appropriate scale. The level should be at the Full mark.

If the level is below the Full mark, add Dexron®II AFT (automatic transaxle fluid) as necessary, with the engine running, through the dipstick tube. Do not overfill, as this may cause the transaxle to malfunction and damage itself.

DRAIN AND REFILL

Manual

It is recommended that the transaxle lubricant be changed every 30,000 miles. You may also want to change it if you have bought your car used or if it has been driven in water deep enough to reach the transaxle case.

1. The oil should be HOT before it is drained. NOTE: *If the vehicle is driven until the engine is at normal operating temperature, the oil should be hot enough.*

2. Remove the filler plug from the left-side of the transaxle to provide a vent.

3. The drain plug is located on the bottom of the transaxle case. Place a pan under the drain plug and remove it.

CAUTION: *The oil will be HOT. Push up against the threads as you unscrew the plug to prevent leakage.*

4. Allow the oil to drain completely. Clean off the plug and replace it, then tighten until it is just snug.

5. Fill the transaxle with gear oil through the filler plug hole. Use API service GL-4 gear oil

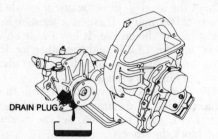

DRAIN PLUG

Manual transaxle drain plug

of the proper viscosity (see the "Viscosity Chart" in the section for recommendations). This oil usually comes in a squeeze bottle with a long nozzle. If yours isn't, use a plastic squeeze bottle (the type used in the kitchen). Refer to the "Capacities" chart for the amount of oil needed.

6. The oil level should come up to the edge of the filler hole. You can stick your finger in to verify this. Watch out for sharp threads.

7. Replace the filler plug. Dispose of the old oil in the same manner as old engine oil. Take a drive in the vehicle, stop and check for leaks.

Automatic

The fluid should be changed accordingly every 30,000 miles. If the vehicle is normally used in severe service, such as start-and-stop driving, trailer towing or the like, the interval should be halved. The fluid must be hot before it is drained; a 20 minute drive should accomplish this.

1. There is no drain plug; the fluid pan must be removed. Partially remove the pan screws until the pan can be pulled down at one corner. Place a container under the transaxle, lower a rear corner of the pan and allow the fluid to drain.

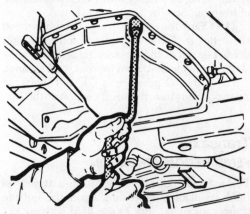

Removing the pan to drain the automatic transaxle

2. After draining, remove the pan screws completely, then the pan and gasket.

3. Clean the pan thoroughly and allow it to air dry. If you wipe it out with a rag, be sure there is no lint left behind to clog the oil passages.

4. Install the pan using a new gasket and a small bead of RTV sealant; be sure to apply sealant around the outside of the pan bolt holes. Tighten the pan screws evenly in rotation from the center outwards, to 3–5 ft. lbs.

5. It is a good idea to measure the amount of fluid drained to determine how much fresh fluid to add. This is because some part of the

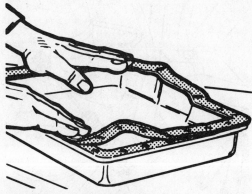

Installing a new pan gasket

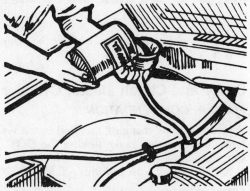

Adding fluid through the transaxle dipstick tube

transaxle, such as the torque converter, will not drain completely and using the dry refill amount specified in the Capacities chart may lead to overfilling. Fluid is added through the dipstick tube. Make sure that the funnel, hose or whatever your are using is completely clean and dry before pouring transaxle fluid through it. Use Dexron®II automatic transaxle fluid.

6. Replace the dipstick after filling. Start the engine and allow it to idle. DO NOT race the engine.

7. After the engine has idled for a few minutes, shift the transaxle slowly through the gears, then return the lever to Park. With the engine idling, check the fluid level on the dip stick. It should be between the "H" and "L" marks. If below "L", add sufficient fluid to raise the level to between the marks.

8. Drive the car until the transaxle is at operating temperature. The fluid should be at the "H" mark. If not, add sufficient fluid until this is the case. Be careful not to overfill; overfilling causes slippage, overheating and seal damage.

NOTE: *If the drained fluid is discolored (brown or black), thick or smells burnt, serious transaxle problems due to overheating*

should be suspected. Your car's transaxle should be inspected by a transaxle specialist to determine the cause.

Coolant

FLUID RECOMMENDATION

The cooling fluid should be changed every 24,000 miles. When replacing the fluid, use a mixture of 50% water and 50% ethylene glycol antifreeze.

LEVEL CHECK

Check the coolant level every time you change the oil. Check for loose connections and signs of deterioration of the coolant hoses. Maintain the coolant level ¾–1¼ in. below the level of the filler neck when the engine is cold.

CAUTION: *Never remove the radiator cap when the vehicle is hot or overheated. Wait until it has cooled. Place a thick cloth over the radiator cap to shield yourself from the heat and turn the radiator cap, SLIGHTLY, until the sound of escaping pressure can be heard. DO NOT turn any more; allow the pressure to release gradually. When no more pressure can be heard escaping, remove the cap with the heavy cloth, CAUTIOUSLY.*

NOTE: *Never add cold water to an overheated engine while the engine is not running.*

After filling the radiator, run the engine until it reaches normal operating temperature, to make sure that the thermostat has opened and all the air is bled from the system.

DRAINING, FLUSHING AND REFILLING

To drain the cooling system, allow the engine to cool down **BEFORE ATTEMPTING TO REMOVE THE RADIATOR CAP**. Then turn the cap until it hisses. Wait until all pressure is off the cap before removing it completely.

CAUTION: *To avoid burns and scalding, always handle a warm radiator cap with a heavy rag.*

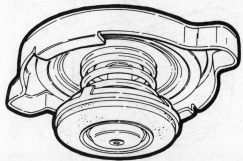

Always check the gasket in the radiator cap when checking coolant level

1. At the dash, set the heater TEMP control lever to the fully HOT position.

2. With the radiator cap removed, drain the radiator by loosening the petcock at the bottom of the radiator. Flush the radiator with water until the fluid runs clear.

NOTE: *On the Stanza models, remove the heater inlet hose from the connector pipe at the left rear of the cylinder block to drain completely. After draining, reconnect the hose to the pipe.*

3. Close the petcock, then refill the system with a 50/50 mix of ethylene glycol antifreeze; fill the system to ¾–1¼ in. from the bottom of the filler neck. Reinstall the radiator cap.

NOTE: *If equipped with a fluid reservoir tank, fill it up to the MAX level.*

4. Operate the engine at 2,000 rpm for a few minutes and check the system for signs of leaks.

NOTE: *If you have replaced or repaired any cooling system component on the Stanza models (1983 and later), the system must be bled. Insert a 0.12 in. pin into the 3-way valve, located at the firewall, and push it in as far as it will go. While pushing in on the pin, fill the radiator up to the filler opening.*

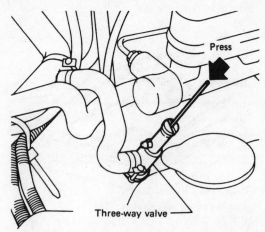

Using the 3-way valve to bleed the cooling system

Replace the radiator cap and fill the reservoir.

Brake and Clutch Master Cylinder

FLUID RECOMMENDATION

When adding or changing the fluid in the systems, use a quality brake fluid of the DOT 3 specifications.

NOTE: *Never reuse old brake fluid.*

LEVEL CHECK

Check the levels of brake fluid in the brake and clutch master cylinder reservoirs every 3,000 miles. The fluid level should be maintained to

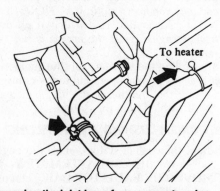

Removing the inlet hose from connector pipe

Typical brake master cylinder reservoir

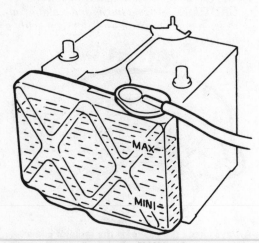

Fill the reservoir up to the MAX level

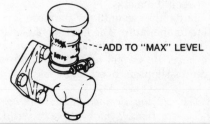

Typical clutch master cylinder

JUMP STARTING A DEAD BATTERY

The chemical reaction in a battery produces explosive hydrogen gas. This is the safe way to jump start a dead battery, reducing the chances of an accidental spark that could cause an explosion.

Jump Starting Precautions

1. Be sure both batteries are of the same voltage.
2. Be sure both batteries are of the same polarity (have the same grounded terminal).
3. Be sure the vehicles are not touching.
4. Be sure the vent cap holes are not obstructed.
5. Do not smoke or allow sparks around the battery.
6. In cold weather, check for frozen electrolyte in the battery. Do not jump start a frozen battery.
7. Do not allow electrolyte on your skin or clothing.
8. Be sure the electrolyte is not frozen.

CAUTION: *Make certain that the ignition key, in the vehicle with the dead battery, is in the OFF position. Connecting cables to vehicles with on-board computers will result in computer destruction if the key is not in the OFF position.*

Jump Starting Procedure

1. Determine voltages of the two batteries; they must be the same.
2. Bring the starting vehicle close (they must not touch) so that the batteries can be reached easily.
3. Turn off all accessories and both engines. Put both cars in Neutral or Park and set the handbrake.
4. Cover the cell caps with a rag—do not cover terminals.
5. If the terminals on the run-down battery are heavily corroded, clean them.
6. Identify the positive and negative posts on both batteries and connect the cables in the order shown.
7. Start the engine of the starting vehicle and run it at fast idle. Try to start the car with the dead battery. Crank it for no more than 10 seconds at a time and let it cool off for 20 seconds in between tries.
8. If it doesn't start in 3 tries, there is something else wrong.
9. Disconnect the cables in the reverse order.
10. Replace the cell covers and dispose of the rags.

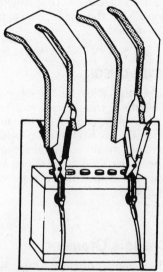

Side terminal batteries occasionally pose a problem when connecting jumper cables. There frequently isn't enough room to clamp the cables without touching sheet metal. Side terminal adaptors are available to alleviate this problem and should be removed after use.

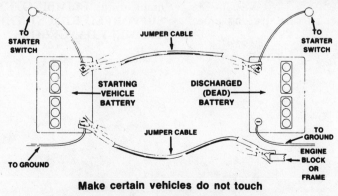

TO STARTER SWITCH   JUMPER CABLE   TO STARTER SWITCH

STARTING VEHICLE BATTERY   DISCHARGED (DEAD) BATTERY

TO GROUND   JUMPER CABLE   TO GROUND   ENGINE BLOCK OR FRAME

Make certain vehicles do not touch

This hook-up for negative ground cars only

a level not below the bottom line on the reservoirs and not above the top line. Any sudden decrease in the level in either of the three reservoirs (two for the brakes and one for the clutch) indicates a probable leak in that particular system and the possibility of a leak should be checked out.

Power Steering System

FLUID RECOMMENDATION

When adding or changing the power steering fluid, use Dexron® AFT (Automatic Transmission Fluid); the system uses approximately 1⅛ qts. of fluid.

LEVEL CHECK

Check the oil level in the reservoir by checking the side of the dipstick marked "HOT" after running the vehicle or the side marked "COLD" when the car has not been used. In each case, the fluid should reach the appropriate full line. Check the fluid level often. See Chapter 7, "Suspension and Steering" for system bleeding procedures.

Chassis Greasing

The manufacturer doesn't install lubrication fittings in lube points on the steering linkage or suspension. You can buy metric threaded fittings to grease these points or use a pointed, rubber tip end on your grease gun. Lubricate all joints equipped with a plug, every 24,000 miles, with NLGI No. 2 (Lithium base) grease. Replace the plugs after lubrication.

Wheel Bearings

Refer to the wheel bearings packing procedure, in Chapter 8, "Brakes".

PUSHING AND TOWING

All manual transaxle vehicles, non-California and Canadian can be push started; automatic transaxles may not be push started. Check to make sure that the bumpers of both vehicles are aligned so neither will be damaged. Be sure that all electrical system components are turned OFF (headlights, heater blower and etc.). Turn on the ignition switch. Place the shift lever in 3rd or 4th gear and push in the clutch pedal. At about 15 mph, signal the driver of the pushing vehicle to fall back, depress the accelerator pedal and release the clutch pedal slowly. The engine should start.

The manufacturer advises against trying to tow-start your vehicle for fear of ramming the tow vehicle when the engine starts.

Both types of transaxles may be towed for short distances and at speeds of no more than 20 mph (automatic) or 50 mph (manual). If the car must be towed a great distance, it should be done with the drive wheels off the ground.

JUMP STARTING

Jump starting is the favored method of starting a car with a dead battery. Make sure that the cables are properly connected, negative-to-negative and positive-to-positive or you stand a chance of damaging the electrical systems of both vehicles.

JACKING

Never use the tire changing jack for anything other than that. If you intend to use this tool to perform your own maintenance, a good scissors or small hydraulic jack and two sturdy jackstands would be a wise purchase. Always chock the wheels when changing a tire or working beneath the vehicle. It cannot be overemphasized, **CLIMBING UNDER A CAR SUPPORTED BY JUST THE JACK IS EXTREMELY DANGEROUS.**

Tune-Up and Performance Maintenance

2

TUNE-UP PROCEDURES

The following procedures are specific ones in case your vehicle needs more than a regular tune-up. See Chapter 9, Troubleshooting, for engine troubleshooting procedures.

The following procedures will show you exactly how to tune your vehicle. For 1976–79 models, the manufacturer recommends a tune-up, including distributor points (unless equipped with electronic ignition) and spark plugs every 12,000 miles.

In 1980, a new, more durable spark plug began use in all models sold in the United States. The manufacturer recommends that the new plugs be replaced every 30,000 miles or 24 months, which ever comes first. Certain 1980 Canadian vehicles still use the conventional 12 month, 12,000 mile spark plugs. All U.S.A. (1980 and later) models have electronic ignition systems, so there are no breaker points and condenser to replace.

Even though the manufacturer suggests a 30,000 mile, 24 month spark plug replacement span for 1980 and later U.S.A. models, it would be wise to remove the plugs and inspect them every 12,000 miles.

If you're experiencing some specific problem with your engine, refer to Chapter 9, Troubleshooting, then follow the programmed format until you pinpoint the trouble. If you're just doing a tune-up to restore your vehicle's pep and economy, proceed with the following steps.

It might be noted that the tune-up is a good time to take a look around the engine compartment for problems in the making, such as oil and fuel leaks, deteriorating radiator or heater hoses, loose and/or frayed fan belts and etc.

Spark Plugs

A typical spark plug consists of a metal shell surrounding a ceramic insulator. A metal elec-

trode extends downward through the center of the insulator and protrudes a small distance. Located at the end of the plug and attached to the side of the outer metal shell is the side electrode. The side electrode bends in at a 90° angle, so that its tip is even with and parallel to, the tip of the center electrode. The distance between these two electrodes (measured in thousandths of an inch) is called the spark plug gap. The spark plug in no way produces a spark but merely provides a gap across which the current can arc. The coil produces anywhere from 20,000–40,000 volts, which travels to the distributor where it is distributed through the spark plug wire to the spark plugs. The current passes along the center electrode, then jumps the gap to the side electrode and ignites the air/fuel mixture in the combustion chamber.

Spark plug life and efficiency depend upon the condition of the engine and the temperatures to which the plug is exposed. Combustion chamber temperatures are affected by many factors such as compression ratio of the engine, air/fuel mixtures, exhaust emission equipment and the type of driving you do. Spark plugs are designed and classified by number according to the heat range at which they will operate most efficiently.

HEAT RANGE

While the spark plug heat range has always seemed to be somewhat of a mystical subject for many people, in reality, the entire subject is quite simple. Basically, it boils down to this; the amount of heat the plug absorbs is determined by the length of the lower insulator. The longer the insulator (or the further it extends into the engine), the hotter the plug will operate; the shorter the insulator the cooler it will operate. A plug that absorbs little heat and remains too cool will quickly accumulate deposits of oil and carbon since it is not hot enough to burn them off. This leads to plug fouling and consequently to misfiring. A plug that absorbs

Tune-Up Specifications

When analyzing compression test results, look for uniformity among cylinders, rather than specific pressures.

Year	Model	Spark Plug Type	Gap (in.)	Distributor Point Dwell (deg)	Point Gap (in.)	Ignition Timing (deg) MT	AT	Fuel Pump Pressure (psi)	Idle Speed (rpm) MT	AT[1]	Valve Clearance In	Ex
1976	F10	BP-5ES	.031–.035	49–55	.018–.022	10B	—	3.8	700	—	.014 Hot	.014 Hot
	F10 Calif.	BP-5ES	.031–.035	Electronic	[2]	10B	—	3.8	700	—	.014 Hot	.014 Hot
1977	F10	BPR5ES-11	.039–.043	49–55	.018–.022	10B	—	3.8	700	—	.014 Hot	.014 Hot
	F10 Calif.	BPR5ES	.031–.035	Electronic	[2]	10B	—	3.8	700	—	.014 Hot	.014 Hot
1978	F10	BP5ES-11	.039–.043	Electronic	[2]	10B	—	3.8	700	—	.014 Hot	.014 Hot
1979	F10	BP5ES-11 [4]	.039–.043	Electronic	[8]	10B [3]	—	3.8	700	—	.014 Hot	.014 Hot
1980	310	BPR5ES-11 [4]	.039–.043	Electronic	[8]	8B	—	3.8	750	—	.014 Hot	.014 Hot
1981	310	BPR5ES-11 [4]	.039–.043	Electronic	[8]	5B	—	3.8	750	—	.014 Hot	.014 Hot
1982	310	BPR5ES-11 [4]	.039–.043	Electronic	[8]	2A [5]	2A [5]	3.8	750	750 [6]	.011 Hot	.011 Hot
	Stanza	[7]	.039–.043	Electronic	[8]	0	—	3.8	650	—	.012 Hot	.012 Hot
1983	Stanza	[7]	.089–.043	Electronic	[8]	0	0	3.8	650	650	.012 Hot	.012 Hot
	Pulsar	BPR5ES-11 [4]	.039–.043	Electronic	[8]	5A	5A	3.8	750	650	.011 Hot	.011 Hot
1984	Stanza	[7]	.039–.043	Electronic	[8]	0	0	3.8	750 [9]	700 [9]	.012 Hot	.012 Hot
	Pulsar	BPR5ES-11 [4][10]	.039–.043	Electronic	[8]	15B [11][14]	8B [11][14]	3.8	800 [12][15][20]	650 [13][16][21]	.011 Hot	.011 Hot
1985–86	Stanza	[17][18]	.039–.043	Electronic	[8]	4B [19]	0 [19]	3.8	750 [9]	700 [9]	.012 Hot	.012 Hot
	Pulsar	BPR5ES-11	.039–.043	Electronic	[8]	15B [11]	8B [11]	3.8	800 [12][20]	650 [13][21]	.011 Hot	.011 Hot

[1] In Drive
[2] Reluctor gap: .008–.016
[3] Calif.: 5B
[4] Canada: BPR-5ES; gap .031–.035
[5] Canada: 4A
[6] Canada: AT 650
[8] Reluctor gap: .012–.020
[9] Canada: 650
[10] E15ET engine (Canada): BPR6ES-11
[11] Calif and Canada: 5A
[12] Calif and Canada: 750
[13] Calif and Canada: 650
[16] E15ET engine (Canada): 650
[17] Intake side: BCPR6ES-11; Exhaust side: BCPR5ES-11
[18] (Canada) intake side: BPR6ES-11; exhaust side: BPR5ES-11
[19] Canada: 0

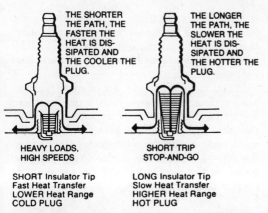

THE SHORTER THE PATH, THE FASTER THE HEAT IS DISSIPATED AND THE COOLER THE PLUG.

THE LONGER THE PATH, THE SLOWER THE HEAT IS DISSIPATED AND THE HOTTER THE PLUG.

HEAVY LOADS, HIGH SPEEDS

SHORT TRIP STOP-AND-GO

SHORT Insulator Tip
Fast Heat Transfer
LOWER Heat Range
COLD PLUG

LONG Insulator Tip
Slow Heat Transfer
HIGHER Heat Range
HOT PLUG

Spark plug heat ranges

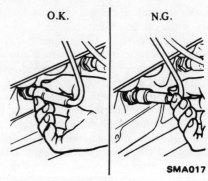

O.K.   N.G.

SMA017

Spark plug wire removal

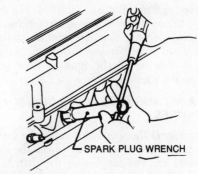

SPARK PLUG WRENCH

Spark plug removal

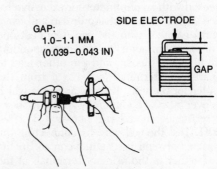

GAP:
1.0–1.1 MM
(0.039–0.043 IN)

SIDE ELECTRODE

GAP

Spark plug gap adjustment

too much heat will have no deposits but due to the excessive heat, the electrodes will burn away quickly and in some instances, preignition may result. Preignition takes place when plug tips get so hot that they glow sufficiently to ignite the fuel/air mixture before the actual spark occurs. This early ignition will usually cause a pinging during low speeds and heavy loads. In severe cases, the heat may become high enough to start the fuel/air mixture burning throughout the combustion chamber rather than just to the front of the plug as in normal operation. At this time, the piston is rising in the cylinder making its compression stroke. The burning mass is compressed and an explosion results, forcing the piston back down in the cylinder while it is still trying to go up. Obviously, something must go and it does–pistons are often damaged.

The general rule of thumb for choosing the correct heat range when picking a spark plug is: if most of your driving is long distance, high speed travel, use a colder plug; if most of your driving is stop and go, use a hotter plug. Factory-installed plugs are, of course, compromise plugs, since the factory has no way of knowing what sort of driving you do. It should be noted that most people never have the need to change their plugs from the factory recommended heat range.

REMOVAL AND INSTALLATION

NOTE: *The Stanza has two spark plugs in each cylinder; the plugs are of different heat ranges–the exhaust side uses the colder plug. All eight plugs should be replaced at every tune-up for maximum fuel efficiency and power. Unplug and remove each spark plug one at a time from the high tension harness to avoid confusing the wiring.*

1. Grasp the spark plug boot and pull it straight out. Don't pull on the wire. If the boot(s) are cracked, replace them.

2. Place the spark plug socket firmly on the plug. Turn the spark plug out of the cylinder head in a counterclockwise direction.

CAUTION: *The cylinder head is aluminum, which is easily stripped. Remove the plugs ONLY when the engine is cold.*

NOTE: *If removal is difficult, loosen the plug only slightly and drip penetrating oil onto the threads. Allow the oil time enough to work and then unscrew the plug. Proceeding in this manner will prevent damaging the cylinder head threads. Be sure to keep the socket straight to avoid breaking the ceramic insulator.*

3. Continue to remove the remaining spark plugs.

4. Inspect the plugs using the Color Insert

section illustrations and then clean or discard them according to condition.

New spark plugs come pre-gapped but double check the setting or reset them if you desire a different gap. The recommended spark plug gap is listed in the Tune-Up Specifications chart. Use a spark plug wire gauge for checking the gap. The wire should pass through the electrode with just a slight drag. Never attempt to adjust the plug gap with a flat-bladed feeler gauge; a false reading will result. Using the electrode bending tool on the end of the gauge, bend the side electrode to adjust the gap. Never attempt to adjust the center electrode. Lightly oil the threads of the replacement plug and install it hand-tight. It is a good practice to use a torque wrench to tighten the spark plugs on any vehicle, especially the aluminum head type. Torque the spark plugs to 14–22 ft. lbs. Install the ignition wire boots firmly on the spark plugs.

CHECKING AND REPLACING SPARK PLUG WIRES

Visually inspect the spark plug cables for burns, cuts or breaks in the insulation. Check the spark plug boots and the nipples on the distributor cap and coil. Replace any damaged wiring. If no physical damage is obvious, the wires can be checked with an ohmmeter for excessive resistance. Remove the distributor cap and leave the wires connected to the cap. Connect one lead of the ohmmeter to the corresponding electrode inside the cap and the other lead to the spark plug terminal (remove it from the spark plug for the test). Replace any wire which shows over 50,000Ω. Generally speaking, however, resistance should run between 35,000–50,000Ω. Test the coil wire by connecting the ohmmeter between the center contact in the cap and either of the primary terminals at the coil. If the total resistance of the coil and the cable is more than 25,000Ω, remove the cable from the coil and check the resistance of the cable. If the resistance is higher than 15,000Ω, replace the cable. It should be remembered that wire resistance is a function of length and

that the longer the cable, the greater the resistance. Thus, if the cables on your car are longer than the factory originals, resistance will be higher and quite possibly outside of these limits.

When installing a new set of spark plug cables, replace the cables one at a time so there will be no mix-up. Start by replacing the longest cable first. Install the boot firmly over the spark plug. Route the wire exactly the same as the original. Insert the nipple firmly into the tower on the distributor cap. Repeat the process for each cable.

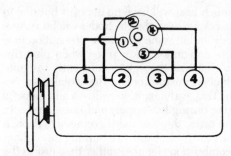

A-series engines—firing order: 1-3-4-2

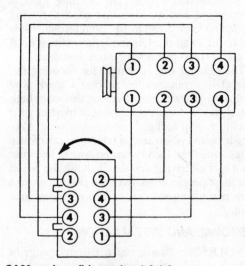

CA20 engine—firing order: 1-3-4-2

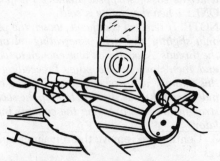

Checking plug wire resistance with an ohmmeter

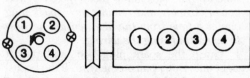

E15, E16 engine—firing order: 1-3-4-2

Breaker Points and Condenser

NOTE: *Certain 1976–1977 and virtually all 1978 and later models are equipped with electronic, breakerless ignition systems. See the following section for maintenance procedures.*

INSPECTION OF THE POINTS

1. Disconnect the high-tension wire from the top of the distributor and the coil.

2. Remove the distributor cap by prying off the spring clips on the sides of the cap.

3. Remove the rotor from the distributor shaft by pulling it straight up. Examine the condition of the rotor. If it is cracked or the metal tip is excessively worn or burned, it should be replaced. Clean the tip with fine emery paper.

4. Pry open the contacts of the points with a screwdriver and check the condition of the contacts. If they are excessively worn, burned or pitted, they should be replaced.

5. If the points are in good condition, adjust them, then replace the rotor and the distributor cap. If the points need to be replaced, follow the replacement procedure given below.

REPLACEMENT OF THE BREAKER POINTS AND CONDENSER

1. Remove the coil's high-tension wire from the top of the distributor cap. Remove the distributor cap and place it out of the way. Remove the rotor from the distributor shaft by pulling up.

2. Remove the points assembly attaching screws, the condenser and the points.

NOTE: *A magnetic screwdriver or one with a holding mechanism will come in handy here, so that you don't drop a screw into the distributor and have to remove the entire distributor to retrieve it.*

3. After the points are removed, wipe off the cam and apply new cam lubricant. If you don't the points will wear out in a few thousand miles.

4. Slip the new set of points onto the locating dowel and install the screws that hold the assembly onto the plate. Don't tighten them all the way yet, since you'll only have to loosen them to set the point gap.

5. Install the new condenser and attach the condenser lead to the points.

6. Set the point gap and dwell (see the following sections).

ADJUSTMENT OF THE BREAKER POINTS WITH A FEELER GAUGE

1. If the contact points of the assembly are not parallel, bend the stationary contact so that they make contact across the entire surface of the contacts. Bend only the stationary bracket part of the point assembly; not the movable contact.

2. Turn the engine until the rubbing block of the points is on one of the high points of the distributor cam. You can do this by either turning the ignition switch to the Start position and releasing it quickly (bumping the engine) or by using a wrench on the crankshaft pulley bolt.

3. Place the correct size feeler gauge between the contacts (see the Tune-Up Chart). Make sure that it is parallel with the contact surfaces.

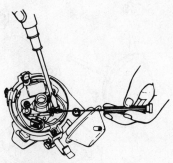

Adjusting point gap

4. With your free hand, insert a screwdriver into the eccentric adjusting screw, then twist the screwdriver to either increase or decrease the gap to the proper setting.

5. Tighten the adjustment lockscrew and recheck the contact gap to make sure that it didn't change when the lockscrew was tightened.

6. Replace the rotor, the distributor cap and the high-tension wire from the top of the distributor to the coil. Make sure that the rotor is firmly seated all the way onto the distributor shaft and that the tab of the rotor is aligned with notch in the shaft. Align the tab in the base of the distributor cap with the notch in the distributor body. Make sure that the cap is firmly seated on the distributor and that the retainer clips are in place. Make sure that the end of the high-tension wire is firmly installed in the top of the distributor and the coil.

Dwell Angle

The dwell angle or cam angle is the number of degrees that the distributor cam rotates while the points are closed. There is an inverse relationship between dwell angle and point gap. Increasing the point gap will decrease the dwell angle and vice-versa. Checking the dwell angle with a meter is a far more accurate method of

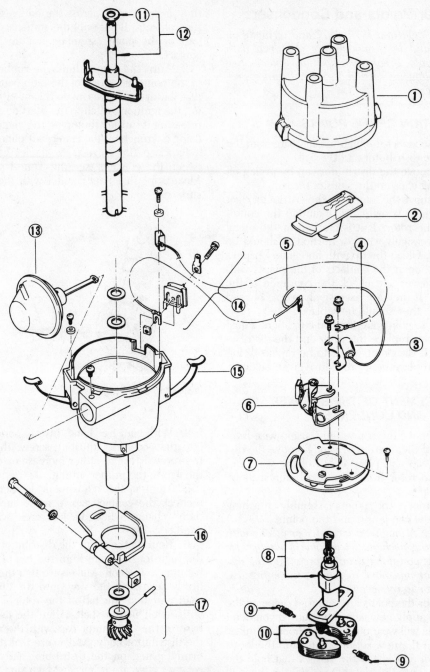

1. Cap	7. Breaker plate
2. Rotor	8. Cam assembly
3. Condenser	9. Governor spring
4. Ground wire	10. Governor weight
5. Lead wire	11. Thrust washer
6. Breaker points	12. Shaft assembly

13. Vacuum control assembly
14. Terminal assembly
15. Clamp
16. Retaining plate
17. Gear set

Point type distributor

measuring point opening than the feeler gauge method.

After setting the point gap to specification with a feeler gauge as described above, check the dwell angle with a meter. Attach the dwell meter according to the manufacturer's instruction sheet. The negative lead is grounded and the positive lead is connected to the primary wire terminal which runs from the coil to the distributor. Start the engine, let it idle and reach operating temperature, then observe the dwell on the meter. The reading should fall within the allowable range. If it does not, the gap will have to be reset or the breaker points will have to be replaced.

ADJUSTMENT OF THE BREAKER POINTS WITH A DWELL METER

1. Adjust the points with a feeler gauge as previously described.

2. Connect the dwell meter to the ignition circuit as according to the manufacturer's instructions. One lead of the meter is connected to a ground and the other lead is connected to the distributor post on the coil. An adapter is usually provided for this purpose.

3. If the dwell meter has a set line on it, adjust the meter to zero the indicator.

4. Start the engine.

NOTE: *Be careful when working on any vehicle while the engine is running. Make sure that the transaxle is in Neutral and that the parking brake is applied. Keep hands, clothing, tools and the wires of the test instruments clear of the rotating fan blades.*

5. Observe the reading on the dwell meter. If the reading is within the specified range, turn off the engine and remove the dwell meter.

NOTE: *If the meter does not have a scale for 4 cylinder engines, multiply the 8 cylinder reading by two.*

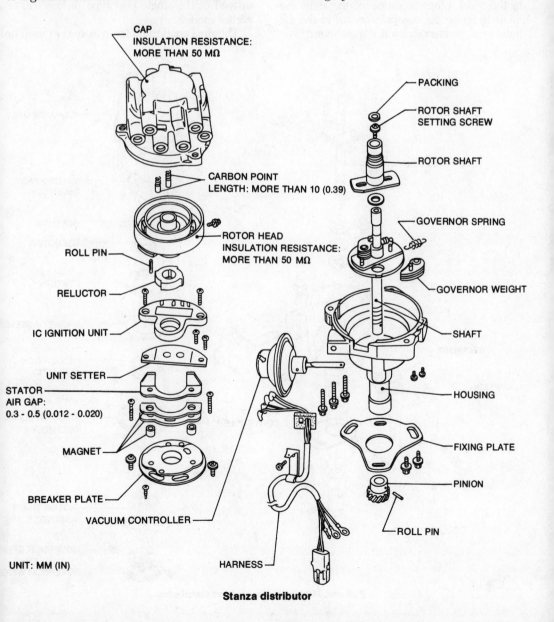

CAP
INSULATION RESISTANCE:
MORE THAN 50 MΩ

PACKING

ROTOR SHAFT
SETTING SCREW

ROTOR SHAFT

CARBON POINT
LENGTH: MORE THAN 10 (0.39)

GOVERNOR SPRING

ROLL PIN

ROTOR HEAD
INSULATION RESISTANCE:
MORE THAN 50 MΩ

RELUCTOR

GOVERNOR WEIGHT

IC IGNITION UNIT

SHAFT

UNIT SETTER

STATOR
AIR GAP:
0.3 - 0.5 (0.012 - 0.020)

HOUSING

MAGNET

FIXING PLATE

BREAKER PLATE

PINION

VACUUM CONTROLLER

ROLL PIN

UNIT: MM (IN)

HARNESS

Stanza distributor

6. If the reading is above the specified range, the breaker point gap is too small. If the reading is below the specified range, the gap is too large. In either case, the engine must be stopped and the gap adjusted in the manner previously covered. After making the adjustment, start the engine and check the reading on the dwell meter. When the correct reading is obtained, disconnect the dwell meter.

7. Check and/or adjust the ignition timing.

Electronic Ignition

DESCRIPTION

The electronic ignition system differs from the conventional breaker points system in form only; its function is exactly the same–to supply a spark to the spark plugs at precisely the right moment to ignite the compressed gas in the cylinders and create mechanical movement.

Located in the distributor, in addition to the normal rotor cap, is a spoked rotor (reluctor) which fits on the distributor shaft where the breaker points cam is found on non-electronic ignitions. The rotor (reluctor) revolves with the rotor head, as it passes a pickup coil inside the distributor body, it breaks a high flux field, which occurs in the space between the reluctor and the pickup coil. The breaking of the field allows current to flow to the pickup coil. Primary ignition current is then cut off by the electronic ignition unit, allowing the magnetic field in the ignition coil to collapse, creating the spark which the distributor passes on to the spark plug.

The 1979–82 IC ignition system uses a ring type pickup coil which surrounds the reluctor instead of the single post type pickup coil on earlier models.

The dual spark plug ignition system used on

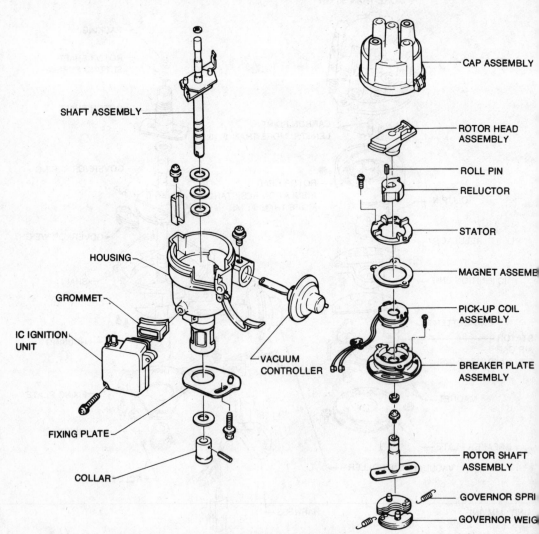

F10 and 310 electronic ignition distributor

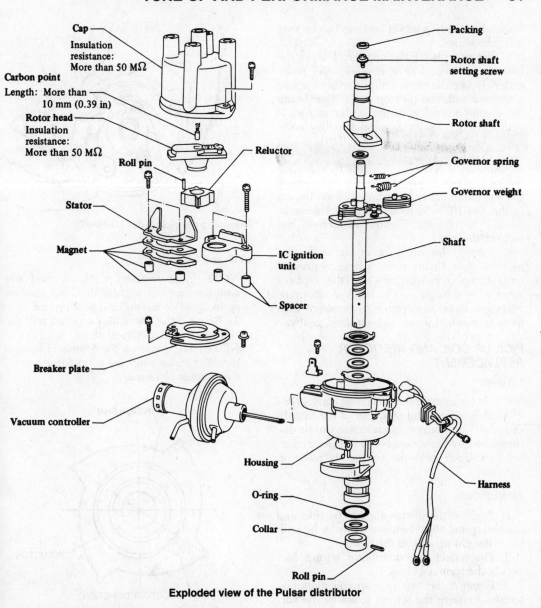

Cap
Insulation
resistance:
More than 50 MΩ

Carbon point
Length: More than
10 mm (0.39 in)

Rotor head
Insulation
resistance:
More than 50 MΩ

Roll pin

Stator

Magnet

Breaker plate

Vacuum controller

Reluctor

IC ignition unit

Spacer

Packing

Rotor shaft setting screw

Rotor shaft

Governor spring

Governor weight

Shaft

Housing

O-ring

Collar

Roll pin

Harness

Exploded view of the Pulsar distributor

the Stanza (1982 and later) uses two ignition coils and each cylinder has two spark plugs which fire simultaneously. In this manner the engine is able to consume large quantities of recirculated exhaust gas which would cause a single spark plug cylinder to misfire and idle roughly.

Since no points or condenser are used and the dwell is determined by the electronic unit, no adjustments are necessary. The ignition timing is checked in the usual way; unless the distributor is disturbed, it is not likely to ever change very much.

Service consists of inspection of the distributor cap, rotor and ignition wires, replacing them when necessary. These parts can be expected to last for at least 40,000 miles. In ad-

dition, the reluctor air gap should be checked periodically.

REPLACEMENT AND AIR GAP ADJUSTMENT

1. The distributor cap is held on by two spring clips. Release them with a screwdriver and lift the cap straight up and off, with the wires attached. Inspect the cap for cracks, carbon tracks or a worn center contact. Replace it if necessary; transfer the wires one at a time from the old cap to the new one.

2. Pull the rotor head (not the spoked reluctor) straight up to remove. Replace it if its contacts are worn, burned or pitted; DO NOT file the contacts. To replace, press it firmly onto

the shaft. It only goes on one way, so be sure it is fully seated.

3. Before replacing the rotor head, check the reluctor air gap. *Use a non-magnetic feeler gauge.* Rotate the engine until a reluctor spoke is aligned with the pick-up coil (either bump the engine around with the starter or turn it with a wrench on the crankshaft pulley bolt). The gap should measure 0.008–0.016 in. for 1976–78 or 0.012–0.020 in. for 1979 and later. Adjustment, if necessary, is made by loosening the pickup coil mounting screws and shifting the coil either closer to or farther from the reluctor. On 1979–82 models, center the stator around the reluctor. Tighten the screws and recheck the gap.

4. Inspect the wires for cracks or brittleness. Replace them one at a time to prevent cross-wiring, carefully pressing the replacement wires into place. The cores of electronic wires are more susceptible to breakage than those of standard wires, so treat them gently.

PICK-UP COIL AND RELUCTOR REPLACEMENT

1976–81

The reluctor cannot be removed on early 1976–77 models—it is an integral part of the distributor shaft. Non-removable reluctors can be distinguished by the absence of a roll pin (retaining pin) which locks the reluctor in place on the shaft.

PICK-UP COIL

1. Remove the distributor cap by releasing the two spring clips. Remove the rotor by pulling it straight up and off the shaft.
2. Disconnect the distributor wiring harness at the terminal block.
3. Remove the two pick-up coil mounting screws. Remove the screws retaining the wiring harness to the distributor.
4. Remove the pick-up coil.
5. To replace the pick-up coil, reverse the removal procedure but leave the mounting screws slightly loose to facilitate the air gap adjustment.

RELUCTOR—WITH ROLL PIN

1. Remove the distributor cap, the rotor and the pick-up coil.
2. Use two screwdrivers or pry bars to pry the reluctor from the distributor shaft. Be extremely careful not to damage the reluctor teeth. Remove the roll pin.
3. To replace, press the reluctor firmly onto the shaft. Install a new roll pin with the slit facing away from the distributor shaft; DO NOT reuse the old roll pin.

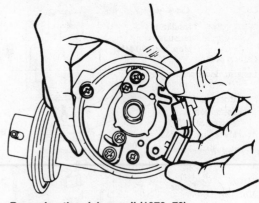

Removing the pickup coil (1976–78)

1982 and Later

NOTE: *The engines of this period are equipped with a slightly different ignition system and do not utilize a pick-up coil.*

1. Remove the distributor cap and pull the rotor from the distributor shaft.

NOTE: *The rotor on the Stanza is held to the distributor shaft by a retaining screw, which must be removed.*

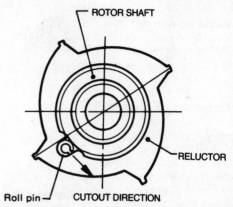

View of the reluctor, roll pin and distributor shaft (1982 and later)

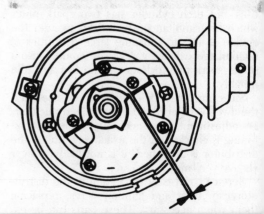

Checking the air gap (1982 and later)

2. Remove the wiring harness and the vacuum controller from the housing.

3. Using two flat bladed screwdrivers, place one on each side of the reluctor and pry it from the distributor shaft.

CAUTION: *When removing the reluctor, be careful not to damage or distort the teeth.*

4. Remove the roll pin from the reluctor.

NOTE: *If it is necessary to remove the IC unit, remove the breaker plate assembly and separate the IC unit from it.*

5. To install, reverse the removal procedures. Adjust the air gap between the reluctor and the stator.

Ignition Timing

CAUTION: *When performing this or any other operation with the engine running, be very careful of the alternator belt and pulleys. Make sure that your timing light wires don't interfere with the belt.*

Ignition timing is an important part of the tune-up. It is always adjusted after the points are gapped (dwell angle changed), since altering the dwell affects the timing. Three basic types of timing lights are available, the neon, the DC and the AC powered. Of the three the DC light is the most frequently used by professional tuners. The bright flash put out by the DC light makes the timing marks stand out on even the brightest of days. Another advantage of the DC light is that you don't need to be near an electrical outlet. Neon lights are available for a few dollars but their weak flash makes it necessary to use them in a fairly dark work area. One neon light lead is attached to the spark plug and the other to the plug wire. The DC light attaches to the spark plug and the wire with an adapter and two clips attach to the battery posts for power. The AC unit is similar, except that the power cable is plugged into a house outlet.

Ignition timing is the measurement, in degrees of crankshaft rotation, of the point at which the spark plugs fire in each of the cylinders. It is measured in degrees before or after Top Dead Center (TDC) of the compression stroke. Ignition timing is controlled by turning the distributor body in the engine.

Ideally, the air/fuel mixture in the cylinder will be ignited by the spark plug just as the piston passes TDC of the compression stroke. If this happens, the piston will be beginning its downward motion of the power stroke just as the piston passes TDC of the compression stroke. If this happens, the piston will be beginning its downward motion of the power stroke just as the compressed and ignited air/fuel mixture starts to expand. The expansion of the air/fuel mixture then forces the piston down on the power stroke and turns the crankshaft.

Because it takes a fraction of a second for the spark plug to ignite the mixture in the cylinder, the spark plug must fire a little before the piston reaches TDC. Otherwise, the mixture will not be completely ignited as the piston passes TDC and the full power of the explosion will not be used by the engine.

The timing measurement is given in degrees of crankshaft rotation before or after the piston reaches TDC (ATDC) (BTDC). If the setting for the ignition timing is 5° BTDC, the spark plug must fire 5° before each piston reaches TDC. This only holds true, however, when the engine is at idle speed.

As the engine speed increases, the pistons go faster. The spark plugs have to ignite the fuel even sooner, if it is to be completely ignited when the piston reaches TDC. To do this, the distributor has a means to advance the timing of the spark as the engine speed increases. This is accomplished by centrifugal weights within the distributor and a vacuum diaphragm, mounted on the side of the distributor. It is necessary to disconnect the vacuum line from the diaphragm when the ignition timing is being set.

The timing is best checked with a timing light. This device is connected in series with the No. 1 spark plug. The current which fires the spark plug also causes the timing light to flash.

The timing marks are located at the front crankshaft pulley and consist of a notch on the crankshaft rotation attached to the front cover.

When the engine is running, the timing light is aimed at the marks on the flywheel pulley and the pointer.

IGNITION TIMING ADJUSTMENT

1. If equipped with a point type distributor, set the dwell to the proper specification. If equipped with electronic ignition type distributor, check and/or adjust the reluctor air gap.

2. Locate the timing marks on the crankshaft pulley and the front of the engine.

3. Clean off the timing marks so that you can see them.

4. Use chalk or white paint to color the mark on the crankshaft pulley and the mark on the scale which will indicate the correct timing when aligned with the notch on the crankshaft pulley.

5. Attach a tachometer and a timing light to the engine, according to the manufacturer's instructions.

6. Disconnect and plug the vacuum line at the distributor vacuum diaphragm.

NOTE: *On the A14 (1976–79), the E16 (1984 and later, except Calif. and Canada) and the*

34 TUNE-UP AND PERFORMANCE MAINTENANCE

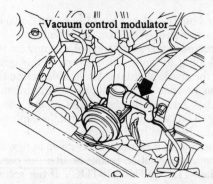

Location of the vacuum control module, E16 engine

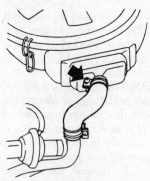

Disconnect the air injection hose when timing the engine—E16 engine (Canada)

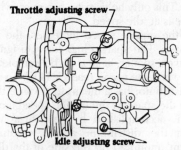

Location of the throttle and the idle adjusting screws—all engines, except E15ET

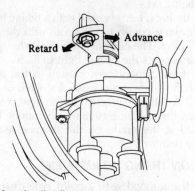

Turning the distributor to adjust the timing

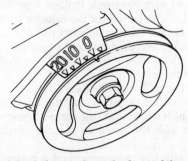

View of the timing marks at the front of the engine

E15ET (1984, Canada) engines, leave the vacuum line connected to the distributor vacuum diaphragm. On the Pulsar, E15ET (1984, Canadian Turbo) engines, disconnect

the Idle Speed Control (ISC) valve harness connector. On the Pulsar, E16 (1984 and later, except Calif. and Canada) engines, disconnect the Vacuum Control Modulator (VCM) valve harness connector to adjust the idle speed, then reconnect the harness and make sure that the idle speed is within the proper range.

7. Check to make sure that all of the wires clear the fan and then start the engine. Allow the engine to reach normal operating temperature.

CAUTION: *Be sure to block the wheels and set the parking brake; if equipped with an automatic transaxle, place the shift selector in the Drive position.*

8. Adjust the idle to the correct setting.

NOTE: *Before checking and/or adjusting the timing, make sure the electrical switches, such as: the headlights, the radiator cooling fan, the heater blower and the air conditioning are turned OFF; if equipped with power steering, make sure that the wheels are faced straight ahead.*

9. Aim the timing light at the timing marks at the front of the engine cover. If the timing marks are aligned when the light flashes, the timing is correct. Turn off the engine, then remove the tachometer and the timing light.

10. If the timing marks are not aligned, proceed with the following steps:

    a. Turn off the engine.

    b. Loosen the distributor lockbolt, just enough, so that the distributor can be turned with a little effort.

    c. Start the engine. Keep the wires of the timing light clear of the fan.

    d. With the timing light aimed at the crankshaft pulley and the timing plate on the engine, turn the distributor in the direction of rotor rotation to retard the spark and in the opposite direction to advance the spark. Align the marks on the pulley and the engine with the flashes of the timing light.

e. Tighten the hold-down bolt. Remove the tachometer and the timing light.

Valve Lash

Valve adjustment determines how far the valves enter the cylinder and how long they stay open and closed.

If the valve clearance is too large, part of the lift of the camshaft will be used in removing the excessive clearance. Consequently, the valve will not be opening as far as it should. This condition has two effects:

a. The valve train components will emit a tapping sound as they take up the excessive clearance.

b. The engine will perform poorly for the valves will not open fully and allow the proper amount of gases to flow through the cylinders.

If the valve clearance is too small, the valves will open too far and not fully seat in the cylinder head when they close. When a valve seats itself in the cylinder head, it does two things:

a. It seals the combustion chamber so that none of the gases in the cylinder escape.

b. It cools itself by transferring some of the heat it absorbs from the combustion process, through the cylinder head into the engine's cooling system.

If the valve clearance is too small, the engine will run poorly because of the gases escaping from the combustion chamber. The valves will also become overheated and warped, since they cannot transfer heat unless they are touching the valve seat in the cylinder head.

NOTE: *While all valve adjustments must be made as accurately as possible, it is better to have the valve adjustment slightly loose than slightly tight, as a burned valve may result from overly tight adjustments.*

VALVE ADJUSTMENT

1. Run the engine until it reaches normal operating temperature. Oil temperature, not water temperature, is critical to valve adjustment. With this in mind, make sure the engine is fully warmed up since this is the only way to make sure the parts have reached their full expansion. Generally speaking, this takes around fifteen minutes. After the engine has reached normal operating temperature, shut it off.

2. Purchase a new valve cover gasket before removing the valve cover. The new silicone gasket sealers are just as good or better if you can't find a gasket.

3. Note the location of any hoses or wires which may interfere with valve cover removal, disconnect and move them aside. Remove the bolts which hold the valve cover in place.

A series
Valve adjustment—

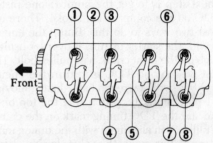

310 E-series and Pulsar valve adjustment

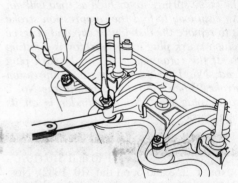

Typical valve adjustment with a feeler gauge

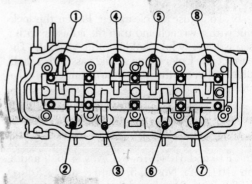

CA20 valve sequence—Stanza model

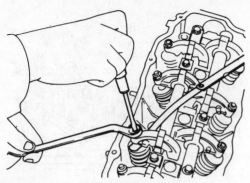

Adjusting the valves—Stanza model

4. After the valve cover has been removed, the next step is to get the number one piston at TDC on the compression stroke. There are at least two ways to do this: Bump the engine over with the starter or turn it over by using a wrench on the front crankshaft pulley bolt. The easiest way to find TDC is to turn the engine over slowly with a wrench (after first removing No. 1 plug) until the piston is at the top of its stroke and the TDC timing mark on the crankshaft pulley is in alignment with the timing mark pointer. At this point, the valves for No. 1 cylinder should be closed.

NOTE: *Make sure both valves are closed with the valve springs up as high as they will go. An easy way to find the compression stroke is to remove the distributor cap and observe which spark plug lead the rotor is pointing to. If the rotor points to No. 1 spark plug lead, No. 1 cylinder is on its compression stroke. When the rotor points to the No. 2 spark plug lead, No. 2 cylinder is on its compression stroke.*

5. Set the No. 1 piston at TDC of the compression stroke, then check and/or adjust the valve clearance on the F10 and 310 (1976–81), Nos. 1, 2, 3 and 5; on the 310 (1982), Nos. 1, 2, 3 and 6; on the Pulsar (1983 and later), Nos. 1, 2, 3 and 6; on the Stanza (1982), Nos. 1, 4, 6 and 7; on the Stanza (1983 and later), Nos. 1, 2, 4 and 6.

6. To adjust the clearance, loosen the locknut with a wrench and turn the adjuster with a screwdriver while holding the locknut. The correct size feeler gauge should pass with a slight drag between the rocker arm and the valve stem.

7. Turn the crankshaft one full revolution to position the No. 4 piston at TDC of the compression stroke. Check and/or adjust the valves (counting from the front to the rear) on the F10 and 310 (1976–81), Nos. 4, 6, 7 and 8; on 310 (1982), Nos. 4, 5, 7 and 8; on the Stanza (1982), Nos. 2, 3, 5 and 8; on the Stanza (1983

and later), Nos. 3, 5, 7 and 8; on the Pulsar (1983 and later), Nos. 4, 5, 7 and 8.

8. Replace the valve cover.

Carburetor

IDLE SPEED AND MIXTURE ADJUSTMENT

NOTE: *1980 and later models require a CO Meter to adjust their mixture ratios, therefore, no procedures concerning this adjustment are given. Also, many California models have a plug over their mixture control screw. It is suggested that in both of these cases, mixture adjustment to be left to a qualified technician.*

CAUTION: *When checking the idle speed, set the parking brake and block the drive wheels.*

NOTE: *Make sure that all of the electrical equipment is turned OFF, including: The headlights, the heater blower and the air conditioning.*

F10 Models (1976–78)

1. Connect a tachometer to the engine according the manufacturer's instructions.

2. Start the engine and operate it until it reaches operating temperatures.

3. Operate it at 2,000 rpm for five minutes under no load, then idle for ten minutes.

NOTE: *If the cooling fan is operating, wait until it stops.*

4. For U.S.A. models, disconnect and plug the air hose from the air check valve. For Canada models, disconnect and plug the air induction pipe at the air cleaner.

5. Race the engine to 1,500–2,000 rpm a few times under no-load, then run it for one minute at idle.

6. If the idle speed is not correct, adjust the throttle adjusting screw at the carburetor.

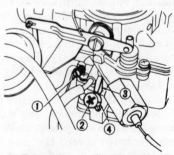

1. Throttle adjusting screw
2. Idle adjusting screw
3. Idle limiter cap
4. Stopper

Carburetor adjusting screws (1976–81)

7. When the idle speed is correct, stop the engine, reconnect the removed hose and disconnect the tachometer.

310 Models (1979–82)

1. Connect a tachometer to the engine according the manufacturer's instructions.

2. Start the engine and run it until it reaches normal operating temperatures.

3. For Canadian models, stop the engine, then disconnect and plug the air induction hose at the air filter. Start the engine and run it at idle speed for two minutes.

4. Operate it at 2,000 rpm for two minutes under no load, then idle for one minute.

NOTE: *If the cooling fan is operating, wait until it stops.*

5. If equipped with a manual transaxle, place the shift selector in Neutral; if equipped with an automatic transaxle, place the shift selector in Drive.

6. If the idle speed is not correct, adjust the throttle adjusting screw at the carburetor.

7. When the idle speed is correct, stop the engine and disconnect the tachometer, then reconnect the air induction hose (if removed).

Stanza Models (1982 and Later)

1. Connect a tachometer to the engine according the manufacturer's instructions.

2. Start the engine and run it until it reaches normal operating temperatures.

3. Operate it at 2,000 rpm for two minutes under no load, then idle for one minute.

NOTE: *If the cooling fan is operating, wait until it stops.*

4. If equipped with a manual transaxle, place the shift selector in Neutral; if equipped with an automatic transaxle, place the shift selector in Drive.

5. If the idle speed is not correct, adjust the throttle adjusting screw at the carburetor.

6. When the idle speed is correct, stop the engine and disconnect the tachometer.

Pulsar—E16 Engine (1983 and Later)

1. Connect a tachometer to the engine according the manufacturer's instructions.

2. Start the engine and run it until it reaches normal operating temperatures.

3. Operate it at idle for two minutes under no-load, then race to 2,000–3,000 a few times and allow it to return to idle speed.

4. Turn OFF the engine.

NOTE: *For U.S.A. models, disconnect the vacuum control modulator harness connector. For Canada models, disconnect and plug the air induction hose at the air filter; also, for Canada models (1984 and later), disconnect and plug the throttle opener control valve*

vacuum hose at the throttle opener control valve side.

5. Start the engine and check the idle speed.

NOTE: *If the cooling fan is operating, wait until it stops.*

6. If equipped with a manual transaxle, place the shift selector in Neutral; if equipped with an automatic transaxle, place the shift selector in Drive.

7. If the idle speed is not correct, adjust the throttle adjusting screw at the carburetor.

8. When the idle speed is correct, stop the engine, reconnect the vacuum control modulator and the throttle opener control valve vacuum hose (if equipped), then disconnect the tachometer.

THROTTLE BODY

Stanza (1984 and Later)

1. Connect a tachometer to the engine, according to the manufacturer's instructions.

2. Start and operate the engine until it reaches normal operating temperatures. Operate the engine for five minutes under no load.

NOTE: *Engage the parking brake and block the drive wheels. If equipped with a manual transaxle, place the shift selector in the Neutral position. If equipped with an automatic transaxle, place the shift selector in the Drive position.*

3. Check and/or adjust the engine speed. If

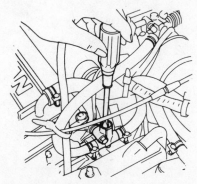

Adjusting the idle speed by turning the idle speed adjusting screw

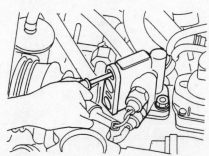

Adjusting the E15ET engine throttle adjusting screw

necessary to adjust, turn the idle speed adjusting screw.

4. With the idle speed adjusted, stop the engine and disconnect the tachometer.

Pulsar Turbo (1984, Canadian)

1. Connect a tachometer to the engine, according to the manufacturer's instructions.

2. Start and run the engine until it reaches normal operating temperatures. Operate the engine at 2,000 rpm, for two minutes under no-load.

3. Race the engine to 2,000–3,000 rpm a few times and allow it to go to idle speed.

NOTE: *Engage the parking brake and block the drive wheels. If equipped with a manual transaxle, place the shift selector in the Neutral position. If equipped with an automatic transaxle, place the shift selector in the Drive position.*

4. Check and/or adjust the engine speed. If necessary to adjust, turn the throttle adjusting screw.

5. With the idle speed adjusted, stop the engine and disconnect the tachometer.

Engine and Engine Rebuilding

3

UNDERSTANDING THE ENGINE ELECTRICAL SYSTEM

The engine electrical system can be broken down into three separate and distinct systems: (1) the starting system, (2) the charging system and (3) the ignition system.

Battery and Starting System

The battery is the first link in the chain of mechanisms which work together to provide cranking of the automobile engine. In most modern cars, the battery is a lead-acid electrochemical device consisting of six two-volt (2V) subsections connected in series so the unit is capable of producing approximately 12V of electrical pressure. Each subsection or cell consists of a series of positive and negative plates held a short distance apart in a solution of sulfuric acid and water. The two types of plates are of dissimilar metals. A chemical reaction occurs which produces current flow from the battery when its positive and negative terminals are connected to an electrical appliance such as a lamp or motor. The continued transfer of electrons would eventually convert the sulfuric acid in the electrolyte to water and make the two plates identical in chemical composition. As electrical energy is removed from the battery, its voltage output tends to drop. Thus, measuring the battery voltage and the battery electrolyte composition are two ways of checking the ability of the unit to supply power.

During the starting of the engine, electrical energy is removed from the battery. However, if the charging circuit is in good condition and the operating conditions are normal, the power removed from the battery will be replaced by the generator (alternator), which will force electrons back into the battery, reversing the normal flow and restoring the battery to its original chemical state.

The battery and the starting motor are linked by very heavy electrical cables, designed to minimize resistance to the flow of current. Generally, the major power supply cable that leaves the battery goes directly to the starter, while other electrical system needs are supplied by a smaller cable. During the starter operation, power flows from the battery to the starter, which is grounded through the car's frame and the battery's negative grounded strap.

The starting motor is a specially designed, direct current electric motor capable of producing a very great amount of power for its size. One thing that allows the motor to produce a great deal of power is its tremendous rotating speed. It drives the engine through a tiny pinion gear (attached to the starter's armature), which drives the very large flywheel ring gear at a greatly reduced speed. Another factor allowing it to produce so much power is that only intermittent operation is required of it. Thus, little allowance for air circulation is required and the windings can be built into a very small space.

The starter solenoid is a magnetic device which employs the small current supplied by the starting switch circuit of the ignition switch. This magnetic action moves a plunger which mechanically engages the starter and electrically closes the heavy switch which connects it to the battery. The starting switch circuit consists of the starting switch, contained within the ignition switch, a transaxle neutral safety switch or clutch pedal switch and the wiring necessary to connect these with the starter solenoid or relay.

A pinion, which is a small gear is mounted to a one-way drive clutch. This clutch is splined to the starter armature shaft. When the ignition switch is moved to the Start position, the solenoid plunger slides the pinion toward the flywheel ring gear by a collar and spring. If the teeth on the pinion and the flywheel match properly, the pinion will engage the flywheel immediately. If the gear teeth butt one another, the spring will be compressed and force the gears to mesh as soon as the starter turns far enough to allow them to do so. As the solenoid plunger reaches the end of its travel, it closes the contacts that connect the battery and starter, then the engine is cranked.

As soon as the engine starts, the flywheel ring gear begins turning fast enough to drive the pinion at an extremely high rate of speed. At this point, the one-way clutch begins, allowing the pinion to spin faster than the starter shaft so that the starter will not operate at excessive speed. When the ignition switch is released from the Start position, the solenoid is de-energized and a spring contained within the solenoid assembly pulls the gear out of mesh and interrupts the current flow to the starter.

Some starters employ a separate relay, mounted away from the starter, to switch the motor and solenoid current on and off. The relay thus replaces the solenoid electrical switch but does not eliminate the need to mechanically engage the starter drive gears. The relay is used to reduce the amount of current the starting switch must carry.

The Charging System

The automobile charging system provides electrical power for operation of the vehicle's ignition and starting systems and all the electrical accessories. The battery serves as an electrical surge or storage tank, storing (in chemical form) the energy originally produced by the engine-driven generator. The system also provides a means of regulating generator output to protect the battery from being overcharged and to avoid excessive voltage to the accessories.

The storage battery is a chemical device incorporating parallel lead plates in a tank containing a sulfuric acid-water solution. Adjacent plates are slightly dissimilar and the chemical reaction of the two dissimilar plates produces electrical energy when the battery is connected to a load such as the starter motor. The chemical reaction is reversible, so that when the alternator is producing a voltage (electrical pressure) greater than that produced by the battery, electricity is forced into the battery and it is returned to its fully charged state.

The alternator is driven mechanically, through V-belts, by the engine crankshaft. It consists of two coils of fine wire, one stationary (the stator) and the other movable (the rotor). The rotor may also be known as the armature and consists of fine wire wrapped around an iron core which is mounted on a shaft. The electricity which flows through the two coils of wire (provided initially by the battery in some cases) creates an intense magnetic field around both rotor and stator, this interaction between the two fields creates voltage, allowing the alternator to power the accessories and charge the battery.

Alternators, being more efficient than generators, can be rotated at higher speeds and have fewer brush problems. In a alternator, the field rotates while all of the current produced passes ONLY through the stator windings. The brushes bear against the continuous slip rings rather than a commutator. This causes the current produced to periodically reverse the direction of its flow. Diodes (electrical one-way switches) block the flow of the current from traveling in the wrong direction. A series of diodes are wired together to permit the alternating flow of the stator to be converted into a pulsating but unidirectional flow at the alternator output. The alternator's field is wired in series with the voltage regulator.

The regulator consists of several circuits. Each circuit has a core or a magnetic coil of wire, which operates as a switch. Each switch is connected to a ground through one or more resistors. The coil of wire responds directly to the system voltage. When the voltage reaches the required level, the magnetic field, created by the winding of the wire, closes the switch and inserts a resistance into the field circuit, thus reducing the output. The contacts of the switch cycle open and close many times each second to precisely control voltage.

SAFETY PRECAUTIONS

Observing these precautions will ensure safe handling of the electrical system components and avoid damage to the vehicle's electrical system:

A. Be *absolutely* sure of the polarity of a booster battery before making connections. Connect the cables positive-to-positive and negative-to-negative. Connect the positive cables first and then make the last connection to a ground on the body of the booster vehicle, so that arcing cannot ignite hydrogen gas that may have accumulated near the battery. Even momentary connection of a booster battery with the polarity reversed will damage the alternator diodes.

B. Disconnect both vehicle battery cables before attempting to charge a battery.

C. Never ground the alternator output or battery terminal. Be cautious when using metal tools around a battery to avoid creating a short circuit between the terminals.

D. Never ground the field circuit between the alternator and the regulator.

E. Never run an alternator without a load, unless the field circuit is disconnected.

F. Never attempt to polarize an alternator.

G. Keep the regulator cover in place when taking the voltage and current limiter readings.

H. Use insulated tools when adjusting the regulator.

Troubleshooting the Electronic Ignition System

F10 Model (1976–78)

The main difference between the 1976–77 and the 1978 systems are: (1) the 1976–77 system uses an external ballast resistor located next to the ignition coil and (2) the earlier system uses a wiring harness with individual eyelet connectors to the electronic unit, while the later system uses a multiple plug connector. You will need an accurate voltmeter and ohmmeter for these tests, which must be performed in the order given:

1. Check all of the connections for corrosion, looseness, breaks and etc., then correct, if necessary. Clean and gap the spark plugs.

2. Disconnect the harness (connector of the plug) from the electronic unit. Turn the ignition switch ON. Set the voltmeter to the DC 50v range.

 a. Connect the positive (+) voltmeter lead to the black/white wire terminal and the negative (−) lead to the black wire terminal. Battery voltage should be obtained. If not, check the black/white and the black wires for continuity; check the battery terminals for corrosion; check the battery state of charge.

 b. Connect the voltmeter positive (+) lead to the blue wire and the negative (−) lead to the black wire. Battery voltage should be obtained. If not, check the blue wire for continuity; check the ignition coil terminals for corrosion or looseness; check the coil for continuity. On the 1976–77 models also check the external ballast resistor.

3. Disconnect the harness from the electronic control unit. Using an Ohmmeter, set it in the X10 range, then connect it to the red and green wire terminals. The resistance should be 720Ω. If the reading is far more or less, replace the distributor pick-up coil.

4. Disconnect the anti-dieseling solenoid valve connector (refer to Chapter 4). Using a voltmeter, set it to the AC 2.5v range, then connect the leads to the red and green terminals of the electronic control harness. When the starter is cranked, the needle should deflect slightly. If not replace the distributor pick-up coil.

5. Reconnect the ignition coil and the electronic control unit. Leave the anti-dieseling solenoid valve wire disconnected. Unplug the high tension lead (coil-to-distributor) from the distributor and hold it $\frac{1}{8}$–$\frac{1}{4}$ in. from the cylinder head with a pair of insulated pliers and a heavy glove. When the engine is cranked, a spark should be observed. If not, check the lead and replace, if necessary. If still no spark, replace the electronic control unit.

6. Reconnect all of the wires. Using a voltmeter, set it on the DC 50v range.

 a. 1976–77: Connect the voltmeter (+) lead to the blue electronic control harness connector and the (−) lead to the black wire. The harness should be attached to the control unit.

 b. 1978: Connect the voltmeter (+) lead to the (−) terminal of the ignition coil and the (−) lead to ground.

 c. Once the ignition switch is turned ON, the meter should indicate battery voltage. If not, replace the electronic control unit.

310 Model (1979–81)

1. Make a check of the power supply circuit. Turn the ignition OFF and disconnect the wiring connector from the distributor unit. Turn the ignition ON. Using a voltmeter, set it on DC 50v range, then measure the voltage at the B terminal of the connector in turn by touching the positive probe of the voltmeter to it and touching the negative probe to a ground, such as the engine. The battery voltage should be indicated. If not, check all of the wiring, the ignition switch and all of the connectors for breaks, corrosion, discontinuity and etc., repair as necessary.

2. To check the pick-coil resistance, turn the ignition OFF, then remove the distributor cap and the ignition rotor. Using an ohmmeter, measure the resistance between the two terminals of the pick-up coil where they are attached to the IC unit. If approximately 400Ω are indicated, the pick-up coil is OK; if the reading is substantially more or less than 400Ω, check the pick-up coil and the wiring to it.

3. Check the pick-up coil output: The engine must be at normal operating temperatures. Using a voltmeter, set it on the AC 5v scale, then attach the (+) lead to the pick-up coil terminal and the (−) lead to a ground. Turn the ignition switch to the Start position. While the engine is cranking, observe the voltmeter needle, if the needle is moving, replace the IC unit; if the needle is steady, check the wiring between the IC unit and the pick-up coil and/or the physical condition of the pick-up coil and the reluctor.

4. With a new pick-up coil installed, install

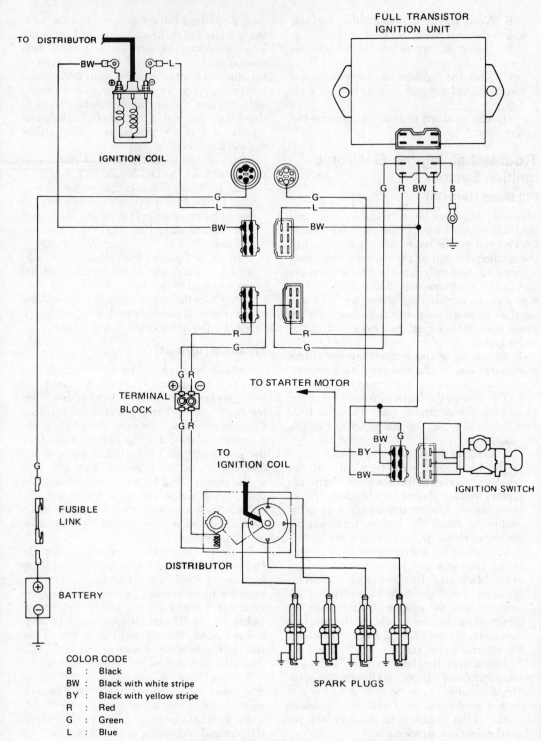

Electronic ignition schematic—1976–77 F10 model

the IC unit. Check for spark at one of the spark plugs (see Step 4.1 in the Troubleshooting Section at the end of this Chapter). If a good spark is obtained, the IC unit is OK; if not, replace the IC unit.

All Models (1982 and Later)

NOTE: *To conduct the following tests, disconnect and remove the distributor cap. When necessary to check the primary and*

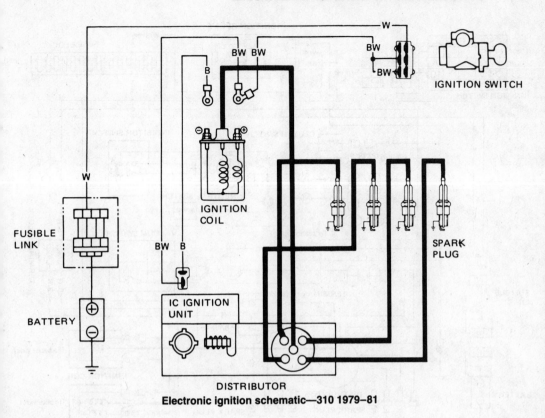

Electronic ignition schematic—310 1979–81

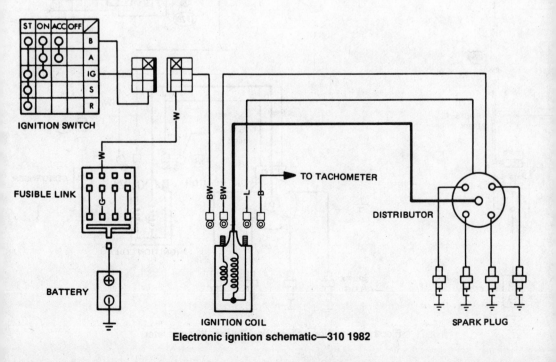

Electronic ignition schematic—310 1982

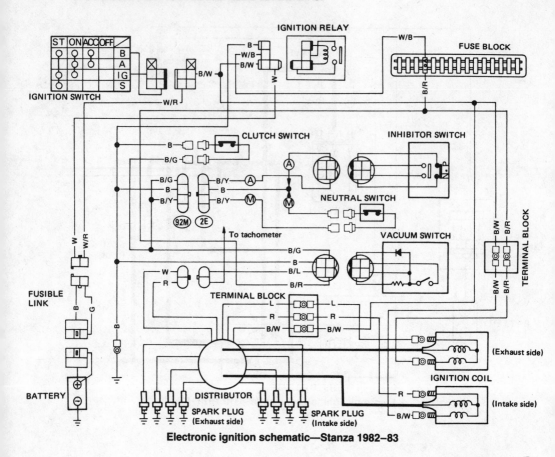

Electronic ignition schematic—Stanza 1982–83

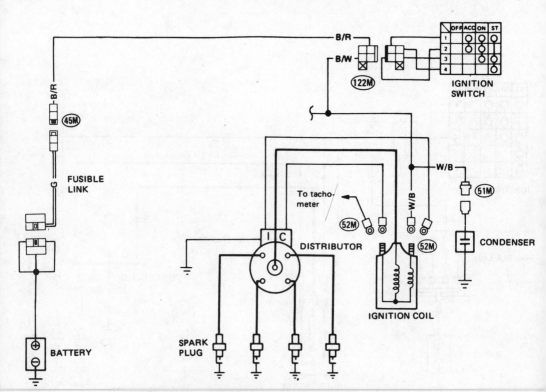

Electronic ignition schematic—Pulsar 1983 and later

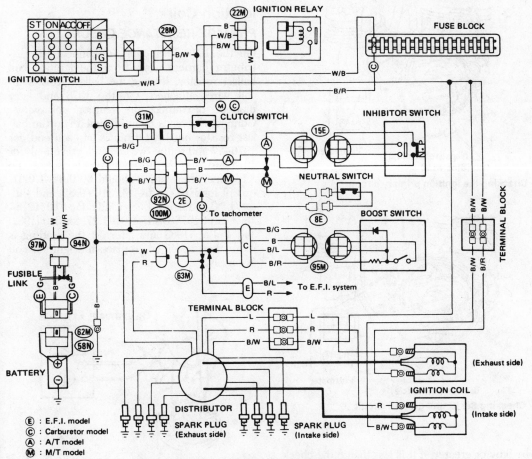

Electronic ignition schematic—Stanza 1984 and later

secondary resistance of the ignition coil, refer to Ignition Coil in this section.

POWER SUPPLY CIRCUIT

At the distributor, pull the black/white wire from the IC unit. Using a voltmeter, set it on the DC 15v scale, then connect the positive (+) lead to the black/white wire and the negative (−) lead to ground. Turn the ignition switch to the ON position. The voltmeter reading should be 11.5–12.5v; if not, check the wiring from the ignition switch to the IC unit. Replace the black/white wire.

POWER SUPPLY CRANKING CIRCUIT

At the distributor, pull the black/white wire from the IC unit. Using a voltmeter, set it on the DC 15v scale, then connect the positive (+) lead to the black/white wire and the negative (−) lead to ground. Pull the high tension wire from the center terminal of the distributor cap and ground it. Turn the ignition switch to the START position. The voltmeter reading should

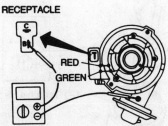

Testing the power supply circuit, for model 310—1979–81

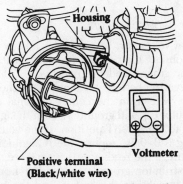

Checking the power supply ignition and cranking circuit

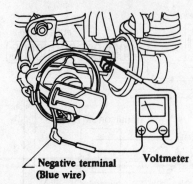

Negative terminal **Voltmeter**
(Blue wire)
Checking the ignition primary circuit

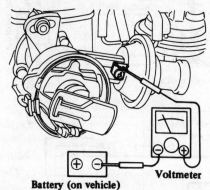

Battery (on vehicle) **Voltmeter**
Checking the IC unit ground circuit

be 8.6v or greater; if it is less than 8.6v, check the ignition switch and the wiring from the ignition switch to the IC unit. Replace the black/white wire.

IGNITION PRIMARY CIRCUIT

At the distributor, pull the blue wire from the IC unit. Using a voltmeter, set it on the DC 15v scale, then connect the positive (+) lead to the blue wire and the negative (−) lead to ground. Turn the ignition switch ON. The voltmeter reading should be 11.5–12.5v; if below 11.5v, check the ignition coil primary circuit.

IC UNIT GROUND CIRCUIT

Using a voltmeter, set it on the DC 5v scale, then connect the positive (+) lead to the distributor ground and the negative (−) lead to the negative battery terminal. Pull the high tension wire from the center terminal of the distributor cap and ground it. Turn the ignition switch to the START position. If the voltmeter reading is 0–0.5v, replace the IC ignition unit assembly; if the reading is 0.5v or more, check the distributor ground, the wiring from the chassis ground to the battery and the battery terminal connectors.

Ignition Coil
PRIMARY RESISTANCE CHECK

On the 1976–77 models, disconnect the distributor harness wires from the ignition coil ballast resistor, leaving the ballast resistor-to-coil wires attached. On the 1978 and later models, disconnect the ignition coil wires. Connect the leads of an ohmmeter to the ballast resistor outside terminals (at each end) for 1976–77 and to the two coil (side) terminals for 1978 and later. With the ohmmeter set on the X1 range, the reading should be 0.84–1.02Ω, except for F10 (1976–78), 310 (1982) and Pulsar (1983 and later); 1.08–1.32Ω, for F10 (1976–78, except 1978 USA); 1.04–1.27, for 310 (1982) and Pulsar (1983 and later); if the reading is more than specified, replace the ignition coil assembly.

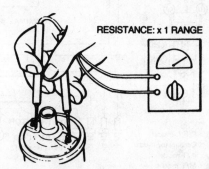

RESISTANCE: x 1 RANGE

Checking the primary circuit of the ignition coil

SECONDARY RESISTANCE CHECK

Turn the ignition key OFF, then remove the high tension and a primary coil wire from the coil. Using an ohmmeter, set it on the X1000 scale. Touch one lead to a primary terminal and the other lead to the center terminal. The resistance should be 8,200–12,400Ω, except F10 (1978, USA), 310 (1982) and Pulsar (1983 and later); 7,300–11,000, for 310 (1982) and Pulsar (1983 and later); and 17,000–23,000Ω, for F10 (1978, USA); if not, replace the ignition coil.

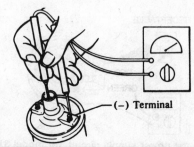

(−) Terminal

Checking the secondary circuit of the ignition coil

Distributor

REMOVAL

1. Unfasten the retaining clips and lift the distributor cap straight up.

NOTE: *It will be easier to install the distributor if the wiring is not disconnected from the cap. If the wires must be removed from the cap, mark their positions to aid in installations.*

2. Disconnect the distributor wiring harness.

3. Disconnect the vacuum lines.

4. Note the position of the rotor in relation to the base. Scribe a mark on the base of the distributor and on the engine block to facilitate reinstallation. Align the marks with the direction the metal tip of the rotor is pointing.

5. Remove the bolt which hold the distributor to the engine.

6. Pull the distributor assembly from the engine.

INSTALLATION

1. Insert the distributor shaft and assembly into the engine. Line up the mark on the distributor and the one on the engine with the metal tip of the rotor. Make sure that the vacuum advance diaphragm is pointed in the same direction as it was pointed originally. This will be done automatically if the marks on the engine and the distributor are lined up with the rotor.

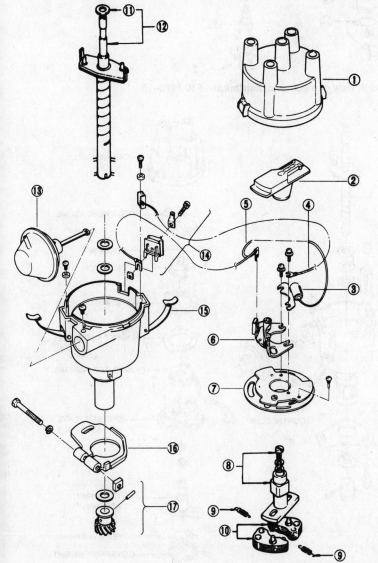

1. Cap
2. Rotor
3. Condenser
4. Ground wire
5. Lead wire
6. Breaker points
7. Breaker plate
8. Cam assembly
9. Governor spring
10. Governor weight
11. Thrust washer
12. Shaft assembly
13. Vacuum control assembly
14. Terminal assembly
15. Clamp
16. Retaining plate
17. Gear set

Exploded view of the single point distributor—F10 1976–77

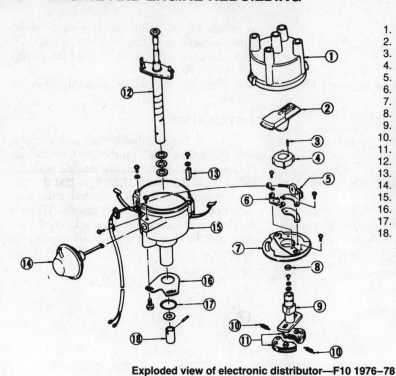

1. Cap assembly
2. Rotor head assembly
3. Roll pin
4. Reluctor
5. Pick-up coil
6. Contactor
7. Breaker plate assembly
8. Packing
9. Rotor shaft
10. Governor spring
11. Governor weight
12. Shaft assembly
13. Cap setter
14. Vacuum controller
15. Housing
16. Fixing plate
17. O-ring
18. Collar

Exploded view of electronic distributor—F10 1976–78

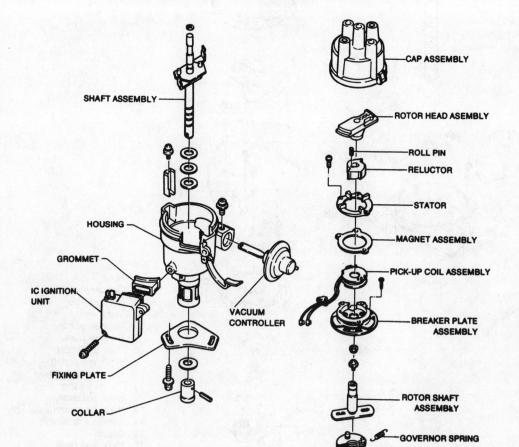

Exploded view of electronic distributor—310 1979–81

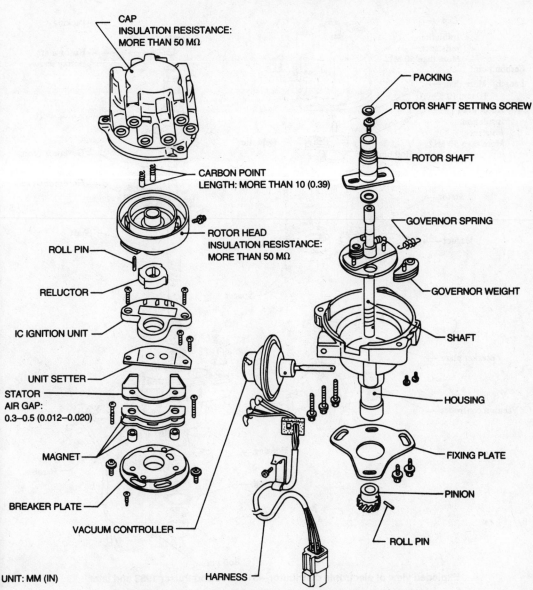

CAP
INSULATION RESISTANCE:
MORE THAN 50 MΩ

PACKING

ROTOR SHAFT SETTING SCREW

ROTOR SHAFT

CARBON POINT
LENGTH: MORE THAN 10 (0.39)

GOVERNOR SPRING

ROTOR HEAD
INSULATION RESISTANCE:
MORE THAN 50 MΩ

ROLL PIN

RELUCTOR

GOVERNOR WEIGHT

IC IGNITION UNIT

SHAFT

UNIT SETTER

STATOR
AIR GAP:
0.3–0.5 (0.012–0.020)

HOUSING

MAGNET

FIXING PLATE

BREAKER PLATE

PINION

VACUUM CONTROLLER

ROLL PIN

UNIT: MM (IN)

HARNESS

Exploded view of electronic distributor—Stanza 1982 and later

2. Install the distributor hold-down bolt and clamp. Leave the screw loose so that you can move the distributor with heavy hand pressure.

3. Connect the primary wire to the coil. Install the distributor cap on the distributor housing. Secure the distributor cap with the spring clips.

4. Install the spark plug wires if removed. Make sure that the wires are pressed all the way into the top of the distributor cap and firmly onto the spark plug.

5. Adjust the point dwell (non-electronic) and set the ignition timing.

NOTE: *If the crankshaft has been turned or the engine disturbed in any manner (disas-* *sembled and/or rebuilt) while the distributor was removed or if the marks were not drawn, it will be necessary to initially time the engine. Follow the procedure given below.*

INSTALLATION–ENGINE DISTURBED

1. It is necessary to place the No. 1 cylinder in the firing position to correctly install the distributor. To locate this position, the ignition timing marks on the crankshaft front pulley are used.

2. Remove the No. 1 cylinder spark plug. Turn the crankshaft until the piston in the No. 1 cylinder is moving up on the compression stroke. This can be determined by placing your

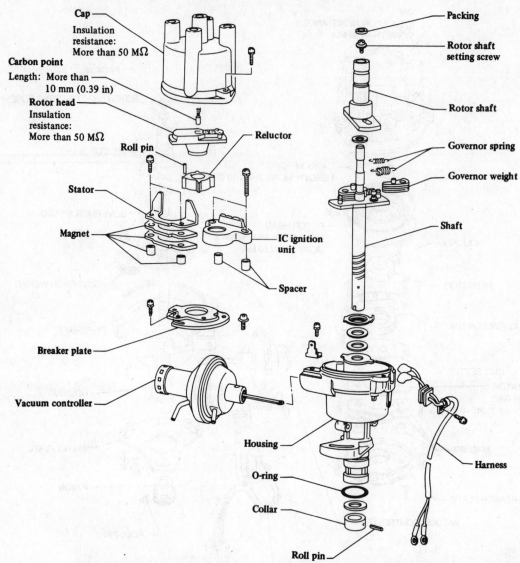

Cap
Insulation resistance: More than 50 MΩ

Carbon point
Length: More than 10 mm (0.39 in)

Rotor head
Insulation resistance: More than 50 MΩ

Roll pin

Stator

Magnet

Breaker plate

Vacuum controller

Packing

Rotor shaft setting screw

Rotor shaft

Governor spring

Governor weight

Shaft

Reluctor

IC ignition unit

Spacer

Housing

O-ring

Collar

Roll pin

Harness

Exploded view of electronic distributor—310 1982 and Pulsar 1983 and later

thumb over the spark plug hole and feeling the air being forced out of the cylinder. Stop turning the crankshaft when the timing marks that are used to time the engine are aligned.

3. Oil the distributor housing lightly where the distributor bears on the cylinder block.

4. Install the distributor with the rotor, which is mounted on the shaft, pointing toward the No. 1 spark plug terminal on the distributor cap. Of course you won't be able to see the direction in which the rotor is pointing if the cap is on the distributor.

NOTE: *Lay the cap on top of the distributor and make a mark on the side of the distributor housing just below the No. 1 spark plug terminal. Make sure that the rotor points toward that mark when you install the distributor.*

5. When the distributor shaft has reached the bottom of the hole, move the rotor back and forth slightly until the driving lug on the end of the shaft enters the slots cut in the end of the oil pump shaft and the distributor assembly slides down into place.

6. When the distributor is correctly installed, the breaker points (non-electronic) should be in such a position that they are just ready to break contact. This is accomplished by rotating the distributor body after it has been installed in the engine. Once again, line up the marks that you made before the distributor was removed from the engine.

7. Install the distributor hold-down bolt.

8. Install the spark plug and continue from Step 3 of the proceeding distributor installation procedure.

Alternator
ALTERNATOR PRECAUTIONS

To prevent damage to the alternator and regulator, the following precautionary measures must be taken when working with the electrical system.

1. Never reverse the battery connections.

2. Booster batteries for starting must be connected properly. Make sure that the posi-

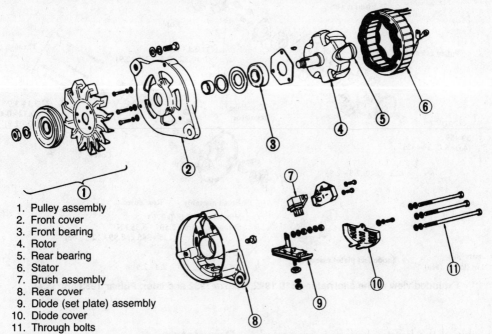

1. Pulley assembly
2. Front cover
3. Front bearing
4. Rotor
5. Rear bearing
6. Stator
7. Brush assembly
8. Rear cover
9. Diode (set plate) assembly
10. Diode cover
11. Through bolts

Exploded view of the alternator—F10 1976–77

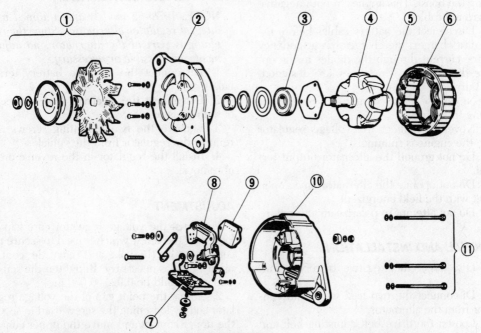

1. Pulley assembly
2. Front cover
3. Front bearing
4. Rotor
5. Rear bearing
6. Stator
7. Diode (Set plate) assembly
8. Brush assembly
9. IC voltage regulator
10. Rear cover
11. Through bolt

Integral regulator type alternator

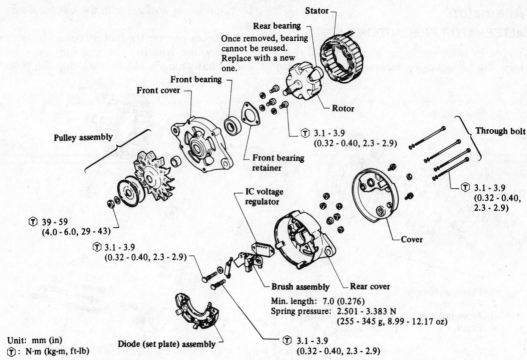

Stator

Rear bearing
Once removed, bearing
cannot be reused.
Replace with a new
one.

Front bearing
Front cover

Rotor

Pulley assembly

⊤ 3.1 - 3.9
(0.32 - 0.40, 2.3 - 2.9)

Through bolt

Front bearing
retainer

⊤ 3.1 - 3.9
(0.32 - 0.40,
2.3 - 2.9)

IC voltage
regulator

⊤ 39 - 59
(4.0 - 6.0, 29 - 43)

Cover

⊤ 3.1 - 3.9
(0.32 - 0.40, 2.3 - 2.9)

Brush assembly   Rear cover

Min. length: 7.0 (0.276)
Spring pressure: 2.501 - 3.383 N
(255 - 345 g, 8.99 - 12.17 oz)

Unit: mm (in)
⊤ : N·m (kg-m, ft-lb)

Diode (set plate) assembly

⊤ 3.1 - 3.9
(0.32 - 0.40, 2.3 - 2.9)

Exploded view of the alternator—310 1982, Stanza 1982 and later, Pulsar 1983 and later

tive cable of the booster battery is connected to the positive terminal of the battery that is getting the boost. This applies to both negative and ground cables.

3. Disconnect the battery cables before using a fast charger; the charger has a tendency to force current through the diodes in the opposite direction for which they are designed. This burns out the diodes.

4. Never use a fast charger as a booster for starting the vehicle.

5. Never disconnect the voltage regulator while the engine is running.

6. Do not ground the alternator output terminal.

7. Do not operate the alternator on an open circuit with the field energized.

8. Do not attempt to polarize an alternator.

REMOVAL AND INSTALLATION

1. Disconnect the negative battery terminal.

2. Disconnect the two lead wires and connector from the alternator.

3. Loosen the drive belt adjusting bolt and remove the belt.

4. Unscrew the alternator attaching bolts and remove the alternator from the vehicle.

5. Install the alternator in the reverse order of removal.

Regulator

REMOVAL AND INSTALLATION

NOTE: *1978–82 models are equipped with integral regulator alternators. Since the regulator is part of the alternator, no adjustments are possible or necessary.*

1. Disconnect the negative battery terminal.

2. Disconnect the electrical lead connector of the regulator.

3. Remove the two mounting screws and remove the regulator from the vehicle.

4. Install the regulator in the reverse order of removal.

ADJUSTMENT

1. Adjust the voltage regulator core gap by loosening the screw which is used to secure the contact set on the yoke and move the contact up or down as necessary. Retighten the screw. The gap should be 0.024–0.039 in.

2. Adjust the point gap of the voltage regulator coil by loosening the screw used to secure the upper contact and move the upper contact up or down. The point gap is 0.014–0.018 in.

3. The core gap and point gap on the charge relay coil is or are adjusted in the same manner as previously outlined for the voltage regulator coil. The core gap is to be set at 0.031–0.039

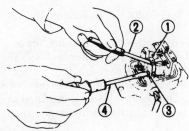

1. Contact set
2. Thickness gauge
3. 4 mm (0.157 in) dia. screw
4. Phillips screwdriver

Adjusting the core gap

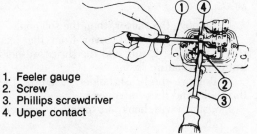

1. Feeler gauge
2. Screw
3. Phillips screwdriver
4. Upper contact

Adjusting the point gap

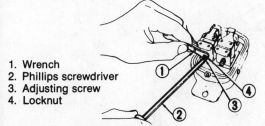

1. Wrench
2. Phillips screwdriver
3. Adjusting screw
4. Locknut

Adjusting the regulated voltage

in. and the point gap adjusted to 0.012–0.016 in.

4. The regulated voltage is adjusted by loosening the locknut and turning the adjusting screw clockwise to increase or counter-clockwise to decrease the regulated voltage. The voltage should be between 14.3–15.3 volts at 68°F.

Starter

In 1978, a gear reduction starter was introduced on some Canadian and United States models. The differences between the gear reduction and conventional starters are: the gear reduction starter has a set of ratio reduction gears while the conventional starter does not; the brushes on the gear reduction starter (except for 310–1982, Pulsar–1983 and later) are located on a plate behind the starter drive housing, while the conventional and the gear reduction (for 310–1982, Pulsar–1983 and later) starter brushes are located at the rear cover. The extra gears on the gear reduction starter make the starter pinion gear turn at about half the speed of the starter, giving the starter twice the turning power of a conventional starter.

REMOVAL AND INSTALLATION

1. Disconnect the negative battery cable from the battery.

2. Disconnect the starter wiring at the starter, taking note of the positions for correct reinstallation.

3. Remove the bolts attaching the starter to the engine and remove the starter from the vehicle.

Alternator and Regulator Specifications

Model	Year	Alternator Identification Number	Rated Output @ 5000 RPM	Output @ 2500 RPM (not less than)	Brush Length (in.)	Brush Spring Tension (oz.)	Regulated Voltage
F-10	1976–77	LT150-26 ①	50	37.5	0.295	9.0–12.2	14.3–15.3
	1978	LR150-36	50	40	0.295	8.99–12.7	14.3–15.3
		LR160-46 ②	60	45	0.295	8.99–12.17	14.4–15.0
310 U.S.A.	1979–80	LR160-46	60	40	0.295	8.99–12.17	14.4–15.0
310 Canada	1979–80	LR150-36	50	40	0.295	8.99–12.17	14.4–15.0
310 U.S.A.	1981–82	LR160-125	50	42	0.295	8.99–12.17	14.4–15.0
310 Canada	1981–82	LR150-99	50	40	0.295	8.99–12.17	14.4–15.0
Stanza	1982–86	LR160-104	60	50	0.295	8.99–12.17	14.4–15.1
	1985–86	LR170-14	70	50	0.295	8.99–12.17	14.4–15.0
Pulsar	1983–86	LR150-125B	50	42	0.295	8.99–12.17	14.4–15.0
	1984	LR160-121	60	50	0.295	8.99–12.17	14.4–15.0

① Uses external voltage regulator
② With air conditioning

4. Install the starter in the reverse order of removal.

BRUSH REPLACEMENT
Non-Reduction Gear Type

1. With the starter out of the vehicle, remove the bolts holding the solenoid to the top of the starter and remove the solenoid.

2. To remove the brushes, remove the two thru-bolts, the two rear cover attaching screws (some models) and the rear cover.

3. Using a wire hook, lift the brush springs to separate the brushes from the commutator.

4. Install the brushes in the reverse order of removal.

Reduction Gear Type

F10 (1978), 310 (1979–81) AND STANZA (1982 AND LATER) MODELS

1. Remove the starter, then the solenoid.

2. Remove the thru-bolts and the rear cover. The rear cover can be pried off with a screw-driver, be careful not to damage the O-ring or gasket.

3. Remove the starter housing, armature and brush holder from the center housing. They can be removed as an assembly.

4. Remove the positive side brush from its holder. The positive brush is insulated from the brush holder and its lead wire is connected to the field coil.

5. Using a wire hook, lift the negative brush from the commutator and remove it from the holder.

6. Installation is the reverse of the removal.

310 (1982) AND PULSAR (1983 AND LATER) MODELS

1. Remove the starter, then the solenoid.

2. Remove the dust cover from the rear cover, then the E-ring and the thrust washers from the armature shaft.

3. Remove the brush holder setscrews, the thru-bolts and the rear cover.

4. Using a wire hook, lift springs to separate

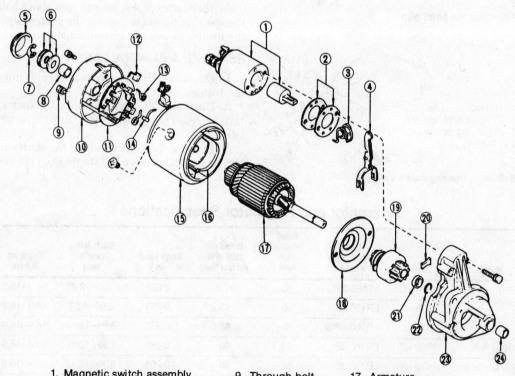

1. Magnetic switch assembly
2. Dust cover (Adjusting washer)
3. Torsion spring
4. Shift lever
5. Dust cover
6. Thrust washer
7. E-ring
8. Rear cover metal
9. Through bolt
10. Rear cover
11. Brush holder
12. Brush (−)
13. Brush spring
14. Brush (+)
15. Yoke
16. Field coil
17. Armature
18. Center bracket
19. Pinion assembly
20. Dust cover
21. Pinion stopper
22. Stopper clip
23. Gear case
24. Gear case metal

Exploded view of the non-reduction gear starter for F10 (1976–78) and 310 (1979–81)

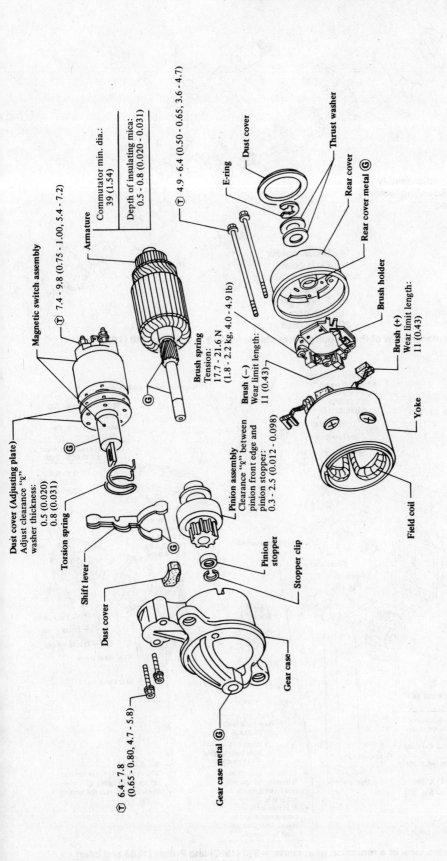

Dust cover (Adjusting plate)
Adjust clearance "ℓ"
washer thickness:
0.5 (0.020)
0.8 (0.031)

Magnetic switch assembly

Ⓣ 7.4 - 9.8 (0.75 - 1.00, 5.4 - 7.2)

Armature

Commutator min. dia.:
39 (1.54)

Depth of insulating mica:
0.5 - 0.8 (0.020 - 0.031)

Ⓣ 4.9 - 6.4 (0.50 - 0.65, 3.6 - 4.7)

E-ring

Dust cover

Rear cover

Thrust washer

Rear cover metal Ⓖ

Brush holder

Brush spring
Tension:
17.7 - 21.6 N
(1.8 - 2.2 kg, 4.0 - 4.9 lb)

Brush (−)
Wear limit length:
11 (0.43)

Brush (+)
Wear limit length:
11 (0.43)

Pinion assembly
Clearance "ℓ" between
pinion front edge and
pinion stopper:
0.3 - 2.5 (0.012 - 0.098)

Yoke

Field coil

Torsion spring

Shift lever

Dust cover

Pinion
stopper

Stopper clip

Gear case

Ⓣ 6.4 - 7.8
(0.65 - 0.80, 4.7 - 5.8)

Gear case metal Ⓖ

Unit: mm (in)
Ⓣ : N·m (kg-m, ft-lb)
Ⓖ : High-temperature grease point

Exploded view of a non-reduction gear starter—1982 and later

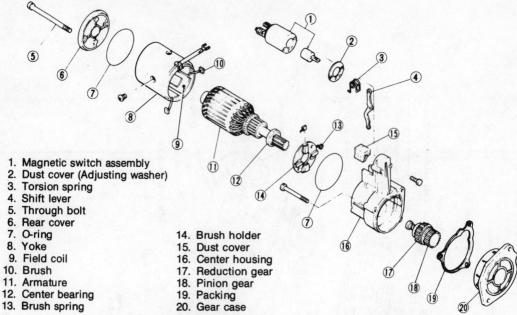

1. Magnetic switch assembly
2. Dust cover (Adjusting washer)
3. Torsion spring
4. Shift lever
5. Through bolt
6. Rear cover
7. O-ring
8. Yoke
9. Field coil
10. Brush
11. Armature
12. Center bearing
13. Brush spring
14. Brush holder
15. Dust cover
16. Center housing
17. Reduction gear
18. Pinion gear
19. Packing
20. Gear case

Exploded view of the reduction gear starter for F10 (1978) and 310 (1979–81)

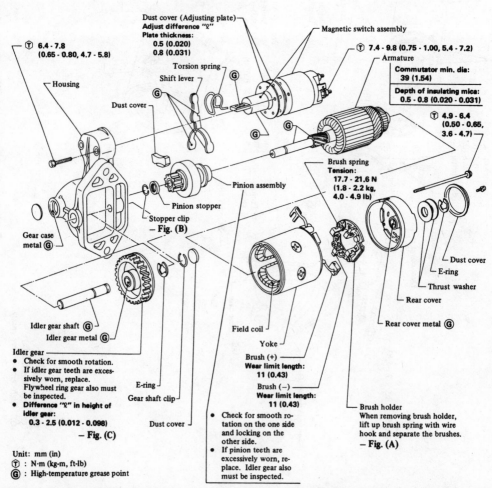

Dust cover (Adjusting plate)
Adjust difference "ℓ"
Plate thickness:
0.5 (0.020)
0.8 (0.031)

Torsion spring
Shift lever

Dust cover

Housing

Ⓣ 6.4 - 7.8
(0.65 - 0.80, 4.7 - 5.8)

Magnetic switch assembly

Ⓣ 7.4 - 9.8 (0.75 - 1.00, 5.4 - 7.2)
Armature

Commutator min. dia:
39 (1.54)

Depth of insulating mica:
0.5 - 0.8 (0.020 - 0.031)

Ⓣ 4.9 - 6.4
(0.50 - 0.65,
3.6 - 4.7)

Brush spring
Tension:
17.7 - 21.6 N
(1.8 - 2.2 kg,
4.0 - 4.9 lb)

Pinion assembly

Pinion stopper

Stopper clip
— Fig. (B)

Gear case
metal Ⓖ

Dust cover
E-ring
Thrust washer
Rear cover
Rear cover metal Ⓖ

Idler gear shaft Ⓖ
Idler gear metal Ⓖ

Field coil
Yoke

Brush (+)
Wear limit length:
11 (0.43)

Brush (−)
Wear limit length:
11 (0.43)

Brush holder
When removing brush holder,
lift up brush spring with wire
hook and separate the brushes.
— Fig. (A)

Idler gear
- Check for smooth rotation.
- If idler gear teeth are excessively worn, replace.
  Flywheel ring gear also must be inspected.
- Difference "ℓ" in height of idler gear:
  0.3 - 2.5 (0.012 - 0.098)
  — Fig. (C)

E-ring
Gear shaft clip
Dust cover

- Check for smooth rotation on the one side and locking on the other side.
- If pinion teeth are excessively worn, replace. Idler gear also must be inspected.

Unit: mm (in)
Ⓣ : N·m (kg-m, ft-lb)
Ⓖ : High-temperature grease point

Exploded view of a reduction gear starter—310 (1982) and Pulsar (1983 and later)

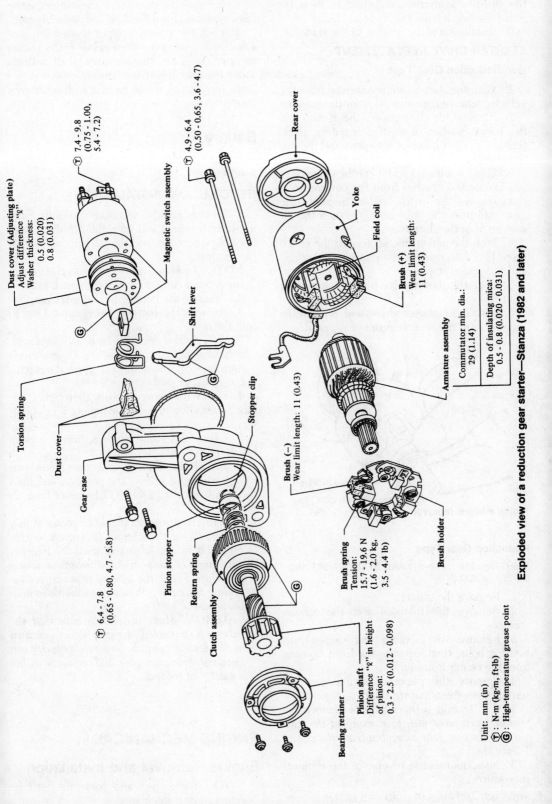

Dust cover (Adjusting plate)
Adjust difference "ℓ"
Washer thickness:
0.5 (0.020)
0.8 (0.031)

Ⓣ 7.4 - 9.8
(0.75 - 1.00,
5.4 - 7.2)

Ⓣ 4.9 - 6.4
(0.50 - 0.65, 3.6 - 4.7)

Rear cover

Magnetic switch assembly

Yoke

Field coil

Brush (+)
Wear limit length:
11 (0.43)

Shift lever

Ⓖ

Torsion spring

Dust cover

Gear case

Stopper clip

Ⓖ

Ⓖ

Brush (−)
Wear limit length: 11 (0.43)

Armature assembly

Commutator min. dia.:
29 (1.14)

Depth of insulating mica:
0.5 - 0.8 (0.020 - 0.031)

Ⓣ 6.4 - 7.8
(0.65 - 0.80, 4.7 - 5.8)

Pinion stopper

Return spring

Clutch assembly

Ⓖ

Brush spring
Tension:
15.7 - 19.6 N
(1.6 - 2.0 kg,
3.5 - 4.4 lb)

Brush holder

Bearing retainer

Pinion shaft
Difference "ℓ" in height
of pinion:
0.3 - 2.5 (0.012 - 0.098)

Unit: mm (in)
Ⓣ : N·m (kg-m, ft-lb)
Ⓖ : High-temperature grease point

Exploded view of a reduction gear starter—Stanza (1982 and later)

the brushes from the commutator, then remove the brush holder.

5. Installation is the reverse of the removal.

STARTER DRIVE REPLACEMENT

Non-Reduction Gear Type

1. With the starter motor removed from the vehicle, remove the solenoid from the starter.

2. Remove the dust cover, the E-ring and the thrust washers from the armature shaft. Remove the brush holder setscrews and the two thru-bolts.

3. Using a wire hook, lift the brush springs to separate the brushes from the commutator, then remove the brush holder. Separate the gear case from the yoke housing, then the armature from the shift lever.

4. Push the pinion stopper toward the clutch assembly, then remove the pinion stopper clip and the pinion stopper.

5. Slide the starter drive from the armature shaft.

6. Install the starter drive and reassemble the starter in the reverse order of removal.

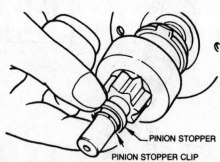

PINION STOPPER
PINION STOPPER CLIP

Pinion stopper removal

Reduction Gear Type

F10 (1978), 310 (1979–81) AND STANZA (1982 AND LATER) MODELS

1. Remove the starter.

2. Remove the solenoid and the torsion spring.

3. Remove the center housing-to-front housing bolts, then separate the front housing from the center housing.

4. Remove the pinion/reduction gear assembly from the armature shaft.

NOTE: *It may be necessary to remove the shift lever pivot pin, to disconnect the pinion/reduction gear assembly from the armature shaft.*

5. Installation is the reverse of the removal procedures.

310 (1982) AND PULSAR (1983 AND LATER) MODELS

1. Remove the starter from the vehicle, then the solenoid from the starter.

2. Remove the thru-bolts, then separate the front gear case from the field coil assembly case.

3. Push the pinion stopper toward the pinion clutch assembly, then remove the pinion stopper clip from the armature shaft and remove the pinion/clutch assembly.

4. Installation is the reverse of the removal procedures.

Battery

Refer to Chapter One for details on battery maintenance.

REMOVAL AND INSTALLATION

1. Disconnect the negative (ground) cable from the terminal and then the positive cable. Special pullers are available to remove the cable clamps.

NOTE: *To avoid sparks, always disconnect the ground cable first and connect it last.*

2. Remove the battery hold-down clamp.

3. Remove the battery, being careful not to spill the acid.

NOTE: *Spilled acid can be neutralized with a baking soda/water solution. If you somehow get acid into your eyes, flush it out with lots of water and get to a doctor.*

4. Clean the battery posts thoroughly before reinstalling or when installing a new battery.

5. Clean the cable clamps, using a wire brush, both inside and out.

6. Install the battery and the hold-down clamp or strap. Connect the positive, and then the negative cable. DO NOT hammer them in place.

NOTE: *The terminals should be coated lightly (externally) with vasoline to prevent corrosion. There are also felt washers impregnated with an anti-corrosion substance which are slipped over the battery posts before installing the cables; these are available in auto parts stores.*

CAUTION: *Make absolutely sure that the battery is connected properly before you turn on the ignition switch. Reversed polarity can burn out your alternator and regulator within a matter of seconds.*

ENGINE MECHANICAL

Engine Removal and Installation

NOTE: *The engine and transaxle must be removed as a single unit.*

CAUTION: *On EFI equipped models, release the fuel pressure in the system before disconnecting the fuel lines.*

Battery and Starter Specifications

All cars use 12 volt, negative ground electrical systems

Year	Model	Battery Amp Hour Capacity	Starter						Brush Spring Tension (oz)	Min Brush Length (in)
			Lock Test			No Load Test				
			Amps	Volts	Torque (ft. lbs.)	Amps	Volts	RPM		
1976–78	F10	60	Not Recommended			60	12	7,000 U.S.A.	49–64	0.47
1978	F10 Canada	100	Not Recommended			100 RG	12	4,300 Canada	49–64	0.43
1979–81	310	60 / 100 RG	Not Recommended			60 / 100	11.5 / 11	7,000 U.S.A. / 3,900 Canada	50–64 / 56–70	0.47 / 0.43
1982	310	60 U.S.A.	Not Recommended			60	11.5	7,000	64–78	0.43
		60 Canada ①	Not Recommended			60	11.5	7,000	64–78	0.43
		60 Canada ②	Not Recommended			60	11.5	6,000	64–78	0.43
1982–86	Stanza	60 / 100 RG	Not Recommended			60 U.S.A. / 100 Canada (U.S. option)	11.5 / 11	7,000 U.S.A., / 3,900 Canada	64–78 / 56–70	0.43 / 0.43
1983–86	Pulsar	60 ①	Not Recommended			60	11.5	7,000	64–78	0.43
1983	Pulsar	60 ②	Not Recommended			60 U.S.A.	11.5	7,000	64–78	0.43
1983	Pulsar	60 ②	Not Recommended			60 Canada	11.5	2,000	64–78	0.43
1984	Pulsar	60 ①	Not Recommended			60 Canada	11.5	2,350	64–78	0.43

RG: Reduction Gear type starter
① Manual Transmission
② Auto. Transmission

General Engine Specifications

Year	Model	Type (model)	Engine Displacement Cu In. (cc)	Carburetor Type	Horsepower (SAE) @ rpm	Torque @ rpm (ft. lbs.)	Bore x Stroke (in.)	Compression Ratio	Normal Oil Pressure (psi)
1976–78	F10	OHV 4 (A14)	85.2 (1397)	Dual throat downdraft	80 @ 6,000	83 @ 3,600	2.99 x 3.03	8.5:1	43–50
1979–80	310	OHV 4 (A14)	85.2 (1397)	Dual throat downdraft	65 @ 5,600	75 @ 3,600	2.99 x 3.03	8.9:1	43–50
1981	310	OHV 4 (A15)	90.8 (1488)	Dual throat downdraft	65 @ 5200	82 @ 2800	2.992 x 3.228	8.9:1	43–50
1982	310	OHC 4 (E15)	90.8 (1488)	Dual throat downdraft	67 @ 5200	85 @ 3200	2.92 x 3.228	9.0:1	50–57
1982–83	Stanza	OHC 4 (CA20)	120.4 (1974)	Dual throat downdraft	88 @ 5200	112 @ 2800	3.33 x 3.46	8.5:1	50–60
1984–86	Stanza (U.S.A.)	OHC 4 (CA20E)	120.4 (1974)	EFI	120 @ 5200	116 @ 3200	3.33 x 3.46	8.5:1	57 @ 4000
	Stanza (Canada)	OHC 4 (CA20S)	120.4 (1974)	Dual throat downdraft	88 @ 5200	112 @ 2800	3.33 x 3.46	8.5:1	57 @ 4000
1984	Pulsar Turbo (Canada)	OHC 4 (E15ET)	90.8 (1488)	EFI	100 @ 5200	152 @ 3200	2.99 x 3.23	8.0:1	50–57
1983–86	Pulsar	OHC 4 (E16)	97.6 (1597)	Dual throat downdraft	69 @ 5200	92 @ 3200	2.99 x 3.46	9.4:1	50–57

NOTE: Specifications given are for United States except California.

Crankshaft and Connecting Rod Specifications
All measurements given in inches

Year	Engine Model	Crankshaft					Connecting Rod Bearings		
		Main Brg Journal Dia	Main Brg Oil Clearance	Shaft End-Play	Thrust on No.	Journal Dia	Oil Clearance	Side Clearance
1976–78	A14	1.966–1.967	0.0008–0.002	0.002–0.006	3	1.7701–1.7706	0.0008–0.002	0.008–0.012
1979–81	A14, A15	1.9666–1.9671	0.001–0.0035	0.002–0.0059	3	1.7701–1.7706	0.0012–0.0031	0.004–0.008
1982	E15	1.9663–1.9671	①	0.002–0.007	3	1.5730–1.5738	0.0012–0.0024	0.004–0.0146
1982–86	CA20, CA20S, CA20E	2.0847–2.0852	0.0016–0.0024	0.002–0.007	3	1.7701–1.7706	0.0008–0.0024	0.008–0.012
1983–86	E16	1.9663–1.9671	①	0.0020–0.0071	3	1.5730–1.5738	0.0012–0.0024	0.0040–0.0146
1984	E15ET	1.9663–1.9671	②	0.0020–0.0071	3	1.5730–1.5738	0.0006–0.0023	0.0040–0.0146

① #1 & 5: 0.0012–0.0030
#2, 3, 4: 0.0012–0.0036

② #1 & 5: 0.0012–0.0030
#2 & 4: 0.0011–0.0035
#3: 0.0012–0.0036

Piston and Ring Specifications

All measurements in inches

Year	Engine Model	Piston Clearance	Ring Gap			Ring Side Clearance		
			Top Compression	Bottom Compression	Oil Control	Top Compression	Bottom Compression	Oil Control
1976–78	A14	0.0009–0.002	0.008–0.014	0.006–0.012	0.012–0.035	0.002–0.003	0.001–0.002	Combined ring
1979–80	A14	0.0010–0.0018	0.008–0.014	0.006–0.012	0.012–0.035	0.002–0.003	0.001–0.002	0.0039 ②
1981	A15	0.0010–0.0018	0.0079–0.0138	0.0059–0.0118	0.0118–0.0354	0.0016–0.0028	0.0012–0.0024	0.0039 ②
1982	E15	0.0009–0.0017	0.0079–0.0138	0.0059–0.0018	0.0118–0.0354	0.0016–0.0029	0.0012–0.0025	0.0020–0.0057
1982–84	CA20, CA20E, CA20S	0.0010–0.0018	0.0098–0.0157	0.0059–0.0118	0.0118–0.0354	0.0016–0.0029	0.0012–0.0025	0.0020–0.0057
1985–86	CA20E CA20S	0.0010–0.0018	0.0098–0.0138	0.0059–0.0098	0.0080–0.0240	0.0016–0.0029	0.0012–0.0025	0.0020–0.0057
1983–86	E16	0.0009–0.0017	0.0079–0.0138	0.0059–0.0118	0.0118–0.0354	0.0016–0.0029	0.0012–0.0025	0.0020–0.0057
1984	E15ET	0.0016–0.0024	①	0.0059–0.0098	0.0079–0.0236	0.0016–0.0029	0.0012–0.0025	0.0020–0.0049

① Grade 1 & 2: 0.0079–0.0102 (Yellow)
Grade 3, 4 & 5: 0.0055–0.0079
② Limit

Valve Specifications

Year	Model	Seat Angle (deg)	Spring Test Pressure lbs. @ in.	Free Length (in.)	Stem-to-Guide Clearance (in.)		Stem Diameter (in.)	
					Intake	Exhaust	Intake	Exhaust
1976–78	A14	45°	52.7 @ 1.189	1.83	0.0006–0.0018	0.0016–0.0028	0.3138–0.3144	0.3128–0.3134
1979–81	A14, A15	45°30′	52.7 @ 1.19	1.83	0.0006–0.0018	0.0016–0.0028	0.3138–0.3144	0.3128–0.3134
1982	E15	45°30′	128 @ 1.189	1.839	0.0008–0.0020	0.0018–0.0030	0.2744–0.2750	0.2734–0.2740
1982–86	CA20, CA20E, CA20S	45°30′	①	②	0.0008–0.0021	0.0016–0.0029	0.2742–0.2748	0.2734–0.2740
1983–86	E16	45°30′	51.66 @ 1.543	1.839	0.0008–0.0020	0.0018–0.0030	0.2744–0.2750	0.2734–0.2740
1984	E15ET	③	51.66 @ 1.543	1.839	0.0008–0.0020	0.0018–0.0030	0.2744–0.2750	0.2734–0.2740

① Inner: 24 @ 1.38   ② Inner: 1.7362
  Outer: 47 @ 1.58   Outer: 1.9677

Torque Specifications

All readings in ft. lbs.

Year	Engine Model	Cylinder Head Bolts	Main Bearing Bolts	Rod Bearing Bolts	Crankshaft Pulley Bolt	Flywheel to Crankshaft Bolts	Manifolds	
							Intake	Exhaust
1976–78	A14	51–54	36–43	23–27	108–145	54–61	11–14	11–14
1979–81	A14, A15	51–54	36–43	23–27	108–145	58–65	11–14	11–14
1982	E15	51–54	36–43	23–27	83–108	58–65	11–14	11–14
1982	CA20	51–58	33–40	22–27	90–98	72–80	13–16	13–17
1983	CA20	58–65	33–40	22–27	90–98	72–80	13–16	13–17
1984–86	CA20E CA20S	①	33–40	24–27	90–98	72–80	14–19	14–22
1983–86	E-16	②	36–43	23–27	83–108	58–65	12–15	12–15
1984	E15ET	②	36–43	23–27	83–108	58–65	12–15	12–15

① a. Torque to 22 ft. lbs.
  b. Torque to 58 ft. lbs.
  c. Loosen all bolts
  d. Torque to 22 ft. lbs.
  e. Torque to 54–61 ft. lbs.

② 1st step: 29–33
  2nd step: 51–54

1. Mark the location of the hinges on the hood and then remove the hood.

2. Disconnect the battery cables and remove the battery.

3. Drain the coolant from the radiator, then remove the radiator and the heater hoses.

4. Remove the air cleaner-to-rocker cover hose and the air cleaner cover, then place a clean rag in the carburetor or throttle body opening to keep out the dirt.

NOTE: *Disconnect and label all the necessary vacuum hoses and electrical connectors, for reinstallation purposes.*

5. If equipped, disconnect the air pump cleaner and remove the carbon canister.

6. Remove the auxiliary fan, the washer tank and the radiator grille. Remove the radiator together with the fan motor assembly.

7. On 1976–81 models, remove the slave cylinder from the clutch housing; on 1982 and later models, remove the clutch control wire from the transaxle. Remove the right and the left buffer rods. Disconnect the speedometer cable from the transaxle and plug the hole with a clean rag.

NOTE: *On the Stanza (1982 and later), re-*

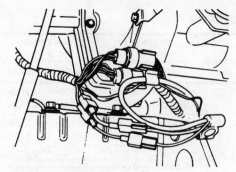

F10 engine harness connector

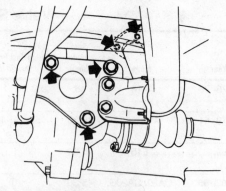

F10, 310 exhaust pipe removal

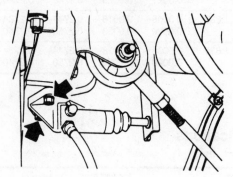

F10, 310 slave cylinder

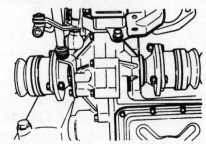

F10 and 310 (1979–81) axle shaft removal

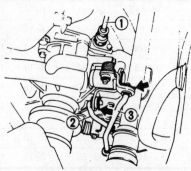

1. Speedometer cable
2. Shift rod
3. Select rod

F10 and 310 (1979–81) speedometer cable and shift rod removal

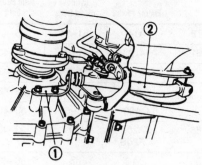

1. Link support
2. Radius link

F10 radius link support

move the EGR vacuum control valve with the bracket from the body.

8. If equipped with AC, loosen the idler pulley nut and the adjusting bolt, then remove the compressor belt. Remove the compressor to one side and suspend on a wire. Remove the condenser and the receiver drier and place them on the right fender.

NOTE: *If equipped with A/C, DO NOT AT-TEMPT TO UNFASTEN ANY OF THE RE-FRIGERANT HOSES. See Chapter One for additional warnings. If equipped with power steering, loosen the idler pulley nut and ad-*

justing bolt, then remove the drive belt and the power steering pulley.

9. If equipped with a manual transaxle, disconnect the transaxle shifting rods by removing the spring pins (1976–81) or the securing bolts (1982 and later). If equipped with an automatic transaxle, disconnect the mounting bracket and the control wire from the transaxle.

10. Attach the engine sling, tool Nos. 10005M4900 and 10006M4900 (1976–81), 1000501M00 and 1000623M00 (310, 1982 and Pulsar, 1983 and later) or 10005D0100 and 10007D0100 (Stanza, 1982 and later) at each end of the engine block. Connect a chain or cable to the engine slingers.

11. Unbolt the exhaust pipe from the ex-

haust manifold. There are three bolts which attach the pipe to the manifold and bolts which attach the pipe support to the engine.

12. On 1976–81 models, unbolt the axle shafts from the transaxle flanges; on the 1982 and later models, refer to Chapter 6, Clutch and Transaxle for the axle shaft, removal and installation procedures, then remove the axle shafts.

13. Remove the radius link support bolt, then lower the transaxle shift selector rods.

14. Unbolt the engine from the engine and the transaxle mounts.

15. Using an overhead lifting device, attach it to the engine lifting sling and remove the engine and transaxle assembly from the vehicle.

NOTE: *When removing the engine, be careful not to knock it against the adjacent parts.*

16. Separate the engine from the transaxle.

17. Installation is the reverse of removal. Adjust the accelerator control and refill the cooling system.

NOTE: *If the buffer rod length has not been altered, it should still be correct. Shims are placed under the engine mounts, be sure to replace the exact ones in the correct places.*

Rocker Arm Cover
REMOVAL AND INSTALLATION

1. Remove or disconnect any electrical lines, hoses or tubes which may interfere with the removal procedures.

NOTE: *It may be necessary to remove the air cleaner (carburetor models) or the air duct (EFI and turbo models).*

2. Remove the rocker arm cover-to-cylinder head acorn nuts (310, 1982 and Pulsar, 1983 and later) or mounting screws (all others), then lift the cover from the cylinder head.

3. Using a putty knife, clean the gasket mounting surfaces.

4. To install, use a new gasket and/or RTV sealant, then the rocker arm cover. Torque the cover-to-cylinder head bolts to 8.4–13.2 inch lbs. or the acorn nuts to 35.0–69.6 inch lbs.

Rocker Arm Shaft
REMOVAL AND INSTALLATION

1. Refer the Rocker Arm Cover, Removal and Installation procedure in this section and remove the cover.

NOTE: *The CA20 engine uses two rocker arm shafts.*

2. Loosen the valve rocker adjusting nuts, then turn the adjusting screws to separate them from the push rods.

3. Evenly, loosen the rocker shaft bolts, then

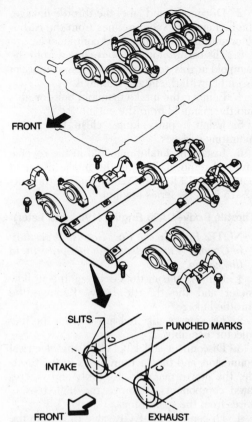

Exploded view of the CA20 engine rocker shafts, other 1982 and later models are similar

remove the bolts and lift the rocker shafts from the cylinder head.

NOTE: *If it is necessary to remove the rocker arms from the shafts, perform the following procedures: on 1976–81 models, remove the rocker arm shaft mounting bolts, then slide the shaft mounts, the rocker arms and the springs; on 1982 and later models, remove the shaft bolts and the spring clips, then slide the rocker arms from the shaft. Be sure to keep the parts in order for reassembly purposes.*

4. To install, reverse the removal procedures. Torque the rocker arm shaft bracket bolts to 14–18 ft.lb. (A-series engines), 12–15 ft.lb. (E-series engines) and 13–16 ft.lb. (CA20 engine). Adjust the valve clearance.

NOTE: *To adjust the valve clearance, refer to the Valve Adjustment procedures in this section.*

Intake Manifold
REMOVAL AND INSTALLATION
Carburetor–E-Series and CA20 Engines

1. Remove the air cleaner assembly together with all of the hoses.

2. Disconnect and label the throttle linkage, the fuel and the vacuum lines from the carburetor and the intake manifold components.

3. The carburetor can be removed from the manifold at this point or can be removed as an assembly with the intake manifold.

4. Remove the intake manifold bolts or nuts and the manifold from the engine.

5. Using a putty knife, clean the gasket mounting surfaces.

6. Install the intake manifold in the reverse order of removal. Torque the intake manifold bolts to 14–19 ft.lb. (CA20 engine) or the nuts 12–15 ft.lb. (E-series engine).

Throttle Body–CA20 Engine (1984 and Later)

NOTE: *Refer to the Fuel Release Procedure in Chapter 4 and release the fuel pressure in the system.*

1. Remove the air duct between the air flow meter and the throttle body. Remove the throttle linkage.

2. Disconnect the fuel line(s) from the fuel injector assembly.

3. Disconnect and label all of the electrical connectors and the vacuum hoses to the throttle, the intake manifold assembly and the related components. Remove the high tension wires from the spark plugs.

4. Disconnect the EGR valve tube from the exhaust manifold. Remove the intake manifold mounting brackets.

5. Remove the mounting bolts and separate the intake manifold from the cylinder head.

6. Using a putty knife, clean the gasket mounting surfaces.

7. To install, use a new gasket and reverse the removal procedures. Torque the intake manifold mounting bolts to 14–19 ft.lb.

Turbocharged–1984 (Only) E15ET Engine

NOTE: *Refer to the Fuel Release Procedure in Chapter 4 and release the fuel pressure.*

1. Disconnect the air intake duct between the air filter and the air pipe, then the air intake duct between the air pipe and the turbocharger. Remove the air inlet duct between the turbocharger and the throttle body. Remove the air pipe.

2. Disconnect and label all of the electrical connectors and the vacuum hoses to the throttle, the intake manifold assembly and the related components. Remove the high tension wires from the spark plugs.

3. Disconnect the EGR valve tube from the exhaust manifold and the fuel line(s) from the fuel injector assembly.

NOTE: *For clearance purposes, it may be necessary to remove the throttle body and the collector chamber from the intake manifold; if the fuel injector assembly is in the way, remove it.*

4. Remove the intake manifold mounting nuts and the intake manifold.

5. Using a putty knife, clean the gasket mounting surfaces.

6. To install, use new gasket(s) and reverse the removal procedures. Torque the intake manifold-to-cylinder head nuts to 12–15 ft.lb., the intake manifold-to-collector chamber bolts to 2.9–4.3 ft.lb. and the air pipe bolt(s) to 6.5–10.1 ft.lb.

Exhaust Manifold
REMOVAL AND INSTALLATION
Carbureted–E-Series and CA20 Engines
Throttle Body—CA20 Engine (1984 and Later)

1. Remove the air cleaner assembly, if necessary for access. Remove the heat shield.

2. Disconnect the high tension wires from the spark plugs on the exhaust side of the engine.

3. Disconnect the exhaust pipe from the exhaust manifold.

4. On the carbureted models, remove the air induction and/or the EGR tubes from the exhaust manifold. On the throttle body model, disconnect the exhaust gas sensor electrical connector.

5. Remove the exhaust manifold mounting nuts and the manifold from the cylinder head.

6. Using a putty knife, clean the gasket mounting surfaces.

7. To install, use new gaskets and reverse the removal procedures. Torque the exhaust manifold nuts to 14–22 ft.lb. (CA20 engine) or 12–15 ft.lb. (E-series engine) and air induction and/or the EGR tube fitting-to-exhaust manifold to 25–33 ft.lb. (CA20 engine) or 29–43 ft.lb. (E-series engine).

Turbocharged–1984 (Only) E15ET Engine

1. Refer to the Turbocharger, Removal and Installation procedure in this section and remove the turbocharger.

2. Remove the exhaust manifold's heat shields, the exhaust manifold from the cylinder head.

3. Using a putty knife, clean the gasket mounting surfaces.

4. To install, use new gaskets and reverse the removal procedures. Torque the exhaust manifold-to-cylinder head bolts to 12–15 ft.lb., the turbocharger-to-exhaust manifold nuts to 22–25 ft.lb., the exhaust outlet-to-turbo nuts to 22–25 ft.lb., the converter's mounting bracket bolt to 14–18 ft.lb. (10mm) or 6.5–10.1 ft.lb. (8mm), the oil pressure tube fitting-to-turbo to 14–22 ft.lb.

ENGINE OVERHAUL

Most engine overhaul procedures are fairly standard. In addition to specific parts replacement procedures and complete specifications for your individual engine, this chapter also is a guide to accepted rebuilding procedures. Examples of standard rebuilding practice are shown and should be used along with specific details concerning your particular engine.

Competent and accurate machine shop services will ensure maximum performance, reliability and engine life. Procedures marked with the symbol shown above should be performed by a competent machine shop, and are provided so that you will be familiar with the procedures necessary to a successful overhaul.

In most instances it is more profitable for the do-it-yourself mechanic to remove, clean and inspect the component, buy the necessary parts and deliver these to a shop for actual machine work.

On the other hand, much of the rebuilding work (crankshaft, block, bearings, pistons, rods, and other components) is well within the scope of the do-it-yourself mechanic.

Tools

The tools required for an engine overhaul or parts replacement will depend on the depth of your involvement. With a few exceptions, they will be the tools found in a mechanic's tool kit (see Chapter 1). More indepth work will require any or all of the following:
  • a dial indicator (reading in thousandths) mounted on a universal base
  • micrometers and telescope gauges
  • jaw and screw-type pullers
  • scraper
  • valve spring compressor
  • ring groove cleaner
  • piston ring expander and compressor
  • ridge reamer
  • cylinder hone or glaze breaker

  • Plastigage®
  • engine stand

Use of most of these tools is illustrated in this chapter. Many can be rented for a one-time use from a local parts jobber or tool supply house specializing in automotive work.

Occasionally, the use of special tools is called for. See the information on Special Tools and the Safety Notice in the front of this book before substituting another tool.

Inspection Techniques

Procedures and specifications are given in this chapter for inspecting, cleaning and assessing the wear limits of most major components. Other procedures such as Magnaflux and Zyglo can be used to locate material flaws and stress cracks. Magnaflux is a magnetic process applicable only to ferrous materials. The Zyglo process coats the material with a flourescent dye penetrant and can be used on any material. Check for suspected surface cracks can be more readily made using spot check dye. The dye is sprayed onto the suspected area, wiped off and the area sprayed with a developer. Cracks will show up brightly.

Overhaul Tips

Aluminum has become extremely popular for use in engines, due to its low weight. Observe the following precautions when handling aluminum parts:
  • Never hot tank aluminum parts (the caustic hot-tank solution will eat the aluminum)
  • Remove all aluminum parts (identification tag, etc.) from engine parts prior to hot-tanking.
  • Always coat threads lightly with engine oil or anti-seize compounds before installation, to prevent seizure.
  • Never over-torque bolts or spark plugs, especially in aluminum threads.

Stripped threads in any component can be repaired using any of several commercial repair kits (Heli-Coil, Microdot, Keenserts, etc.)

When assembling the engine, any parts that will be in frictional contact must be prelubed to provide lubrication at initial start-up. Any product specifically formulated for this purpose can be used, but engine oil is not recommended as a pre-lube.

When semi-permanent (locked, but removable) installation of bolts or nuts is desired, threads should be cleaned and coated with Loctite® or other similar, commercial non-hardening sealant.

Repairing Damaged Threads

Several methods of repairing damaged threads are available. Heli-Coil® (shown here), Keenserts® and Microdot® are among the most widely used. All involve basically the same principle—drilling out stripped threads, tapping the hole and installing a pre-wound insert—making welding, plugging and oversize fasteners unnecessary.

Two types of thread repair inserts are usually supplied—a standard type for most Inch Coarse, Inch Fine, Metric Coarse and Metric Fine thread sizes and a spark plug type to fit most spark plug port sizes. Consult the individual manufacturer's catalog to determine exact applications. Typical thread repair kits will contain a selection of pre-wound threaded inserts, a tap (corresponding to the outside diameter threads of the insert) and an installation tool. Spark plug inserts usually differ because they require a tap equipped with pilot threads and a combined reamer/tap section. Most manufacturers also supply blister-packed thread repair inserts separately in addition to a master kit containing a variety of taps and inserts plus installation tools.

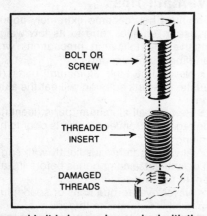

Damaged bolt holes can be repaired with thread repair inserts

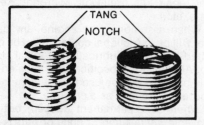

Standard thread repair insert (left) and spark plug thread insert (right)

Before effecting a repair to a threaded hole, remove any snapped, broken or damaged bolts or studs. Penetrating oil can be used to free frozen threads; the offending item can be removed with locking pliers or with a screw or stud extractor. After the hole is clear, the thread can be repaired, as follows:

Drill out the damaged threads with specified drill. Drill completely through the hole or to the bottom of a blind hole

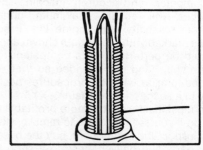

With the tap supplied, tap the hole to receive the thread insert. Keep the tap well oiled and back it out frequently to avoid clogging the threads

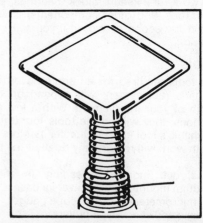

Screw the threaded insert onto the installation tool until the tang engages the slot. Screw the insert into the tapped hole until it is ¼–½ turn below the top surface. After installation break off the tang with a hammer and punch

Standard Torque Specifications and Fastener Markings

In the absence of specific torques, the following chart can be used as a guide to the maximum safe torque of a particular size/grade of fastener.
- There is no torque difference for fine or coarse threads.
- Torque values are based on clean, dry threads. Reduce the value by 10% if threads are oiled prior to assembly.
- The torque required for aluminum components or fasteners is considerably less.

U.S. Bolts

SAE Grade Number	1 or 2			5			6 or 7		
Number of lines always 2 less than the grade number.									
Bolt Size (Inches)—(Thread)	Maximum Torque			Maximum Torque			Maximum Torque		
	Ft./Lbs.	Kgm	Nm	Ft./Lbs.	Kgm	Nm	Ft./Lbs.	Kgm	Nm
¼—20	5	0.7	6.8	8	1.1	10.8	10	1.4	13.5
—28	6	0.8	8.1	10	1.4	13.6			
⁵/₁₆—18	11	1.5	14.9	17	2.3	23.0	19	2.6	25.8
—24	13	1.8	17.6	19	2.6	25.7			
⅜—16	18	2.5	24.4	31	4.3	42.0	34	4.7	46.0
—24	20	2.75	27.1	35	4.8	47.5			
⁷/₁₆—14	28	3.8	37.0	49	6.8	66.4	55	7.6	74.5
—20	30	4.2	40.7	55	7.6	74.5			
½—13	39	5.4	52.8	75	10.4	101.7	85	11.75	115.2
—20	41	5.7	55.6	85	11.7	115.2			
⁹/₁₆—12	51	7.0	69.2	110	15.2	149.1	120	16.6	162.7
—18	55	7.6	74.5	120	16.6	162.7			
⅝—11	83	11.5	112.5	150	20.7	203.3	167	23.0	226.5
—18	95	13.1	128.8	170	23.5	230.5			
¾—10	105	14.5	142.3	270	37.3	366.0	280	38.7	379.6
—16	115	15.9	155.9	295	40.8	400.0			
⅞— 9	160	22.1	216.9	395	54.6	535.5	440	60.9	596.5
—14	175	24.2	237.2	435	60.1	589.7			
1— 8	236	32.5	318.6	590	81.6	799.9	660	91.3	894.8
—14	250	34.6	338.9	660	91.3	849.8			

Metric Bolts

Relative Strength Marking	4.6, 4.8			8.8		
Bolt Markings						
Bolt Size Thread Size x Pitch (mm)	Maximum Torque			Maximum Torque		
	Ft./Lbs.	Kgm	Nm	Ft./Lbs.	Kgm	Nm
6 x 1.0	2–3	.2–.4	3–4	3–6	.4–.8	5–8
8 x 1.25	6–8	.8–1	8–12	9–14	1.2–1.9	13–19
10 x 1.25	12–17	1.5–2.3	16–23	20–29	2.7–4.0	27–39
12 x 1.25	21–32	2.9–4.4	29–43	35–53	4.8–7.3	47–72
14 x 1.5	35–52	4.8–7.1	48–70	57–85	7.8–11.7	77–110
16 x 1.5	51–77	7.0–10.6	67–100	90–120	12.4–16.5	130–160
18 x 1.5	74–110	10.2–15.1	100–150	130–170	17.9–23.4	180–230
20 x 1.5	110–140	15.1–19.3	150–190	190–240	26.2–46.9	160–320
22 x 1.5	150–190	22.0–26.2	200–260	250–320	34.5–44.1	340–430
24 x 1.5	190–240	26.2–46.9	260–320	310–410	42.7–56.5	420–550

CHECKING ENGINE COMPRESSION

A noticeable lack of engine power, excessive oil consumption and/or poor fuel mileage measured over an extended period are all indicators of internal engine wear. Worn piston rings, scored or worn cylinder bores, blown head gaskets, sticking or burnt valves and worn valve seats are all possible culprits here. A check of each cylinder's compression will help you locate the problems.

As mentioned in the "Tools and Equipment" section of Chapter 1, a screw-in type compression gauge is more accurate than the type you simply hold against the spark plug hole, although it takes slightly longer to use. It's worth it to obtain a more accurate reading. Follow the procedures below for gasoline and diesel-engined cars.

Gasoline Engines

1. Warm up the engine to normal operating temperature.
2. Remove all spark plugs.

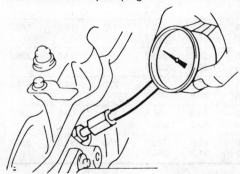

The screw-in type compression gauge is more accurate

3. Disconnect the high-tension lead from the ignition coil.
4. On carbureted cars, fully open the throttle either by operating the carburetor throttle linkage by hand or by having an assistant "floor" the accelerator pedal. On fuel-injected cars, disconnect the cold start valve and all injector connections.
5. Screw the compression gauge into the No. 1 spark plug hole until the fitting is snug.
NOTE: *Be careful not to crossthread the plug hole. On aluminum cylinder heads use extra care, as the threads in these heads are easily ruined.*
6. Ask an assistant to depress the accelerator pedal fully on both carbureted and fuel-injected cars. Then, while you read the compression gauge, ask the assistant to crank the engine two or three times in short bursts using the ignition switch.

7. Read the compression gauge at the end of each series of cranks, and record the highest of these readings. Repeat this procedure for each of the engine's cylinders. Compare the highest reading of each cylinder to the compression pressure specifications in the "Tune-Up Specifications" chart in Chapter 2. The specs in this chart are maximum values.

A cylinder's compression pressure is usually acceptable if it is not less than 80% of maximum. The difference between each cylinder should be no more than 12–14 pounds.

8. If a cylinder is unusually low, pour a tablespoon of clean engine oil into the cylinder through the spark plug hole and repeat the compression test. If the compression comes up after adding the oil, it appears that that cylinder's piston rings or bore are damaged or worn. If the pressure remains low, the valves may not be seating properly (a valve job is needed), or the head gasket may be blown near that cylinder. If compression in any two adjacent cylinders is low, and if the addition of oil doesn't help the compression, there is leakage past the head gasket. Oil and coolant water in the combustion chamber can result from this problem. There may be evidence of water droplets on the engine dipstick when a head gasket has blown.

Diesel Engines

Checking cylinder compression on diesel engines is basically the same procedure as on gasoline engines except for the following:

1. A special compression gauge adaptor suitable for diesel engines (because these engines have much greater compression pressures) must be used.
2. Remove the injector tubes and remove the injectors from each cylinder.
NOTE: *Don't forget to remove the washer underneath each injector; otherwise, it may get lost when the engine is cranked.*

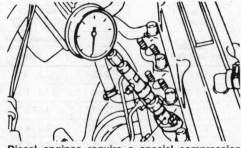

Diesel engines require a special compression gauge adaptor

3. When fitting the compression gauge adaptor to the cylinder head, make sure the bleeder of the gauge (if equipped) is closed.
4. When reinstalling the injector assemblies, install new washers underneath each injector.

Combination Manifold

REMOVAL AND INSTALLATION

A-Series (1976–1981)

1. Remove the air cleaner assembly together with all of the hoses.

2. Disconnect and label the throttle linkage, the fuel and the vacuum lines from the carburetor and the intake manifold components.

3. The carburetor can be removed from the manifold at this point or can be removed as an assembly with the intake manifold.

4. Disconnect the intake and exhaust manifold as an assembly. Loosen the intake manifold attaching nuts, working from the two ends toward the center and then remove them.

5. Using a putty knife, clean the gasket mounting surfaces.

6. To install, use new gaskets and reverse the removal procedures. Torque the intake manifold-to-cylinder head nuts to 11–14 ft.lb., the intake-to-exhaust manifold nuts/bolts to 11–14 ft.lb. and the carburetor-to-manifold nuts 2.9–4.3 ft.lb.

Turbocharger

REMOVAL AND INSTALLATION

E15ET–1984 Pulsar

1. Disconnect the air inlet and the outlet pipes from the turbocharger.

2. Disconnect the oil pressure tube and the oil return hose from the turbocharger. Disconnect the high tension wires from the spark plugs.

3. Remove the catalytic converter heat shield, then the converter's mounting bracket.

4. Remove the exhaust outlet-to-turbocharger mounting nuts and separate the outlet from the turbocharger.

5. Remove the turbocharger-to-exhaust manifold mounting nuts and lift the turbocharger from the exhaust manifold.

6. Using a putty knife, clean the gasket mounting surfaces.

7. To install, use new gaskets and reverse the removal procedures. Torque the turbocharger-to-exhaust manifold nuts to 22–25 ft.lb., the exhaust outlet-to-turbo nuts to 22–25 ft.lb., the converter's mounting bracket bolt to 14–18 ft.lb. (10mm) or 6.5–10.1 ft.lb. (8mm), the oil pressure tube fitting-to-turbo to 14–22 ft.lb.

Cylinder Head

REMOVAL AND INSTALLATION

NOTE: *To prevent distortion or warping of the cylinder head, allow the engine to cool completely before removing the head bolts.*

A-Series

1. Disconnect the negative battery cable.

2. Drain the coolant, then remove the upper radiator hose, the water outlet elbow and the thermostat.

3. Remove the air cleaner, the carburetor, the rocker arm cover and the manifold assembly.

4. Remove the spark plugs. Disconnect the temperature gauge electrical connector.

5. Loosen the rocker arm assembly adjusting bolts, then remove the rocker arm assembly and the push rods (keep the push rods in order).

6. Remove the cylinder head bolts and the cylinder head. If necessary, rap the head with a mallet to loosen it from the block. After removing the cylinder head, discard the gasket.

7. Using a putty knife, clean the gasket mounting surfaces.

NOTE: *Install the cylinder head gasket with the side marked Top facing upwards.*

CAUTION: *The No. 1, right-side center, head bolt is smaller in diameter than the others. Since it acts as the oil passageway for the rocker components, it must be inserted in the correct hole or the valve train will seize after a few hundred miles.*

8. To assemble, use new gaskets and reverse the removal procedures. Torque the cylinder head bolts to 51–54 ft.lb. (in three steps), the rocker arm mounting bolts to 15–18 ft.lb. and the manifold assembly nuts to 11–14 ft.lb. Adjust the valves to the cold setting of 0.010 inch. Refill the cooling system.

NOTE: *Torque the head bolts (in sequence) using three steps: first, to 20 ft.lb., second, to 40 ft.lb. and third, to 51–54 ft.lb.*

9. Start and warm the engine, then re-

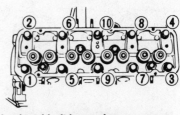

A series head bolt loosening sequence

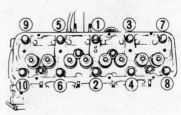

A series head bolt tightening sequence

torque the head bolts and readjust the valves clearances to the HOT specifications.

NOTE: *Retorque the head bolts after 600 miles of driving. Check the valve clearances after torquing, as this may disturb the settings.*

CA20 and E-Series–Overhead Camshaft Engines

CAUTION: *Before disassembling the engine, be sure to place the No. 1 cylinder on the TDC of the compression stroke.*

1. Refer to the Timing Belt, Removal and Installation procedure in this section and remove the timing belt.

NOTE: *On the CA20 EFI and the E15ET Turbo models, release the pressure in the fuel system before disconnecting the fuel lines.*

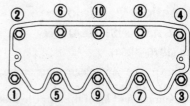

E series head bolt loosening sequence

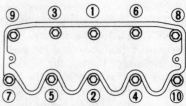

E series head bolt tightening sequence

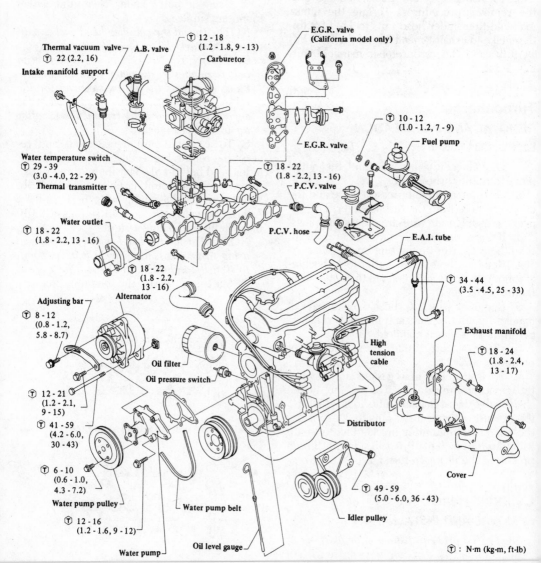

CA20 engine outer components

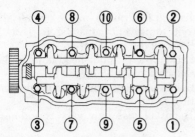

CA20 head bolt loosening sequence

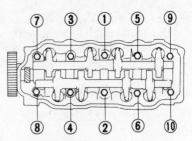

CA20 head bolt tightening sequence

2. Remove the high tension wires from the spark plugs. Disconnect and label all of the necessary vacuum lines and electrical connectors, which will interfere with the cylinder head removal. Drain the cooling system.

3. On the carburetor models, remove the air cleaner, the carburetor and the intake manifold. On the EFI models, remove the air intake duct between the throttle body and the air flow meter, then the throttle body, the air

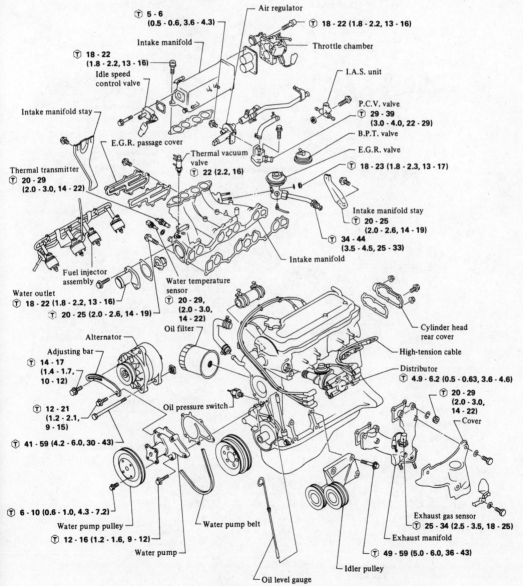

Exploded view of the CA20 EFI engine outer components—1984 and later

plenum and the intake manifold as an assembly. On the Turbo models, remove the turbocharger, then the throttle body, the collector, the fuel rail and the intake manifold as an assembly.

4. Disconnect and remove the exhaust manifold.

5. Remove the distributor. If equipped with a mechanical fuel pump on the cylinder head, remove it, to prevent damaging it.

6. Remove the valve cover.

7. Loosen the cylinder head bolts in the sequence shown, then lift off the head.

8. Using a putty knife, clean the gasket mounting surfaces.

9. To install, use new gaskets and reverse

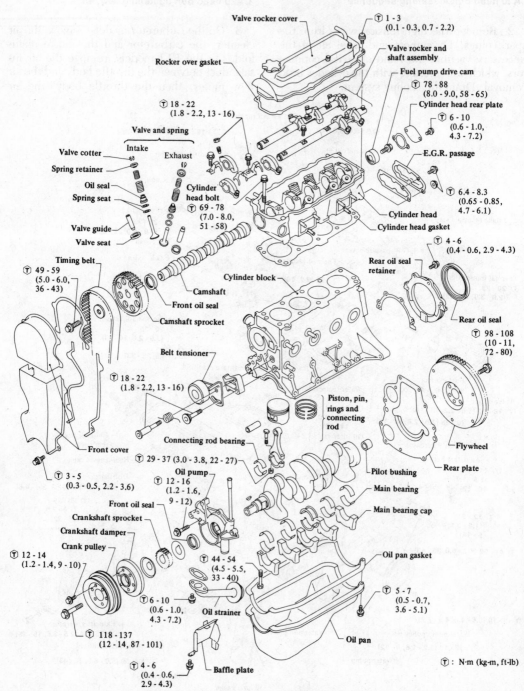

CA20 engine internal components

removal procedures. Torque the cylinder head bolts (in five steps) to 51–58 ft.lb. (CA20, 1982), 58–65 ft.lb. (CA20, 1983–84), 54–61 ft.lb. (CA20, 1985 and later) or 51–54 ft.lb. (E-series). Adjust the valves and refill the cooling system.

NOTE: *When tightening the cylinder head, torque it (in sequence) in five steps: (1) 22 ft.lb., (2) 51 ft.lb., (3) loosen all bolts completely, (4) 22 ft.lb., (5) final torquing pressure. On the CA20 (1984 and later) models, torque all bolts an additional 90–95° clock-*

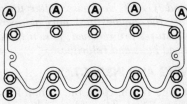

Final torquing sequence for the 1984 and later, E-Series engine

wise; on the E-series (1984 and later), torque the particular bolts an additional (A) 45°, (B)

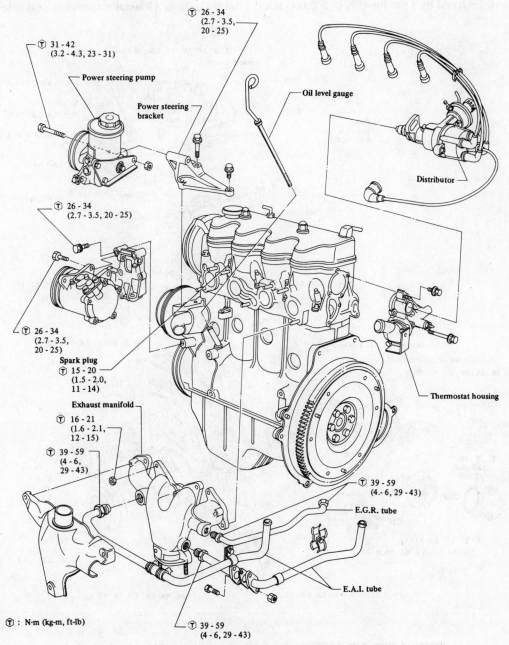

E series engine outer components

55° and (C) 40° clockwise. After torquing, operate the engine until normal operating temperatures are reached, loosen the cylinder head bolts and retorque.

CLEANING AND INSPECTION

Using a wire brush, clean the carbon from the cylinder head, then check it for cracks and flaws.

Make sure that the cylinder head and the block surfaces are clean. Check the cylinder head surface for flatness, using a straightedge and a feeler gauge. If the cylinder head and/or the block are warped more than 0.004 in., it must be trued by a machine shop; if this is not done, there will probably be a compression or water leak.

Valves and Springs
VALVE ADJUSTMENT

1. Run the engine until it reaches normal operating temperature. Oil temperature, not water temperature, is critical to valve adjustment. With this in mind, make sure the engine is fully warmed up since this is the only way to make sure the parts have reached their full expansion. Generally speaking, this takes

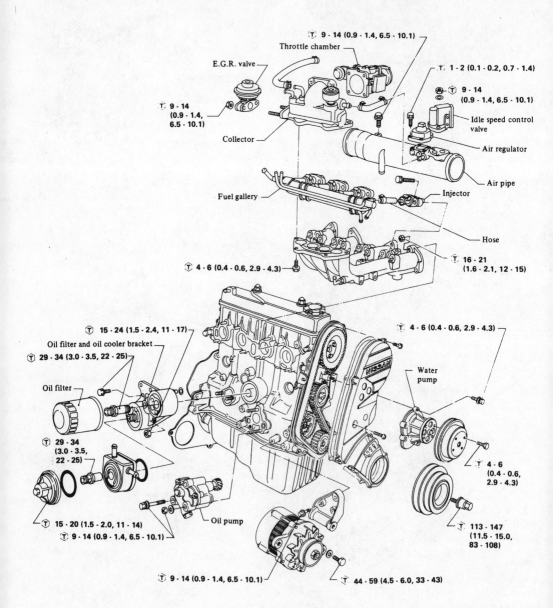

Exploded view of the E15ET engine outer components—1984 turbocharged

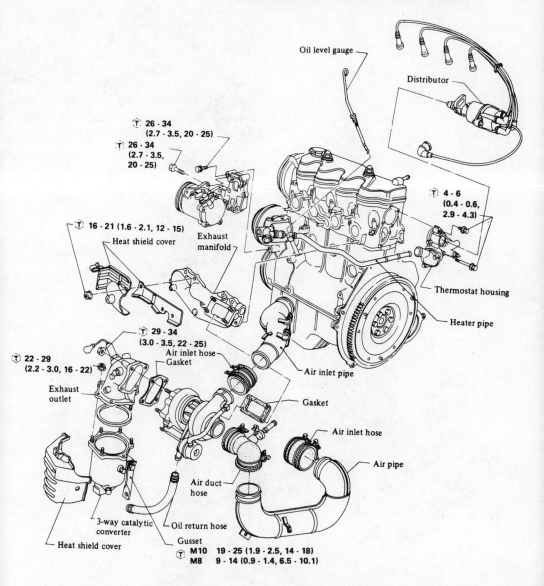

Oil level gauge

Distributor

Ⓣ 26 - 34
(2.7 - 3.5, 20 - 25)

Ⓣ 26 - 34
(2.7 - 3.5,
20 - 25)

Ⓣ 4 - 6
(0.4 - 0.6,
2.9 - 4.3)

Ⓣ 16 - 21 (1.6 - 2.1, 12 - 15)

Heat shield cover

Exhaust
manifold

Thermostat housing

Heater pipe

Ⓣ 29 - 34
(3.0 - 3.5, 22 - 25)

Air inlet hose
Gasket

Ⓣ 22 - 29
(2.2 - 3.0, 16 - 22)

Exhaust
outlet

Air inlet pipe

Gasket

Air inlet hose

Air pipe

Air duct
hose

3-way catalytic
converter

Oil return hose

Heat shield cover

Gusset
Ⓣ M10 19 - 25 (1.9 - 2.5, 14 - 18)
M8   9 - 14 (0.9 - 1.4, 6.5 - 10.1)

Ⓣ : N·m (kg-m, ft-lb)

Exploded view of the E15ET engine outer components—1984 turbocharged

around fifteen minutes. After the engine has reached normal operating temperature, shut it off.

NOTE: *To see the valve arrangements, refer to Valve Lash in Chapter 2.*

2. Purchase a new valve cover gasket before removing the valve cover. The new silicone gasket sealers are just as good or better if you can't find a gasket.

3. Note the location of any hoses or wires which may interfere with valve cover removal, disconnect and move them aside. Remove the bolts which hold the valve cover in place.

4. After the valve cover has been removed, the next step is to get the number one piston

at TDC on the compression stroke. There are at least two ways to do this: Bump the engine over with the starter or turn it over by using a wrench on the front crankshaft pulley bolt. The easiest way to find TDC is to turn the engine over slowly with a wrench (after first removing No. 1 plug) until the piston is at the top of its stroke and the TDC timing mark on the crankshaft pulley is in alignment with the timing mark pointer. At this point, the valves for No. 1 cylinder should be closed.

NOTE: *Make sure both valves are closed with the valve springs up as high as they will go. An easy way to find the compression stroke is to remove the distributor cap and observe*

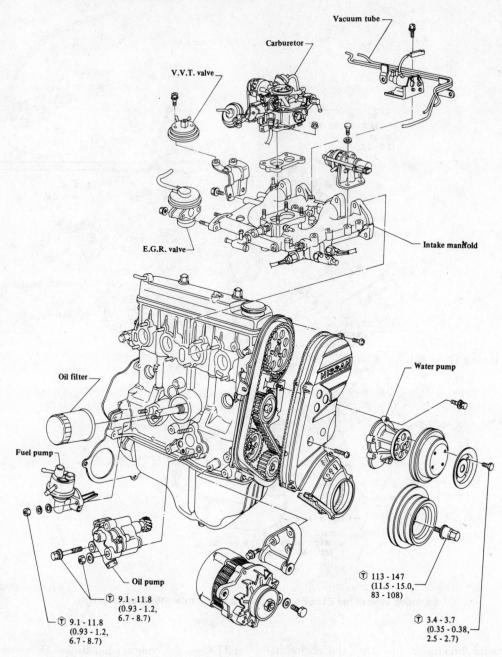

E-series engine outer components

which spark plug lead the rotor is pointing to. If the rotor points to No. 1 spark plug lead, No. 1 cylinder is on its compression stroke. When the rotor points to the No. 2 spark plug lead, No. 2 cylinder is on its compression stroke.

5. Set the No. 1 piston at TDC of the compression stroke, then check and/or adjust the valve clearance on the F10 and 310 (1976–

81), Nos. 1, 2, 3 and 5; on the 310 (1982), Nos. 1, 2, 3 and 6; on the Pulsar (1983 and later), Nos. 1, 2, 3 and 6; on the Stanza (1982), Nos. 1, 4, 6 and 7; on the Stanza (1983 and later), Nos. 1, 2, 4 and 6.

6. To adjust the clearance, loosen the locknut with a wrench and turn the adjuster with a screwdriver while holding the locknut. The correct size feeler gauge should pass with a slight

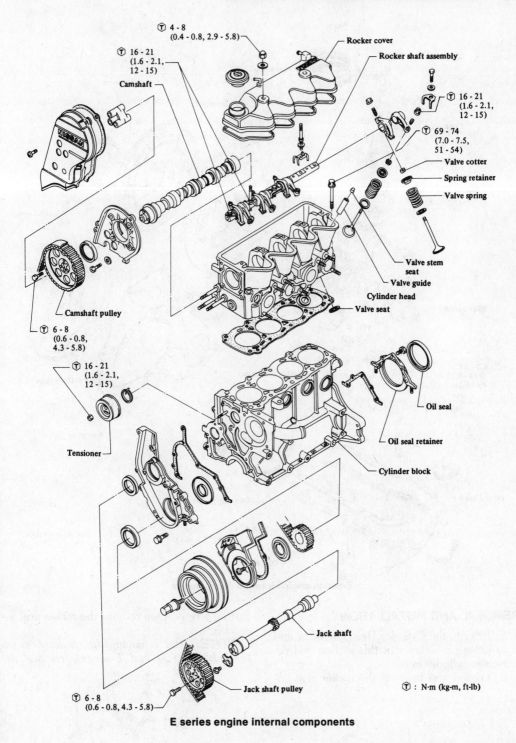

Ⓣ 4 - 8
(0.4 - 0.8, 2.9 - 5.8)

Ⓣ 16 - 21
(1.6 - 2.1,
12 - 15)

Camshaft

Rocker cover

Rocker shaft assembly

Ⓣ 16 - 21
(1.6 - 2.1,
12 - 15)

Ⓣ 69 - 74
(7.0 - 7.5,
51 - 54)

Valve cotter

Spring retainer

Valve spring

Valve stem
seat

Valve guide

Cylinder head

Camshaft pulley

Valve seat

Ⓣ 6 - 8
(0.6 - 0.8,
4.3 - 5.8)

Ⓣ 16 - 21
(1.6 - 2.1,
12 - 15)

Oil seal

Oil seal retainer

Tensioner

Cylinder block

Jack shaft

Ⓣ : N·m (kg-m, ft-lb)

Ⓣ 6 - 8
(0.6 - 0.8, 4.3 - 5.8)

Jack shaft pulley

E series engine internal components

drag between the rocker arm and the valve stem.

7. Turn the crankshaft one full revolution to position the No. 4 piston at TDC of the compression stroke. Check and/or adjust the valves (counting from the front to the rear) on the F10 and 310 (1976–81), Nos. 4, 6, 7 and 8; on 310 (1982), Nos. 4, 5, 7 and 8; on the Stanza (1982), Nos. 2, 3, 5 and 8; on the Stanza (1983 and later), Nos. 3, 5, 7 and 8; on the Pulsar (1983 and later), Nos. 4, 5, 7 and 8.

8. Replace the valve cover.

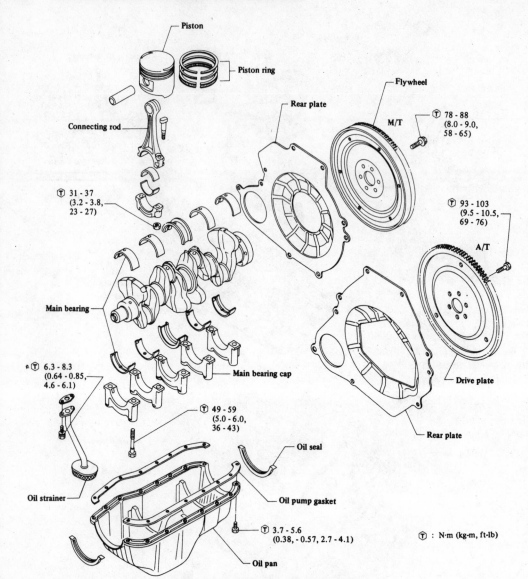

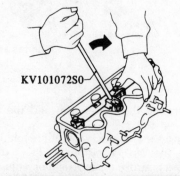

E-series engine internal components

Labels in diagram:
- Piston
- Piston ring
- Flywheel
- Connecting rod
- Rear plate
- M/T
- 78 - 88 (8.0 - 9.0, 58 - 65)
- 31 - 37 (3.2 - 3.8, 23 - 27)
- 93 - 103 (9.5 - 10.5, 69 - 76)
- A/T
- Main bearing
- Main bearing cap
- 6.3 - 8.3 (0.64 - 0.85, 4.6 - 6.1)
- 49 - 59 (5.0 - 6.0, 36 - 43)
- Drive plate
- Oil seal
- Rear plate
- Oil strainer
- Oil pump gasket
- 3.7 - 5.6 (0.38, - 0.57, 2.7 - 4.1)
- : N·m (kg-m, ft-lb)
- Oil pan

REMOVAL AND INSTALLATION

1. Refer to the Cylinder Head, Removal and Installation procedures in this section and re-move the cylinder head.

2. Loosen and back off the rocker arm ad-justing screws, then remove the rocker arm assembly.

NOTE: *After removing the rocker arm assembly (CA20 and E-series), remove the*

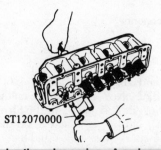

ST12070000

Compressing the valve spring—A-series engine

KV101072S0

Compressing the valve spring—E-series engine

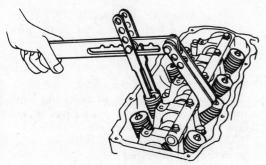

Compressing the valve spring—CA20 engine

spring retainers and the rocker arms from the shaft(s) (be sure to keep the parts in order), then reinstall the rocker arm shaft.

3. Using the spring compression tool No. ST12070000 (A-series), No. KV101092S0 (CA20) or No. KV101072S0 (E-series), compress the valve springs. Remove the valve keeper, then relieve the spring pressure. Remove the springs, the valve seals and the valves.

4. To install, use new oil seals and reverse the removal procedures. Tighten the rocker shaft bolts to 14–18 ft.lb. on the A-series engines; 13–16 ft.lb. on CA20 engines; 13–15 ft.lb. on E-series engines, in a circular sequence. Adjust the valves.

NOTE: *The intake/exhaust valve springs are the uneven pitch type. That is, the springs have narrow coils at the bottom and wide*

Measuring the valve stem diameter

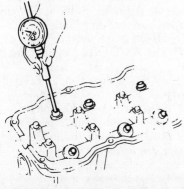

Using a dial indicator (inside) to measure the valve guide inner diameter

coils at the top. The narrow coils (painted white) must be the side making contact on the cylinder head surface.

INSPECTION

Before the valves can be properly inspected, the stem, the lower end of the stem, the entire valve face and head must be cleaned. An old valve works well for chipping carbon from the valve head, a wire brush, a gasket scraper or a putty knife can be used for cleaning the valve face and/or the area between the face and the lower stem. DO NOT scratch the valve face during cleaning. Clean the entire stem with a rag soaked in thinners to remove all of the varnish and gum.

Thorough inspection of the valves requires the use of a micrometer and a dial indicator. If these instruments are not available, the parts should be taken to a reputable machine shop for inspection. Refer to the Valve Specifications chart, for the valve stem and stem-to-guide specifications.

Using a dial indicator, measure the inside diameter of the valve guides at their bottom, midpoint and top positions, at 90° apart. Subtract the valve stem measurement; if the clearance exceeds that listed in the specifications chart under Stem-to-Guide Clearance, replace the valve(s).

Check the top of each valve for pitting and unusual wear due to improper rocker adjustment, etc. The stem tip can be ground flat if it is worn but no more that 0.020 in. can be removed; if this limit must be exceeded to make the tip flat and square, then the valve must be replaced. If the valve stem tips are ground, make sure that the valve is fixed securely into the jig, so that the tip contacts the grinding wheel squarely at exactly 90°.

REFACING

Valve refacing should only be handled by a reputable machine shop, as the experience and equipment needed to do the job are beyond that of the average owner/mechanic. During the course of a normal valve job, refacing is necessary when simply lapping the valves into their seats will not correct the seat and face wear. When the valves are reground (resurfaced), the valve seats must also be recut, again requiring special equipment and experience.

CHECK SPRINGS

1. Place the valve spring on a flat, clean surface, next to a square.

2. Measure the height of the spring and rotate it against the edge of the square to measure the distortion (out-of-roundness). If the spring height between springs varies or the

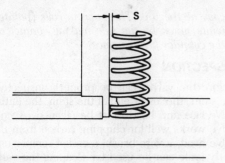

Measuring the spring height and squareness. Make sure the closed coils face downward

Testing the spring pressure

distortion exceeds more than 1/16 in., replace the spring(s). The valve spring squareness should not exceed: 0.087 in. (outer) or 0.075 in. (inner).

3. A valve spring tester is needed to test the spring pressure. Compare the tested pressure with the pressures listed in the Valve Specifications chart in this section.

Valve Seats

INSPECTION

Check the valve seat inserts for evidence of pitting or excessive wear at the valve contact surface. Because the cylinder head must be machined to accept the new seat inserts, consult an engine specialist or machinist about this work.

REMOVAL AND INSTALLATION

CAUTION: *To prevent damaging the other cylinder head components, completely disassemble the head.*

1. The old valve seat can be removed by machining it from the head or by heating the head in an 302–320°F (150–160°C) oil bath, then driving it from the head with a punch.

NOTE: *When removing the valve insert, be careful not to damage the cylinder head surface.*

2. Select a valve insert replacement and check the outside diameter, then ream the cylinder head recess at room temperature.

3. Heat the cylinder head to 302–320°F (150–160°C) in an oil bath, then press in the new valve seat, until it seats in the recess.

CUTTING THE SEATS

1. Allow the cylinder head to cool to room temperature. Using a valve seating tool kit, cut a new valve contact surface on the valve seat.

NOTE: *When repairing the valve seat, make sure that the valve and the guide are in good condition; if wear is evident, replace the valve and/or the guide, then correct the valve seat.*

2. To complete the operation, use valve grinding compound and lap the valve to the seat.

3. To install the removed components, reverse the removal procedures.

Lapping the valve seat and the valve

Valve Guides

REMOVAL AND INSTALLATION

1. Using a 2-ton press or a hammer and a suitable driving tool, drive the old valve guide from the cylinder head, in the rocker cover to combustion chamber direction.

NOTE: *Heating the cylinder head to 302–392°F (150–200°C) will facilitate the operation.*

2. Using the Valve Guide Reamer tool KV11081000 (F10) or ST11081000 (all other models), ream the valve guide hole.

3. Using a new valve guide, press it into the cylinder head and ream the guide hole with the proper size reamer.

4. Using a valve seating tool kit, cut a new valve contact on the valve seat.

5. To install the removed components, reverse the removal procedures.

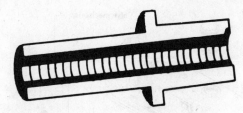

Cross-section view of a knurled valve guide

KNURLING

Valve guides which are not excessively worn or distorted may in some cases, be knurled rather than reamed. Knurling is a process in which metal inside the valve guide bores is displaced and raised (forming a very fine crosshatch pattern), thereby reducing clearance. Knurling also provides for excellent oil control. The possibility of knurling rather than reaming the guides should be discussed with a machinist.

Timing Chain/Belt Cover
REMOVAL AND INSTALLATION
A-Series—Overhead Valve Engines

It may be necessary to raise the vehicle, then remove the wheel assembly and the splash shield.

1. Disconnect the negative battery cable. Drain the cooling system.

2. Loosen the alternator adjustment and remove the drive belt.

NOTE: *It may be necessary to remove the alternator and the mounting bracket(s). If equipped with A/C, an air pump or power steering, loosen the adjustment(s) and remove the drive belt(s).*

3. Using a socket and a long handle, remove the crankshaft pulley nut, the washer and the pulley.

NOTE: *On certain models, it is recommended that the oil pan be removed or loosened before the front cover is removed.*

4. Remove the water pump pulley and the water pump. Remove the timing chain cover.

5. Replace the crankshaft oil seal in the cover. Most models use a felt seal.

6. Using a putty knife, clean the gasket mounting surfaces.

7. To install, use new gaskets, sealant and reverse the removal procedures. Torque the timing chain cover bolts to 4–5 ft.lb., the water pump bolts to 7–10 ft.lb., the oil pan bolts to 11–14 ft.lb. and the crankshaft pulley bolt to 108–145 ft.lb. Adjust the drive belts and refill the cooling system.

CA20 and E-Series—Overhead Cam Engine

It may be necessary to raise the vehicle, then remove the wheel assembly and the splash shield.

1. Disconnect the negative battery cable.

2. Loosen the alternator adjustment, then remove the drive belt and the adjusting bracket.

NOTE: *If equipped with A/C, an air pump or power steering, loosen the adjustment(s) and remove the drive belt(s).*

3. Using a socket and a long handle, remove the crankshaft pulley nut and the pulley.

4. Remove the water pump pulley. Remove the timing chain cover upper and lower covers.

NOTE: *The front crankshaft oil seal can only be replaced when the crankshaft sprocket is removed, refer the to the Timing Belt, Removal and Installation procedures in this section for details.*

5. Using a putty knife, clean the gasket mounting surfaces.

6. To install, use new gaskets and reverse the removal procedures. Torque the timing chain cover bolts to 2.5–4 ft.lb., the water pump pulley bolts to 4.5–7 ft.lb. (CA20) or 3–4 ft.lb. (E-series) and the crankshaft pulley bolt to 90–98 ft.lb. (CA20) or 83–108 ft.lb. (E-series). Adjust the drive belts and refill the cooling system.

Timing Belt and/or Chain
REMOVAL AND INSTALLATION
A-Series—Overhead Valve Engines

It is recommended that this operation be done with the engine removed from the vehicle.

1. Refer to the Timing Chain Cover, Removal and Installation procedures in this section and remove the cover.

2. Remove the oil throw and the chain tensioner.

3. Turn the crankshaft so that the dowel pin hole in the camshaft sprocket is facing the crankshaft sprocket and the crankshaft sprocket is facing directly away from the camshaft sprocket (see illustration).

4. Remove the camshaft sprocket retaining bolt.

5. Pull off the camshaft sprocket with the timing chain, if necessary, ease off the crankshaft sprocket.

NOTE: *If possible, remove both sprockets and the timing chain as an assembly. Be careful not to lose the shims from behind the crankshaft sprocket.*

6. Using a putty knife, clean the gasket mounting surface.

7. To install, insert the sprockets tempo-

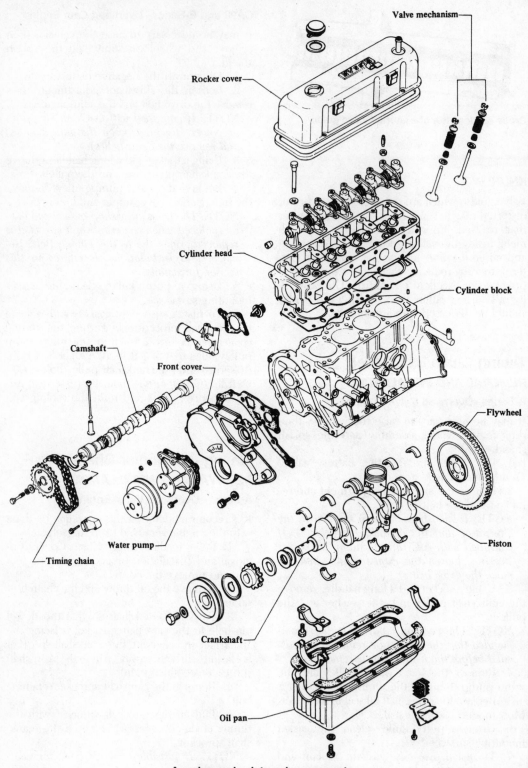

Valve mechanism

Rocker cover

Cylinder head

Cylinder block

Camshaft

Front cover

Flywheel

Water pump

Piston

Timing chain

Crankshaft

Oil pan

A-series engine internal components

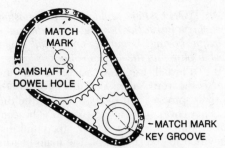

A series engine timing mark alignment

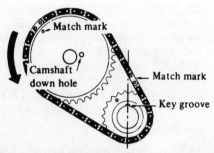

Timing chain sprocket positions with the No. 1 piston at TDC—A-series engine

Correct projection "L":
Less than
15 mm (0.59 in)

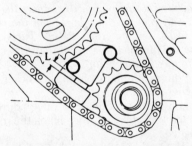

Measuring the chain tensioner gap—A-series engine

rarily and make sure that they are parallel; adjust by shimming under the crankshaft sprocket.

8. Assemble the sprockets with the chain, aligning them.

9. Turn the crankshaft counter-clockwise until the crankshaft keyway and the No. 1 piston are at the TDC (see illustration); the engine is timed correctly. Replaced the oil slinger with the concave surface to the front.

NOTE: *If installation is correct, the camshaft sprocket marks must be aligned between the shaft centers when the No. 1 piston is at TDC.*

10. To complete the installation, use a new gasket, sealant and reverse the removal procedures. Torque the camshaft sprocket retaining

bolt to 29–35 ft.lb., the chain tensioner bolt to 4–6 ft.lb. and the timing cover to 4–5 ft.lb.

NOTE: *If the timing chain tensioner adjusting gap L, is greater than 0.59 inch, replace the timing chain.*

CA20 and E-Series—Overhead Camshaft Engines

1. Refer to the Timing Belt Cover, Removal and Installation procedures, in this section and remove the timing cover.

2. If necessary, remove the spark plug, then turn the crankshaft to position the No. 1 piston at TDC of the compression stroke.

NOTE: *Note the position of the timing marks on the camshaft sprocket, the timing belt and the crankshaft sprocket (see illustrations). Most CA20 engine, camshaft sprockets are similiar in design to the E-series engine; if*

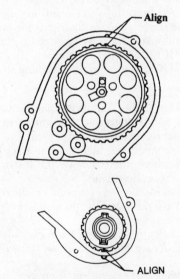

E series engine valve timing mark alignment

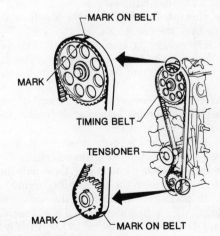

CA20 valve timing mark alignment

necessary, *install the camshaft sprocket exactly as the E-series engine.*

3. Loosen and/or remove the timing belt tensioner. Mark the rotation direction of the timing belt, then remove it from the sprockets.

4. To remove the front oil seal, pull off the crankshaft sprocket, then pry out the oil seal with a small pry bar (be careful not to scratch the crankshaft).

5. Clean the oil seal mounting surface.

6. To install, use a new oil seal, gaskets and reverse the removal procedures. Torque the tensioner pulley bolts to 13–16 ft.lb. (CA20) or 12–15 ft.lb. (E-series), the timing cover bolts to 2.5–4 ft.lb., the crankshaft pulley bolt to 90–98 ft.lb. (CA20) or 83–108 ft.lb. (E-series).

Camshaft and Bushings

REMOVAL AND INSTALLATION

For the following procedures, the engine should be removed from the vehicle and installed on an engine stand. Remove the right-side engine mount and install the Engine Attachment tool No. KV10102500 (all engines), plus No. KV10107110 (E-series) to the attaching studs.

A-Series

1. Refer to the Timing Belt and/or Chain, Removal and Installation procedures in this section and remove the timing chain.

2. Disconnect the high tension wires from the spark plugs, then remove the distributor assembly from the engine.

3. Remove the rocker arm cover, the rocker arm shaft assembly and the push rods (keep the rods in order).

NOTE: *Before removing the rocker arm assembly, loosen and back off the valve adjusters.*

4. Drain the engine oil. Remove the oil pump and the filter assembly, then invert the engine and remove the oil pan.

5. Remove the clutch and the flywheel assembly from the crankshaft.

6. Disconnect the connecting rods from the crankshaft (DO NOT remove the piston assemblies from the engine) and the crankshaft from the engine block.

NOTE: *When removing the connecting rod and the crankshaft bearings, be certain to keep the parts in order.*

7. Remove the camshaft sprocket bolt, then separate the sprocket from the camshaft. Remove the camshaft thrust plate, then pull the camshaft out through the front of the engine.

8. If necessary to replace the camshaft bearings, use a hammer and the Camshaft Bearing Drift tool No. ST16110000, to drive out and install the bearings in the cylinder block.

CAUTION: *After replacing the camshaft bearings, finish the bearing inner diameters by line boring. Using sealant install a new welch plug into the cylinder block.*

9. To install, use new gaskets, sealant and reverse the removal procedures. Torque the camshaft sprocket bolt to 29–35 ft.lb., the timing chain cover bolts to 3.5–5 ft.lb., the camshaft locating plate to 3–4 ft.lb., the crankshaft pulley bolt to 108–145 ft.lb., the main bearing cap bolts to 36–43 ft.lb., the connecting rod cap bolts to 23–27 ft.lb. and the rocker shaft bracket bolts to 14–18 ft.lb. Adjust the valves and the drive belts, then refill the cooling and the lubrication systems. Start the engine, then check and/or adjust the timing.

10. With the camshaft mounted in the cylinder block, mount a dial indicator on the sprocket bolt and check the end play; if it exceeds 0.0039 in., replace the locating plate.

CA20 and E-Series

1. Refer to the Timing Belt and/or Chain, Removal and Installation procedures in this section and remove the timing belt.

2. Disconnect the high tension wires from the spark plugs, then remove the distributor from front-left side (CA20) or the rear (E-series) of the cylinder head.

NOTE: *On the CA20 engine, if equipped with a mechanical fuel pump, disconnect the fuel lines and remove the pump from the cylinder head. On the 1984 Pulsar Turbo, remove the air inlet pipe from the turbocharger to the throttle body.*

3. Remove the hoses from the rocker arm cover, then the cover.

4. Loosen the rocker arm valve adjusting screws and back them off, then lift off the rocker arm shaft(s).

NOTE: *On the CA20 engine, remove the triangular cover plate from the rear of the cylinder head, then remove the bolt and the fuel pump drive cam from the rear of the camshaft.*

5. Remove the camshaft sprocket-to-camshaft bolt(s), then the sprocket from the camshaft. On the E-series engine, remove the upper backing plate and separate it from the cylinder head.

6. On the CA20 engine, pry the oil seal from the cylinder head. On the E-series engine, pry the oil seal from the backing plate.

7. Remove the camshaft by moving it toward the front of the engine, be careful not the damage the bearing surfaces.

NOTE: *Since these engines DO NOT use replaceable camshaft bearings, overhaul is performed by replacement of the camshaft or the cylinder head. Check the camshaft bearing surfaces (in the cylinder head) with an internal micrometer and the bearing surfaces (of the camshaft) with a micrometer.*

8. To install, use a new oil seal, gaskets, and reverse the removal procedures. Torque the camshaft sprocket-to-camshaft bolt to 36–43 ft.lb. (CA20, 1982–83), 58–65 ft.lb. (CA20, 1984 and later) or 4.5–6 ft.lb. (E-series, 1982–83), 6.5–9 ft.lb. (E-series, 1984 and later), the fuel pump drive cam bolt to 58–65 ft.lb. (CA20), the triangular cover plate to 4–7 ft.lb. (CA20), the rocker arm shaft-to-cylinder head bolts to 13–15 ft.lb., the rocker arm cover bolts to 1–2 ft.lb. (CA20) or nuts to 3–6 ft.lb. (E-series), the timing cover bolts to 9–10 ft.lb. (CA20) or 3–4 ft.lb. (E-series) and the crankshaft pulley bolt 90–98 ft.lb. (CA20) or 83–108 ft.lb. (E-series).

9. Adjust the valves, the timing belt and the equipment drive belt tension. Check and/or adjust the idle speed and the timing.

10. With the camshaft mounted in the cylinder block, mount a dial indicator on the sprocket bolt and check the end play. On the CA20 engine, if the end play exceeds 0.008 in., replace the cylinder head or the camshaft. On the E-series engine, if the end play exceeds 0.016 in., replace the faulty parts.

CHECKING CAMSHAFT

Place the camshaft on a set of V-blocks, supported by the outermost bearing surfaces. Place a dial micrometer, with it's finger resting on the center bearing surface, then turn the camshaft to check the bearing runout; the runout should not exceed 0.0039 in., if it does exceed the limit, replace the camshaft.

Check the camshaft bearing surfaces (in the engine) with an internal micrometer and the bearing surfaces (of the camshaft) with a micrometer.

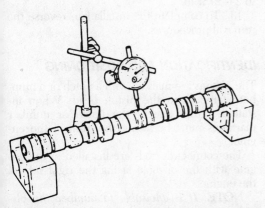

Checking the camshaft runout using a dail micrometer

Jackshaft
REMOVAL AND INSTALLATION
E-Series Engine

1. Refer to the Timing Belt and/or Chain, Removal and Installation procedures in this section and remove the timing belt.

2. Pull the crankshaft sprocket from the crankshaft. Remove the jackshaft sprocket bolts, then separate the sprocket from the jackshaft.

3. Remove the lower locating plate from the cylinder block. Remove the jackshaft and the crankshaft oil seals from the locating plate.

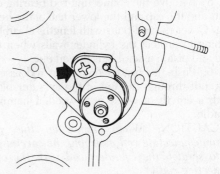

Removing the jackshaft retaining plate

4. Remove the jackshaft locating plate, then pull the shaft out through the front of the cylinder block.

5. Check the jackshaft bearing diameters (in the cylinder block) with an internal micrometer and the bearing diameters (of the jackshaft) with a micrometer; the clearance should not exceed 0.0059 in., if it does exceed the limit, replace the jackshaft bearings.

6. Use a hammer and a brass drift, to remove and install the jackshaft bearings in the cylinder block.

NOTE: *Be sure to align the oil hole in the bearing with the hole in the cylinder block. After installation, check the bearing clearances. Using sealant, install a new welch plug into the cylinder block.*

7. To install, use new oil seals, gaskets and reverse the removal procedures. Torque the jackshaft sprocket bolts to 6.5–9 ft.lb., the oil pump bolts to 5.8–7.2 ft.lb., the tensioner pulley bolts to 12–15 ft.lb., the timing cover bolts to 2.5–4 ft.lb., the crankshaft pulley bolt to 83–108 ft.lb. Adjust the timing belt and the drive belt tensions.

Pistons and Connecting Rods
REMOVAL AND INSTALLATION

It is recommended that the engine be removed from the vehicle and mount it on an engine stand, before removing the pistons and connecting rods from the engine.

1. Refer to the Cylinder Head, Removal and Installation procedures in this section and remove the cylinder head.

2. Using a ridge reamer tool, remove the carbon buildup from the top of the cylinder wall.

3. Drain the lubricant from the engine. Invert the engine on the stand, then remove the oil pan, the oil strainer and the pickup tube.

4. Position the piston to be removed at the bottom of its stroke, so that the connecting rod bearing cap can be easily reached.

5. Remove the connecting rod bearing cap nuts and the cap and the lower half of the bearing. Cover the rod bolts with lengths of rubber tubing to protect the cylinder walls when the rod and piston assembly is driven out.

6. Push the piston/connecting rod assembly, out through the top of the cylinder block with a length of wood or a wooden hammer handle.

CAUTION: *When removing the piston/connecting rod assembly, be careful not to scratch the cylinder wall with the connecting rod.*

7. Keep all of the components from each cylinder together and install them in the cylinder from which they were removed.

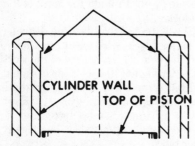

Ridge caused by cylinder wear

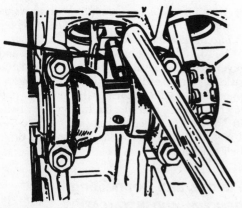

Driving out the piston assemblies with a wooden hammer handle. Note the tubing covering the rod bolts (arrow)

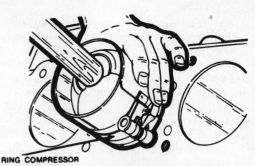

RING COMPRESSOR

Lubricate the components, compress the rings and drive the piston into the bore

8. Lubricate all of the piston/connecting rod components with engine oil, including the bearing face of the connecting rod and the outer face of the pistons with engine oil.

NOTE: *See the illustrations for the correct positioning of the piston rings.*

9. Turn the crankshaft until the rod journal of the particular cylinder you are working on is brought to the TDC position.

10. Clamp the piston/ring assembly into a ring compressor, the notched mark or number (on the piston head) must face the front of the engine and the oil hole (on the side of the connecting rod) must face the right-side of the engine; push the piston/connecting rod assembly into the cylinder bore until the big bearing end of the connecting rod seats on the rod journal of the crankshaft.

CAUTION: *Use care not to scratch the cylinder wall with the connecting rod.*

11. Push down on the piston/connecting rod assembly, while turning the crankshaft (the connecting rod rides around on the crankshaft rod journal), until the crankshaft rod journal is at the BDC (bottom dead center).

12. Align the mark on the connecting rod bearing cap with that on the connecting rod and torque the connecting rod bearing cap bolts to 24–27 ft.lb.

13. To complete the installation, reverse the removal procedures.

IDENTIFICATION AND POSITIONING

The pistons are marked with a notch or a number stamped on the piston head. When installed in the engine the notch or number markings must be facing the front of the engine.

The connecting rods are installed in the engine with the oil hole facing the right-side of the engine.

NOTE: *It is advisable to number the pistons, connecting rods and bearing caps in some manner so that they can be reinstalled*

CA20 piston and rod alignment

FRONT MARK
(NOTCH)

OIL HOLE

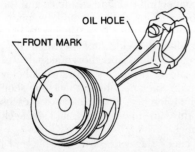

E series engine piston and rod alignment

OIL HOLE

FRONT MARK

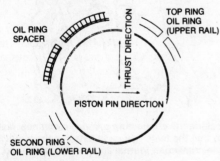

A series engine piston and rod alignment

OIL JET HOLE

NUMBER

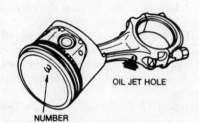

A-series piston ring arrangement

OIL RING
SPACER

TOP RING
OIL RING
(UPPER RAIL)

THRUST DIRECTION

PISTON PIN DIRECTION

SECOND RING
OIL RING (LOWER RAIL)

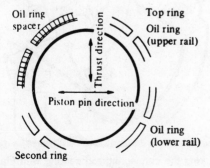

E-series—piston ring positioning

Oil ring
spacer

Top ring

Oil ring
(upper rail)

Thrust direction

Piston pin direction

Oil ring
(lower rail)

Second ring

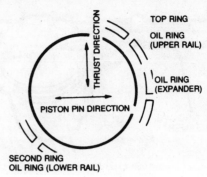

CA20 engine—piston ring positioning

TOP RING

OIL RING
(UPPER RAIL)

THRUST DIRECTION

OIL RING
(EXPANDER)

PISTON PIN DIRECTION

SECOND RING
OIL RING (LOWER RAIL)

in the same cylinder, facing in the same direction from which they are removed.

PISTON RING REPLACEMENT

A piston ring expander is necessary for removing and installing the piston rings (to avoid damaging them). When the rings are removed, clean the ring grooves using an appropriate ring groove cleaning tool, using care not to cut too deeply. Use solvent to thoroughly remove all of the carbon and varnish deposits.

When installing the rings, make sure that the stamped mark on the ring is facing upwards. Install the bottom rings first, then the upper ones last. Be sure to use a ring expander, to keep from breaking the rings.

CLEANING AND INSPECTION

Clean the piston after removing the rings (Refer to Piston Ring Replacement), by scraping the carbon from the top of the piston (DO NOT scratch the piston surface). Use a broken piston ring or a ring cleaning tool, to clean out the ring grooves. Clean the entire piston with solvent and a brush (NOT a wire brush).

With the piston thoroughly cleaned, place both compression rings on each piston. Using a feeler gauge, check the side clearance of the piston rings. If the side clearance is too large, replace the piston; if the side clearance is too small, cut the land areas a little larger.

Removing the piston rings with a ring expander

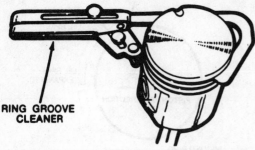

RING GROOVE CLEANER

Using a ring groove cleaning tool to properly clean the ring grooves

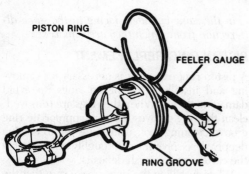

PISTON RING

FEELER GAUGE

RING GROOVE

Measuring the piston-to-ring side clearance

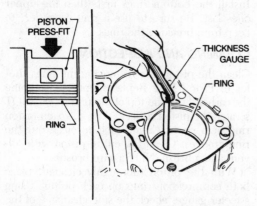

PISTON PRESS-FIT

THICKNESS GAUGE

RING

RING

Measuring the piston-to-bore and the piston ring end gap

Using a feeler gauge to check the ring end gap, lubricate the cylinder wall, then (using an inverted piston) drive the new ring(s) approximately 1–2 inches below the top of the cylinder bore.

NOTE: *If the ring gap is too small, carefully remove the rings and file the ends until the proper gap is acquired.*

PISTON PIN REPLACEMENT

The piston pin, the piston and the connecting rod are held together as an assembly, by pressing piston pin into the connecting rod. An arbor press and a special pin removing stand tool

No. ST13040000 (F10), KV10105300 (310, 1979–81), KV101070S0 (Stanza) or KV10107400 (310, 1982 and Pulsar), are used for removing and installing the piston pin.

NOTE: *The piston pin should slide smoothly into the piston, using hand pressure, at room temperature.*

ROD BEARING REPLACEMENT

The connecting rod side clearance and the big-end bearing inspection should be performed while the rods are still installed in the engine. Determine the clearance between the connecting rod sides and the crankshaft, using a feeler gauge. If the side clearance is below the minimum tolerance, have a machine shop correct the tolerance; if the clearance is excessive, substitute an unworn rod and recheck the clearance.

To check the connecting rod big-end bearing clearances, remove the rod bearing caps one at a time. Using a clean, dry shop rag, thoroughly clean all of the oil from the crank journal and the bearing insert in the cap.

NOTE: *The Plastigage® gauging material you will be using to check the clearances with, is soluble in oil; therefore any oil on the journal or bearing could result in an incorrect reading.*

Lay a strip of Plastigage® across the bearing

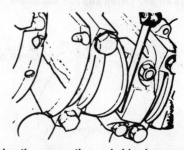

Checking the connecting rod side clearance. Make sure that the feeler gauge is between the shoulder of the crankshaft journal and the side of the rod.

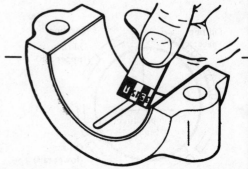

Checking the connecting rod bearing with Plastigage®

insert. Reinsert the bearing cap and retorque to specifications.

Remove the rod cap and determine the bearing clearance by comparing the width of the now flattened Plastigage® to the scale on the Plastigage® envelope. The journal taper is determined by comparing the width of the strip near its ends. Rotate the crankshaft 90° and re-test, to determine the journal eccentricity.

CAUTION: *DO NOT rotate the crankshaft with Plastigage® installed, for an incorrect reading will result.*

If the clearances are not within the toler-ances, the bearing inserts must be replaced with ones of the correct oversize or undersize and/or the crankshaft must be ground. If installing new bearing inserts, make sure that the tabs fit cor-rectly into the notch of the bearing cap and rod. Lubricate the face of each insert before install-ing them onto the crankshaft.

Rear Main Oil Seal
REMOVAL AND INSTALLATION

1. Remove the engine and transaxle assem-bly from the vehicle.
2. Remove the transaxle from the engine.
3. Remove the clutch/flywheel assembly (M/T) or the driveplate (A/T) from the crank-shaft.
4. Using a small pry bar, pry the rear main oil seal from around the crankshaft.
5. Apply lithium grease around the sealing

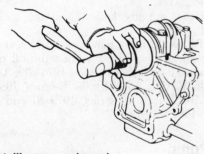

Installing rear main seal

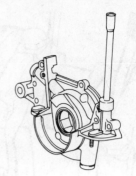

CA20 oil pump

lip of the oil seal and install the seal by driving it into the cylinder block using an oil seal in-stallation tool.

6. To complete the installation, reverse the removal procedures.

Crankshaft and Main Bearing
REMOVAL AND INSTALLATION

1. Refer to the Piston and Connecting Rod, Removal and Installation procedures, in this section and remove the connecting rod bear-ings from the crankshaft.

NOTE: *It may not be necessary to remove the piston/connecting rod assemblies from the cylinder block.*

2. On the A-series engine, remove the tim-ing chain and the flywheel from the engine. On the CA20 engine, remove the oil pump from the front of the engine block, then the clutch/flywheel assembly (M/T) or driveplate (A/T), the rear oil seal retainer and the rear plate. On the E-series engine, remove the jackshaft sprocket, the crankshaft sprocket, the front-side rear timing plate, then the clutch/flywheel as-sembly (M/T) or driveplate (A/T), the rear oil seal retainer and the rear plate.

3. Check the crankshaft thrust clearance (end play) before removing the crankshaft from the engine block. Using a pry bar, pry the crank-shaft forward to the extent of its travel and measure the clearance at the No. 3 main bear-

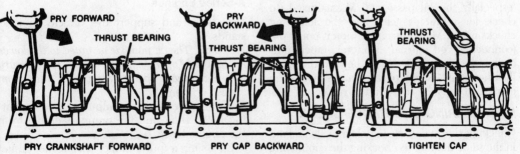

Checking the crankshaft thrust bearing clearance

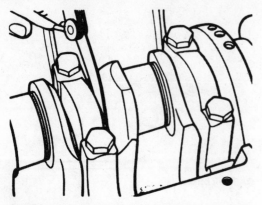

Checking the end-play of the crankshaft with a feeler gauge

ing. Pry the crankshaft rearward to the extent of its travel and measure the clearance on the other side of the bearing.

NOTE: *If the clearance is greater than specified, the thrust bearing must be replaced. When removing the crankshaft bearing caps, be sure to keep the bearing together with the caps, unless new bearings are going to be installed.*

4. Remove the crankshaft bearing caps, the cap bearings and the crankshaft from the engine.

5. To install, check the clearances with the Plastigage® method, then replace the bearings (if necessary) and reverse the removal procedures. Torque the crankshaft bearing cap bolts to 33–40 ft.lb. (CA20 engine), 36–43 ft.lb. (A and E-series engines).

6. To complete the installation, reverse the removal procedures.

NOTE: *When torquing the main bearing caps, start with the center bearing and work towards both ends at the same time.*

INSPECTION

The crankshaft inspection and servicing should be handled exclusively by a reputable machinist, for most necessary procedures require a dial indicator, fixing jigs and a large micrometer; also machine tools, such as: crankshaft grinder. The crankshaft should be throughly cleaned (especially the oil passages), Magnafluxed (to check for minute cracks) and the following checks made: Main journal diameter, crank pin (connecting rod journal) diameter, taper, out-of-round and run-out. Wear, beyond the specification limits, in any of these areas means the crankshaft must be reground or replaced.

MAIN BEARING CLEARANCE CHECK

Checking the main bearing clearances is done in the same manner as checking the connecting rod big-end clearances.

1. With the crankshaft installed, remove the main bearing cap. Clean all of the oil from the bearing insert (in the cap and the crankshaft journal), for the Plastigage® material is oil-soluble.

2. Lay a strip of Plastigage® across the full width of the bearing cap and install the bearing cap, then torque the cap to specifications.

NOTE: *DO NOT rotate the crankshaft with the Plastigage® installed.*

3. Remove the bearing cap and compare the scale on the Plastigage® envelope with the flattened Plastigage® material in the bearing. The journal taper is determined by comparing the width of both ends of the Plastigage® material. Rotate the crankshaft 90° and retest, to determine eccentricity.

4. Repeat the procedure for the remaining bearings. If the bearing journal and insert appear to be in good shape (with no unusual wear visible) and are within tolerances, no further main bearing service is required. If unusual wear is evident and/or the clearances are outside specifications, the bearings must be replaced and the cause of their wear determined.

Oil Pan

REMOVAL AND INSTALLATION

To remove the oil pan it will be necessary to unbolt the motor mounts and jack the engine to gain clearance.

1. Drain the oil from the crankcase.

2. Remove the attaching screws, the oil pan and the gasket.

3. Using a putty knife, clean the gasket mounting surfaces.

4. To install, use a new gasket and reverse the removal procedures. Torque the oil pan screws to 11–14 ft.lb. (A-series, 1976–78), 3.6–5.1 ft.lb. (CA20), 2.7–4.1 ft.lb. (E-series, 1982–83), 2.9–4.3 ft.lb. (A-series, 1979–81 and E-series, 1984 and later).

Oil Pump

REMOVAL AND INSTALLATION

A-Series Engines

1. Raise and support the vehicle on jackstands.

NOTE: *The oil pump is mounted to the lower right-side of the cylinder block. If necessary to have more space, remove the filter from the oil pump.*

2. Remove the oil pump-to-engine mounting bolts, then pull the pump assembly from the engine block.

3. Using a putty knife, clean the gasket mounting surfaces.

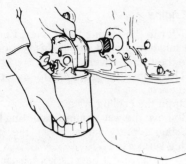

A series oil pump removal

4. Fill the pump housing with petroleum jelly.

5. To install, use a new gasket and reverse the removal procedures. Torque the oil pump mounting bolts to 6.5–10 ft.lb. Start the engine and check for oil leaks.

E-Series Engine

1. Raise and support the vehicle on jackstands.

NOTE: *The oil pump is mounted to the lower right-side of the cylinder block.*

2. Remove the oil pump-to-engine mounting bolts, then pull the pump assembly from the engine block.

3. Using a putty knife, clean the gasket mounting surfaces.

4. Fill the pump housing with petroleum jelly.

5. To install, use a new gasket and reverse the removal procedures. Torque the oil pump mounting bolts to 5.8–7.2 ft.lb. Start the engine and check for oil leaks.

CA20 Engine

1. Refer to the Timing Belt, Removal and Installation procedures in this section and remove the timing belt.

2. Remove the crankshaft sprocket and the key.

3. Remove the oil pump bolts and oil pump.

NOTE: *When the oil pump is removed it is recommended to change the front oil seal.*

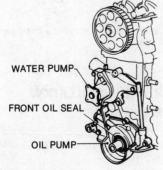

WATER PUMP

FRONT OIL SEAL

OIL PUMP

CA20 oil pump installed

4. Using a putty knife, clean the gasket mounting surfaces.

5. To install, use a new gasket and reverse the removal procedures. Fill the pump with clean engine oil and rotate it several times prior to installation. Torque the oil pump bolts to 9–12 ft.lb.

Flywheel and Ring Gear
REMOVAL AND INSTALLATION
F10 and 310 (1979-81)

NOTE: *The clutch/flywheel assembly can be serviced without disturbing any adjacent units. The clutch cover and the pressure plate are balanced as an assembly; if replacement of either part becomes necessary, replace both parts as an assembly.*

1. Refer to the Clutch, Removal and Installation procedures in Chapter 6 and remove the clutch cover assembly.

2. Remove the flywheel-to-crankshaft bolts and the flywheel.

NOTE: *If necessary the clutch disc should be inspected and/or replaced at this time; the clutch lining wear limit is 0.012 inch above the rivet heads.*

3. To install, reverse the removal procedures. Torque the flywheel-to-crankshaft bolts to 58–65 ft.lb., the clutch cover-to-flywheel bolts and the bearing housing-to-clutch housing bolts to 4.3–7.2 ft.lb.

Stanza and Pulsar

1. If equipped with a manual transaxle, refer to the Clutch, Removal and Installation procedures in Chapter 6, then remove the transaxle and the clutch assembly. If equipped with an automatic transaxle, refer to the Automatic Transaxle, Removal and Installation procedures in Chapter 6, then remove the transaxle and the torque converter.

2. For manual transaxles, remove the flywheel-to-crankshaft bolts and the flywheel. For automatic transaxles, remove the drive plate-to-crankshaft bolts and the drive plate.

3. To install, reverse the removal procedures. Torque the flywheel-to-crankshaft bolts to 72–80 ft.lb. (Stanza) or 58–65 ft.lb. (Pulsar); torque the drive plate-to-crankshaft bolts to 72–80 ft.lb. (Stanza) or 69–76 ft.lb. (Pulsar).

Water Pump
REMOVAL AND INSTALLATION
A-Series Engines

1. Drain the engine coolant into a clean container.

2. Remove the drive belt, then pulley from the water pump hub.

3. Remove the water pump bolts and the pump (with the gasket) from the timing chain cover.

4. Using a putty knife, clean the gasket mounting surfaces.

5. To install, use a new gasket, sealant and reverse the removal procedures. Torque the pump bolts to 6.5–10 ft.lb. Adjust the drive belt and refill the cooling system. Start the engine and check for leaks.

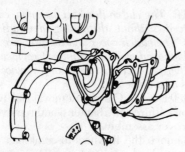

A series water pump removal

E-Series Engines

1. Drain the cooling system.

2. Remove the power steering drive belt and the power steering pump.

NOTE: *When removing the power steering pump, do not disconnect the pressure hoses or drain the system.*

3. Remove the water pump/alternator drive belt.

4. Remove the alternator mounting bolts and move it aside.

5. Remove the water pump pulley, then the water pump and the gasket.

6. Using a putty knife, clean the gasket mounting surfaces.

7. To install, use a new gasket, sealant and reverse the removal procedures. Torque the water pump bolts to 6.5–10 ft.lb. Adjust the drive belts and refill the cooling system. Start the engine and check for leaks.

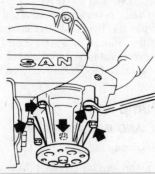

E series water pump removal

CA20 Engine

1. Refer to the Timing Belt Cover, Removal and Installation procedures in this section and remove the timing cover.

NOTE: *It may be necessary to remove the timing belt.*

2. Drain the cooling system.

3. Remove the water pump mounting bolts.

4. Using a putty knife, clean the gasket mounting surfaces.

5. To install, use a new gasket, sealant and reverse the removal procedures. Torque the water pump bolts to 9–12 ft.lb., the water pump pulley bolts to 4.3–7.2 ft.lb., the alternator brace-to-water pump bolt to 9–15 ft.lb. and the alternator adjusting bolt to 10–12 ft.lb. Adjust the drive belt(s) and refill the cooling system. Start the engine and check for leaks.

Thermostat

REMOVAL AND INSTALLATION

All Engines

1. Drain the engine coolant into a clean container so that the level is below the thermostat housing.

2. Disconnect the upper radiator hose at the water outlet.

3. Loosen the two securing nuts and remove the water outlet, gasket and the thermostat from the thermostat housing.

4. Using a putty knife, clean the gasket mounting surface.

5. To install, use a new gasket, sealant and reverse the removal procedures.

NOTE: *Install the thermostat with the spring toward the inside of the engine and the air bleeder or jiggle valve facing upwards.*

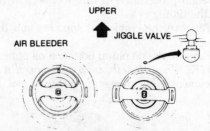

1980 and later thermostat: place the jiggle valve toward the top

Radiator

REMOVAL AND INSTALLATION

A-Series Engines

NOTE: *On some models, it may be necessary to remove the front grille.*

1. Drain the engine coolant into a clean container.

2. Disconnect the upper and lower radiator hoses and the expansion tank hose.

3. Disconnect the fan motor electrical connectors. Remove the fan motor assembly retaining bolts and lift the assembly out of the engine compartment.

4. Remove the radiator mounting bolts and the radiator.

5. To install, reverse the removal procedures. Refill the cooling system. Operate the engine and check for leaks.

E-Series Engine

1. Drain the cooling system.

2. Unbolt and set aside the power steering pump. DO NOT disconnect the power steering pressure hoses or drain the system.

3. Disconnect the upper and lower radiator hoses.

4. Remove the lower hose adapter.

5. If equipped with an automatic transaxle, disconnect and cap the cooling lines at the radiator.

6. Disconnect the fan motor wires and remove the fan assembly. Remove the radiator.

7. To install, reverse the removal procedures. Refill the radiator and the automatic transaxle (if equipped). Start the engine and check for leaks.

CA20 Engine

1. Drain the cooling system.

2. Disconnect the upper and lower radiator hoses and the coolant reserve tank hose.

3. Disconnect the water temperature switch connector and the fan wiring. Disconnect the fan assembly and remove it from the engine compartment.

4. If equipped with an automatic transaxle, disconnect and cap the cooling lines at the radiator.

5. Remove the radiator.

6. To install, reverse the removal procedures. Refill the radiator and the automatic transaxle (if equipped). Start the engine and check for leaks.

Emission Controls and Fuel System

EMISSION CONTROLS

There are three types of automotive pollutants: crankcase fumes, exhaust gases and gasoline evaporation. The equipment that is used to limit these pollutants is commonly called emission control equipment.

Crankcase Emission Controls

The crankcase emission control equipment consists of a positive crankcase ventilation valve (PCV), an oil filler cap (sealed) and hoses (connected to the equipment). The CA20 engines use an external oil separator (in the PCV line) to keep excess oil in the crankcase, away from the PCV valve.

OPERATION

When the engine is running, a small portion of the gases which are formed in the combustion chamber during combustion, leak by the piston rings and enter the crankcase. Since these gases are under pressure they tend to escape from the crankcase and enter into the atmosphere. If these gases were allowed to remain in the crankcase for any length of time, they would contaminate the engine oil and cause sludge to build up. If the gases are allowed to escape into the atmosphere, they would pollute the air, for they contain unburned hydrocarbons. The crankcase emission control equipment recycles these gases back into the engine combustion chamber where they are burned.

Crankcase gases are recycled in the following manner: when the engine is running, clean filtered air (from the carburetor air filter) is drawn into the crankcase or the rocker cover, through a hose. As the air passes through the crankcase it mixes with combustion gases, then carries them (out of the crankcase) through the PCV valve and into the intake manifold. After they enter the intake manifold they are drawn into the combustion chamber and burned.

The most critical component in the system is the PCV valve. This vacuum controlled valve regulates the amount of gases which are recycled into the combustion chamber. At low engine speeds, the valve is partially closed, limiting the flow of gases into the intake manifold. At increased engine speeds, the valve opens to admit greater quantities of the gases into the intake manifold. If the valve should become blocked or plugged, the gases will be prevented from escaping from the crankcase by the normal route. Since these gases are under pressure, they will find their own way out of the crankcase. This alternate route is usually a weak oil seal or gasket in the engine. As the gas escapes by the gasket, it also creates an oil leak. Besides causing oil leaks, a clogged PCV valve also allows these gases to remain in the crankcase for an extended period of time, promoting the formation of sludge in the engine.

TESTING AND SERVICE

To check the PCV system, inspect the PCV valve, the air filter(s), the hoses, the connections and the oil separator (CA20 engine); check for leaks, plugged valve(s) and/or filters, then replace or tighten, as necessary.

To check the PCV valve, remove it and blow through both of its ends. When blowing from the intake manifold side, very little air should pass through it. When blowing from the crankcase or valve cover side, air should pass through freely.

> NOTE: *If the valve fails to function as outlined, replace it with a new one; DO NOT attempt to clean or adjust it.*

To check the hoses, use compressed air to free them or replace them. If the air filters are dirty, replace them.

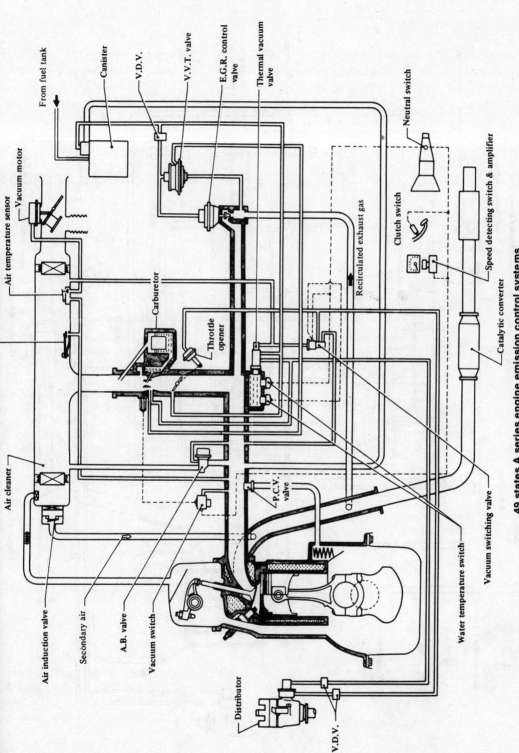

From fuel tank

Air temperature sensor

Vacuum motor

Canister

V.D.V.

V.V.T. valve

E.G.R. control valve

Thermal vacuum valve

Neutral switch

Carburetor

Throttle opener

Recirculated exhaust gas

Clutch switch

Speed detecting switch & amplifier

Air cleaner

Catalytic converter

P.C.V. valve

Air induction valve

Secondary air

A.B. valve

Vacuum switch

Water temperature switch

Vacuum switching valve

Distributor

V.D.V.

49 states A series engine emission control systems

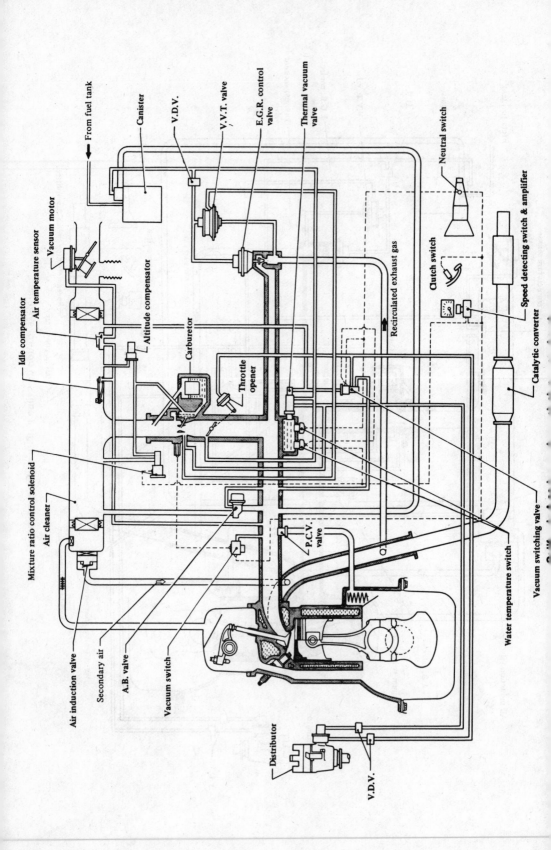

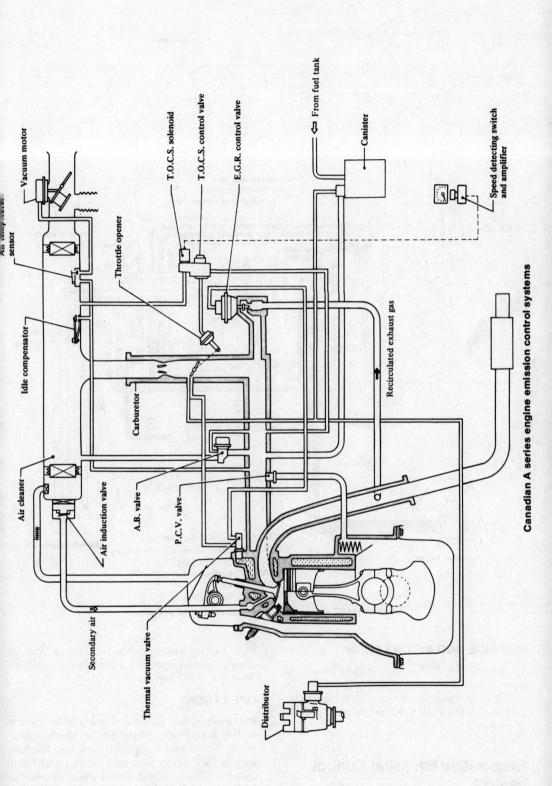

Vacuum motor

Air temp. intake
sensor

T.O.C.S. solenoid

T.O.C.S. control valve

E.G.R. control valve

Throttle opener

Idle compensator

Air cleaner

Carburetor

A.B. valve

P.C.V. valve

Air induction valve

Secondary air

Thermal vacuum valve

Distributor

From fuel tank

Canister

Speed detecting switch
and amplifier

Recirculated exhaust gas

Canadian A series engine emission control systems

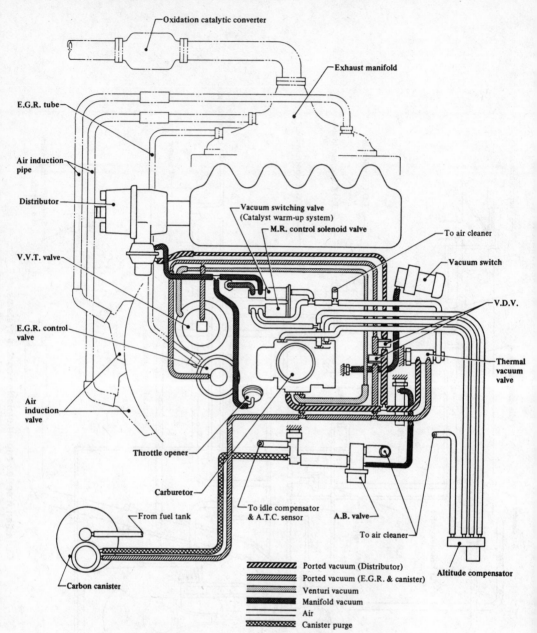

E-series (1982, Calif.) engine emission control systems

REMOVAL AND INSTALLATION

To remove the PCV valve, simply loosen the hose clamp and remove the valve from the manifold-to-crankcase hose and intake manifold. Install the PCV valve in the reverse order of removal.

Evaporative Emission Control System

The system consists of sealed fuel tank, vapor-liquid separator (certain models only), vapor vent line, carbon canister, vacuum signal line, a canister purge line and a float bowl vent line (E-series, 1982 and later).

OPERATION

In operation, fuel vapors and/or liquid are routed to the liquid/vapor separator or check valve, where liquid fuel is directed back into the fuel tank as fuel vapors flow into the charcoal filled canister. The charcoal absorbs and stores the fuel vapors when the engine is not running or at idle. When the throttle valves are opened, vacuum from above the throttle valves is routed

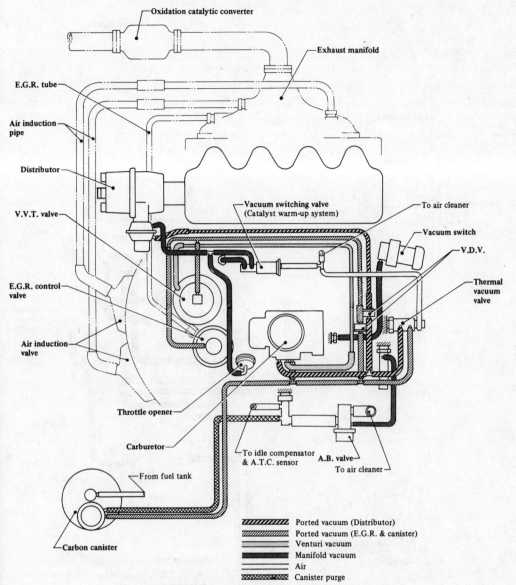

E-series (1982, 49 states) engine emission control systems

through a vacuum signal line to the purge control valve on the canister. The control valve opens, the fuel vapors move from the canister through a purge line, into the intake manifold and the combustion chambers.

INSPECTION AND SERVICE

Check the hoses for proper connections and damage. Replace as necessary. Check the vapor separator tank for fuel leaks, distortion and dents, then replace as necessary.

Carbon Canister and Purge Control Valve

To check the operation of the carbon canister purge control valve, disconnect the rubber hose between the canister control valve and the T-fitting, at the T-fitting. Apply vacuum to the hose leading to the control valve. The vacuum condition should be maintained indefinitely. If the control valve leaks, remove the top cover of the valve and check for a dislocated or cracked diaphragm. If the diaphragm is damaged, a repair kit containing a new diaphragm, retainer and spring is available, replace it.

The carbon canister has an air filter in the bottom of the canister. The filter element should be checked once a year or every 12,000 miles; more frequently if the car is operated in dusty areas. Replace the filter by pulling it out of the bottom of the canister and installing a new one.

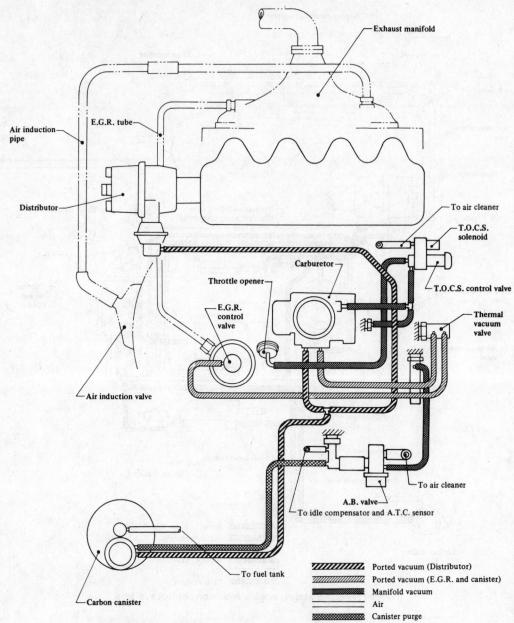

Air induction pipe

E.G.R. tube

Exhaust manifold

Distributor

To air cleaner

T.O.C.S. solenoid

Carburetor

Throttle opener

T.O.C.S. control valve

E.G.R. control valve

Thermal vacuum valve

Air induction valve

To air cleaner

A.B. valve

To idle compensator and A.T.C. sensor

To fuel tank

Carbon canister

	Ported vacuum (Distributor)
	Ported vacuum (E.G.R. and canister)
	Manifold vacuum
	Air
	Canister purge

E-series (1982 and later, Canada) engine emission control systems

REMOVAL AND INSTALLATION

Removal and installation of the various evaporative emission control system components consists of disconnecting the hoses, loosening retaining screws and removing the part which is to be replaced or checked. Install in the reverse order. When replacing hose, make sure that it is fuel and vapor resistant.

Spark Timing Control System
Except 1985 Pulsar

The spark timing control system has been used in different forms since 1972. The first system, Transmission Controlled Spark System (TCS) was used on most vehicles, through 1979. This system consists of a thermal vacuum valve, a vacuum switching valve, a high gear detecting

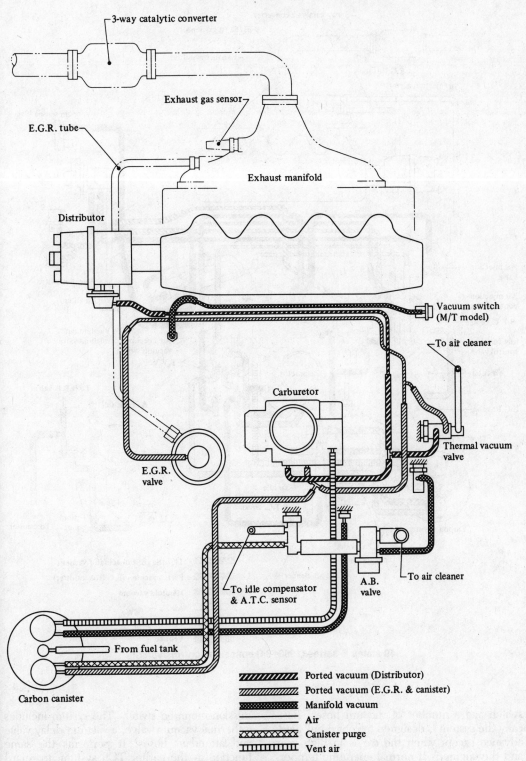

3-way catalytic converter

Exhaust gas sensor

E.G.R. tube

Exhaust manifold

Distributor

Vacuum switch
(M/T model)

To air cleaner

Carburetor

Thermal vacuum
valve

E.G.R.
valve

To idle compensator
& A.T.C. sensor

A.B.
valve

To air cleaner

From fuel tank

Carbon canister

	Ported vacuum (Distributor)
	Ported vacuum (E.G.R. & canister)
	Manifold vacuum
	Air
	Canister purge
	Vent air

California E-series (1983 and later) emission control system

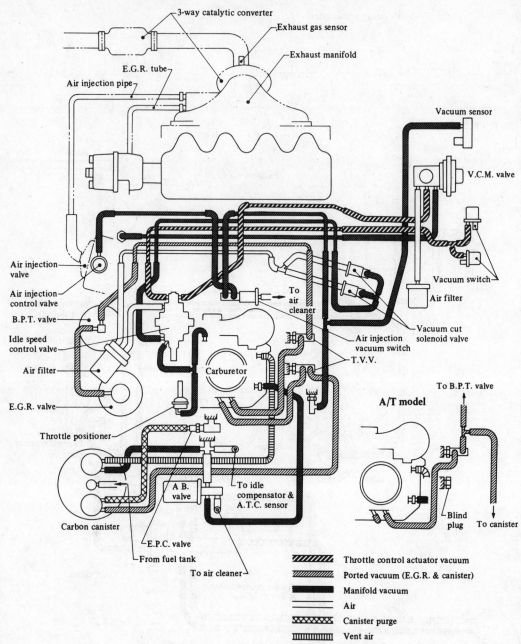

49 states E-series (1983–84) emission control system

switch and a number of vacuum hoses. Basically the system is designed to retard full spark advance except when the car is in high gear and the engine is at normal operating temperature. At all other times, the spark advance is retarded to one degree or another.

The 1980 and later, Spark Timing Control System replaces the TCS system. The major difference is that it works solely from engine water temperature changes rather than a trans-mission-mounted switch. The system includes a thermal vacuum valve, a vacuum delay valve and attendant hoses. It performs the same function as the earlier TCS system; to retard full spark advance at times when high levels of pollutants would otherwise be given off.

The system is designed to control the distributor vacuum advance under varying driving conditions to reduce the HC and the NOx emissions.

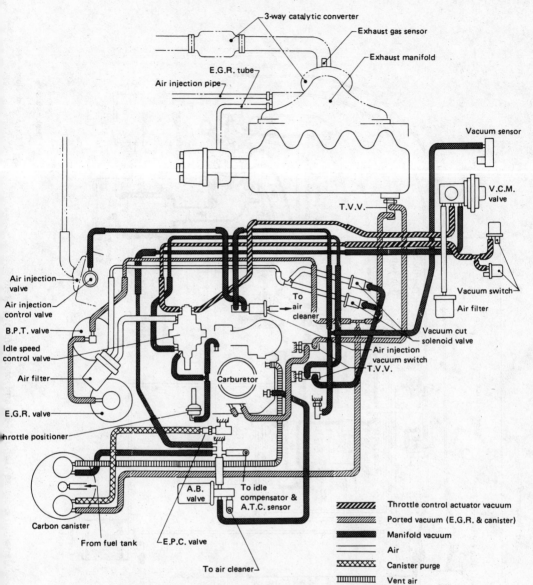

49 states E-series (1985 and later) emission control system

Legend:
- Throttle control actuator vacuum
- Ported vacuum (E.G.R. & canister)
- Manifold vacuum
- Air
- Canister purge
- Vent air

1985 Pulsar

The igniton timing is controlled by the central electronic control unit adjusting the engine operating conditions: as the best ignition timing in each driving condition and is determined by the electric signal calculated in the unit.

The information signals (used to determine the engine timing) are received from the water temperature, the engine rpm, the engine load and etc. The electronic control unit sends signals to the power transistor (of the ignition coil) and controls the ignition timing.

The distributor is equipped with a sensor and a signal rotor plate (photo-electric), which detects the position of the crankshaft and sends a signal to the control unit to control the various operations. The signal rotor plate has 360 (at 1° intervals) slots surrounding the outer edge (for detecting the rpm and ignition timing control) and 4 (at 90° intervals) slots on a inner circle (for detecting the piston TDC). When the signal rotor plate cuts the light signal between the Light Emitting Diode (LED) and the Photo Diode, an alternate voltage is created and sent to the control unit.

INSPECTION AND ADJUSTMENTS

Except 1985 Pulsar

Normally the TCS and Spark Timing Control systems should be trouble-free. However, if you

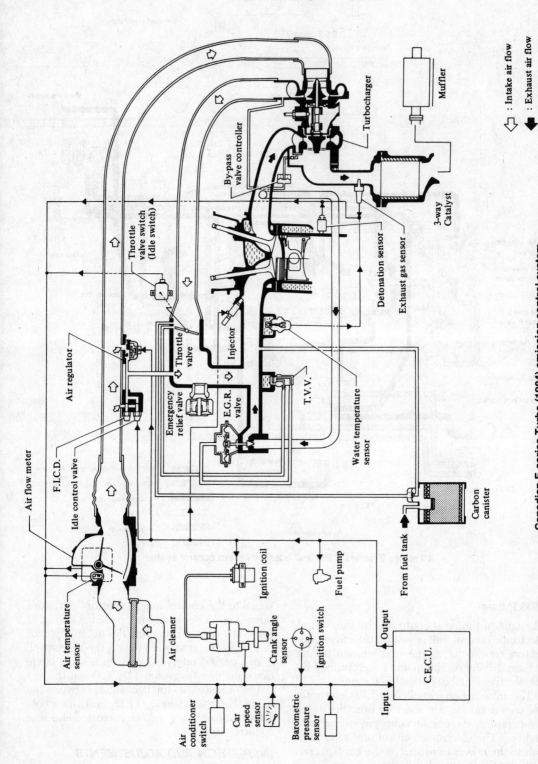

Canadian E-series Turbo (1984) emission control system

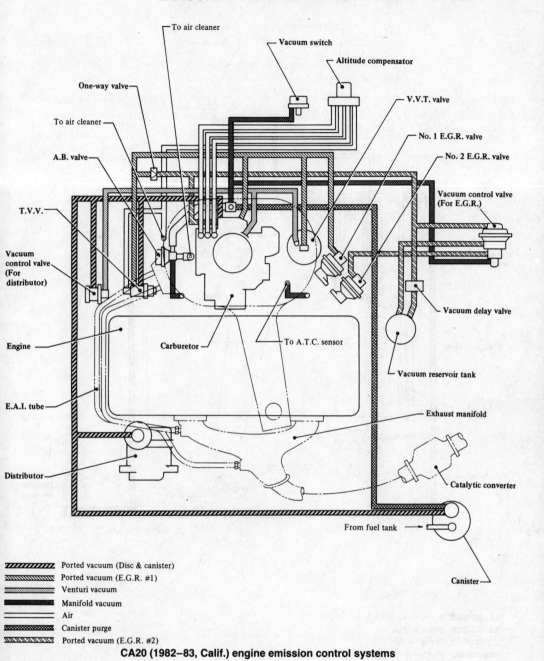

To air cleaner

Vacuum switch

Altitude compensator

One-way valve

V.V.T. valve

To air cleaner

No. 1 E.G.R. valve

A.B. valve

No. 2 E.G.R. valve

Vacuum control valve (For E.G.R.)

T.V.V.

Vacuum control valve (For distributor)

Vacuum delay valve

Engine

Carburetor

To A.T.C. sensor

Vacuum reservoir tank

E.A.I. tube

Exhaust manifold

Distributor

Catalytic converter

From fuel tank

Canister

▨▨▨	Ported vacuum (Disc & canister)
▨▨▨	Ported vacuum (E.G.R. #1)
▨▨▨	Venturi vacuum
▬▬▬	Manifold vacuum
═══	Air
▨▨▨	Canister purge
▨▨▨	Ported vacuum (E.G.R. #2)

CA20 (1982–83, Calif.) engine emission control systems

suspect a problem in the system, first check to make sure all wiring (if equipped) and hoses are connected and free from dirt. Also check to make sure the distributor vacuum advance is working properly. If everything appears OK, connect a timing light to the engine and make sure the initial timing is correct. On vehicles with the TCS system, run the engine until it reaches normal operating temperature, then have an assistant sit in the car and shift the transmission through all the gears slowly. If the system is functioning properly, the timing will be 10°–15° advanced in high gear (compared to the other gear positions). If the system is still not operating correctly, you will have to check for continuity at all the connections with a test light.

To test the Spark Timing Control System, connect a timing light and check the ignition timing while the temperature gauge is in the

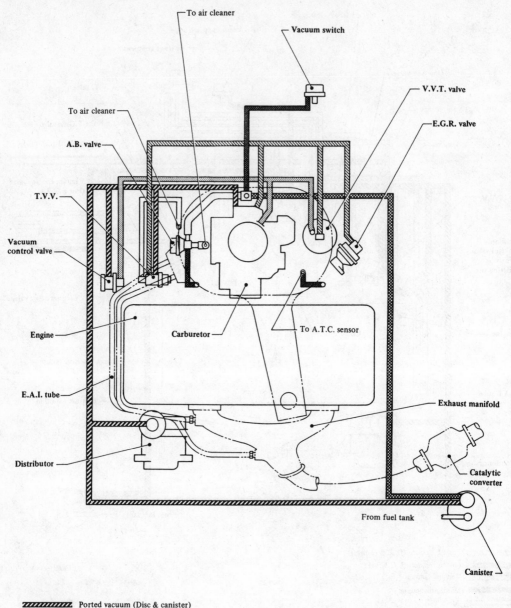

To air cleaner

Vacuum switch

V.V.T. valve

E.G.R. valve

To air cleaner

A.B. valve

T.V.V.

Vacuum control valve

Engine

Carburetor

To A.T.C. sensor

E.A.I. tube

Exhaust manifold

Distributor

Catalytic converter

From fuel tank

Canister

Ported vacuum (Disc & canister)
Ported vacuum
Venturi vacuum
Manifold vacuum
Air
Canister purge

CA20 (1982 and later, 49 states) engine emission control systems

cold position; the timing should be normal or advanced. Allow the engine to run with the timing light attached until the temperature needle reaches the center of the gauge. As the engine is warming up, check with the timing light to make sure the ignition timing retards.

When the engine reaches normal operating temperature, the ignition timing should advance from its previous position. If the ignition timing does not change, replace the thermal vacuum valve or the vacuum control valve (CA20, 1982 and later).

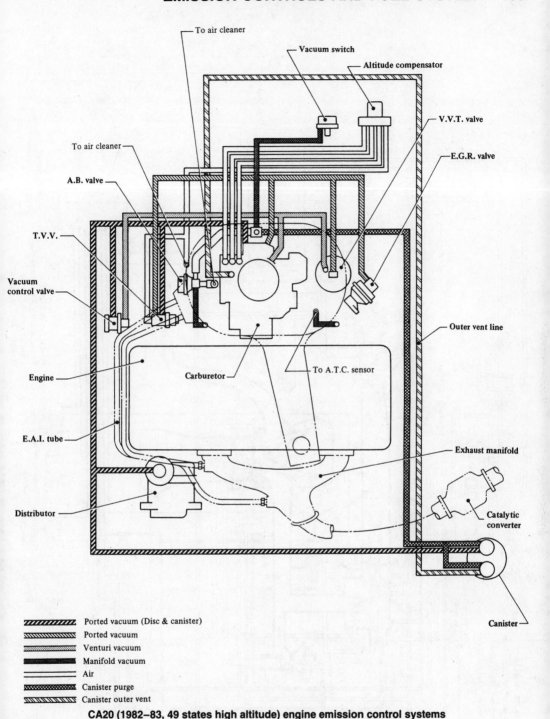

To air cleaner

Vacuum switch

Altitude compensator

V.V.T. valve

E.G.R. valve

To air cleaner

A.B. valve

T.V.V.

Vacuum control valve

Engine

Carburetor

To A.T.C. sensor

Outer vent line

E.A.I. tube

Exhaust manifold

Distributor

Catalytic converter

Canister

- ///// Ported vacuum (Disc & canister)
- \\\\ Ported vacuum
- Venturi vacuum
- ▓▓▓ Manifold vacuum
- Air
- Canister purge
- Canister outer vent

CA20 (1982–83, 49 states high altitude) engine emission control systems

NOTE: *The CA20 (carbureted) engines utilize a vacuum control valve, which is controlled by the velocity of the air moving through the carburetor to retard the spark.*

1985 Pulsar

The ignition timing is automatically controlled by the control unit and adjustment is unnecessary.

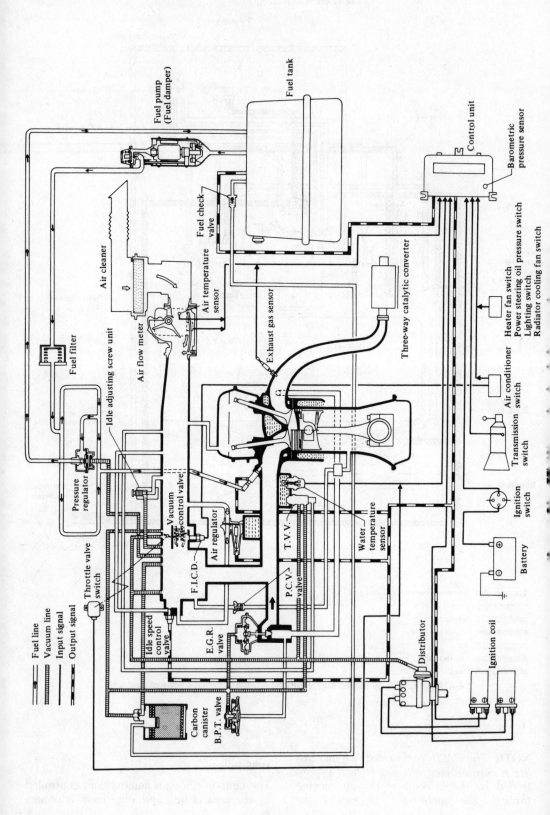

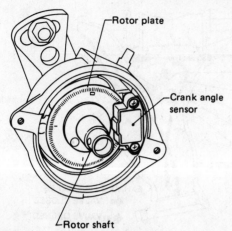

View of the signal rotor system, Pulsar (1985) distributor

Spark Plug Switching Control System–CA20 Engine

The system consists of an ignition control unit (installed in the distributor), a vacuum switch (connected to the intake manifold), a clutch switch and a neutral switch (M/T) or an inhibitor switch (A/T).

The system is designed to change the ignition system from a 2 plug ignition system to a 1 plug system, during heavy load driving conditions, to reduce engine noise; it also advances the ignition timing by a specified value, during the 1 plug operation.

INSPECTION

1. Disconnect the inhibitor switch connector (A/T) or the clutch switch connector (M/T).

2. Disconnect the vacuum hose from the vacuum switch, then connect a vacuum source and gauge to the switch.

3. Connect a timing light to the high tension cable of the exhaust side.

4. Apply (−)5.91 in. Hg (vacuum) to the switch and start the engine.

5. Reduce the vacuum gradually, make sure that the timing light does not brighten or dim when the vacuum reaches (−)3.15 in. Hg or

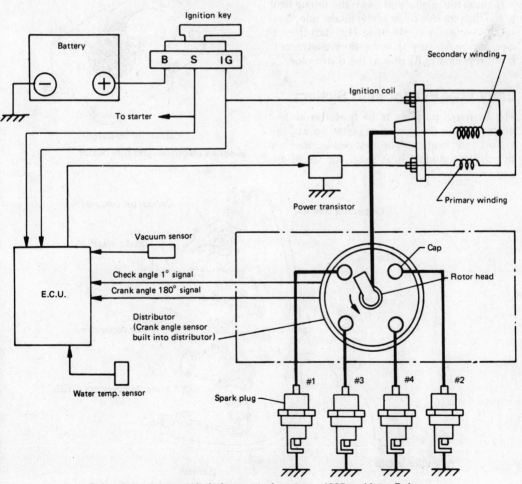

Schematic of the spark timing control system—1985 and later Pulsar

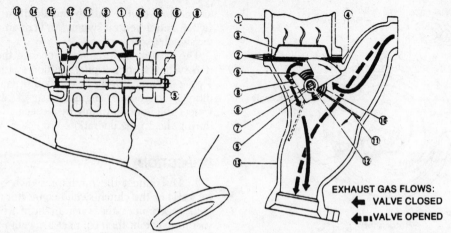

EXHAUST GAS FLOWS:
◀— VALVE CLOSED
◀■▪ VALVE OPENED

1. Intake manifold
2. Stove gasket
3. Manifold stove
4. Heat shield plate

5. Snap ring
6. Counterweight
7. Key
8. Stopper pin

9. Screw
10. Thermostat spring
11. Heat control valve
12. Control valve shaft

13. Exhaust manifold
14. Cap
15. Bushing
16. Coil spring

A-series heat riser type fuel heater

less. If necessary, check and replace each component.

6. Stop the engine and move the timing light to the high tension cable of the intake side, then set the vacuum to $(-)5.91$ in Hg, start the engine and make sure that the timing advances. If not replace the IC unit in the distributor.

Early Fuel Evaporation System

The system's purpose is to heat the air/fuel mixture when the engine is below normal operating temperature. The A-series engines use an exhaust manifold heat riser, the CA20 en-

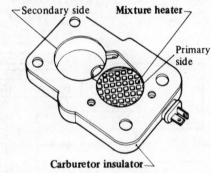

Secondary side — Mixture heater —
Primary side
Carburetor insulator —
E-series electrical-grid fuel heater

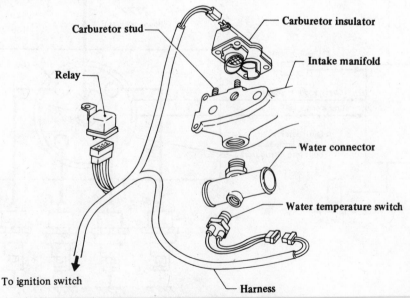

Carburetor stud
Carburetor insulator
Relay
Intake manifold
Water connector
Water temperature switch
To ignition switch
Harness
CA20 coolant water heated fuel heater

gines use a coolant water style heater and the E-series use an electric-grid style heater. The only adjustment necessary (A-series) is to occasionally lubricate the counterweight, otherwise, the system should be trouble-free; the other systems are trouble-free.

Throttle Opener Control System (TOCS)/Boost Control Deceleration Device (BCDD)

The Throttle Opener Control System (TOCS) is used on A-series (except 1980 and later, Calif.)

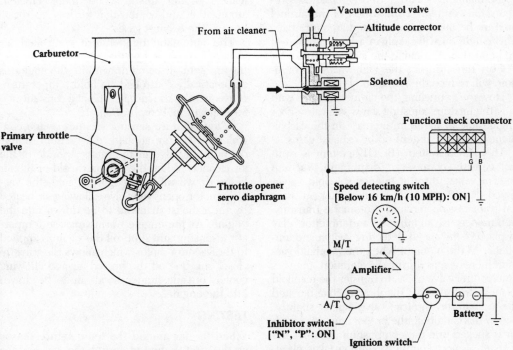

A-series and E-series throttle opener control system

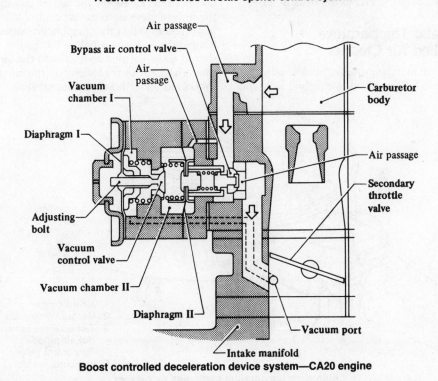

Boost controlled deceleration device system—CA20 engine

and the E-series engines; the Boost Control Deceleration Device (BCDD) is used on the CA20 engines. The purpose of both systems is to reduce hydrocarbon emissions during coasting conditions.

OPERATIONS

High manifold vacuum during coasting prevents the complete combustion of the air/fuel mixture because of the reduced amount of air. This condition will result in a large amount of HC emission. Enriching the air/fuel mixture for a short time (during the high vacuum condition) will reduce the emission of the HC.

However, enriching the air/fuel mixture with only the mixture adjusting screw will cause poor engine idle or invite an increase in the carbon monoxide (CO) content of the exhaust gases.

The TOCS system (BCDD system is similar) consists of a servo diaphragm, vacuum control valve, throttle opener solenoid valve, speed detecting switch and amplifier on manual transmission models. Automatic transmission models use an inhibitor and inhibitor relay in place of the speed detecting switch and amplifier. At the moment when the manifold vacuum increases, as during deceleration, the vacuum control valve opens to transfer the manifold vacuum to the servo diaphragm chamber and the carburetor throttle valve opens slightly. Under this condition, the proper amount of fresh air is sucked into the combustion chamber. As a result, a more thorough ignition takes place, burning much of the HC in the exhaust gases.

Automatic Temperature Controlled Air Cleaner

The rate of fuel atomization varies with the temperature of the air that the fuel is being mixed with. The air/fuel ratio cannot be held constant for efficient fuel combustion with a wide range of air temperatures. Cold air being drawn into the engine causes a denser and richer air/fuel mixture, inefficient fuel atomization, thus, more hydrocarbons in the exhaust gas. Hot air being drawn into the engine causes a leaner air/fuel mixture and more efficient atomization and combustion for less hydrocarbons in the exhaust gases.

The automatic temperature controlled air cleaner is designed so that the temperature of the ambient air being drawn into the engine is automatically controlled, to hold temperature, consequently, the fuel/air ratio at a constant rate for efficient fuel combustion.

A temperature sensing vacuum switch controls the vacuum applied to a vacuum motor, operating a valve in the intake snorkle of the air cleaner. When the engine is cold or the air being drawn into the engine is cold, the vacuum motor opens the valve, allowing air heated by the exhaust manifold to be drawn into the engine. As the engine warms up, the temperature sensing unit shuts off the vacuum applied to the vacuum motor which allows the valve to close, shutting off the heated air and allowing cooler, outside (under hood) air to be drawn into the engine.

TESTING

When the air around the temperature sensor of the unit mounted inside the air cleaner housing reaches 100°F, the sensor should block the flow of vacuum to the air control valve vacuum motor. When the temperature around the temperature sensor is below 100°F, the sensor should allow vacuum to pass onto the air valve vacuum motor thus blocking off the air cleaner snorkle to under hood (unheated) air.

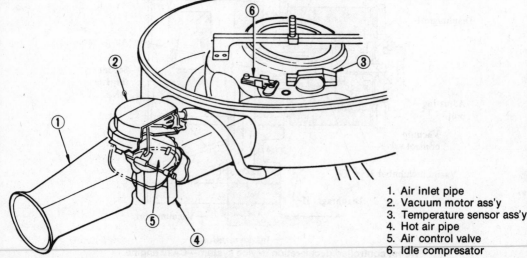

1. Air inlet pipe
2. Vacuum motor ass'y
3. Temperature sensor ass'y
4. Hot air pipe
5. Air control valve
6. Idle compresator

Automatic temperature controlled air cleaner

When the temperature around the sensor is above 118°F, the air control valve should be completely open to under hood air.

If the air cleaner fails to operate correctly, check for loose or broken vacuum hoses. If the hoses are not the cause, replace the vacuum motor in the air cleaner.

Exhaust Gas Recirculation (EGR)

The system is used on all models. Exhaust gas recirculation is used to reduce combustion temperatures in the engine, thereby reducing the oxides of nitrogen emissions.

An EGR valve is mounted on the center of the intake manifold. The recycled exhaust gas is drawn into the intake manifold through the exhaust manifold heat stove and EGR valve. A vacuum diaphragm is connected to a timed signal port at the carburetor flange.

OPERATIONS

As the throttle valve is opened, vacuum is applied to the EGR valve vacuum diaphragm. When the vacuum reaches about 2 in. Hg, the diaphragm moves against spring pressure and is in a fully up position at 8 in. Hg of vacuum. As the diaphragm moves up, it opens the exhaust gas metering valve which allows exhaust gas to be pulled into the engine intake manifold. The system does not operate when the engine is idling because the exhaust gas recirculation would cause a rough idle.

A thermal vacuum valve inserted in the engine thermostat housing controls the application of the vacuum to the EGR valve. When the engine coolant reaches a predetermined temperature, the thermal vacuum valve opens and allows vacuum to be routed to the EGR valve. Below the predetermined temperature, the thermal vacuum valve closes and blocks vacuum to the EGR valve.

Some models have a Back Pressure Transducer (BPT) valve installed between the EGR valve and the thermal vacuum valve. The BPT valve has a diaphragm which is raised or lowered by exhaust back pressure. The diaphragm opens or closes an air bleed, which is connected into the EGR vacuum line. High pressure results in higher levels of EGR, because the diaphragm is raised, closing off the air bleed, which allows more vacuum to reach and open the EGR valve. Thus, the amount of recirculated exhaust gas varies with exhaust pressure.

Some models use a Venturi Vacuum Transducer (VVT) valve. The VVT valve monitors exhaust pressure and carburetor vacuum in order to activate the diaphragm which controls the throttle vacuum applied to the EGR control valve. This system expands the operating range of the EGR unit, as well as increasing the EGR flow rate.

Many vehicles are equipped with an EGR warning system which signals via a light in the dashboard that the EGR system may need service. The EGR warning light should come on every time the starter is engaged as a test to make sure the bulb is not blown. The system uses a counter which works in conjunction with the odometer and lights the warning signal after the vehicle has traveled a predetermined number of miles.

To reset the counter, which is mounted in the engine compartment, remove the grommet installed in the side of the counter, insert the tip of a small screwdriver into the hole and press down on the knob inside the hole, then reinstall the grommet.

TESTING

1. Remove the EGR valve and apply enough vacuum to the diaphragm to open the valve.
2. The valve should remain open for over 30 seconds after the vacuum is removed.
3. Check the valve for damage, such as warpage, cracks and excessive wear around the valve and seat.
4. Clean the seat with a brush and compressed air, then remove any deposits from around the valve and port (seat).
5. To check the operation of the thermal vacuum valve, remove the valve from the engine and apply vacuum to the valve ports; it should not allow vacuum to pass.
6. Place the valve in a container of water with a thermometer and heat the water. When the temperature of the water reaches 134°–145°F,

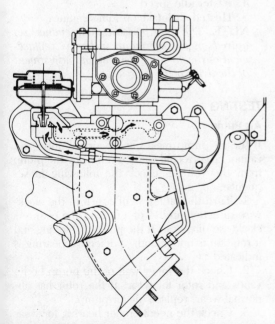

Typical EGR system

remove the valve and apply vacuum to the ports; the valve should allow vacuum to pass.

7. To test the BPT valve, disconnect the two vacuum hoses from the valve. Plug one of the ports. While applying pressure to the bottom of the valve, apply vacuum to the unplugged port and check for leakage. If any exists, replace the valve.

8. To check the VVT valve, disconnect the top and bottom center hoses and apply a vacuum to the top hose. Check for leaks. If a leak is present, replace the valve.

Mixture Ratio Rich-Lean and EGR Large-Small Exchange System (1980–82 California Engines)

This system controls the air/fuel mixture ratio and the amount of recirculated exhaust gas (manual transmission models only) in accordance with the engine coolant temperature and car speed. The system consists of a vacuum switching valve, a power valve, a speed detecting switch located in the speedometer, a speed detecting switch amplifier and a water temperature switch.

When the coolant temperature is above 122°F and the car is traveling at least 40 mph, the vacuum switching valve is on and acts to lean down the fuel mixture; a small amount of EGR is being burned. When the coolant temperature is above 122°F but the vehicle is traveling less than 40 mph, the vacuum switching valve is off and allows the mixture to enrichen; a large amount of EGR is being burned. When coolant temperature is below 122°F, the vacuum switching valve is always on and acts to lean down the fuel mixture.

TESTING

Warm up the engine and raise the drive wheels off the ground; support the raised end of the vehicle with jack stands and block the wheels still on the ground. Start the engine, shift the transmission into TOP speed and maintain a speedometer speed higher than 50 MPH. Pinch off the vacuum switching valve-to-air cleaner hose, then see if the engine speed decreases and operates erratically. Shift the transmission into 3rd speed and run the vehicle at a speed lower than 30 MPH. Disconnect the vacuum switching valve-to-power valve hose, at the power valve and plug the open end with your finger. The engine should operate erratically. If the expected engine reaction in both of these tests does not happen, check all of the wiring connections and hoses for breaks and/or blockage.

Air Injection Reactor System (1976–80)

It is difficult to completely burn the air/fuel mixture through normal combustion in the combustion chambers. Under certain operating conditions, unburned fuel is exhausted into the atmosphere.

The air injection reactor system is designed so that ambient air, pressurized by the air pump, is injected through the injection nozzles into the exhaust ports near each exhaust valve. The exhaust gases are at high temperatures and ignite when brought into contact with the oxygen. Unburned fuel is then burned in the exhaust ports and manifold.

The 1976 California models utilized a secondary system consisting of an air control valve, which limits the injection of secondary air and an emergency relief valve, which controls the supply of secondary air. This system protects the catalytic converter from overheating. In 1977, the function of both valves was combined in the Combined Air Control (CAC) valve.

All engines with an air pump system have a series of minor alterations to accommodate the system. These are:

1. Special close-tolerance carburetor. Most engines require a slightly rich idle mixture adjustment.
2. Distributor with special advance curve. Ignition timing is retarded about 10° at idle in most cases.
3. Cooling system changes such as: a larger fan, a higher fan speed and a thermostatic fan clutch; this is required to offset the increase in temperature caused by retarded timing at idle.
4. Faster idle speed.
5. Heated air intake on some engines.
NOTE: *The only periodic maintenance required on the air pump system is replacement of the air filter element and adjustment of the drive belt.*

TESTING
Air Pump

If the air pump makes an abnormal noise and cannot be corrected without removing the pump from the vehicle, check the following in sequence:

1. Turn the pulley ¾ of a turn in the clockwise direction and ¼ of a turn in the counterclockwise direction. If the pulley is binding and if rotation is not smooth, a defective bearing is indicated.
2. Check the inner wall of the pump body, vanes and rotor for wear. If the rotor has abnormal wear, replace the air pump.
3. Check the needle roller bearing for wear

and damage. If the bearings are defective, the air pump should be replaced.

4. Check and replace the rear side seal if abnormal wear or damage is noticed.

5. Check and replace the carbon shoes holding the vanes if they are found to be worn or damaged.

6. A deposit of carbon particles on the inner wall of the pump body and vanes is normal, but should be removed with compressed air before reassembling the air pump.

Check Valve

Remove the check valve from the air pump discharge line. Test it for leakage by blowing air into the valve from the air pump side and from the air manifold side. Air should only pass through the valve from the air pump side if the valve is functioning normally. A small amount of air leakage from the manifold side can be overlooked. Replace the check valve if it is found to be defective.

Anti-Backfire Valve

Disconnect the rubber hose connecting the mixture control valve with the intake manifold and plug the hose. If the mixture control valve is operating correctly, air will continue to blow out the mixture control valve for a few seconds after the accelerator pedal is fully depressed (engine running) and released quickly. If air continues to blow out for more than five seconds, replace the mixture control valve.

Air Pump Relief Valve

Disconnect the air pump discharge hose leading to the exhaust manifold. With the engine running, restrict the air-flow coming from the pump. The air pump relief valve should vent the pressurized air to the atmosphere if it is working properly.

NOTE: *When performing this test do not completely block the discharge line of the air pump as damage may result if the relief valve fails to function properly.*

Air Injection Nozzles

Check around the air manifold for air leakage with the engine running at 2,000 rpm. If air is leaking from the eye joint bolt, retighten or replace the gasket. Check the air nozzles for restrictions by blowing air into the nozzles.

Hoses

Check and replace hoses if they are found to be weakened or cracked. Check all hose connections and clips. Be sure that the hoses are not in contact with other parts of the engine.

Emergency Air Relief Valve

1. Warm up the engine.
2. Check all hoses for leaks, kinks, improper connections and etc.
3. Run the engine up to 2000 rpm, under no load; no air should be discharged from the valve.
4. Disconnect the intake manifold-to-air relief valve hose. Run the engine to 2000 rpm; air should be discharged from the valve, if not, replace it.

Combined Air Control Valve

1. Check all hoses for leaks, kinks and improper connections.
2. Thoroughly warm the engine.
3. With the engine idling, check for air discharge from the relief opening in the air cleaner case.
4. Disconnect and plug the vacuum hose from the valve; air should be discharged from the valve with the engine idling. If the disconnected vacuum hose is not plugged, the engine will stumble.
5. Connect a hand-operated vacuum pump to the vacuum fitting on the valve and apply 7.8–9.8 in. Hg of vacuum. Run the engine speed to 3000 rpm; no air should be discharged from the valve.
6. Disconnect and plug the air hose at the check valve, with the conditions as in the preceding step. This should cause the valve to discharge air. If not, or if any of the conditions in this procedure are not met, replace the valve.

Air Induction System (1981 and Later)

The air induction system is used to send fresh secondary air to the exhaust manifold by utilizing vacuum created by the exhaust pulsation in the manifold. The system consists of a dual or single set of reed valves connected to the air filter housing, with tube(s) leading to the exhaust manifold.

NOTE: *The air induction system is used on the carburetor models ONLY.*

OPERATION

The exhaust pressure usually pulsates in response to the opening and closing of the exhaust valve and it periodically decreases below atmospheric pressure. If a secondary air intake pipe is opened to the atmosphere under a vacuum condition, secondary air can then be drawn into the exhaust manifold in proportion of the vacuum. Because of this, the air induction system is able to reduce the CO and HC content in the exhaust gases. The system consists of two

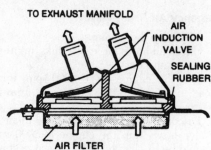

TO EXHAUST MANIFOLD

AIR INDUCTION VALVE

SEALING RUBBER

AIR FILTER

Cross-sectional view of the air induction valve

air induction valves, a filter, hoses and EAI tubes.

TESTING

Disconnect the air induction tube from the tube leading to the exhaust manifold. Place the tube to your mouth, then suck on the tube (air should move freely through the valve); try to blow through the tube (air should not flow through it). If the valve does not respond correctly, replace it.

Fuel Shut-Off System

On the 1980–81, carburetor models, a fuel shut-off system was introduced. The system consist of: a vacuum switch, a speed detecting switch, clutch switch, transaxle neutral switch, neutral relay and a fuel shut-off relay.

NOTE: *The 1982 and later, carburetor models, utilize the Electronic Control Unit (ECU) to control the operation of the anti-dieseling solenoid.*

OPERATION

The system is operated by an anti-dieseling solenoid valve in the carburetor which is controlled by a vacuum switch. When the intake manifold vacuum increases to an extremely high level (which it does during deceleration), the fuel flow of the slow system is shut off by the anti-dieseling solenoid valve. When the intake manifold vacuum drops to a low level, the fuel flow of the slow system is resupplied.

The fuel shut-off system is further controlled by the clutch switch and gear position switches such as the neutral switch (M/T) and the inhibitor switch (A/T) to ensure that fuel cannot be shut off even it the manifold vacuum is high enough to trigger the normal fuel shut-off operation.

Electric Choke

The purpose of the electric choke, is to shorten the time the choke is in operation after the en-

gine is started, thus shortening the time of high HC output.

An electric heater warms the bimetal spring which controls the opening and closing of the choke valve. The heater starts to heat as soon as the engine starts.

Catalytic Converter

This system is used on all 1976–78 California models and all 1979 and later models. The catalytic converter is a muffler-like container built into the exhaust system. The catalyst element consists of individual pellets or a honeycomb monolithic substrate coated with a noble metal such as platinum, palladium, rhodium or a combination. When the exhaust gases come into contact with the catalyst, it changes residual HC, CO and NO in the exhaust gas into CO_2, H_2O and N, before the exhaust gas is discharged into the atmosphere.

All models equipped with an air pump use an emergency air relief valve as a catalyst protection device. When the temperature of the catalyst goes above maximum operating temperature, the temperature sensor signals the switching module to activate the emergency air relief valve. This stops air injection into the exhaust manifold and lowers the temperature of the catalyst.

Certain 1976–78 catalyst-equipped models have a floor temperature warning system which emits a warning, if the catalytic converter or engine becomes overly hot or malfunctions, causing floor temperature to rise. The system consists of: a relay (located under the passenger seat) and a light (installed on the instrument panel). The lamp illuminates when the floor temperatures become abnormally high, due to converter or engine malfunction. The light also comes on when the ignition switch is turned to Start, to check its operation. The 1979 and later models, do not have the warning system.

All models with the 3-way converter have an oxygen sensor warning light on the dashboard, which illuminates at the first 30,000 mile internal signaling the need for oxygen sensor replacement. The oxygen sensor is part of the Mixture Ration Feedback System.

No regular maintenance is required for the catalytic converter system, except for periodic replacement of the Air Induction System filter (if equipped). The Air Induction System is used to supply the converter with fresh air; oxygen present in the air is used in the oxidation process.

Precautions

1. Use ONLY unleaded fuel.
2. Avoid prolonged idling; the engine should

run no longer than 20 min. at curb idle and not longer than 10 min. at fast idle.

3. Do not disconnect any of the spark plug leads while the engine is running.

4. Make engine compression checks as quickly as possible.

Mixture Ratio Feedback System

The need for better fuel economy coupled to increasingly strict emission control regulations dictates a more exact control of the engine air/fuel mixture. The manufacturer has developed this system which is installed on all 1984 and later models.

The principle of the system is to control the air/fuel mixture exactly, so that a more complete combustion can occur in the engine and more thorough oxidation and reduction of the exhaust gases can occur in the catalytic converter. The object is to maintain a stoichiometric air/fuel mixture, which is chemically correct for theoretically complete combustion.

The components used in the system include an oxygen sensor, installed in the exhaust manifold upstream of the converter, a catalytic converter, an electronic control unit and the fuel injection system.

It should be noted that proper operation of the system is entirely dependent on the oxygen sensor. Thus, if the sensor is not replaced at the correct interval or if the sensor fails during normal operation, the engine fuel mixture will be incorrect, resulting in poor fuel economy, starting problems or stumbling and stalling of the engine when warm.

Oxygen Sensor

The oxygen sensor is built into the exhaust manifold, it monitors the density of the oxygen in the exhaust gas. The sensor consists of a closed-end tube made of ceramic zirconia and other components. Porous platinum electrodes cover the tubes inner and outer surfaces. The tubes outer surface is exposed to the exhaust gases in the exhaust manifold, while its inner surface is exposed to normal air.

FUEL SYSTEM

Mechanical Fuel Pump

The fuel pump is a mechanically operated, diaphragm-type driven by the fuel pump eccentric on the camshaft. The pump is located on the lower right side (A-series and E-series), on the right rear-side of the cylinder head (CA20).

REMOVAL AND INSTALLATION

1. Disconnect the fuel lines from the fuel pump. Be sure to keep the line leading from the fuel tank up high to prevent the excess loss of fuel.

2. Remove the two fuel pump mounting nuts and the fuel pump assembly from the right-side of the engine.

3. To install, use a new gasket, sealant and reverse the removal procedures. Torque the fuel pump bolts to 7–9 ft.lb.

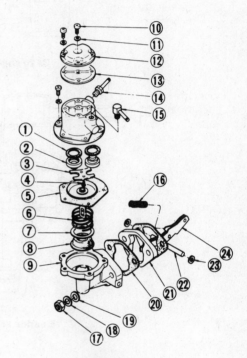

1. Packing
2. Valve assembly
3. Retainer
4. Screw
5. Diaphragm assembly
6. Diaphragm spring
7. Retainer
8. Diaphragm assembly
9. Complete-body lower
10. Screw
11. Washer-spring
12. Fuel pump cap
13. Cap gasket
14. Connector-inlet
15. Connector-outlet
16. Rocker arm spring
17. Nut
18. Washer-spring
19. Washer-plain
20. Gasket
21. Spacer
22. Rocker pin
23. Spacer
24. Rocker arm

A series engine fuel pump

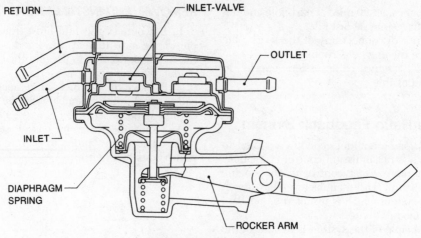

CA20 engine fuel pump

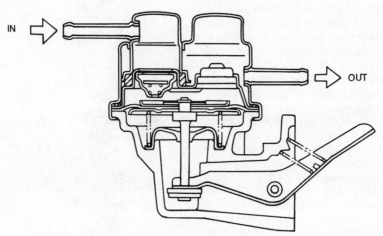

E series engine fuel pump

TESTING

Static Pressure

1. Disconnect the fuel line at the carburetor. Using a T-connector, connect two rubber hoses to the connector, then install it between the fuel line and the carburetor fitting.

NOTE: *When disconnecting the fuel line, be sure to place a container under the line to catch the excess fuel which will be present.*

2. Connect a fuel pump pressure gauge to the T-connector and secure it with a clamp.

3. Start the engine and check the pressure at various speeds. The pressure should be 3.0–3.8 psi (1976–83) or 2.8–3.8 psi (1984 and later). There is usually enough gas in the float bowl to perform this test.

4. If the pressure is OK, perform a capacity test. Remove the gauge and the T-connector assembly, then reinstall the fuel line to the carburetor.

Capacity Test

1. Disconnect the fuel line from the carburetor and place the line in a graduated container.

2. Fill the carburetor float bowl with gas.

3. Start the engine and run it for one minute at about 1,000 rpm (A-series and CA20) or 600 rpm (E-series). The pump should deliver 16 oz./min. (A-series), 51 oz./min. (CA20) or 44 oz./min. (E-series).

Electrical Fuel Pump

The Stanza (1984 and later) EFI system fuel pump is located under the vehicle in front of the fuel tank, it is combined with the fuel damper. The Pulsar (1984) Turbo system fuel pump is located in the fuel tank.

The fuel pumps are of a wet type, where the vane rollers are directly coupled to the motor,

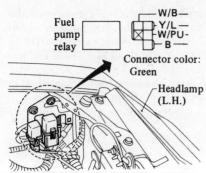

Location of fuel pump relay—Pulsar (Turbo)

which is filled with fuel. A relief valve in the pump is designed to open at 44–64 psi, should a malfunction arise in the system.

NOTE: *Before disconnecting the fuel lines or any of the fuel system components, refer to Fuel Pressure Release procedures, in this section and release the fuel pressure.*

REMOVAL AND INSTALLATION

Stanza–EFI System

1. Disconnect the negative battery cable.
2. Raise and support the rear of the vehicle on jackstands.
3. Disconnect the electrical connector from the fuel pump.
4. Place fuel container under the fuel lines, then disconnect the fuel lines and drain the excess fuel into the container.
5. Remove the mounting braces and the fuel pump from the vehicle.

6. To install, use new gaskets and reverse the removal procedures.

Pulsar Turbo

1. Disconnect the negative battery cable.
2. Open the trunk lid, disconnect the fuel gauge electrical connector and remove the fuel tank inspection cover.
3. Disconnect the fuel outlet and the return hoses.
4. Using a large driving tool and a hammer, drive the fuel tank locking ring in the counterclockwise direction.
5. Remove the locking ring and the O-ring, then lift the fuel pump assembly from the fuel tank. Plug the opening with a clean rag to prevent dirt from entering the system.
NOTE: *When removing the fuel tank gauge unit, be careful not to damage or deform it. Install a new O-ring.*
6. To install, use a new O-ring and reverse the removal procedures.

TESTING

1. Disconnect the fuel hose from the metal pipe leading from the fuel filter, then install the Pressure Gauge tool J-25400-34 between the metal pipe and the fuel filter hose. Place the gauge, so it can be read from the driver's seat.
2. Start the engine and read the fuel pressure, it should be 30 psi (at idle) or 37 psi (engine accelerated).
NOTE: *If the reading is not correct, replace the pressure regulator and repeat the check-*

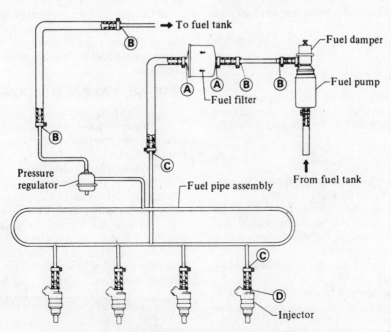

Description of the Stanza EFI fuel system—Pulsar (Turbo) similar

ing procedure. If the pressure is below specifications, check for clogged or deformed fuel lines; if necessary, replace the fuel pump or check valve.

Fuel Pressure Regulator

The pressure regulator is located on the fuel return side of the fuel injection rail, under the fuel rail (Stanza–EFI system) or next to the oil filter (Pulsar–Turbo).

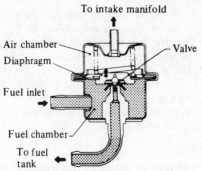

Cross-sectional view of the pressure regulator

Stanza–EFI System

1. Refer to the Fuel Pressure Release procedures, in this section and release the fuel pressure.
2. Remove the vacuum tubes and the EFI harness.
3. Remove the air regulator and the PCV valve assembly.
4. Remove the bolts retaining the fuel pipe assembly and the injectors.
5. Remove the fuel pipe assembly with the injectors.

Pulsar Turbo

To replace it, remove the fuel line clamps, the hoses and the mounting bracket. To install, use new hose clamps and reverse the removal procedures.

TESTING

NOTE: *This test is to be performed in combination with the fuel pressure test.*

1. Disconnect the fuel pressure regulator vacuum hose from the intake manifold and connect to the Variable Vacuum Source tool J-23738.
2. At the fuel pump relay harness, jump connectors W/B and W/PU.
3. Turn the ignition switch to the ON position and observe the fuel pressure as the vacuum is changed.
4. With the vacuum at 0 in. Hg, the fuel

pressure should be 36–37 psi; increase the vacuum to 5 in. Hg, the fuel pressure should be 33–35 psi; increase the vacuum to 10 in. Hg, the fuel pressure should be 31–32 psi; increase the vacuum to 15 in. Hg, the fuel pressure should be 29–30 psi; increase the vacuum to 20 in. Hg, the fuel pressure should be 26–28 psi.

5. Turn the ignition switch to the OFF position.
6. With the testing complete, remove the test equipment and the jumper wire, then replace hoses.

FUEL PRESSURE RELEASE PROCEDURE

Stanza–EFI System

1. Start the engine.
2. Under the passenger seat, disconnect the black and the white body harness connectors.
3. After the engine stalls, crank it over a few times, then turn the ignition switch OFF.
4. Reconnect the body harness connectors.

Pulsar Turbo

1. Start the engine.
2. At the left front fender, disconnect the electrical connector of the fuel pump relay.
3. After the engine stalls, crank it over a few times, then turn the ignition switch OFF.
4. Reconnect the electrical connector to the fuel pump relay.

Carburetor

The carburetor used is a two-barrel down-draft type with a low-speed (primary) side and a high-speed (secondary) side.

All models have an electrically-operated anti-dieseling solenoid. As the ignition switch is turned off, the valve is energized and shuts off the supply of fuel to the idle circuit of the carburetor.

REMOVAL AND INSTALLATION

1. Remove the air cleaner.
2. Disconnect the electrical connector(s), the fuel and the vacuum hoses from the carburetor.
3. Remove the throttle lever.
4. Remove the four nuts and washers retaining the carburetor to the manifold.
5. Lift the carburetor from the manifold.
6. Remove and discard the gasket used between the carburetor and the manifold.
7. To install, use a new base gasket and reverse the removal procedures. Torque the carburetor mounting nuts to 9–13 ft. lb.

THROTTLE LINKAGE ADJUSTMENT

1. Disconnect the negative battery cable.
2. Remove the air cleaner.

3. Open the automatic choke valve by hand, while turning the throttle valve by pulling the throttle lever, then set the choke valve in the open position.

NOTE: *If equipped with a vacuum controlled throttle positioner, use a vacuum hand pump to retract the the throttle positioner rod.*

4. Adjust the throttle cable at the carburetor bracket, so that a 0.04–0.08 in. of free pedal play exists.

DASHPOT ADJUSTMENT

A dashpot is used on carburetors with automatic transaxles and some manual transaxles. The dashpot slowly closes the throttle on automatic transmissions to prevent stalling and serves as an emission control device on all late model vehicles.

The dashpot should be adjusted to contact the throttle lever on deceleration at approximately 2,000–2,300 rpm (A-series), 1,400–1,600 rpm (CA20), 2,300–2,500 rpm (E15) engines, 1,900–2,100 rpm (E16, A/T) or 2,250–2,450 (E16, M/T).

NOTE: *Before attempting to adjust the dashpot, make sure the idle speed, timing and mixture adjustments are correct.*

1. Loosen the locknut (turn the dash pot, if necessary) and make sure the engine speed drops smoothly from 2,000-to-1,000 rpm in 3 seconds.

2. If the dash pot has been removed from the carburetor, it must be adjusted when installed. Adjust the gap between the primary throttle valve and the inner carburetor wall, when the dash pot stem comes in contact with the throttle arm. The dash pot gap is 0.0260–0.0338 in. (M/T) or 0.0194–0.0271 in. (A/T).

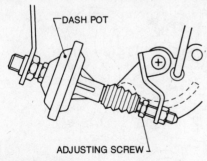

Dashpot adjustment

SECONDARY THROTTLE LINKAGE ADJUSTMENT

All carburetors discussed in this book are two stage type carburetors. On this type of carburetor, the engine runs on the primary barrel most of the time, with the secondary barrel

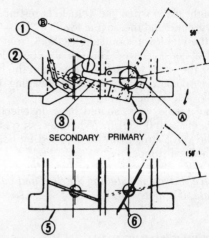

1. Roller
2. Connecting lever
3. Return plate
4. Adjust plate
5. Throttle chamber
6. Throttle valve

Secondary throttle linkage adjustment

being used for acceleration purposes. When the throttle valve on the primary side opens to an angle of approximately 50° (from its fully closed position), the secondary throttle valve is pulled open by the connecting linkage. The 50° angle of throttle valve opening works out to a clearance measurement of 0.23 in. (F10 model), 0.218–241 in. (310 model, 1979–80), 0.22–0.25 in. (310 model, 1981–82), 0.29–0.33 in. (Stanza) or 0.224–0.27 in. (Pulsar, Calif.) between the throttle valve and the carburetor body. The easiest way to measure this is to use a drill bit. Drill bits from size H-to-P (standard letter size drill bits) should fit. Check the appendix in the back of the book for the exact size of the various drill bits. If an adjustment is necessary, bend the connecting link between the two linkage assemblies.

NOTE: *The Pulsar carburetor is equipped with a tang on the adjusting link, bend the tang to adjust the clearance.*

FLOAT LEVEL ADJUSTMENT

The fuel level is normal if it is within the lines on the window glass of the float chamber (or

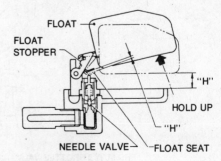

Float level adjustment

the sight glass) when the vehicle is resting on level ground and the engine is off.

If the fuel level is outside the lines, remove the float housing cover. Have an absorbent cloth under the cover to catch the fuel from the fuel bowl. Adjust the float level by bending the needle seat on the float.

The needle valve should have an effective stroke of about 0.0591 in. When necessary, the needle valve stroke can be adjusted by bending the float stopper.

NOTE: *Be careful not to bend the needle valve rod when installing the float and baffle plate, if removed.*

FAST IDLE ADJUSTMENT

Except Stanza

NOTE: *On the Stanza models, the fast idle cam lever is located next to the fast idle cam screw, so the choke cover does not have to be removed. On the 1985 Stanza, disconnect the Fast Idle Breaker harness at the carburetor.*

1. Remove the carburetor from the vehicle.

NOTE: *On the Pulsar (1984 Calif.), disconnect the harness cover from the auto-choke heater cover, the vacuum hose from the vacuum break diaphragm (install a plug after pushing the vacuum break stem toward the diaphragm), then move the throttle lever counter-clockwise (fully). Go to Step No. 4.*

2. Remove the choke cover, then place the fast idle arm on the 2nd step of the fast idle cam. Using the correct wire gauge, measure the clearance A between the throttle valve and the wall of the throttle valve chamber (at the center of the throttle valve). Check it against the following specifications:

- 1976 F10: 0.0315–0.0346 in.
- 1977–78 F10: 0.0287–0.0343 in.
- 1979–80 310: 0.0283–0.0350 in.
- 1981 310: 0.0287–0.0343 in.
- 1982 310: 0.0287–0.0343 in. (M/T)
  0.0393–0.0449 in (A/T)
- 1982–86 Stanza: 0.0260–0.0315 in. (M/T)
  0.0319–0.0374 in. (A/T)
- 1983 Pulsar: USA 0.0311–0.0367 in. (M/T)
  0.0425–0.0481 in. (A/T)
  Canada 0.0255–0.0311 in. (M/T)
  0.0366–0.0422 in. (A/T)
- 1984–86 Pulsar: USA 0.0300–0.0378 in. (M/T)
  0.0414–0.0492 in. (A/T)
  Canada 0.0214–0.0324 in. (M/T)
  0.0355–0.0433 in. (A/T)

M/T means manual transmission. A/T means automatic transmission.

NOTE: *The first step of the fast idle adjustment procedure is not absolutely necessary.*

3. Install the carburetor on the engine.

4. Start the engine, warm it to operating temperatures and check the fast idle rpm. The cam should be at the 2nd step.

- 1976 F10: 2,450–2,650 rpm
- 1977–78 F10: 1900–2700 rpm
- 1979–81 310: 49 states 2400–3200 rpm
  Calif. 2300–3100 rpm
  Canada 1900–2700 rpm
- 1982 310: 49 states 2400–3200 rpm
  Calif. 2300–3100 rpm
  Canada 1900–2700 rpm (M/T)
  2400–3200 rpm (A/T)

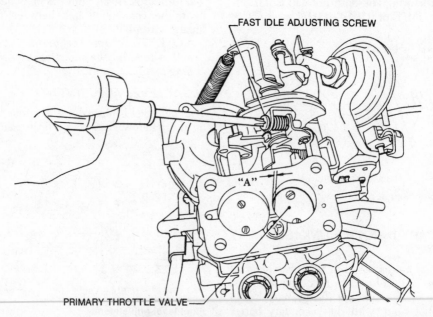

FAST IDLE ADJUSTING SCREW

"A"

PRIMARY THROTTLE VALVE

E series fast idle adjustment

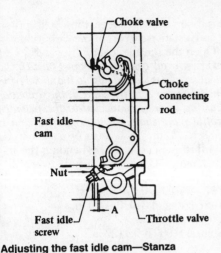

Adjusting the fast idle cam—Stanza

FAST IDLE BREAKER ADJUSTMENT
Stanza (1985–86)

1. Start the engine and warm it to operating temperatures without racing it.

2. Check the engine speed and the breaker operation, it should be high revolution at the start, then idle speed when warm.

3. Disconnect the fast idle breaker harness connector at the carburetor. Using an ohmmeter, check the fast idle breaker for continuity; place one lead on the breaker's ground wire and the other lead on the No. 8 pin of the harness connector.

NOTE: *Checking is performed when the breaker is cold (less than 68°F) and the choke plate closed.*

4. If there is no continuity, replace the breaker.

5. If an ohmmeter is not available, check the breaker with the engine running (harness connector installed), if the breaker does not warm up, replace it.

- 1985–86 Stanza: 2,400–2,700 rpm (M/T)
  2,800–3,100 rpm (A/T)
- 1983 Pulsar: 49 states 2,400–3,200 rpm (M/T)
  2,700–3,500 rpm (A/T)
  Calif. 2,600–3,400 rpm (M/T)
  2,900–3,700 rpm (A/T)
  Canada 1900–2700 rpm (M/T)
  2400–3200 rpm (A/T)
- 1984–86 Pulsar: Calif. 2,600–3,400 rpm (M/T)
  2,900–3,700 rpm (A/T)
  Canada 1900–2700 rpm (M/T)
  Canada 2400–3200 rpm (A/T)

5. To adjust the fast idle speed, turn the fast idle adjusting screw counterclockwise to increase the fast idle speed and clockwise to decrease the fast idle speed.

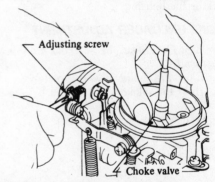

Adjusting the cam follow lever—Stanza

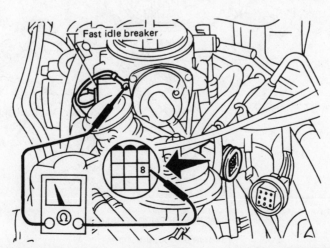

Checking the continuity of the fast idle breaker—Stanza 1985 and later

CAM FOLLOW LEVER ADJUSTMENT
Stanza

Hold the choke plate closed, turn the adjusting screw until there is no clearance between the cam follow lever and the fast idle cam.

AUTOMATIC CHOKE ADJUSTMENT

1. With the engine cold, make sure the choke is fully closed (press the accelerator pedal all the way to the floor and release).

2. Check the choke linkage for binding. The choke plate should be easily opened and closed with your finger. If the choke sticks or binds, it can usually be freed with a liberal application of a carburetor cleaner made for the purpose. A couple of quick squirts of the right stuff normally does the trick; if not, the carburetor will have to be disassembled for repairs.

3. The choke is correctly adjusted when the index mark on the choke housing (notch) aligns with the center mark on the carburetor body. If the setting is incorrect, loosen the three screws clamping the choke body in place and rotate the choke cover left or right until the marks align. Tighten the screws carefully to avoid cracking the housing.

CHOKE UNLOADER ADJUSTMENT

NOTE: *The choke must be cold for this adjustment.*

1. Close the choke valve completely.
2. Hold the choke valve closed by stretch-ing a rubber band between the choke piston lever and a stationary part of the carburetor.
3. Open the throttle lever fully.

NOTE: *On all vehicles (except Stanza), the unloader cam is located next to the choke plate adjusting lever. On the Stanza, the unloader adjusting lever is connected to the primary throttle plate shaft, an intermediate cam is connected to the choke lever by a choke rod.*

4. Adjustment is made by bending the unloader tongue. Gauge the gap between the choke plate and the carburetor body to:
- 1976–77 F10: 0.079 in.
- 1987 F10 and 310: 0.0929 in.
- Pulsar: 0.1165 in.
- Stanza: 0.0807–0.1122 in.

VACUUM BREAK ADJUSTMENT

1. With the engine cold, close the choke completely.
2. Pull the vacuum break stem straight up as far as it will go.
3. Check the clearance between the choke plate and the carburetor wall.

Clearance should be:
- 1976–77 F10: 0.0567–0.0614 in.
- 1978 F10 and 1979–80 310: 0.0709–0.0780 in.
- 1981–82 310: 0.0634–0.0704 in. USA 0.0552–0.0622 in. Canada
- 1982–86 Stanza: 0.1228–0.1465 in. (above 68°F), 0.0650–0.0886 in. (below 41°F)

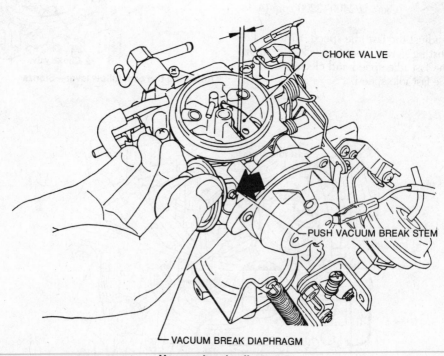

CHOKE VALVE

PUSH VACUUM BREAK STEM

VACUUM BREAK DIAPHRAGM

Vacuum break adjustment

• 1983–86 Pulsar: 0.523–0.681 in. (below 63°F), 0.0945–0.1103 in. (above 75°F)

4. On the F10 and the 310 (1979–80), the adjustment is made by bending the connecting rod. Adjustment is made on Canadian models by bending the connecting rod; on USA 310 (1981–82) models by removing the plastic plug from the adjusting screw hole and turning the adjusting screw. On the Pulsar and the Stanza models, adjustment is made by bending the tang at the choke plate lever assembly.

NOTE: *On the Pulsar and the Stanza models, remove the choke cover, then connect a rubber band to the choke lever to hold it shut.*

ACCELERATOR PUMP ADJUSTMENT

If a smooth constant stream of fuel is not injected into the carburetor bore when the throttle is opened, the accelerator pump needs adjustment.

NOTE: *The Stanza accelerator pump is of a different design and is not adjustable; if it is not operating correctly, replace it.*

1. Remove the carburetor from the engine.
2. Check the gap between the primary throttle valve and the inner wall of the carburetor when the pump lever comes in contact with the piston pin. This is the stroke limiter gap. It should be 0.05 in. If not, bend the stroke limiter.
3. Fill the carburetor bowl with fuel.
4. Fully open the choke.
5. Place a calibrated container under the throttle bore. Slowly open and close the throttle (full open to full closed) ten times keeping the throttle open 3 seconds each time. Measure the amount of fuel in the container. The amount should be 0.3–0.5 ml or 0.010–0.018 oz. If not, and the stroke limiter gap is correct, replace the accelerator pump unit.

ANTI-DIESELING SOLENOID

Check this valve if the engine continues to run after the key has been turned off.

1. Run the engine at idle speed and disconnect the lead wire at the anti-dieseling solenoid. The engine should stop.
2. If the engine does not stop, check the harness for current at the solenoid. If current is present, replace the solenoid. Installation torque for the solenoid is 13–25 ft.lb. for CA20 engines and 13–16 ft.lb. for all other engines.

OVERHAUL

Efficient carburetion depends greatly on careful cleaning and inspection during overhaul, since dirt, gum, water and/or varnish in or on the carburetor parts are often responsible for poor performance.

Overhaul your carburetor in a clean, dust free area. Carefully disassemble the carburetor, referring often to the exploded views. Keep all similar and look-alike parts segregated during disassembly and cleaning to avoid accidental interchange during assembly. Make a note of all jet sizes.

When the carburetor is disassembled, wash all the parts (except diaphragms, electric choke units, pump plunger and any other plastic, leather, fiber or rubber parts) in clean carburetor solvent. Do not leave parts in the solvent any longer than is necessary to sufficiently loosen

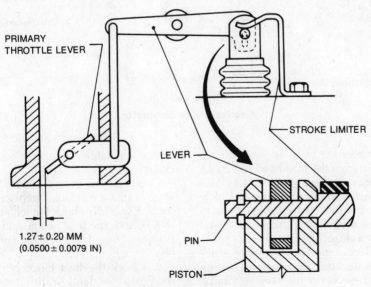

PRIMARY THROTTLE LEVER

STROKE LIMITER

LEVER

PIN

PISTON

1.27 ± 0.20 MM
(0.0500 ± 0.0079 IN)

Accelerator pump adjustment

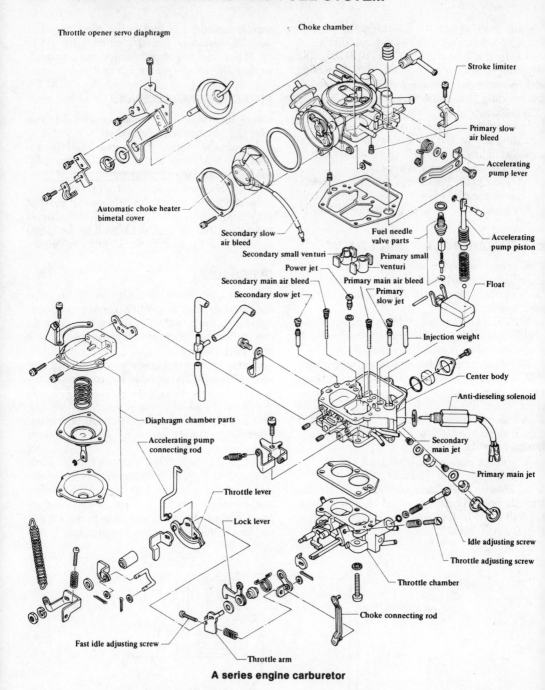

Throttle opener servo diaphragm

Choke chamber

Stroke limiter

Primary slow air bleed

Accelerating pump lever

Accelerating pump piston

Automatic choke heater bimetal cover

Secondary slow air bleed

Fuel needle valve parts

Secondary small venturi

Primary small venturi

Power jet

Secondary main air bleed

Primary main air bleed

Float

Secondary slow jet

Primary slow jet

Injection weight

Diaphragm chamber parts

Center body

Anti-dieseling solenoid

Accelerating pump connecting rod

Secondary main jet

Primary main jet

Throttle lever

Lock lever

Idle adjusting screw

Throttle adjusting screw

Throttle chamber

Choke connecting rod

Fast idle adjusting screw

Throttle arm

A series engine carburetor

the deposits. Excessive cleaning may remove the special finish from the float bowl and choke valve bodies, leaving these parts unfit for service. Rinse all parts in clean solvent and blow them dry with compressed air to allow them to air dry. Wipe clean all cork, plastic, leather and fiber parts with a clean, lint-free cloth.

Blow out all passages and jets with compressed air, be sure that there are no restrictions or blockages. Never use wire or similar tools for cleaning purposes; clean the jets and

valves separately, to avoid accidental interchange.

Check all the parts for wear or damage. If wear or damage is found, replace the defective parts. Especially check the following:

1. Check the float needle and seat for wear. If wear is found, replace the complete assembly.

2. Check the float hinge pin for wear and the float(s) for dents or distortion. Replace the float if fuel has leaked into it.

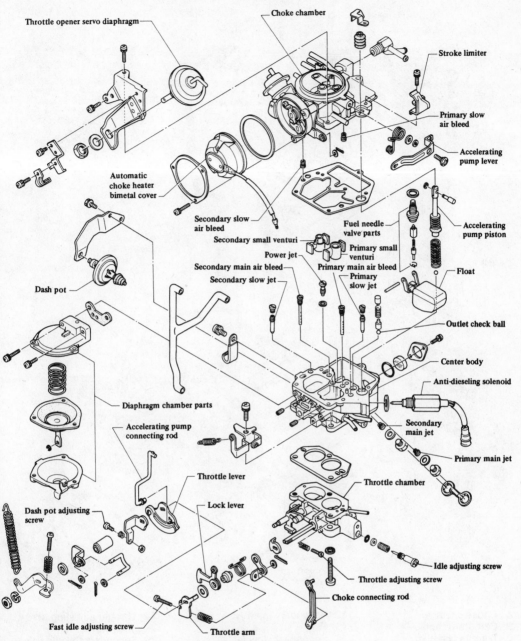

Throttle opener servo diaphragm

Choke chamber

Stroke limiter

Primary slow air bleed

Accelerating pump lever

Automatic choke heater bimetal cover

Accelerating pump piston

Secondary slow air bleed

Fuel needle valve parts

Secondary small venturi

Primary small venturi

Power jet

Dash pot

Secondary main air bleed

Primary main air bleed

Secondary slow jet

Primary slow jet

Float

Outlet check ball

Center body

Diaphragm chamber parts

Anti-dieseling solenoid

Accelerating pump connecting rod

Secondary main jet

Primary main jet

Throttle lever

Throttle chamber

Dash pot adjusting screw

Lock lever

Idle adjusting screw

Throttle adjusting screw

Choke connecting rod

Fast idle adjusting screw

Throttle arm

E series engine carburetor

3. Check the throttle and choke shaft bores for wear or an out-of-round condition. Damage or wear to the throttle arm, shaft or shaft bore will often require replacement of the throttle body. These parts require a close tolerance of fit; wear may allow air leakage, which could affect starting and idling.

NOTE: *Throttle shafts and bushings are not included in overhaul kits. They can be purchased separately.*

4. Inspect the idle mixture adjusting needles for burrs or grooves. Any such condition requires replacement of the needle, since you will not be able to obtain a satisfactory idle.

5. Test the accelerator pump check valves. They should pass air one way but not the other. Test for proper seating by blowing and sucking on the valve. Replace the valve if necessary. If the valve is satisfactory, wash the valve again to remove breath moisture.

6. Check the bowl cover for warped surfaces with a straightedge.

7. Closely inspect the valves and seats for wear and/or damage, replacing as necessary.

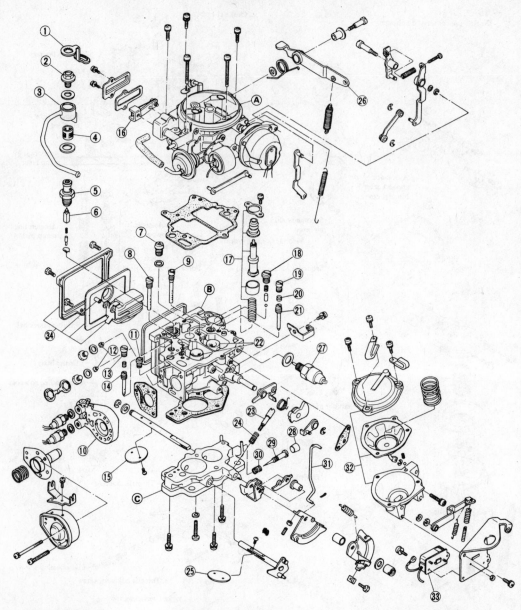

A. Choke chamber
B. Carburetor body
C. Throttle chamber
1. Lock lever
2. Filter set screw
3. Fuel nipple
4. Fuel filter
5. Needle valve body
6. Needle valve
7. Power valve
8. Secondary main air bleed
9. Primary main air bleed
10. B.C.D.D.
11. Secondary slow air bleed
12. Secondary main jet
13. Plug
14. Secondary slow jet
15. Primary throttle valve
16. Idle compensator
17. Accelerating pump parts
18. Plug for accelerating
    mechanism
19. Plug
20. Spring
21. Primary slow jet
22. Primary and secondary small
    venturi
23. Throttle adjusting screw
24. Throttle adjusting screw
    spring
25. Secondary throttle valve
26. Accelerating pump lever
27. Anti-dieseling solenoid valve
28. Blind plug
29. Idle adjusting screw
30. Idle adjusting screw spring
31. Choke connecting rod
32. Diaphragm chamber parts
33. Throttle valve switch
34. Float

CA20 engine carburetor

Carburetor Specifications

Year	Engine	Vehicle Model	Carb Model	Main Jet #		Main Air Bleed #		Slow Jet #		Float Level (in.)	Power Jet #
				Primary	Secondary	Primary	Secondary	Primary	Secondary		
1976	A14 California	F10	DCH306-17	105	145	95	80	45	50	0.75	40
	A14 (Federal)	F10	DCH306-16	103	145	95	80	45	50	0.75	40
1977	A14 California	F10	DCH306-17A	106	145	95	80	45	50	0.75	40
	A14 (Federal)	F10	DCH306-16A	105	145	95	80	45	50	0.75	40
1978	A14 (California)	F10	DCH306-65	106	145	95	80	45	50	0.75	40
	A14 (Federal)	F10	DCH306-64	105	145	95	80	45	50	0.75	40
1979	A14 (California)	310	DCH306-75	107	145	95	80	45	50	0.75	43
	A14 (Federal)	310	DCH306-76	105	145	110	80	45	50	0.75	40
1980	A14 (California)	310	DCH306-112	107	145	80	80	45	50	0.75	38
	A14 (Federal)	310	DCH306-102	107	143	65	60	45	50	0.75	43
1981	A15 (Federal)	310	DCR306-103	114	125	80	80	45	50	0.75	35
	A15 (California)	310	DCR306-113	113	125	60	80	45	50	0.75	35
	A15 (Canada)	310	DCR306-123	100	145	70	80	43	70	0.75	40

Carburetor Specifications (continued)

Year	Vehicle Model	Engine	Carb Model	Main Jet #		Main Air Bleed #		Slow Jet #		Float Level (in.)	Power Jet #
				Primary	Secondary	Primary	Secondary	Primary	Secondary		
1982	310	E15 (Federal)	DCR306-130	116	125	80	80	45	50	0.47	38
	310	E15 (California)	DCR306-140	114	125	60	80	45	50	0.47	38
	310	E15 (Canada)	DCR306-150MT	100	120	70	60	43	80	0.47	40
	310	E15 (Canada)	DCR306-151AT	100	120	70	60	43	80	0.47	40
	Stanza	CA20 (Fed. & Canada)	DCR342-33	111	160	90	60	47	100	0.91	45
	Stanza	CA20 (California)	DCR342-31	113	160	90	60	47	100	0.91	45
1983	Stanza	CA20 ① (Federal)	DCR342-25	111	160	95	60	47	100	0.91	45
	Stanza	CA20 (Calif.)	DCR342-37 ① DCR342-38 ②	113	160	95	60	47	100	0.91	45
	Stanza	CA20 ② (Canada)	DCR342-36	113	160	95	60	47	100	0.91	40
	Pulsar	E16 (Calif.)	DFC328-1 ① DFC328-2 ②	91	130	105	60	43	70	0.47	—
	Pulsar	E16 (Federal)	DCZ328-1 ① DCZ328-2 ②	106	133	100	60	43	55	0.47	35
	Pulsar	E16 (Canada)	DCZ328-11 ① DCZ328-12 ②	100	135	110	60	43	65	0.47	35

Carburetor Specifications (continued)

Year	Engine	Vehicle Model	Carb Model	Main Jet # Primary	Main Jet # Secondary	Main Air Bleed # Primary	Main Air Bleed # Secondary	Slow Jet # Primary	Slow Jet # Secondary	Float Level (in.)	Power Jet #
1984	CA20S (Canada)	Stanza	DCR342-35 ① DCR342-36 ②	111	155	95	60	47	100	0.91	45 ① 40 ②
	E16 (Federal)	Pulsar	DFE2832-1 ① DFE2832-2 ②	90 82	105 105	80 110	70 70	43 45	65 65	0.47 0.47	— —
	E16 (Calif.)	Pulsar	DFC328-1F ② DFC328-2F ②	91	130	110	60	43	65	0.47	—
	E16 (Canada)	Pulsar	DCZ328-11F ① DCZ328-12F ②	100	135	110	60	43	65	0.47	35
1985–86	CA20S (Canada)	Stanza	DCR342-35 ① DCR342-36 ②	111	155	95	60	47	100	③	45 ① 40 ②
	E16 (Federal)	Pulsar	DFE2832-5 ① DFE2832-6 ②	90 82	105 105	80 110	70 70	43 45	65 65	0.47 0.47	— —
	E16 (Calif.)	Pulsar	DFC328-1F ② DFC328-2F ②	91	130	110	60	43	65	0.47	—
	E16 (Canada)	Pulsar	DCZ328-11G ① DCZ328-12G ②	100	135	110	60	43	65	0.47	35

① Manual Transmission
② Automatic Transmission
③ Use the sight adjusting glass on the side of the float bowl

8. After the carburetor is assembled, check the choke valve for freedom of operation.

Carburetor overhaul kits are recommended for each overhaul. These kits contain all gaskets and new parts to replace those that deteriorate most rapidly. Failure to replace all parts supplied with the kit (especially gaskets) can result in poor performance later.

Some carburetor manufacturers supply overhaul kits of three basic types: minor repair, major repair and gasket kits. Basically, they contain the following:

Minor Repair Kits:
• All gaskets
• Float needle valve
• Volume control screw
• All diaphragms
• Spring for the pump diaphragm

Major Repair Kits:
• All jets and gaskets
• All diaphragms
• Float needle valve
• Volume control screw
• Pump ball valve
• Main jet carrier
• Float

Gasket Kits:
• All gaskets

After cleaning and checking all components, reassemble the carburetor, using new parts and referring to the exploded view. When reassembling, make sure that all screws and jets are tight in their seats but do not overtighten as the tips will be distorted. Tighten all screws gradually in rotation. Do not tighten needle valves into their seats; uneven jetting will result. Always use new gaskets. Be sure to adjust the float level when reassembling.

Fuel Injection

The electronic fuel injection (EFI) system is an electronic type using various types of sensors to convert engine operating conditions into electronic signals. The generated information is fed to a control unit, where it is analyzed, then calculated electrical signals are sent to the various equipment, to control the idle speed, the timing and amount of fuel being injected into the engine.

REMOVAL AND INSTALLATION

Throttle Chamber

The throttle chamber is located on the intake side of the intake plenum.

1. Disconnect the negative battery cable.
2. Remove the intake duct from the throttle chamber.
3. Disconnect the vacuum hoses and the

electrical harness connector from the throttle chamber. Disconnect the accelerator cable from the throttle chamber.

4. Remove the mounting bolts and the throttle chamber from the intake plenum.
5. To install, use a new gasket and reverse the removal procedures. Torque the throttle chamber bolts to 13–16 ft.lb. Adjust the throttle cable.

Intake Plenum

1. Refer to the Throttle Chamber, Removal and Installation procedures, in this section and remove the throttle chamber from the intake plenum.
2. The idle speed control valve is located at the other end of the intake plenum, either disconnect the vacuum hose and the electrical harness connector or remove the bolts and the unit from the intake plenum.
3. Remove the hoses from the intake plenum.
4. Remove the mounting bolts and the intake plenum from the intake manifold, discard the gasket.
5. Using a putty knife, clean the gasket mounting surfaces.
6. To install, use a new gasket and reverse the removal procedures. Torque the intake plenum-to-intake manifold bolts to 13–16 ft.lb.

Air Flow Meter

The air flow meter is located at the left-front fender. It monitors the quantity and the temperature of the incoming air. The gathered information is sent to the computer so that the correct fuel injection pulse can be determined for the fuel injectors.

1. Move the interfering hoses to one side or disconnect them, then disconnect the air duct from the air flow meter.
2. Disconnect the electrical harness connector from the potentiometer and the electrical connectors from the air sensor.
3. Remove the air flow meter-to-air cleaner assembly mounting bolts and the air flow meter from the vehicle.
4. To install, reverse the removal procedures.

Fuel Injector(s)

1. Refer to the Fuel Pressure Release Procedure in this section and reduce the fuel pressure to zero.
2. Remove the fuel inlet and outlet hoses from the fuel rail.
3. Disconnect the EFI electrical harness from the fuel injectors and the vacuum hose from the fuel pressure regulator, located at the center of the fuel rail.
4. Remove the fuel rail securing bolts, the

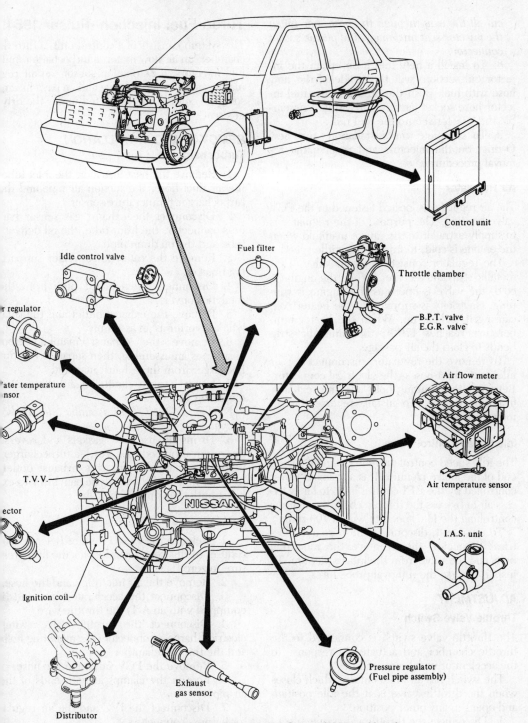

Idle control valve

Fuel filter

r regulator

Throttle chamber

ater temperature
nsor

B.P.T. valve
E.G.R. valve

Air flow meter

T.V.V.

Air temperature sensor

ector

I.A.S. unit

Ignition coil

Distributor

Exhaust
gas sensor

Pressure regulator
(Fuel pipe assembly)

Control unit

NISSAN

Exploded view of the EFI system—Stanza (1984 and later)

ollector at the throttle chamber and the injec-
or securing bolts.

5. Remove the fuel injectors with the fuel
ail assembly.

6. Remove the fuel injector hose-to-fuel rail
·lamp(s), then pull the injector from the fuel
ail.

7. To remove the fuel hose from the injector, use a hot soldering iron, then cut (melt) a
line in the fuel hose (to the braided reinforcement), starting at the injector socket to ¾ in.
long. Remove the hose from the injector, by
hand.

NOTE: *DO NOT allow the soldering iron to*

cut all the way through the hose, nor touch the injector seat or damage the plastic socket connector.

8. To install a new fuel hose, clean the injector tail section, wet the inside of the new hose with fuel, push the hose into the fuel injector hose socket (as far as it will go). Assemble the injector(s) onto the fuel rail.

9. To complete the installation, use new O-rings on the injectors and reverse the removal procedures.

Air Regulator

The air regulator is located fastened to the PCV valve housing. The purpose of the regulator is to supply extra air to the intake manifold when the engine is cold, to improve the idle speed.

The regulator consists of an air valve, a bimetallic strip and a heater. When the engine is cold, the valve is open; as the engine is running, electricity is supplied to the heater coil, causing it to heat up. When the heater temperature reaches 176°F, the bimetalic strip bends to close the air passage.

To remove the regulator, disconnect the air inlet and outlet hoses, the electrical connector. Remove the mounting bolts and the regulator from the engine. To install, reverse the removal procedures.

Idle Speed Control Valve

The idle speed control valve is mounted to one end of the intake plenum. It is a solenoid valve, controlled by the EFI control unit, to allow excess air to by-pass the throttle chamber, thereby controlling the idle speed to within 100 rpm.

To remove it, disconnect the hose and electrical connector, then remove the mounting bolts and the valve from the intake plenum. To install, reverse the removal procedures.

ADJUSTMENT

Throttle Valve Switch

The throttle valve switch is connected to the throttle chamber and actuates in response to the accelerator pedal movement.

The switch has an idle contact, which closes when the throttle valve is at the idle position and opens in any other position.

1. Disconnect the throttle valve switch connector and connect the leads of an ohmmeter to the No. 29 and 30 pin connectors, the ohmmeter reading should be 0Ω.

2. Adjust the idle speed to 850 rpm.

3. Loosen the retaining screw(s).

4. With the engine running at 850 rpm, turn the switch, so that it turns from OFF to ON, tighten the retaining screws.

Turbo Fuel Injection–Pulsar 1984

The system consists of a control unit, a throttle chamber, an air flow meter, a turbocharger unit, fuel injectors, a detonation sensor, an air regulator, an idle control valve and an oxygen sensor. The control unit is located under the driver's seat.

REMOVAL AND INSTALLATION

Turbocharger

1. Remove the heat insulator, the inlet tube, the air duct hose, the suction air pipe and the turbocharger temperature sensor.

2. Disconnect the exhaust gas sensor harness connector, the front tube, the oil delivery tube and the oil drain pipe.

3. Remove the catalytic converter supporting bracket.

4. Disconnect the exhaust pipe from the catalytic converter.

5. Remove the exhaust outlet and the catalytic converter as an assembly.

6. Remove the exhaust manifold/turbocharger as an assembly, then separate the turbocharger from the exhaust manifold.

7. Using a putty knife, clean the gasket mounting surfaces.

NOTE: *DO NOT disassemble the turbocharger.*

8. To install, use new gaskets and reverse the removal procedures. Torque turbocharger-to-exhaust manifold nuts, the exhaust outlet to-turbo nuts and the catalytic converter-to-exhaust outlet nuts to 16–22 ft.lb.

Fuel Injectors

1. Refer to the Fuel Pressure Release procedure, in this section and lower the fuel pressure to zero.

2. Remove the air inlet pipe and the hose.

3. Disconnect the accelerator wire and (if equipped with an A/T) the throttle wire.

4. Disconnect the throttle valve switch electrical harness connector, the mounting bolts and the throttle chamber.

5. Remove the PCV valve and the hose.

6. Loosen the clamps at both ends of the air pipe.

7. Disconnect the IVC and the air regulator harness connectors.

8. Remove the air pipe.

9. Disconnect the harness connectors from the injectors. Remove the fuel hoses. Remove the fuel rail mounting bolts and the fuel injector mounting screws.

10. Remove the fuel rail assembly by pulling out the fuel rail and the injectors.

11. Unfasten the fuel injector-to-fuel rail hose

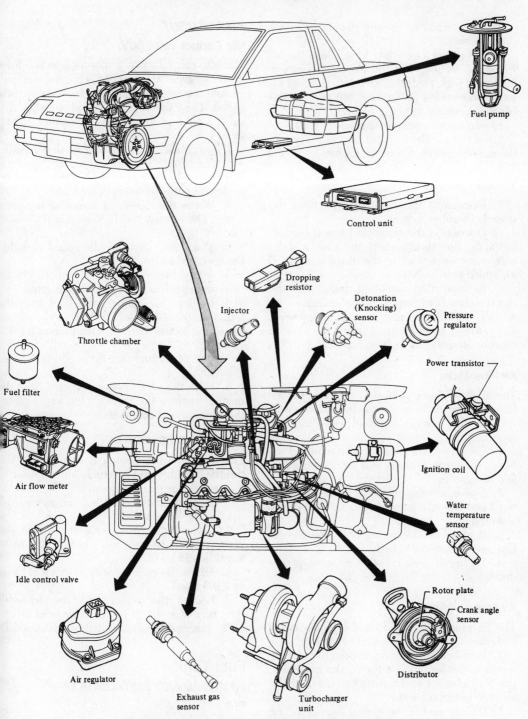

Fuel pump

Control unit

Dropping resistor

Injector

Detonation (Knocking) sensor

Pressure regulator

Throttle chamber

Power transistor

Fuel filter

Ignition coil

Air flow meter

Water temperature sensor

Idle control valve

Rotor plate

Crank angle sensor

Air regulator

Exhaust gas sensor

Turbocharger unit

Distributor

Exploded view of the Turbo EFI system—Pulsar (1984)

clamp and pull the injector from the fuel rail.

NOTE: *When disconnecting the fuel injector from the fuel rail, place a rag under it to prevent fuel splash.*

12. To remove the fuel hose from the injector, use a hot soldering iron, then cut (melt) a line in the fuel hose (to the braided reinforcement), starting at the injector socket to ¾ in. long (up the hose). Remove the hose from the injector, by hand.

NOTE: *DO NOT allow the soldering iron to cut all the way through the hose, nor touch the injector seat or damage the plastic socket connector.*

13. To install a new fuel hose, clean the injector tail section, wet the inside of the new hose with fuel, push the hose into the fuel injector hose socket (as far as it will go). Assemble the injector(s) onto the fuel rail.

14. To install, use new O-rings on the injectors and reverse the order of removal. Turn on the ignition switch and check for fuel leaks.

Throttle Chamber

1. Disconnect the air inlet pipe from the throttle chamber.

2. Disconnect the electrical harness connector (at the throttle chamber), the hoses and the accelerator wire and/or the throttle wire (if equipped with an A/T).

3. Remove the mounting bolts and the throttle chamber from the intake collector.

4. To install, use new gaskets and reverse the removal procedures. Torque the throttle chamber-to-collector bolts to 6.5–10.1 ft.lb.

Air Flow Meter

The air flow meter is located between the air filter and the intake manifold. It's purpose is to measure the quantity and temperature of the incoming air.

1. Disconnect the air duct (at the meter) between the air flow meter and the intake manifold air pipe.

2. Disconnect the electrical harness connector(s) and any hose(s) from the air flow meter assembly.

3. Remove the mounting bolts and the air flow meter from the vehicle.

4. To install, reverse the removal procedures.

Air Pipe

The air pipe is mounted on the intake manifold, directly under the throttle chamber.

1. Disconnect the air ducts from the air flow meter-to-the air pipe (at the intake manifold), the turbocharger-to-throttle chamber and the air pipe-to-turbocharger.

NOTE: *It may be necessary to remove the throttle chamber.*

2. Disconnect the idle speed connector and the air regulator, electrical harnesses and the hose from the intake collector to the air pipe.

3. Remove the mounting bolts and the air pipe.

4. To install, reverse the removal procedures. Torque the air pipe mounting bolts to 6.5–10.1 ft.lb.

ADJUSTMENT
Idle Control Valve (ICV)

The idle control valve is mounted on the fron of the air pipe. It's purpose is to send auxiliar air into the intake collector to increase the id speed. The valve is adjusted and sealed (with rubber plug) at the factory, no further adjust ment is necessary.

If by mistake, the idle control solenoid valv adjusting screw (2nd screw from the top of th ICV) was adjusted, correct the adjustment b performing the following procedure:

1. Warm the engine to operating tempera tures. Disconnect the ICV electrical conne tor.

2. Make sure that the idle speed is withi the specified range.

3. Apply battery voltage to the ICV sole noid (upper solenoid) electrical connector.

4. Remove the rubber plug (2nd from th top) from the adjusting screw. Turn the adjus ing screw so that the idle speed increases 90 120 rpm.

NOTE: *Make sure that the engine is runnin smoothly.*

5. With the adjustment completed, stop th engine, replace the rubber plug and reinsta the ICV harness connector.

Throttle Valve Switch

The throttle valve switch is attached to th throttle chamber and is actuated in response t the accelerator pedal movement.

1. Disconnect the electrical connector fro the throttle valve switch.

2. Connect an ohmmeter to the No. 18 an 25 pins of the throttle valve switch; the resis tance should be 0Ω.

3. Adjust the engine speed so that it is idlin at 1,100 rpm.

4. Loosen the switch's retaining screw(s then turn it so that it just changes from ON t OFF, under no load, then tighten the screws.

Fuel Tank
REMOVAL AND INSTALLATION
F10

1. Disconnect the battery ground cable.

2. Drain the fuel into a suitable container.

3. Disconnect the filler hose, the air ven hose, fuel return hose, and fuel outlet hose.

4. Disconnect the wires from sending unit.

5. Remove the bolts securing the fuel tan and remove the tank.

6. Installation is in the reverse order of re moval.

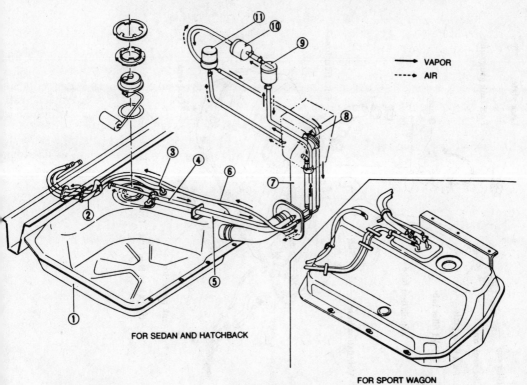

VAPOR
AIR

FOR SEDAN AND HATCHBACK

FOR SPORT WAGON

1. Fuel tank
2. Fuel outlet hose
3. Fuel return hose
4. Evaporation hose to fuel tank

5. Air vent line
6. Evaporation hose to engine
7. Filler hose
8. Filler cap

9. Separator
10. Limit valve
11. Vent cleaner

F10 fuel tank

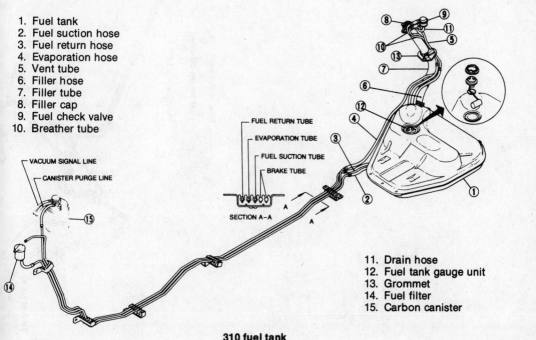

1. Fuel tank
2. Fuel suction hose
3. Fuel return hose
4. Evaporation hose
5. Vent tube
6. Filler hose
7. Filler tube
8. Filler cap
9. Fuel check valve
10. Breather tube

VACUUM SIGNAL LINE
CANISTER PURGE LINE

FUEL RETURN TUBE
EVAPORATION TUBE
FUEL SUCTION TUBE
BRAKE TUBE

SECTION A–A

11. Drain hose
12. Fuel tank gauge unit
13. Grommet
14. Fuel filter
15. Carbon canister

310 fuel tank

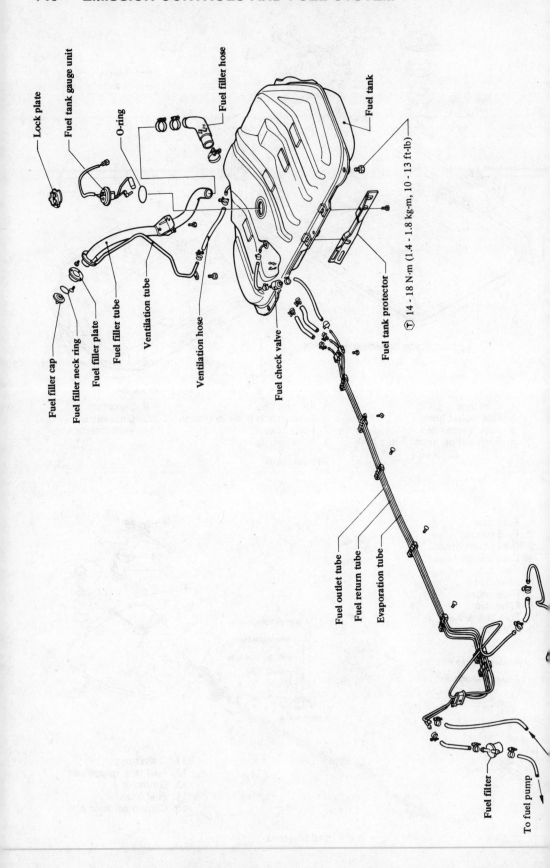

Lock plate

Fuel tank gauge unit

Fuel filler hose

O-ring

Fuel tank

Fuel filler cap

Fuel filler neck ring

Fuel filler plate

Fuel filler tube

Ventilation tube

Ventilation hose

Fuel check valve

Fuel tank protector

Ⓣ 14 - 18 N·m (1.4 - 1.8 kg-m, 10 - 13 ft-lb)

Fuel outlet tube

Fuel return tube

Evaporation tube

Fuel filter

To fuel pump

CHILTON'S
FUEL ECONOMY
& TUNE-UP TIPS

Tune-up • Spark Plug Diagnosis • Emission Controls

Fuel System • Cooling System • Tires and Wheels

General Maintenance

55 WAYS TO IMPROVE FUEL ECONOMY

CHILTON'S FUEL ECONOMY & TUNE-UP TIPS

Fuel economy is important to everyone, no matter what kind of vehicle you drive. The maintenance-minded motorist can save both money and fuel using these tips and the periodic maintenance and tune-up procedures in this Repair and Tune-Up Guide.

There are more than 130,000,000 cars and trucks registered for private use in the United States. Each travels an average of 10-12,000 miles per year, and, and in total they consume close to 70 billion gallons of fuel each year. This represents nearly ⅔ of the oil imported by the United States each year. The Federal government's goal is to reduce consumption 10% by 1985. A variety of methods are either already in use or under serious consideration, and they all affect you driving and the cars you will drive. In addition to "down-sizing", the auto industry is using or investigating the use of electronic fuel delivery, electronic engine controls and alternative engines for use in smaller and lighter vehicles, among other alternatives to meet the federally mandated Corporate Average Fuel Economy (CAFE) of 27.5 mpg by 1985. The government, for its part, is considering rationing, mandatory driving curtailments and tax increases on motor vehicle fuel in an effort to reduce consumption. The government's goal of a 10% reduction could be realized — and further government regulation avoided — if every private vehicle could use just 1 less gallon of fuel per week.

How Much Can You Save?

Tests have proven that almost anyone can make at least a 10% reduction in fuel consumption through regular maintenance and tune-ups. When a major manufacturer of spark plugs sur-

TUNE-UP

1. Check the cylinder compression to be sure the engine will really benefit from a tune-up and that it is capable of producing good fuel economy. A tune-up will be wasted on an engine in poor mechanical condition.

2. Replace spark plugs regularly. New spark plugs alone can increase fuel economy 3%.

3. Be sure the spark plugs are the correct type (heat range) for your vehicle. See the Tune-Up Specifications.

Heat range refers to the spark plug's ability to conduct heat away from the firing end. It must conduct the heat away in an even pattern to avoid becoming a source of pre-ignition, yet it must also operate hot enough to burn off conductive deposits that could cause misfiring.

The heat range is usually indicated by a number on the spark plug, part of the manufacturer's designation for each individual spark plug. The numbers in bold-face indicate the heat range in each manufacturer's identification system.

Manufacturer	Typical Designation
AC	R **45** TS
Bosch (old)	WA **145** T30
Bosch (new)	HR **8** Y
Champion	RBL **15** Y
Fram/Autolite	41**5**
Mopar	P-**62** PR
Motorcraft	BRF-**42**
NGK	BP **5** ES-15
Nippondenso	W **16** EP
Prestolite	14GR **5** 2A

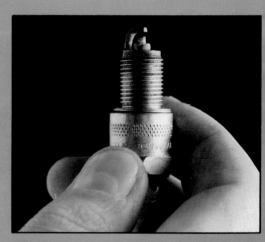

Periodically, check the spark plugs to be sure they are firing efficiently. They are excellent indicators of the internal condition of your engine.

On AC, Bosch (new), Champion, Fram/Autolite, Mopar, Motorcraft and Prestolite, a higher number indicates a hotter plug. On Bosch (old), NGK and Nippondenso, a higher number indicates a colder plug.

4. Make sure the spark plugs are properly gapped. See the Tune-Up Specifications in this book.

5. Be sure the spark plugs are firing efficiently. The illustrations on the next 2 pages show you how to "read" the firing end of the spark plug.

6. Check the ignition timing and set it to specifications. Tests show that almost all cars have incorrect ignition timing by more than 2°.

veyed over 6,000 cars nationwide, they found that a tune-up, on cars that needed one, increased fuel economy over 11%. Replacing worn plugs alone, accounted for a 3% increase. The same test also revealed that 8 out of every 10 vehicles will have some maintenance deficiency that will directly affect fuel economy, emissions or performance. Most of this mileage-robbing neglect could be prevented with regular maintenance.

Modern engines require that all of the functioning systems operate properly for maximum efficiency. A malfunction anywhere wastes fuel. You can keep your vehicle running as efficiently and economically as possible, by being aware of your vehicle's operating and performance characteristics. If your vehicle suddenly develops performance or fuel economy problems it could be due to one or more of the following:

PROBLEM	POSSIBLE CAUSE
Engine Idles Rough	Ignition timing, idle mixture, vacuum leak or something amiss in the emission control system.
Hesitates on Acceleration	Dirty carburetor or fuel filter, improper accelerator pump setting, ignition timing or fouled spark plugs.
Starts Hard or Fails to Start	Worn spark plugs, improperly set automatic choke, ice (or water) in fuel system.
Stalls Frequently	Automatic choke improperly adjusted and possible dirty air filter or fuel filter.
Performs Sluggishly	Worn spark plugs, dirty fuel or air filter, ignition timing or automatic choke out of adjustment.

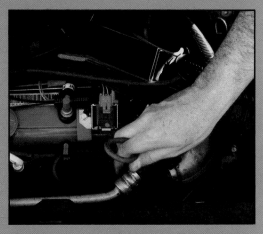

Check spark plug wires on conventional point type ignition for cracks by bending them in a loop around your finger.

Be sure that spark plug wires leading to adjacent cylinders do not run too close together. (Photo courtesy Champion Spark Plug Co.)

7. If your vehicle does not have electronic ignition, check the points, rotor and cap as specified.

8. Check the spark plug wires (used with conventional point-type ignitions) for cracks and burned or broken insulation by bending them in a loop around your finger. Cracked wires decrease fuel efficiency by failing to deliver full voltage to the spark plugs. One misfiring spark plug can cost you as much as 2 mpg.

9. Check the routing of the plug wires. Misfiring can be the result of spark plug leads to adjacent cylinders running parallel to each other and too close together. One wire tends to pick up voltage from the other causing it to fire "out of time".

10. Check all electrical and ignition circuits for voltage drop and resistance.

11. Check the distributor mechanical and/or vacuum advance mechanisms for proper functioning. The vacuum advance can be checked by twisting the distributor plate in the opposite direction of rotation. It should spring back when released.

12. Check and adjust the valve clearance on engines with mechanical lifters. The clearance should be slightly loose rather than too tight.

SPARK PLUG DIAGNOSIS

Normal

APPEARANCE: This plug is typical of one operating normally. The insulator nose varies from a light tan to grayish color with slight electrode wear. The presence of slight deposits is normal on used plugs and will have no adverse effect on engine performance. The spark plug heat range is correct for the engine and the engine is running normally.

CAUSE: Properly running engine.

RECOMMENDATION: Before reinstalling this plug, the electrodes should be cleaned and filed square. Set the gap to specifications. If the plug has been in service for more than 10-12,000 miles, the entire set should probably be replaced with a fresh set of the same heat range.

Oil Deposits

APPEARANCE: The firing end of the plug is covered with a wet, oily coating.

CAUSE: The problem is poor oil control. On high mileage engines, oil is leaking past the rings or valve guides into the combustion chamber. A common cause is also a plugged PCV valve, and a ruptured fuel pump diaphragm can also cause this condition. Oil fouled plugs such as these are often found in new or recently overhauled engines, before normal oil control is achieved, and can be cleaned and reinstalled.

RECOMMENDATION: A hotter spark plug may temporarily relieve the problem, but the engine is probably in need of work.

Incorrect Heat Range

APPEARANCE: The effects of high temperature on a spark plug are indicated by clean white, often blistered insulator. This can also be accompanied by excessive wear of the electrode, and the absence of deposits.

CAUSE: Check for the correct spark plug heat range. A plug which is too hot for the engine can result in overheating. A car operated mostly at high speeds can require a colder plug. Also check ignition timing, cooling system level, fuel mixture and leaking intake manifold.

RECOMMENDATION: If all ignition and engine adjustments are known to be correct, and no other malfunction exists, install spark plugs one heat range colder.

Photos Courtesy Fram Corporation

Carbon Deposits

APPEARANCE: Carbon fouling is easily identified by the presence of dry, soft, black, sooty deposits.

CAUSE: Changing the heat range can often lead to carbon fouling, as can prolonged slow, stop-and-start driving. If the heat range is correct, carbon fouling can be attributed to a rich fuel mixture, sticking choke, clogged air cleaner, worn breaker points, retarded timing or low compression. If only one or two plugs are carbon fouled, check for corroded or cracked wires on the affected plugs. Also look for cracks in the distributor cap between the towers of affected cylinders.

RECOMMENDATION: After the problem is corrected, these plugs can be cleaned and reinstalled if not worn severely.

MMT Fouled

APPEARANCE: Spark plugs fouled by MMT (Methycyclopentadienyl Maganese Tricarbonyl) have reddish, rusty appearance on the insulator and side electrode.

CAUSE: MMT is an anti-knock additive in gasoline used to replace lead. During the combustion process, the MMT leaves a reddish deposit on the insulator and side electrode.

RECOMMENDATION: No engine malfunction is indicated and the deposits will not affect plug performance any more than lead deposits (see Ash Deposits). MMT fouled plugs can be cleaned, regapped and reinstalled.

High Speed Glazing

APPEARANCE: Glazing appears as shiny coating on the plug, either yellow or tan in color.

CAUSE: During hard, fast acceleration, plug temperatures rise suddenly. Deposits from normal combustion have no chance to fluff-off; instead, they melt on the insulator forming an electrically conductive coating which causes misfiring.

RECOMMENDATION: Glazed plugs are not easily cleaned. They should be replaced with a fresh set of plugs of the correct heat range. If the condition recurs, using plugs with a heat range one step colder may cure the problem.

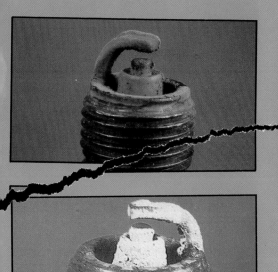

Ash (Lead) Deposits

APPEARANCE: Ash deposits are characterized by light brown or white colored deposits crusted on the side or center electrodes. In some cases it may give the plug a rusty appearance.

CAUSE: Ash deposits are normally derived from oil or fuel additives burned during normal combustion. Normally they are harmless, though excessive amounts can cause misfiring. If deposits are excessive in short mileage, the valve guides may be worn.

RECOMMENDATION: Ash-fouled plugs can be cleaned, gapped and reinstalled.

Detonation

APPEARANCE: Detonation is usually characterized by a broken plug insulator.

CAUSE: A portion of the fuel charge will begin to burn spontaneously, from the increased heat following ignition. The explosion that results applies extreme pressure to engine components, frequently damaging spark plugs and pistons.

Detonation can result by over-advanced ignition timing, inferior gasoline (low octane) lean air/fuel mixture, poor carburetion, engine lugging or an increase in compression ratio due to combustion chamber deposits or engine modification.

RECOMMENDATION: Replace the plugs after correcting the problem.

Photos Courtesy Champion Spark Plug Co.

EMISSION CONTROLS

13. Be aware of the general condition of the emission control system. It contributes to reduced pollution and should be serviced regularly to maintain efficient engine operation.

14. Check all vacuum lines for dried, cracked or brittle conditions. Something as simple as a leaking vacuum hose can cause poor performance and loss of economy.

15. Avoid tampering with the emission control system. Attempting to improve fuel econ-

FUEL SYSTEM

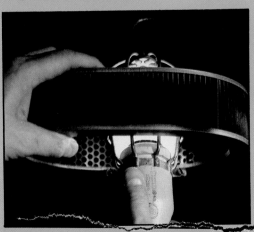

Check the air filter with a light behind it. If you can see light through the filter it can be reused.

Extremely clogged filters should be discarded and replaced with a new one.

18. Replace the air filter regularly. A dirty air filter richens the air/fuel mixture and can increase fuel consumption as much as 10%. Tests show that ⅓ of all vehicles have air filters in need of replacement.

19. Replace the fuel filter at least as often as recommended.

20. Set the idle speed and carburetor mixture to specifications.

21. Check the automatic choke. A sticking or malfunctioning choke wastes gas.

22. During the summer months, adjust the automatic choke for a leaner mixture which will produce faster engine warm-ups.

COOLING SYSTEM

29. Be sure all accessory drive belts are in good condition. Check for cracks or wear.

30. Adjust all accessory drive belts to proper tension.

31. Check all hoses for swollen areas, worn spots, or loose clamps.

32. Check coolant level in the radiator or expansion tank.

33. Be sure the thermostat is operating properly. A stuck thermostat delays engine warm-up and a cold engine uses nearly twice as much fuel as a warm engine.

34. Drain and replace the engine coolant at least as often as recommended. Rust and scale

TIRES & WHEELS

38. Check the tire pressure often with a pencil type gauge. Tests by a major tire manufacturer show that 90% of all vehicles have at least 1 tire improperly inflated. Better mileage can be achieved by over-inflating tires, but never exceed the maximum inflation pressure on the side of the tire.

39. If possible, install radial tires. Radial tires deliver as much as ½ mpg more than bias belted tires.

40. Avoid installing super-wide tires. They only create extra rolling resistance and decrease fuel mileage. Stick to the manufacturer's recommendations.

41. Have the wheels properly balanced.

omy by tampering with emission controls is more likely to worsen fuel economy than improve it. Emission control changes on modern engines are not readily reversible.

16. Clean (or replace) the EGR valve and lines as recommended.

17. Be sure that all vacuum lines and hoses are reconnected properly after working under the hood. An unconnected or misrouted vacuum line can wreak havoc with engine performance.

23. Check for fuel leaks at the carburetor, fuel pump, fuel lines and fuel tank. Be sure all lines and connections are tight.

24. Periodically check the tightness of the carburetor and intake manifold attaching nuts and bolts. These are a common place for vacuum leaks to occur.

25. Clean the carburetor periodically and lubricate the linkage.

26. The condition of the tailpipe can be an excellent indicator of proper engine combustion. After a long drive at highway speeds, the inside of the tailpipe should be a light grey in color. Black or soot on the insides indicates an overly rich mixture.

27. Check the fuel pump pressure. The fuel pump may be supplying more fuel than the engine needs.

28. Use the proper grade of gasoline for your engine. Don't try to compensate for knocking or "pinging" by advancing the ignition timing. This practice will only increase plug temperature and the chances of detonation or pre-ignition with relatively little performance gain.

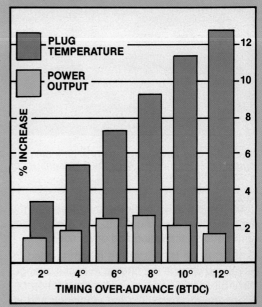

Increasing ignition timing past the specified setting results in a drastic increase in spark plug temperature with increased chance of detonation or preignition. Performance increase is considerably less. (Photo courtesy Champion Spark Plug Co.)

that form in the engine should be flushed out to allow the engine to operate at peak efficiency.

35. Clean the radiator of debris that can decrease cooling efficiency.

36. Install a flex-type or electric cooling fan, if you don't have a clutch type fan. Flex fans use curved plastic blades to push more air at low speeds when more cooling is needed; at high speeds the blades flatten out for less resistance. Electric fans only run when the engine temperature reaches a predetermined level.

37. Check the radiator cap for a worn or cracked gasket. If the cap does not seal properly, the cooling system will not function properly.

42. Be sure the front end is correctly aligned. A misaligned front end actually has wheels going in differed directions. The increased drag can reduce fuel economy by .3 mpg.

43. Correctly adjust the wheel bearings. Wheel bearings that are adjusted too tight increase rolling resistance.

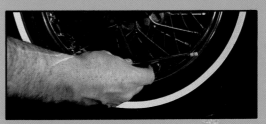

Check tire pressures regularly with a reliable pocket type gauge. Be sure to check the pressure on a cold tire.

GENERAL MAINTENANCE

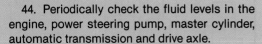

Check the fluid levels (particularly engine oil) on a regular basis. Be sure to check the oil for grit, water or other contamination.

A vacuum gauge is another excellent indicator of internal engine condition and can also be installed in the dash as a mileage indicator.

44. Periodically check the fluid levels in the engine, power steering pump, master cylinder, automatic transmission and drive axle.

45. Change the oil at the recommended interval and change the filter at every oil change. Dirty oil is thick and causes extra friction between moving parts, cutting efficiency and increasing wear. A worn engine requires more frequent tune-ups and gets progressively worse fuel economy. In general, use the lightest viscosity oil for the driving conditions you will encounter.

46. Use the recommended viscosity fluids in the transmission and axle.

47. Be sure the battery is fully charged for fast starts. A slow starting engine wastes fuel.

48. Be sure battery terminals are clean and tight.

49. Check the battery electrolyte level and add distilled water if necessary.

50. Check the exhaust system for crushed pipes, blockages and leaks.

51. Adjust the brakes. Dragging brakes or brakes that are not releasing create increased drag on the engine.

52. Install a vacuum gauge or miles-per-gallon gauge. These gauges visually indicate engine vacuum in the intake manifold. High vacuum = good mileage and low vacuum = poorer mileage. The gauge can also be an excellent indicator of internal engine conditions.

53. Be sure the clutch is properly adjusted. A slipping clutch wastes fuel.

54. Check and periodically lubricate the heat control valve in the exhaust manifold. A sticking or inoperative valve prevents engine warm-up and wastes gas.

55. Keep accurate records to check fuel economy over a period of time. A sudden drop in fuel economy may signal a need for tune-up or other maintenance.

NOTE: *For the F10 Wagon, the removal procedure is the same as that for the sedan and hatchback. However, when removing the fuel tank bolts, it is easier if you start at the three bolts at the front of the tank.*

310

1. Disconnect the battery ground cable.
2. Remove the drain plug and drain the fuel.
3. Disconnect the filler tube and filler hose from the fuel tank.
4. Disconnect the hoses attached to the fuel tank near the filler hose at the bottom front of the tank.
5. Loosen the tension on the parking brake and disconnect the wire on the fuel tank gauge unit.
6. Remove the retaining bolts and remove the tank by sliding it forward and down.

7. To install, reverse the removal procedures.

Pulsar and Stanza

1. Drain the fuel tank.
2. Remove the rear seat cushion.
3. Remove the inspection cover.
4. Disconnect the fuel gauge electrical harness connector.
5. Disconnect the fuel filler and the ventilation hoses. Disconnect the fuel outlet, return and evaporation hoses, at the front of the tank. Plug open fuel lines.
NOTE: *On the Stanza models, remove the tank protector.*
6. Remove the fuel tank mounting bolts and the tank from the vehicle.
7. To install, reverse the removal procedures. Torque the mounting bolts to 20–27 ft.lb.

Chassis Electrical

5

HEATER

Heater Assembly

REMOVAL AND INSTALLATION

F10

1. Disconnect the battery ground cable.
2. Drain the engine coolant and remove the heater hoses.
3. Remove the defroster hoses from each side of the heater assembly.
4. Remove the cable retaining clamps, then the cables for the intake and the floor doors.
5. Disconnect the three pole connector.
6. Remove the four heater retaining screws and the heater.

7. Installation is in the reverse order of the removal procedures.

310

1. Disconnect the negative battery terminal.
2. Set the temperature lever to the HOT position and drain the engine coolant.
3. Remove the instrument panel assembly. See the following section for instructions.
4. Disconnect the control cables, the control rod and the heater motor harness from the heater unit.
5. Disconnect the inlet and the outlet heater hoses from the engine compartment.
6. Remove the two lower and three upper

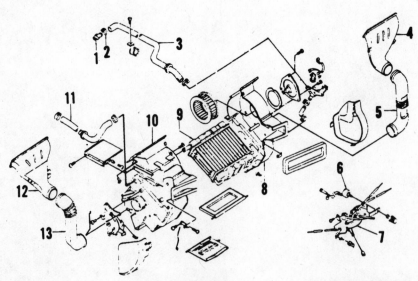

1. Connector
2. Clip
3. Heater hose (inlet)
4. Defroster nozzle (R.H.)
5. Defroster duct (R.H.)
6. Heater switch
7. Heater control
8. Heater case (R.H.)
9. Heater core
10. Heater case (L.H.)
11. Heater hose (outlet)
12. Defroster nozzle (L.H.)
13. Defroster duct (L.H.)

F10 heater assembly

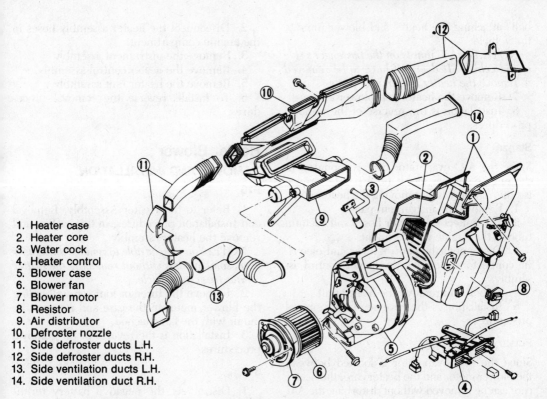

1. Heater case
2. Heater core
3. Water cock
4. Heater control
5. Blower case
6. Blower fan
7. Blower motor
8. Resistor
9. Air distributor
10. Defroster nozzle
11. Side defroster ducts L.H.
12. Side defroster ducts R.H.
13. Side ventilation ducts L.H.
14. Side ventilation duct R.H.

310 heater assembly

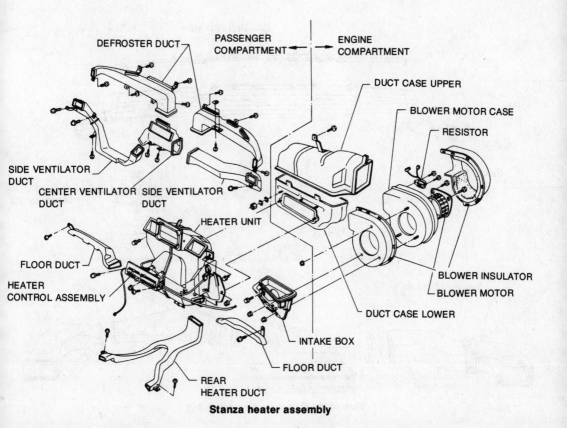

Stanza heater assembly

bolts attaching the heater and blower units to the vehicle.

NOTE:*The A/C unit is on the passenger's side of the vehicle. It does not have to be removed to remove the heater and blower units.*

7. Remove the heater and blower units.

8. Installation is the reverse of the removal procedures.

Stanza

Since the A/C evaporator core is mounted in the engine compartment, no A/C interference is experienced when removing the heater core.

1. Remove the instrument panel.

2. Disconnect the heater hoses and vacuum tube in the engine compartment.

3. Disconnect the control lever and electrical connectors. Remove the heater control assembly.

4. Unbolt and remove the heater unit.

5. Installation is the reverse of the removal procedures.

Pulsar

Since the A/C evaporator is located between the blower motor and the heater core, the heater core can be removed without disturbing the A/C evaporator.

1. Set the TEMP lever to the maximum HOT position and drain the engine coolant.

2. Disconnect the heater assembly hoses in the engine compartment.

3. Remove the instrument assembly.

4. Remove the heater control assembly.

5. Remove the heater unit assembly.

6. To install, reverse the removal procedures.

Heater Blower

REMOVAL AND INSTALLATION

F10

1. Refer to the Heater Assembly, Removal and Installation procedures, in this section and remove the heater assembly.

NOTE: *You may be able to remove the blower on some models without removing the heater unit from the vehicle.*

2. Remove the three or four screws holding the blower motor in the case and remove the motor with the fan attached.

3. Installation is the reverse of the removal procedures.

310

1. Disconnect the negative battery terminal.

2. Remove the instrument panel's lower cover on the driver's side.

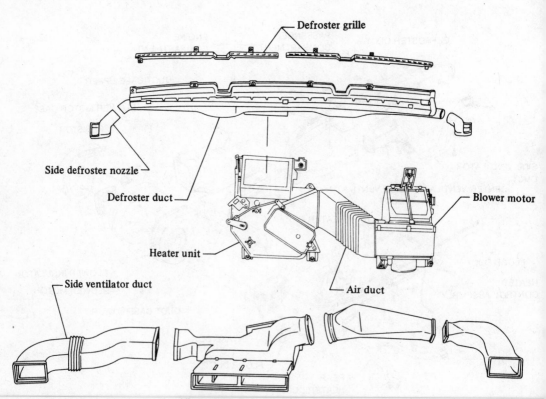

View of the Pulsar heating assembly

Labels: Defroster grille · Side defroster nozzle · Defroster duct · Heater unit · Side ventilator duct · Blower motor · Air duct

3. Disconnect the wiring harness at the blower and wherever else it constricts removal of the blower motor.

4. Remove the control wire and rod from in front of the motor.

5. Remove the three screws holding the control assembly in front of the blower motor and move the assembly out of the way.

6. Remove the three blower motor attaching screws and then remove the blower motor with the fan attached.

7. Installation is the reverse of the removal procedures.

Stanza

1. Working in the engine compartment, disconnect the blower motor insulator upper fasteners.

2. Remove the blower motor retaining bolts.

3. Push the blower motor insulator down by hand and remove the motor.

4. Installation is the reverse of the removal procedures.

Pulsar

The blower motor is located behind the glove box, facing the floor.

1. Disconnect the electrical harness from the blower motor.

2. Remove the retaining bolts from the bottom of the blower unit and lower the blower motor from the case.

3. To install, reverse the removal procedures.

Heater Core
REMOVAL AND INSTALLATION
F10

1. Refer to the Heater Assembly, Removal and Installation procedures, this section and remove the heater assembly.

2. Remove the sealing sponges. Unfasten the seven clips that hold the heater case together.

3. Remove the heater core from the cases.

4. Installation is the reverse of the removal procedures.

310

1. Refer to the Heater Assembly, Removal and Installation procedures, this section and remove the heater assembly.

2. Disconnect the inlet and outlet hoses from the core if you have not done so already.

3. Remove the clips securing the case halves and separate the halves.

4. Remove the heater core.

5. Installation is the reverse of the removal procedures.

Stanza

NOTE: *When refilling the cooling system, be sure to bleed the air from it. Refer to the Draining, Flushing and Refilling procedure in Chapter 1 and bleed the cooling system.*

1. Remove pedal bracket mounting bolts, the steering column mounting bolts, the brake and the clutch pedal cotter pins.

2. Move the pedal bracket and the steering column to the left.

3. Disconnect the air mix door control cable and the heater valve control lever, then remove the control lever.

4. Remove the core cover.

5. Disconnect the hoses at the core. Remove the heater core.

6. Installation is the reverse of the removal procedures.

Pulsar

1. Refer to the Heater Assembly, Removal and Installation procedures, in the section and remove the heater assembly from the vehicle.

2. Remove the heater assembly case bolts and separate the cases, then pull the heater core from the case.

3. To install, reverse the removal procedures. Refill the cooling system.

RADIO

REMOVAL AND INSTALLATION
F10

1. Remove the instrument cluster.

2. Detach all of the electrical connections.

3. Remove the radio knobs and the retaining nuts.

4. Remove the rear support bracket.

5. Remove the radio.

6. To install, reverse the removal procedures.

310 and Stanza

1. Disconnect the negative battery terminal.

2. Remove the center bezel.

3. Loosen and remove the radio retaining screws.

4. Remove the radio and disconnect the antenna feeder cable, the power lines and the speaker connections.

5. To install, reverse the removal procedures.

Pulsar

1. Remove the ash tray and the ash tray bracket.

2. Remove the radio mounting bolts.

3. Remove the instrument panel cover surrounding the radio.

4. Disconnect the electrical harness connector and the antenna plug from the radio.

5. To install, reverse the removal procedures.

WINDSHIELD WIPER

Wiper Switch

REMOVAL AND INSTALLATION

F10

1. Disconnect the negative battery terminal.

2. Reach up under the left side of the dash and disconnect the electrical connector.

3. Disconnect the illumination fiber-scope at the illumination lamp.

4. Remove the knob by pressing and turning it.

5. Remove the retaining nut on the meter cover.

6. Reach up under the instrument panel and remove the wiper switch.

7. To install, reverse the removal procedures.

310

1. Disconnect the negative battery cable.

2. Remove the horn pad, the steering wheel and the steering wheel cover.

3. Disconnect the electrical connectors from the combination switch.

4. Loosen the retaining screw and remove the combination switch assembly.

5. To install, reverse the removal procedures.

Pulsar (1983) and Stanza

1. Remove the steering wheel and the steering column cover.

2. Disconnect all of the combination switch wires.

3. Loosen the retaining screw and remove the combination switch wires.

4. To install, reverse the removal procedures.

Pulsar (1984 and Later)

The wiper switch can be removed without removing the combination switch from the steering column.

1. Remove the steering column cover.

2. Disconnect the wiper switch electrical connector.

3. Remove the wiper switch to combination switch retaining screws.

4. To install, reverse the removal procedures.

Motor and Linkage

REMOVAL AND INSTALLATION

F10

1. Disconnect the battery ground cable.

2. Lift the wiper arms, then remove the attaching nuts and the wiper arms.

3. Remove the meter cover.

4. Remove the glove box.

5. Remove the wiper motor attaching bolts.

6. Remove the ball joint connecting the motor shaft to the wiper link.

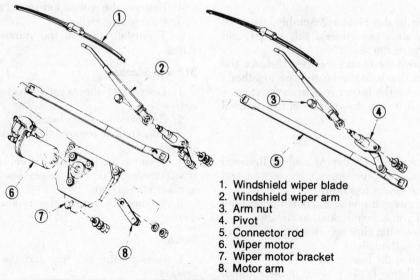

1. Windshield wiper blade
2. Windshield wiper arm
3. Arm nut
4. Pivot
5. Connector rod
6. Wiper motor
7. Wiper motor bracket
8. Motor arm

F10 wiper system

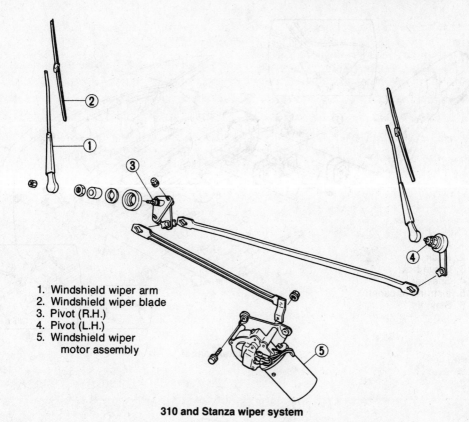

1. Windshield wiper arm
2. Windshield wiper blade
3. Pivot (R.H.)
4. Pivot (L.H.)
5. Windshield wiper
   motor assembly

310 and Stanza wiper system

7. Remove the wiper motor from the dash panel after disconnecting the electrical harness.

8. Remove the wiper pivot bolts from under the dashboard and the linkage.

9. To install, reverse the removal procedures.

NOTE: *Make sure you install the wiper arms in the correct positions by operating the system (without the arms), stopping it, then attach the arms.*

310, Pulsar and Stanza

1. Disconnect the negative battery terminal.

2. Open the hood and disconnect the motor wiring connection.

3. Unbolt the motor from the body.

4. Disconnect the wiper linkage from the motor and remove the motor.

5. To install, reverse the removal procedures.

INSTRUMENT CLUSTER

REMOVAL AND INSTALLATION

F10

1. Disconnect the negative battery terminal.

2. Disconnect the speedometer cable from the back of the speedometer.

3. Remove the package tray and disconnect the heater control cables from the heater.

4. Disconnect all of the wiring harness connectors from the back of the instrument panel after noting their locations and tagging them.

5. Remove the choke knob and nut.

6. Remove the steering column bracket installation bolts.

7. Loosen the instrument panel upper attaching screws.

8. Remove the bolts securing the sides of the instrument panel.

9. Remove the bolts attaching the instrument panel to the pedal bracket.

10. Remove the instrument panel.

11. To install, reverse the removal procedures.

310

1. Disconnect the negative battery terminal.

2. Remove the steering wheel and the steering column covers.

3. Remove the instrument cluster lid by removing its screws.

4. Remove the instrument cluster screws,

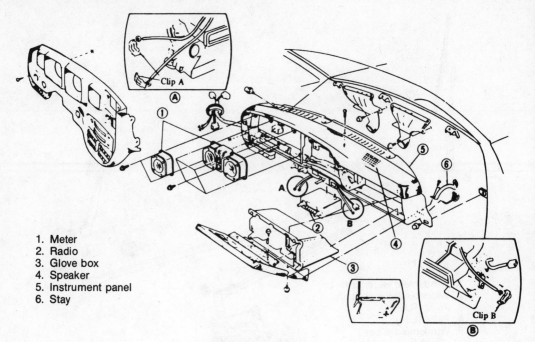

1. Meter
2. Radio
3. Glove box
4. Speaker
5. Instrument panel
6. Stay

F10 instrument panel

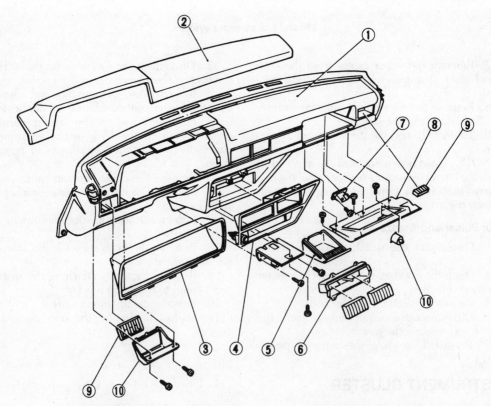

1. Instrument panel	5. Ash tray	9. Side ventilator case
2. Instrument pad	6. Center ventilator	10. Key lock
3. Cluster lid	7. Striker	11. Coin pocket
4. Center bezel	8. Glove lid	

310 instrument panel

then pull the unit out and disconnect all wiring and cables from its rear.

NOTE: *Mark the wires to avoid confusion during assembly; be careful not to damage the printed circuit.*

5. Remove the instrument cluster.

6. To install, reverse the removal procedures.

Stanza

1. Disconnect the negative battery terminal.

SGL models

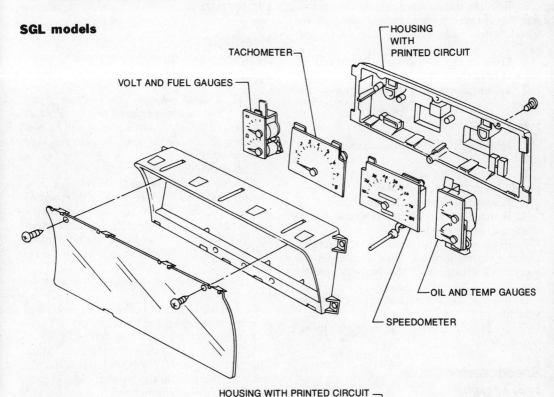

G models

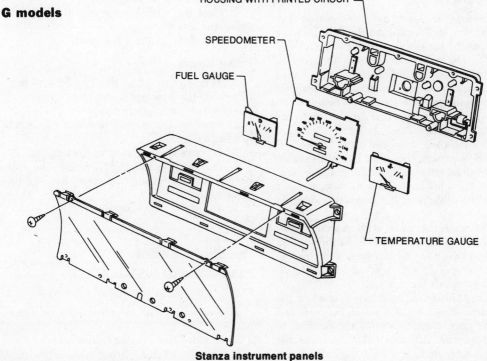

Stanza instrument panels

2. Loosen the tilt adjusting lever and completely lower the steering column.

3. Remove the steering column cover.

4. Remove the mounting screws and slightly tilt the cluster lid forward, then release the lid from the front nails.

5. Remove the instrument cluster screws, pull the cluster forward, then disconnect the speedometer cable and the harness connectors.

6. Pull out the instrument cluster and remove it from the vehicle.

7. To install, reverse the removal procedures.

Pulsar

1. Disconnect the negative battery terminal.

2. Loosen the tilt adjusting lever and completely lower the steering column.

3. Remove the steering column cover.

4. Remove the mounting screws and the instrument cluster hood.

5. Remove the instrument cluster screws, pull the cluster forward, then disconnect the speedometer cable and the harness connectors.

6. Remove the instrument cluster from the vehicle.

7. To install, reverse the removal procedures.

Speedometer Cable
REPLACEMENT

1. Remove any lower dash covers that may be in the way and disconnect the speedometer cable from the back of the speedometer.

NOTE: *On some models it may be easier to remove the instrument cluster to gain access to the cable. On the Stanza and Pulsar, the cable connector-to-instrument cluster has a snap release; simply press on the connector tab to release it.*

2. Pull the cable from the cable housing. If the cable is broken, the other half of the cable will have to be removed from the transaxle end. Unscrew the retaining knob at the transaxle and remove the cable from the transaxle extension housing.

3. Lubricate the cable with graphite powder (sold as speedometer cable lubricant) and feed the cable into the housing. It is best to start at the speedometer end and feed the cable down towards the transaxle.

NOTE: *It is usually necessary to unscrew the transaxle connection and install the cable end to the gear, then reconnect the housing to the transaxle. Slip the cable end into the speedometer and reconnect the cable housing.*

Ignition Switch

Ignition switch removal and installation procedures are covered in Chapter 7; Suspension and Steering.

LIGHTING

Headlights
REMOVAL AND INSTALLATION
Except Pulsar Coupe

NOTE: *Many vehicles have radiator grilles which are unit-constructed to also serve as headlight frames. In this case, it will be necessary to remove the grille to gain access to the headlights.*

1. Remove the grille, if necessary.

2. Remove the headlight retaining ring screws. These are the three or four short screws in the assembly. There are also two longer screws at the top and side of the headlight which are used to aim the headlight. Do not tamper with these or the headlight will have to be re-aimed.

3. Remove the ring on round headlights by turning it clockwise.

4. Pull the headlight bulb from its socket and disconnect the electrical plug.

5. Connect the plug to the new bulb.

6. Position the headlight in the shell. Make sure that the word TOP is, indeed, at the top and that the knobs in the headlight lens engage the slots in the mounting shell.

7. Place the retaining ring over the bulb and install the screws.

8. Install the grille, if removed.

Pulsar Coupe

1. Turn on the retractable headlight switch, then after the headlights are open, disconnect the negative battery terminal.

2. Remove the screws and the clip, then headlight cover.

3. Remove the retaining ring cover.

4. Pull out the headlight, remove the rubber cap and the wiring connector. Remove the headlight.

5. To install, reverse the removal procedures.

Headlight Switch
REMOVAL AND INSTALLATION
F10

1. Disconnect the negative battery terminal.

2. Remove the steering column cover.

3. Disconnect the wiring harness connector.

4. Remove the ignition switch-to-steering column retaining screws and the switch assembly.

5. To install, reverse the removal procedures.

310, Stanza and Pulsar (1983–84)

1. Place the ignition switch in the OFF position and disconnect the negative battery terminal.

2. Remove the steering wheel and the steering column cover.

3. Disconnect the wiring harness from the combination switch.

4. Loosen the retaining screws and remove the combination switch.

5. To install, reverse the removal procedures.

Pulsar (1985 and later)

1. Place the ignition switch in the OFF position and disconnect the negative battery terminal.

2. Remove the steering wheel and the steering column cover.

3. Disconnect the wiring harness from the lighting switch side of the combination switch.

4. Loosen the retaining screws and remove the lighting switch from the combination switch.

5. To install, reverse the removal procedures.

CIRCUIT PROTECTION

Fusible Links

A fusible link(s) is a protective device used in an electrical circuit. When current increases beyond a certain amperage, the fusible metal wire of the link melts, thus breaking the electrical circuit and preventing further damage to the other components and wiring. Whenever a fusible link is melted because of a short circuit, correct the cause before installing a new link.

Use the following chart to locate the fusible link(s).

All fusible links are the plug in kind. To replace them, simply unplug the bad link and insert the new one.

Fuses

On all vehicles (except Stanza), the fuse block is located under the left side of the instrument panel. On the Stanza, the fuse block is located under the glove box, concealed by a protective cover; open the fuse block cover to expose the fuse block.

REMOVAL AND INSTALLATION

The fuses can be easily inspected to see if they are blown. Simply pull the fuse from the block, inspect it and replace it with a new one, if necessary.

CAUTION: *When replacing a blown fuse, be certain to replace it with one of the correct amperage.*

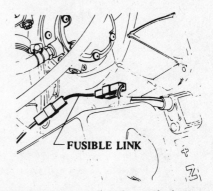

Most fusible links are found near the battery

Fusible Links

Year	Model	Number	Color/Protects	Location
1976–78	F10	2	Red/N.A. Green/N.A.	At positive battery terminal
1979–81	310	4	1 Red/Fuse block 3 Green/Ignition, lights, fan	Mounted on fender well beside battery
1982	310 Stanza	4	1 Red/Fuse block, alternator, air conditioner relay 3 Green/Ignition switch, fan and defogger, lights, carburetor cooling fan (U.S. models)	Mounted on fender well beside battery
1983–86	Stanza Pulsar	—	—	Connected to the battery terminal

Fuse Box and Flasher Location

Year	Model	Fuse Box Location	Flasher Location
1976–78	F10	Below hood release knob	Under driver's side of dashboard ①
1979–82	310	Below hood release knob	Turn signal: Passenger side kick board Hazard: Driver's side of hood release
1982–86	Stanza	Under glove box	On the steering column support, behind the instrument panel
1983–86	Pulsar	Under dash next to driver's kick panel	On the steering column support behind the instrument panel

① Both the turn signal and the hazard flashers are side by side

WIRING DIAGRAMS

Wiring diagrams have been left out of this book. As the vehicles have become more complex, and available with longer and longer option lists, the wiring diagrams have grown in size and complexity also. It has become virtually impossible to provide a readable reproduction in a reasonable number of pages.

MANUAL TRANSAXLE

REMOVAL AND INSTALLATION

F10 and 310 (1979–81)

1. Refer to the Engine, Removal and Installation procedures in Chapter 3, then remove the engine/transaxle assembly from the vehicle.

2. Remove the starter from the engine/transaxle assembly.

3. With the engine/transaxle assembly removed from the vehicle, remove the transaxle-to-engine bolts and separate transaxle from the engine.

NOTE: *The clutch assembly will remain attached to the engine.*

4. To install, reverse the removal procedures.

CAUTION: *If the clutch has been removed, it will have to be re-aligned. When connecting the drive shafts, insert O-rings between the differential side flanges and the drive shafts.*

310 (1982), Pulsar and Stanza

1. Remove the battery.

NOTE: *On the Pulsar and the Stanza, remove the battery holding plate and the radiator reservoir.*

2. Drain the lubricant from the transaxle.

3. Remove the driveshafts from the transaxle.

NOTE: *Take care not to damage the seal lips. After the driveshafts are removed, insert a dummy shaft into each opening so that the side gears don't fall into the case.*

4. Remove the distributor, the air induction tube, the EGR tube and the exhaust manifold cover.

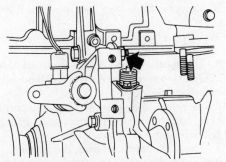

Removing the transmission mounting bracket on F10 and early 310 models

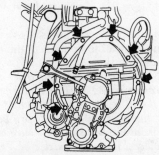

Separating the clutch housing from the engine on F10 and early 310 models

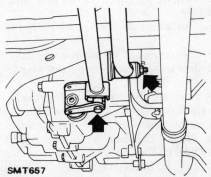

SMT657

Separating the control rod and the support rod on 1982 310

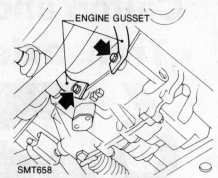

SMT658

Engine gusset removal on 1982 310

SMT659

310 and Stanza right engine mount

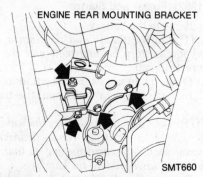

SMT660

310 and Stanza rear mounting bracket

5. Remove the heater hose clamp.

6. Remove the clutch control cable from the lever.

7. Disconnect the speedometer cable at the case.

8. Disconnect all wiring from the case. On the Pulsar and Stanza, remove the wheel well liner.

9. Separate the control and support rods from the case. On the Pulsar and Stanza, disconnect the exhaust pipe at the manifold.

10. Place a jackstand under the engine oil pan to take up the engine weight.

11. Take up the transaxle weight with a floor jack.

12. Remove the engine gusset bolts. On the Pulsar and Stanza, remove the transmission protector.

13. On 5-speed models, remove the engine right side and rear mounting brackets and the starter.

14. Attach a shop crane to the transaxle at the clutch control cable bracket.

15. Unbolt the transaxle from the engine. On 5-speed models, pull the engine to the right and slide the transaxle away from the engine.

16. On the 310, lift the transaxle from the vehicle. On the Pulsar and Stanza, lower the transaxle from the vehicle.

17. To install, reverse the removal procedures. Note the following points:

a. Clean all mating surfaces.

b. Apply EP chassis lube to the splines on the clutch disc and input shaft.

c. Fill transaxle with 80W-90 gear oil. Apply sealant to the threads of the filler and drain plugs.

d. Engine-to-transaxle bolt torque is 12–15 ft.lb.

Halfshaft

REMOVAL AND INSTALLATION

1. Raise the front of the vehicle and support it on jackstands, then remove the wheel and the tire assembly.

2. Remove the caliper assembly.

3. Remove the cotter pin from the drive axle.

4. Using a bar to hold the wheel from turning, loosen the hub nut.

5. Using the Ball Joint Removal tool HT72520000, remove the tie-rod ball joint from the steering knuckle.

6. Remove the control arm-to-steering knuckle, ball joint mounting nuts and separate the ball joint from the control arm.

7. Drain the lubricant from the transaxle.

NOTE: *On the 1976–81 models, remove the drive shaft flange bolts at the transaxle and remove the drive shaft from the transaxle. On the 1982 and later models, use a small pry bar to pry the drive shaft from the transaxle.*

8. Pull the hub/steering knuckle assembly away from the vehicle, to disconnect the drive shaft from the transaxle.

CAUTION: *When removing the drive shaft from the transaxle, DO NOT pull on the drive shaft, for it will separate at the sliding joint (damaging the boot), use a small pry bar to remove it from the transaxle. Be sure to replace the oil seal in the transaxle.*

NOTE: *After removing the drive shaft from the transaxle, be sure to install a holding tool*

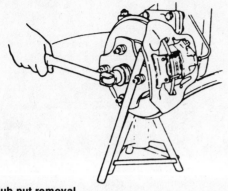

Hub nut removal

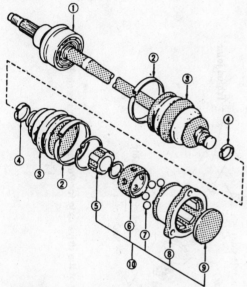

1. Outside joint assembly (Birfield joint)
2. Band
3. Dust cover
4. Band
5. Inner ring
6. Cage
7. Ball
8. Outer ring
9. Plug
10. Inside joint assembly (Double offset joint)

Drive axle—F10 and 310 (1976–81)

to hold the side gear in place while the axle is removed.

9. Use the Drive Shaft Remover tool ST35100000 (F10 and 310 models) or a wheel puller tool (Pulsar and Stanza), to press the drive shaft from the hub/steering knuckle assembly.

10. To install, use a new circlip (on the drive shaft), oil seal (transaxle) and reverse the removal procedures. Torque the control arm-to-ball joint to 40–51 ft.lb. (Stanza) or 40–47 ft.lb. (All Others), the lower ball joint stud nut to 22–29 ft.lb. (F10 and 310), 40–51 ft.lb. (Stanza) or 25–36 ft.lb. (Pulsar), the tie-rod stud nut to

40–47 ft.lb. (F10 and 310), 22–29 ft.lb. (Stanza) or 22–36 ft.lb. (Pulsar) and the hub nut to 145–203 ft.lb. (Stanza) or 87–145 ft.lb. (All Others).

NOTE: *When installing the drive shaft into the transaxle, use Oil Seal Protector tool KV38105500 to protect the oil seal from damage; after installation, remove the tool.*

OVERHAUL

Because of the special tool needed to disassemble and assemble the drive axles, it is recommended that a professional service facility should perform any repairs.

SHIFTER ADJUSTMENT

F10

4-SPEED MODELS

1. The adjustment is made at the shift rods on the transaxle. Loosen the adjusting nuts marked No. 1 and No. 2 in the illustration.

2. Measure the clearance between the shift lever marked No. 3 in the illustration and the transaxle case. Make sure the shift lever is pushed completely into the transaxle case. The clearance is marked A in the illustration.

3. Place the transaxle in 4th gear. Shift lever No. 3 should now be fully downward.

4. Increase the initial clearance A by 0.31 in. (8 mm).

5. Push lever No. 4 fully upward. Now tighten nut No. 1 until it makes contact with trunnion No. 7. then back the nut off one full turn and tighten it with nut No. 2.

5-SPEED MODELS

1. Loosen locknuts Nos. 1, 2, 3 and 4.

2. Make sure shift lever No. 5 is pushed completely into the transaxle case, then move it back 0.31 in. (8 mm).

3. Place the car in 3rd gear.

4. Push select lever No. 6 fully down. Turn nut No. 3 until it comes into contact with trunnion No. 9. Back the nut off one or two turns and then tighten nut No. 3 with nut No. 4.

5. Shift the hand lever into Neutral, then adjust the dimension B of the hand lever assembly to 0.039–0.079 in. and tighten the lock nut No. 1 with No. 2, securely.

310 Models

4-SPEED AND 5-SPEED MODELS

Adjustment can be made by adjusting the select lever.

1. Loosen the adjusting nuts at each end of the control rod lever near the bottom of the linkage.

2. Set the shift control lever in the Neutral position.

3. Fully push the shift lever (transaxle side)

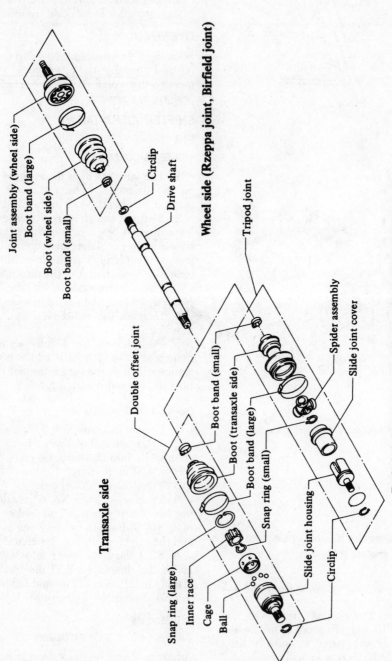

Joint assembly (wheel side)
Boot band (large)
Boot (wheel side)
Boot band (small)
Circlip
Drive shaft

Wheel side (Rzeppa joint, Birfield joint)

Tripod joint
Spider assembly
Slide joint cover

Transaxle side

Double offset joint
Boot band (small)
Boot (transaxle side)
Boot band (large)
Snap ring (small)
Slide joint housing
Circlip

Snap ring (large)
Inner race
Cage
Ball

Exploded view of the drive axle for Pulsar—Stanza is similar

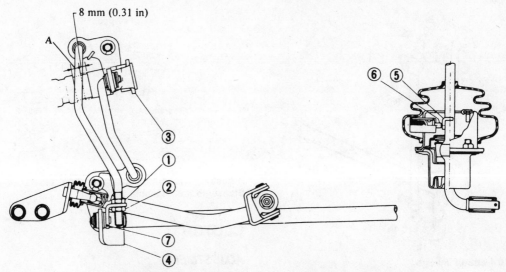

F10 4-speed linkage is adjusted in sequence at the numbered points

in the direction P1, as shown in the illustration. On the 4-speed transaxle, pull the lever back about 0.31 in. (8 mm). On the 5-speed, pull the shift lever back 0.453 in. (11.5 mm). With the select lever held in the above position, move the shift lever in direction P2, which engages the 3rd gear on the 4-speed transaxles and the 2nd gear on the 5-speed transaxles.

4. Push the control rod select lever as far as it will go in direction P3, then turn the upper adjusting nut until it touches the trunnion. Turn the nut a quarter turn more and lock the select lever with the other adjusting nut.

5. Operate the shift control lever to see if it shifts smoothly through the gears.

Pulsar and Stanza

1. Raise and support the front of the vehicle on jackstands.

2. Under the vehicle, at the shift control area, loosen the select stopper securing bolts.

3. Shift the gear selector into 1st gear.

4. Adjust the clearance between the control lever and select stopper by sliding the select stopper so that the clearance is 0.039 in. (1.0 mm).

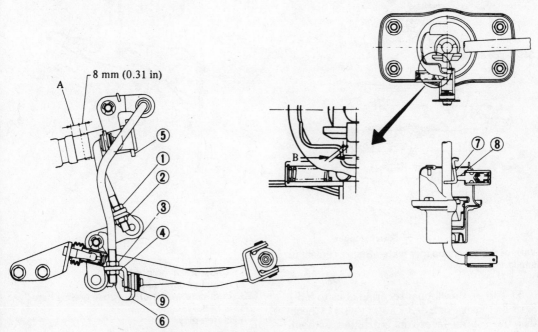

F10 5-speed linkage is adjusted in sequence at the numbered points

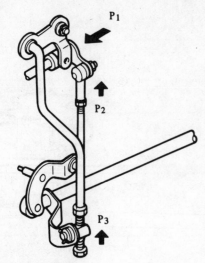

310 4-speed linkage

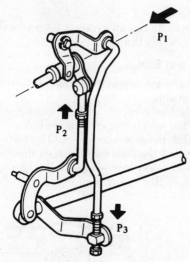

310 5-speed linkage

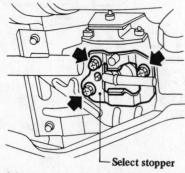

View of the select stopper plate—Stanza (Pulsar is similar)

5. Torque the stopper securing bolts to 5.8–8.0 ft.lb. (Stanza) or 2.3–3.7 ft.lb. (Pulsar). Check that the control lever can be shifted without binding or dragging.

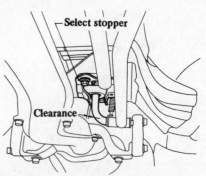

Adjusting the select stopper plate clearance—Stanza (Pulsar is similar)

CLUTCH

ADJUSTMENT

Refer to the Clutch Specifications Chart for clutch pedal height above floor and pedal free play.

The (1976–81) models have an hydraulically operated clutch. Pedal height is usually adjusted with a stopper limiting the upward travel of the pedal. Pedal free-play is adjusted at the clutch master cylinder pushrod. If the pushrod is nonadjustable, free-play is adjusted by placing shims between the master cylinder and the firewall. On a few models, pedal free play can also be adjusted at the operating (slave) cylinder pushrod. Pushrods are available in three lengths for the F10 and the 310.

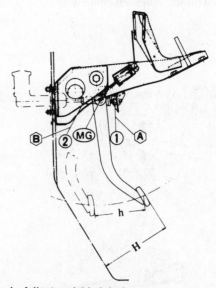

1. Adjust pedal height here
2. Adjust pedal free-play here
MG. Lubricate with multipurpose grease here
H. is pedal height
h. is free-play

Hydraulic clutch adjusting points

Clutch Specifications

Year	Model	Pedal Height Above Floor (in.)	Pedal Free-Play (in.)
1976–78	F10	6.9	0.23–0.55
1979–81	310	7.15	0.04–0.20
1982	310	7.27	0.43–0.83
1982	Stanza	6.00	0.43–0.63
1983–84	Stanza	6.05	0.43–0.63
1985–86	Stanza	6.20	0.47–0.67
1983–84	Pulsar	7.97	0.43–0.83
1985–86	Pulsar	8.33	0.49–0.69

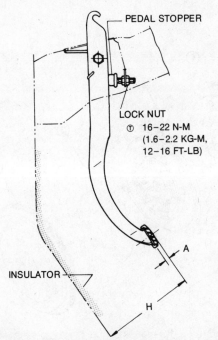

Stanza clutch pedal adjustment: H is the pedal height, A is the pedal free-play

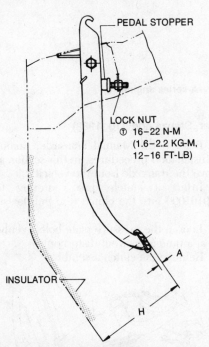

1982 310 clutch pedal adjustment: H is the pedal height, A is the pedal free-play

The (1982 and later) models have a cable-actuated mechanical clutch. The pedal height is adjusted at the clutch switch or the ASCD stop switch (both are located at the top of the clutch pedal). The free-play is adjusted at the cable bracket, located near the clutch release lever on the transaxle.

REMOVAL AND INSTALLATION

F10 and 310 (1979–81)

NOTE: *The clutch/flywheel assembly can be serviced without disturbing any adjacent units. The clutch cover and the pressure plate are balanced as an assembly; if replacement of either part becomes necessary, replace both parts as an assembly.*

1. Disconnect the negative battery cable, the fresh air duct and the high tension coil between the ignition coil and the distributor.

2. Remove the fuel filter from the fuel filter bracket. Remove the clutch operating cylinder from the clutch housing.

3. On the right-side wheel housing, remove the access hole cover protector and the dust cover. Working through the access hole, remove the E-clip (securing the withdrawal lever pin to the bearing housing) and the withdrawal lever.

4. Remove the bearing housing bolts and remove the primary drive gear assembly through the access hole.

5. At the upper section of the clutch housing, remove the bolts and the upper clutch housing section. By turning the flywheel with a pry bar, remove the clutch cover-to-flywheel bolts (loosen the bolts evenly).

6. Lift the clutch cover/disc assembly out through the clutch housing opening; the diaphragm spring can be removed at the same time.

7. Remove the strap holding the pressure plate to the clutch cover and remove the clutch from the center.

NOTE: *The strap must be replaced in the same position it had before removal. Mark the relative position before removal. Installing it out of position will cause an imbal-*

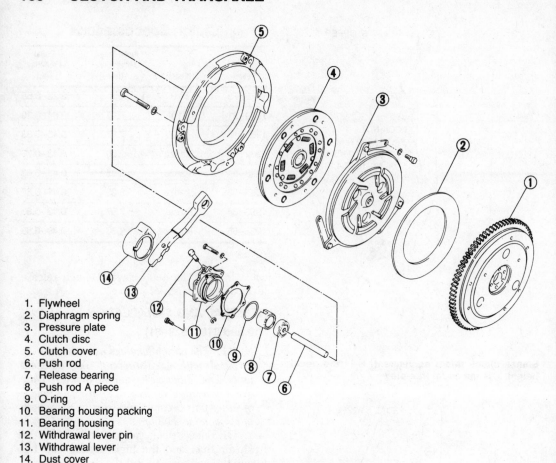

1. Flywheel
2. Diaphragm spring
3. Pressure plate
4. Clutch disc
5. Clutch cover
6. Push rod
7. Release bearing
8. Push rod A piece
9. O-ring
10. Bearing housing packing
11. Bearing housing
12. Withdrawal lever pin
13. Withdrawal lever
14. Dust cover

Exploded view of the clutch unit—A-series engine

ance. If necessary, the clutch disc should be inspected and/or replaced at this time; the clutch lining wear limit is 0.012 inch above the rivet heads.

8. To install, reverse the removal procedures. Torque the clutch cover-to-pressure plate bolts to 5–6 ft.lb. (F10) or 7–9 ft.lb. (310), the flywheel-to-crankshaft bolts to 58–65 ft.lb., clutch cover-to-flywheel bolts and the bearing housing-to-clutch housing bolts to 4.3–7.2 ft.lb.

Pulsar, Stanza and 310 (1982)

1. Refer to the Manual Transaxle, Removal and Installation procedures, in this section and remove the transaxle from the vehicle.

2. Insert a clutch disc centering tool KV30101000 into the clutch disc hub for support.

3. Loosen the pressure plate bolts evenly, a little at a time to prevent distortion.

4. Remove the clutch assembly.

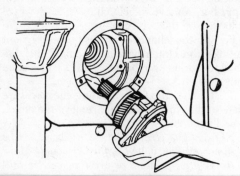

Removing the primary drive gear

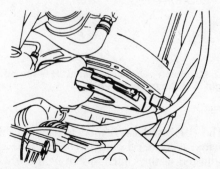

Removing the clutch cover assembly from the clutch housing—A-series engine

5. Installation is the reverse of removal. Apply a light coating of chassis lube to the clutch disc splines and the input shaft. Use a centering tool to aid installation. Torque the pressure plate bolts in a criss-cross pattern, a little at a time each to 12–15 ft.lb. (310) or 16–22 ft.lb. (Pulsar and Stanza).

Clutch Master Cylinder

REMOVAL AND INSTALLATION

1. Disconnect the clutch pedal arm from the pushrod.
2. Disconnect the clutch hydraulic line from the master cylinder.

NOTE: *Take precautions to keep brake fluid from coming in contact with any painted surfaces.*

3. Remove the nuts attaching the master cylinder and remove the master cylinder and pushrod toward the engine compartment side.
4. Install the master cylinder in the reverse order of removal and bleed the clutch hydraulic system.

OVERHAUL

1. Remove the master cylinder from the vehicle.
2. Drain the clutch fluid from the master cylinder reservoir.
3. Remove the boot, the circlip and the pushrod.
4. Remove the stopper, the piston, the cup and the return spring.
5. Clean all of the parts in clean brake fluid.
6. Check the master cylinder and piston for wear, corrosion and scores, then replace the parts as necessary. Light scoring and glaze can

be removed with crocus cloth soaked in brake fluid.

7. Generally, the cup seal should be replaced each time the master cylinder is disassembled. Check the cup and replace it, if it is worn, fatigued or damaged.
8. Check the clutch fluid reservoir, the filler cap, the dust cover and the pipe for distortion and damage, replace the parts as necessary.
9. Lubricate the new parts with clean brake fluid.
10. Reassemble the master cylinder parts in the reverse order of disassembly, taking note of the following:

a. Reinstall the cup seal carefully to prevent damaging the lipped portions.
b. Adjust the height of the clutch pedal after installing the master cylinder in position on the vehicle.
c. Fill the master cylinder and clutch fluid reservoir, then bleed the clutch hydraulic system.

Clutch Slave Cylinder

REMOVAL AND INSTALLATION

1. Remove the slave cylinder attaching bolts and the pushrod from the shaft fork.
2. Disconnect the flexible fluid hose from the slave cylinder and remove the unit from the vehicle.
3. Install the slave cylinder in the reverse order of removal and bleed the clutch hydraulic system.

OVERHAUL

1. Remove the slave cylinder from the vehicle.

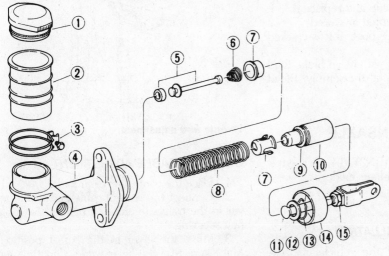

1. Reservoir cap
2. Reservoir
3. Reservoir band
4. Cylinder body
5. Valve assembly
6. Valve spring
7. Spring seat
8. Return spring
9. Piston cup
10. Piston
11. Push rod
12. Stopper
13. Stopper ring
14. Dust cover
15. Nut

Typical master cylinder

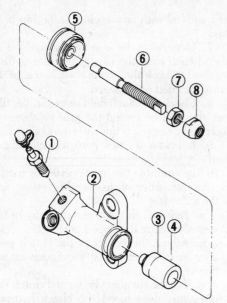

1. Bleeder screw   5. Dust cover
2. Cylinder body   6. Push rod
3. Piston cup   7. Lock nut
4. Piston   8. Push nut

Typical slave cylinder

2. Remove the pushrod and the boot.
3. Force out the piston by blowing compressed air into the slave cylinder at the hose connection.

NOTE: *Be careful not to apply excess air pressure to avoid possible injury.*

4. Clean all of the parts in clean brake fluid.
5. Check and replace the slave cylinder bore and piston if wear or severe scoring exists. Light scoring and glaze can be removed with crocus cloth soaked in brake fluid.
6. Normally, the piston cup should be replaced when the slave cylinder is disassembled. Check the piston cup and replace it, if it is found to be worn, fatigued or scored.
7. Replace the rubber boot, if it is cracked or broken.
8. Lubricate all parts with clean brake fluid and assemble in reverse of disassembly. Bleed the system.

AUTOMATIC TRANSAXLE

The automatic transaxle (RN3F01A, 3-speed) is available on all 1982 and later models.

Oil Pan

REMOVAL AND INSTALLATION

1. Raise and support the vehicle on jackstands.

2. Place a container under the transaxle to catch the oil when the pan is removed.
3. Remove the transaxle pan bolts.

NOTE: *If the pan sticks, bump it with a soft hammer to break it loose.*

4. Using a putty knife, clean the gasket mounting surfaces.
5. To install, use a new gasket, sealant and reverse the removal procedures. Torque the oil pan bolts to 3.6–5.1 ft.lb. Refill the transaxle.

OIL FILTER

1. Refer to the Oil Pan, Removal and Installation procedures, in this section and remove the oil pan.
2. Remove the control valve body, oil strainer plate bolts and the plate.

NOTE: *If the separator plate shows signs of scratches or damage, replace it.*

3. To install, reverse the removal procedures.

THROTTLE WIRE ADJUSTMENT

The throttle wire is adjusted by means of double nuts on the carburetor side.

1. Loosen the adjusting nuts at the carburetor throttle wire bracket.
2. With the throttle fully opened, turn the threaded shaft inward as far as it will go and tighten the 1st nut against the bracket.
3. Back off the 1st nut 1–1½ turns and tighten the 2nd nut against the bracket.
4. The throttle wire stroke between the threaded shaft and the cam should be 1.079-1.236 in.

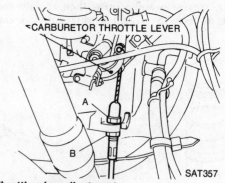

Throttle wire adjustment

CONTROL CABLE ADJUSTMENT

1. Place the control lever in Park.
2. Connect the control cable end to the lever in the transaxle unit and tighten the cable bolt securing.
3. Move the lever to the No. 1 position. Make sure that the lever works smoothly and quietly.

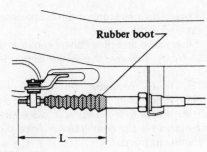

Control cable adjustment

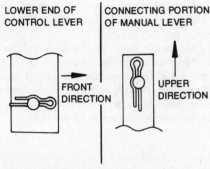

| LOWER END OF CONTROL LEVER | CONNECTING PORTION OF MANUAL LEVER |

Correct positioning of the control lever cotter pin

4. Place the control lever in Park.

5. Make sure that the lever locks in Park. Remove the cable adjusting outer nut and loosen the inner nut. Connect the control cable to the trunnion and install the outer nut.

6. Pull on the cable a couple of times, then tighten the outer nut until it just contacts the bracket. Tighten the inner nut securely. The length of the cable between the inner end of the rubber boot and the outer end of the rod should be 4.75 in.

7. Check all parts to ensure smooth working order. Check the cable spring cotter pin to make sure that it is assembled as shown.

INHIBITOR SWITCH ADJUSTMENT

The inhibitor switch allows the back-up lights to glow when the transaxle is placed in Reverse range and acts as a Neutral switch, by allowing the current to pass to the starter when the transaxle is placed in Neutral or Park.

1. Raise and support the vehicle on jackstands.

2. Loosen the inhibitor switch adjusting screws. Place the select lever in the Neutral position.

3. Using a 0.098 inch dia. pin, place the pin into the adjustment holes on both the inhibitor switch and the switch lever (the switch lever should be as near vertical position as possible).

4. Tighten the adjusting screws to 1.4–1.9 ft.lb. Check the switch for continuity.

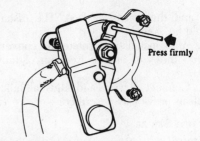

Adjusting the inhibitor switch

BRAKE BAND ADJUSTMENT

1. Refer to the Oil Pan, Removal and Installation procedures in this section and remove the oil pan.

2. Inside the transaxle, loosen the band adjuster locknut.

3. Tighten the anchor end pin locknut to 3–4 ft.lb.

4. Back off the anchor end pin lock nut exactly 2½ turns.

5. Tighten the locknut to 12–16 ft.lb. making absolutely certain that the anchor end pin locknut does not move.

6. Replace the oil pan and refill the transaxle.

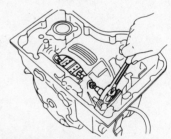

Adjusting the brake band

REMOVAL AND INSTALLATION

310 (1982)

1. Refer to the Engine, Removal and Installation procedures in Chapter 3, then remove the engine and transaxle as an assembly.

2. Remove the converter housing dust cover.

3. Unbolt the flex plate from the converter.

4. Make two chalk marks on the converter and flex plate for reassembly purposes.

5. Remove the starter.

6. Remove the bolts securing the transaxle to the engine and separate the transaxle from the engine.

7. To install, reverse the removal procedures. Note the following:

    a. Align the previously made chalk marks when installing the converter. Measure the distance between the transaxle housing end face and the converter face. The distance should be ⅞ inch.

b. After installation, rotate the converter several times to ensure freedom of movement.

c. Connect all wires and adjust all linkage points as previously described.

Pulsar and Stanza

1. Disconnect the negative battery terminal.

2. Raise and support the front of the vehicle on jackstands.

3. Remove the left-front wheel assembly and the left-front fender protector. Drain the transaxle fluid.

4. Disconnect the drive axles, the speedometer cable, the throttle wire from the carburetor throttle lever.

5. Remove the control cable from the rear of the transaxle, then the oil level gauge tube.

6. Place a floor jack under the transaxle and a support under the engine.

7. Disconnect and plug the oil cooler hoses from the tubes. Remove the torque converter-to-drive plate bolts.

NOTE: *When removing the torque converter-to-drive plate bolts, turn the crankshaft for access to the bolts and place alignment marks on the converter-to-drive plate for alignment purposes.*

8. Remove the engine mount securing bolts and the starter motor.

9. Remove the transaxle-to-engine bolts, pull the transaxle away from the engine and lower it from the vehicle.

10. To install, reverse the removal procedures. Measure the distance between the torque converter and the transaxle housing, it should be more than ⅞ inch. Torque the converter-to-drive plate bolts to 36–51 ft.lb., the converter housing-to-engine to 12–16 ft.lb.

Suspension and Steering

7

FRONT SUSPENSION

All models covered in this book use Mac-Pherson strut front suspension. In this type of suspension, each strut combines the function of coil spring and shock absorber. The spindle is mounted to the lower part of the strut through a single ball joint. No upper suspension arm is required in this design. The spindle and lower control arm is required in this design. The spindle and lower control arm are located fore and aft by tension rods which attach to the chassis.

Springs and Shock Absorbers

TESTING SHOCK ABSORBER ACTION

Shock absorbers require replacement: if the vehicle fails to recover quickly (after a large bump is encountered), if there is a tendency for the vehicle to sway or nose dive excessively or if the suspension is overly susceptible to vibration.

A good way to test the shocks is to intermittently apply downward pressure to one corner of the vehicle until it is moving up and down for almost the full suspension travel, then release it and watch the recovery. If the vehicle bounces slightly about one more time and then comes to rest, the shock absorbers are serviceable. If the vehicle goes on bouncing, the shocks require replacement.

Strut

REMOVAL AND INSTALLATION

F10 and 310

1. Raise the vehicle and support it on jack-stands. Remove the wheel/tire assembly.
2. Disconnect and plug the brake hose.
3. Using the Ball Joint Puller tool HT72520000, disconnect the tie-rod from the strut.
4. Place a jackstand under the control arm to support it.
5. Remove the steering knuckle-to-strut mounting bolts and separate the strut from the steering knuckle.
6. Open the hood and remove the strut-to-body nuts.
7. Remove the strut assembly from the vehicle.
8. To install, reverse the removal procedures. Torque the strut-to-body bolts to 11–17 ft.lb., the strut-to-steering knuckle to 24–33 ft.lb. and the tie-rod ball joint-to-strut to 40–47 ft.lb.

NOTE: *The self-locking nuts holding the top of the strut must be replaced. Bleed the brakes.*

Stanza and Pulsar

1. Raise and support the vehicle on jack-stands.
2. Remove the wheel/tire assembly.
3. Detach the brake tube from the strut.
4. Support the transverse link with a jack-stand.
5. Detach the steering knuckle from the strut.
6. Loosen, but do not remove, the strut piston rod locknut.
7. Support the strut and remove the three upper attaching nuts. Remove the strut from the vehicle.
8. To install, reverse the removal procedures. Torque the strut-to-body nuts to 23–31 ft.lb., the piston rod locknut to 43–54 ft.lb. and the strut-to-knuckle bolts to 56–80 ft.lb. (Stanza) or 72–87 ft.lb. (Pulsar).

OVERHAUL

CAUTION: *The coil springs are under considerable tension and can exert enough force to cause serious injury. Disassemble the struts*

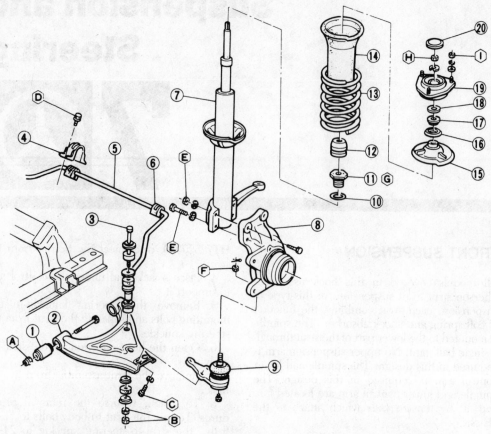

1. Transverse link bushing
2. Transverse link
3. Connecting bolt
4. Stabilizer bracket
5. Stabilizer
6. Stabilizer bushing
7. Strut

8. Knuckle
9. Ball joint
10. O-ring
11. Gland packing assembly
12. Bound bumper
13. Coil spring
14. Dust cover

15. Spring seat
16. Grease seal
17. Thrust seat
18. Thrust plate
19. Mount insulator
20. Insulator cap

F10, 310 front suspension

only if the proper tools are available and use extreme caution.

The coil springs on all models must be removed with the aid of a coil spring compressor. If you don't have one, don't try to improvise by using something else: you could risk injury. The coil spring compressor is Special Tool ST35652001 or variations of that number. Basically, they are all the same tool. These are the recommended compressors, although they are probably not the only spring compressors which will work. Always follow manufacturer's instructions when operating a spring compressor. You can now buy cartridge type shock absorbers for many models: installation procedures are not the same as those given here. In this case, follow the instructions that come with the shock absorbers.

To remove the coil spring, you must first re-move the strut assembly from the vehicle. See above for procedures.

1. Secure the strut assembly in a vise.

2. Attach the spring compressor to the spring, leaving the top few coils free.

3. Remove the dust cap from the top of the strut to expose the center nut, if a dust cap is provided.

4. Compress the spring just far enough to permit the strut insulator to be turned by hand. Remove the self-locking center nut.

5. Take out the strut insulator, strut bearing, oil seal, upper spring seat and bound bumper rubber from the top of the strut. Note their sequence of removal and be sure to assemble them in the same order.

6. Remove the spring with the spring compressor still attached.

Assembly is the reverse of disassembly. Ob-

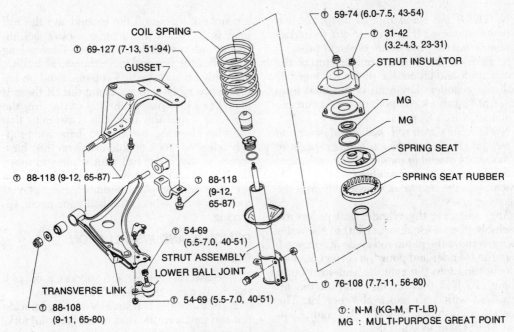

COIL SPRING

① 59-74 (6.0-7.5, 43-54)

① 69-127 (7-13, 51-94)

① 31-42
(3.2-4.3, 23-31)

GUSSET

STRUT INSULATOR

MG

MG

SPRING SEAT

① 88-118 (9-12, 65-87)

① 88-118
(9-12,
65-87)

SPRING SEAT RUBBER

① 54-69
(5.5-7.0, 40-51)

STRUT ASSEMBLY

LOWER BALL JOINT

① 76-108 (7.7-11, 56-80)

TRANSVERSE LINK

① 54-69 (5.5-7.0, 40-51)

① 88-108
(9-11, 65-80)

①: N-M (KG-M, FT-LB)
MG : MULTI-PURPOSE GREAT POINT

Stanza front suspension

serve the following. Make sure you assemble the unit with the shock absorber piston rod fully extended. When assembling, take care that the rubber spring seats, both top and bottom and the spring are positioned in their grooves before releasing the spring.

7. To remove the shock absorber: Remove the dust cap (if equipped) and push the piston rod down until it bottoms. With the piston in this position, loosen and remove the gland packing shock absorber retainer. This calls for the Special Tool ST35500001, but you should be able to loosen it either with a pipe wrench or by tapping it around with a drift.

1. Driveshaft
2. Strut assembly
3. Grease seal
4. Inner sheel bearing
5. Knuckle
6. Spacer
7. Outer wheel bearing
8. Grease seal
9. Rotor
10. Wheel hub
11. Hub nut
12. Ball joint
13. Transverse link assembly

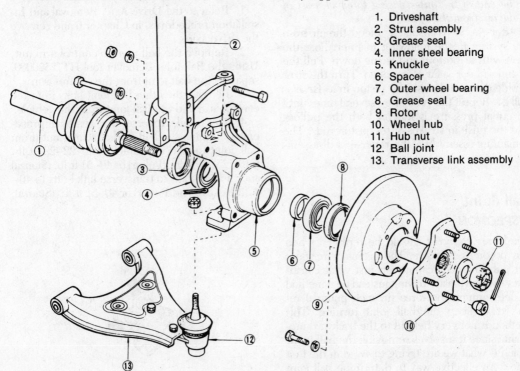

F10, 310 front hub and knuckle

NOTE: *If the gland tube is dirty, clean it before removing it to prevent dirt from contaminating the fluid inside the strut tube.*

8. Remove the O-ring from the top of the piston guide and lift out the piston rod together with the cylinder. Drain all of the fluid from the strut and shock components into a suitable container. Clean all parts.

NOTE: *The piston rod, piston rod guide and cylinder are a matched set: single parts of this shock assembly should not be exchanged with parts of other assemblies.*

Assembly is the reverse of disassembly with the following notes:

After installing the cylinder and piston rod assembly (the shock absorber kit) in the outer casing, remove the piston rod guide (if equipped) from the cylinder and pour the correct amount of new fluid into the cylinder and strut outer casing. To find this amount, consult the instructions with your shock absorber kit. The amount of oil should be listed. Use only Genuine Strut Oil or its equivalent.

NOTE: *It is important that the correct amount of fluid be poured into the strut to assure correct shock absorber damping force.*

Install the O-ring, fluid and any other cylinder components. Fit the gland packing and tighten it after greasing the gland packing-to-piston rod mating surfaces.

NOTE: *When tightening the gland packing, extend the piston rod about 3–5 inches from the end of the outer casing to expel most of the air from the strut.*

After the kit is installed, bleed the air from the system in the following manner: hold the strut with its bottom end facing down. Pull the piston rod out as far as it will go. Turn the strut upside down and push the piston in as far as it will go. Repeat this procedure several times until an equal pressure is felt on both the pullout and the push in strokes of the piston rods. The remaining assembly is the reverse of disassembly.

Ball Joint

INSPECTION

The lower ball joint should be replaced when play becomes excessive. The manufacturer does not publish specifications on just what constitutes excessive play, relying instead on a method of determining the force (in inch pounds) required to keep the ball joint turning. This method is not very helpful to the backyard mechanic since it involves removing the ball joint, which is what we are trying to avoid in the first place. An effective way to determine ball joint play is to jack up the car until the wheel is just

a couple of inches off the ground and the ball joint is unloaded (meaning you can't jack directly underneath the ball joint). Place a long bar under the tire and move the wheel and tire assembly up and down. Keep one hand on top of the tire while you are doing this. If there is over ¼ inch of play at the top of the tire, the ball joint is probably bad. This is assuming that the wheel bearings are in good shape and properly adjusted. As a double check on this, have someone watch the ball joint while you move the tire up and down with the bar. If you can see considerable play, besides feeling play at the top of the wheel, the ball joint needs replacing.

REMOVAL AND INSTALLATION

F10

1. Raise the vehicle and support it on jack stands. Remove the wheel/tire assembly.
2. Remove the ball stud-to-steering knuckle nut and force out the stud with a ball joint fork, being careful not to damage the ball joint dust cover.
3. Remove the ball joint bolts and the ball joint.
4. To install, reverse the removal procedures. Tighten the ball stud-to-steering knuckle nut to 22–29 ft.lb. and the ball joint-to-control arm bolts to 40–47 ft.lb.

310, Pulsar and Stanza

1. Refer to the Drive Axle, Removal and Installation procedures, in Chapter 6 and remove the drive axle.
2. Remove the ball joint-to-control arm nut. Using the Ball Joint Remover tool HT72520000, separate the ball joint from the control arm.
3. Remove the other ball joint bolts from the control arm and the ball joint from the vehicle.
4. To install, reverse the removal procedures. Tighten the ball stud attaching nut (from ball joint-to-steering knuckle) to 22–29 ft.lb. (310), 25–36 ft.lb. (Pulsar) or 40–51 ft.lb. (Stanza) and the ball joint to transverse link bolts to 40–47 ft.lb. (310 and Pulsar) or 40–51 ft.lb. (Stanza).

Ball joint removal

Lower Control Arm (Transverse Link)

REMOVAL AND INSTALLATION

F10 and 310

CAUTION: *Always use new nuts.*
1. Raise and support the car on jackstands.
2. Remove the wheel/tire assembly.
3. Unbolt the control arm from the ball joint.
4. Remove the stabilizer link-to-control arm nut and separate the link from the arm.
5. Unbolt the control arm-to-subframe bolts and remove the control arm from the vehicle.
6. To install, reverse the removal procedures. Torque the control arm-to-sub frame bolts to 42–51 ft.lb., the ball joint-to-control arm nut to 40–47 ft.lb. and the stabilizer link-to-control arm nut to 5.8–8.7 ft.lb.

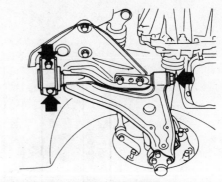

Removing Stanza transverse link

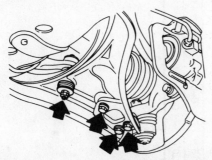

Transverse link attaching points, F10 and 310

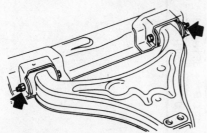

Unbolting transverse link from sub frame on F10 and 310

Stanza

CAUTION: *Always use new nuts when installing the ball joint to the control arm.*
1. Raise and support the vehicle on jackstands.
2. Remove the wheel/tire assembly.
3. Remove the lower ball joint bolts from the control arm.
NOTE: *If equipped with a stabilizer bar, disconnect it from the control arm.*
4. Remove the control arm-to-body bolts.
5. Remove the gusset.
6. Remove the control arm from the vehicle.

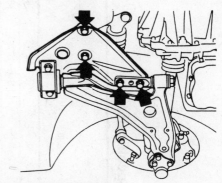

Removing Stanza gusset

7. To install, reverse the removal procedures. Torque the gusset-to-body bolts to 65–87 ft.lb. (Stanza) or 65–80 ft.lb. (Pulsar), the control arm securing nut to 65–80 ft.lb. (Stanza) or 72–87 ft.lb. (Pulsar), the control arm securing bolts to 65–87 ft.lb. (Stanza) or 65–80 ft.lb. (Pulsar), the lower ball joint-to-control arm nuts to 40–51 ft.lb. (Stanza) or 40–47 ft.lb. (Pulsar) and stabilizer bar-to-control arm to 6.7–8.7 ft.lb. (Pulsar).
NOTE: *When installing the link, tighten the nut securing the link spindle to the gusset. Final tightening should be made with the weight of the car on the wheels.*

Front End Alignment

CASTER AND CAMBER

Caster is the tilt of the upper end of the kingpin or the upper ball joint, which results in a slight tilt of the steering axis forward or backward. Rearward tilt is referred to as a positive caster, while forward tilt is referred to as negative caster.

Camber is the inward or outward tilt from the vertical (measured in degrees) of the front wheels at the top. An outward tilt gives the wheel positive camber. Proper camber is critical to assure even tire wear.

Wheel Alignment Specifications

Year	Model	Caster Range (deg)	Caster Preferred Setting (deg)	Camber Range (deg)	Camber Preferred Setting (deg)	Toe-In (in.)	Steering Axle Inclination (deg)	Wheel Pivot Ratio (deg) Inner Wheel	Wheel Pivot Ratio (deg) Outer Wheel
1976–78	F10	20'P–1°50'P	1°05'P	50'P–2°20'P	1°35'P	①	9°15'–10°45'	36°30'–39°30'	31°–34°
1979–82	310	25'P–1°55'P	1°10'P	15'P–1°45'P	1°P	0–0.08	11°10'–12°30'	36°30'–39°30'	29°30'–32°30' ②
1982–84	Stanza	40'P–2°10'P	1°25'P	45'N–45'P	0	0–0.08	13°40'–15°10'	36°–40°	30°–34°
1985–86	Stanza	40'P–2°10'P	25'P	25'N–1°05'P	20'N	0–0.08	13°40'–15°10'	36°–40°	30°–34°
1983	Pulsar	45'P–2°15'P	1°30'P	35'N–1°05'P	15'P	0–0.08	12°10'–13°40'	40°–44°	31°–35°
1984	Pulsar	45'P–2°15'P	1°30'P	35'N–1°05'P	15'P	0–0.08	12°10'–13°40'	40°30'–43°30'	31°30'–34°30'
1985–86	Pulsar	45'P–2°15'P	1°30'P	25'N–1°05P	20'P	0.12–0.20	12°10'–13°40'	③⑤	④⑥

① 0–0.79 Radial tires
0.20–0.28 Bias tires
② Power Steering: 28°30'–31°30'
③ M/T and A/T (power steering): 40°30'–43°30'
④ M/T and A/T (without power steering): 31°30'–34°30'
⑤ A/T (manual steering): 37°30'–40°30'
⑥ A/T (manual steering): 29°30'–32°30'

Since caster and camber are adjusted traditionally by adding or subtracting shims behind the upper control arms. The vehicles covered in this guide have replaced the upper control arm with the MacPherson strut, the only way to adjust caster and camber is to replace bent or worn parts of the front suspension.

TOE

Toe is the amount, measure in a fraction of an inch, that the wheels are closer together at one end than the other. Toe-in means that the front wheels are closer together at the front than the rear; toe-out means the rears are closer than the front. The vehicles are adjusted to have a slight amount of toe-in. Toe-in is adjusted by turning the tie-rod, which has a right-hand thread on one end and a left-hand thread on the other.

You can check your vehicle's toe-in yourself without special equipment if you make careful measurements. The wheels must be straight ahead.

1. Toe-in can be determined by measuring the distance between the center of the tire treads, at the front of the tire and at the rear. If the tread pattern of your car's tires makes this impossible, you can measure between the edges of the wheel rims, but make sure to move the car forward and measure in a couple of places to avoid errors caused by bent rims or wheel runout.

2. If the measurement is not within specifi-

cations, loosen the locknuts at both ends of the tie-rod (the driver's side locknut is left-hand threaded).

3. Turn the top of the tie-rod toward the front of the car to reduce toe-in, or toward the rear to increase it. When the correct dimension is reached, tighten the locknuts and check the adjustment.

NOTE: *The length of the tie-rods must always be equal to each other.*

STEERING ANGLE ADJUSTMENT

The maximum steering angle is adjusted by stopper bolts on the steering arms. Loosen the locknut on the stopper bolt, turn the stopped bolt in or out as required to obtain the proper maximum steering angle and retighten the locknut.

SUSPENSION HEIGHT

Suspension height is adjusted by replacing the springs. Various springs are available for adjustment.

REAR SUSPENSION

Springs

REMOVAL AND INSTALLATION

F10 Station Wagon

1. Raise the vehicle and support it with jackstands.

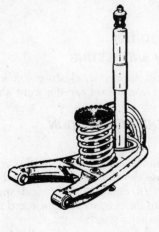

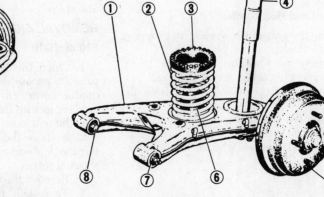

1. Rear arm
2. Coil spring
3. Rubber seat
4. Shock absorber
5. Drum
6. Bumper
7. Bushing
8. Rear arm bolt

F10 sedan and hatchback rear suspension

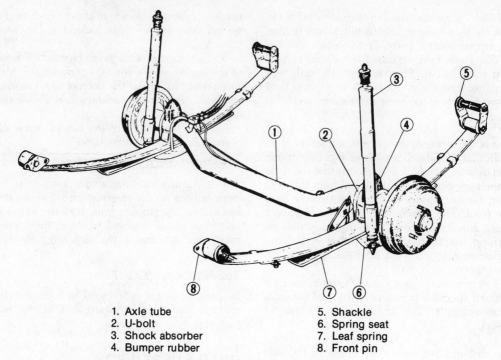

1. Axle tube
2. U-bolt
3. Shock absorber
4. Bumper rubber

5. Shackle
6. Spring seat
7. Leaf spring
8. Front pin

F10 station wagon rear suspension

2. Remove the wheel/tire assembly.

3. Remove the nuts from the lower portion of the shock absorber.

4. Remove the nuts from the U-bolts, then detach the bumper rubbers and the spring seat.

5. Using a floor jack, raise the axle until it clears the leaf spring.

6. Remove the hand brake clamp from the leaf spring.

7. Remove the front pin and shackle, then detach the spring from the body.

8. To install, reverse the removal procedures.

F10 Sedan and Hatchback

1. Raise the rear of the vehicle and support it with jackstands.

2. Remove the wheel/tire assemblies.

3. Support the trailing arm with a jack.

4. Remove the upper and lower shock absorber nuts.

5. Lower the jack slowly and carefully, then remove the coil spring.

6. To install, reverse the removal procedures.

Pulsar

1. Raise and support the rear of the vehicle with jackstands.

2. Remove the wheel/tire assembly.

3. Support the lower end of the rear arm with a jackstand.

4. Remove the lower end bolt from the shock absorber.

5. Slowly, lower the jack and remove the coil spring.

6. To install, reverse the removal procedures. Torque the shock absorber's lower bolt to 51–65 ft.lb.

Shock Absorber

INSPECTION AND TESTING

Inspect and test the rear shock absorbers in the same manner as outlined for the front shock absorbers.

REMOVAL AND INSTALLATION

F10 and 310

1. Open the trunk and remove the cover panel to expose the shock mounts. Pry off the mount covers (if equipped). On leaf spring models, jack up the rear of the vehicle and support the rear axle on stands.

2. Remove the two nuts holding the top of the shock absorber. Unbolt the bottom of the shock absorber.

3. Remove the shock absorber.

4. To install, reverse the removal procedures.

Pulsar

1. Raise and support the rear of the vehicle on jackstands.

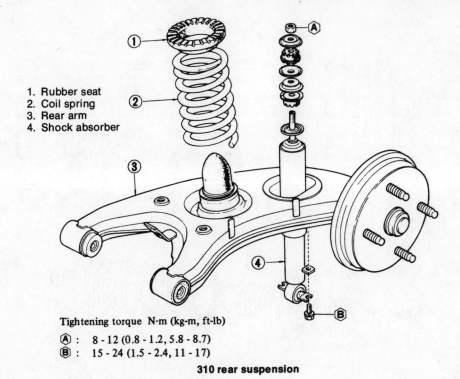

1. Rubber seat
2. Coil spring
3. Rear arm
4. Shock absorber

Tightening torque N·m (kg-m, ft-lb)

Ⓐ : 8 - 12 (0.8 - 1.2, 5.8 - 8.7)

Ⓑ : 15 - 24 (1.5 - 2.4, 11 - 17)

310 rear suspension

2. Remove the upper nut and the lower mounting bolt form the shock absorber.

3. Remove the shock absorber from the vehicle.

4. To install, reverse the removal procedures. Torque the upper shock absorber nut to 6.5–8.7 ft.lb. and the lower shock absorber bolt to 51–65 ft.lb.

Strut

REMOVAL AND INSTALLATION

Stanza

1. Raise and support the rear of the vehicle on jackstands.

2. Remove the wheel/tire assembly.

3. Disconnect the brake tube and the parking brake cable.

4. If necessary, remove the brake assembly and wheel bearing.

5. Detach the parallel links and radius rod from the strut.

6. Support the strut with a jackstand.

7. Remove the strut upper end nuts and the strut from the vehicle.

8. To install, reverse the removal procedures. Torque the strut-to-parallel link nuts to 65–87 ft.lb., the strut-to-radius rod nuts to 54–69 ft.lb. and the strut-to-body nuts to 23–31 ft.lb.

Rear End Alignment

The camber is preset at the factory and cannot be adjusted; if the camber alignment is not within specifications, check the associated parts, then repair or replace them. The camber angle is 0–1½°P.

The only adjustments that can be performed are the toe-in and the vehicle posture.

INSPECTION

Before checking the wheel alignment, be sure to make a preliminary check of all the rear end parts: tire pressure, wheel bearing axial play, shock absorber operation, tighten each rear axle and suspension parts, measure the vehicle height (unloaded) and repair or replace any damaged parts.

TOE-IN ADJUSTMENT–STANZA

The toe-in can be adjusted by varying the position of the parallel link bracket.

1. Position the rear wheels on a turning radius gauge.

2. Temporarily tighten the bracket on one side with the fixing bolt.

3. Turn the rear wheels from left to right, then tighten the bracket with the bolt in the middle of the turning angle.

4. Position the other bracket, so that a toe-in of (-)½°–⅔° (1982–83) or (-)⅔°–½° (1984 and later) is obtained.

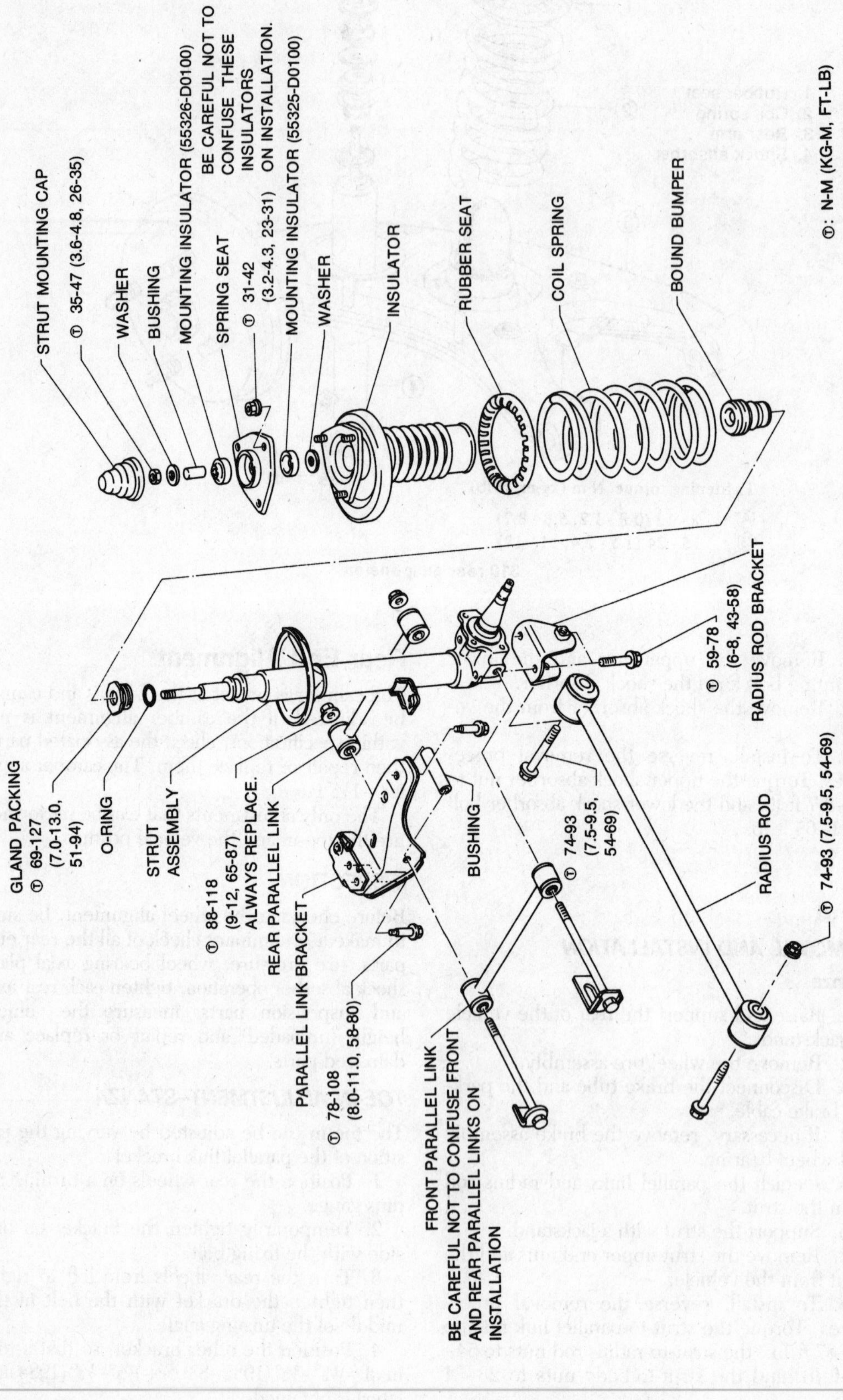

STRUT MOUNTING CAP
Ⓣ 35-47 (3.6-4.8, 26-35)
WASHER
BUSHING
MOUNTING INSULATOR (55326-D0100)
SPRING SEAT
Ⓣ 31-42 (3.2-4.3, 23-31)
MOUNTING INSULATOR (55325-D0100)
WASHER
INSULATOR
RUBBER SEAT
COIL SPRING
BOUND BUMPER

BE CAREFUL NOT TO CONFUSE THESE INSULATORS ON INSTALLATION.

Ⓣ: N-M (KG-M, FT-LB)

GLAND PACKING
Ⓣ 69-127 (7.0-13.0, 51-94)
O-RING
STRUT ASSEMBLY
Ⓣ 88-118 (9-12, 65-87) ALWAYS REPLACE.
REAR PARALLEL LINK
PARALLEL LINK BRACKET
Ⓣ 78-108 (8.0-11.0, 58-80)
FRONT PARALLEL LINK
BE CAREFUL NOT TO CONFUSE FRONT AND REAR PARALLEL LINKS ON INSTALLATION
BUSHING
Ⓣ 74-93 (7.5-9.5, 54-69)
RADIUS ROD
Ⓣ 74-93 (7.5-9.5, 54-69)
RADIUS ROD BRACKET
Ⓣ 59-78 (6-8, 43-58)

Stanza rear suspension

WHEEL BEARING PRELOAD ADJUSTMENT

After the wheel bearing has been replaced, it will be necessary to adjust the wheel bearing preload.

1. Clean all of the parts thoroughly.
2. Lubricate all of the parts with multi-purpose grease.
3. Torque the wheel bearing nut to 18–22 ft.lb. (F10) or 29–33 ft.lb. (all other models).
4. Turn the wheel hub several times in both directions.
5. Retorque the wheel bearing nut.
6. Loosen the wheel bearing nut 90°, align the castle nut slot with the hole in the axle shaft and install a cotter pin.

STEERING

Steering Wheel

REMOVAL AND INSTALLATION

1. Position the wheels in the straight-ahead direction. The steering wheel should be right-side up and level.
2. Disconnect the battery ground cable.
3. Some models have countersunk screws on the back of the steering wheel, remove the screws and pull off the horn pad.
NOTE: *Some models have a horn wire running from the pad to the steering wheel; disconnect it.*
4. Remove the rest of the horn switching mechanism, noting the relative location of the parts. Remove the mechanism only if it hinders subsequent wheel removal procedures.
5. Match-mark the top of the steering column shaft and the steering wheel flange.
6. Remove the attaching nut. Using the Steering Wheel Remover tool ST27180001, pull the steering wheel from the steering column.
CAUTION: *Do not strike the shaft with a hammer, which may cause the column to collapse.*
7. Install the steering wheel in the reverse order of removal, aligning the punch marks; DO NOT drive or hammer the wheel.
8. Tighten the steering wheel nut to 14–18 ft.lb. (F10), 22–25 ft.lb. (310), 29–40 ft.lb. (Pulsar) and 27–38 ft.lb. (Stanza).
9. Reinstall the horn button, pad or ring.

Turn Signal Switch

REMOVAL AND INSTALLATION

On some later models, the turn signal switch is part of a combination switch. The whole unit is removed together.

Except Pulsar (1984 and Later)

1. Refer to the Steering Wheel, Removal and Installation procedures, in this section and remove the steering wheel.
2. Remove the steering column cover(s).
3. Disconnect the electrical connectors from the switch.
4. Remove the retaining screws and the switch from the steering column.
5. To install, reverse the removal procedures.
NOTE: *Many models have turn signal switches that have a tab which must fit into a hole in the steering shaft in order for the system to return the switch to the neutral position after the turn has been made. Be sure to align the tab and the hole when installing.*

Pulsar (1984 and Later)

1. Disconnect the negative battery terminal.
2. Remove the steering column covers.
3. Disconnect the electrical connector from the turn signal side of the combination switch.
4. Remove the retaining screws and separate the turn signal switch from the combination switch.
5. To install, reverse the removal procedures.

Steering Lock/Ignition Lock

REMOVAL AND INSTALLATION

The steering lock/ignition switch assembly is attached to the steering column by special screws whose heads shear off on installation. The screws must be drilled out to remove the assembly.

1. Refer to the Steering Wheel, Removal and Installation procedures, in this section and remove the steering wheel.
2. Remove the steering column cover(s).
3. Using a drill, drill out the self-shear type screws of the steering lock retainer.
NOTE: *The F10 models use only 2 self-shearing screws to hold the steering lock onto the steering column. All other models use 2 self-shearing screws and 2 regular screws.*
4. Remove the screws and the steering lock from the steering column.
5. To install, use new self-shearing screws and reverse the removal procedures. Torque the self-shearing type screws until the heads break off.

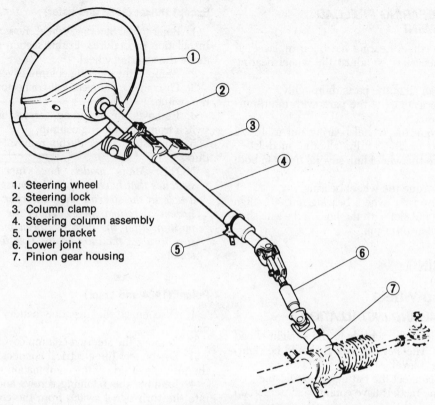

1. Steering wheel
2. Steering lock
3. Column clamp
4. Steering column assembly
5. Lower bracket
6. Lower joint
7. Pinion gear housing

F10 and 310 steering column

Tie-Rod Ends (Steering Side Rods)
REMOVAL AND INSTALLATION

1. Raise the front of the vehicle and support it on jack stands. Remove the wheel/tire assembly.

2. Locate the faulty tie-rod end. It will have a lot of play in it and the dust cover will probably be ripped.

3. Remove the cotter pin and the tie-rod ball joint stud nut. Note the position of the steering linkage.

4. Loosen the tie-rod-to-steering gear locknut.

5. Using the Ball Joint Remover tool HT72520000, remove the tie-rod ball joint from the strut or the steering knuckle.

6. Loosen the locknut and remove the tie-rod end from the tie-rod, counting the number of turns it takes to completely free it.

7. Install the new tie-rod end, turning it in exactly as far as you screwed out the old one. Make sure it is correctly positioned in relationship to the steering linkage.

8. Fit the ball joint and nut, tighten them and install a new cotter pin. Torque the ball joint stud nut to 40–47 ft.lb. (F10 and 310),

22–29 ft.lb. (Stanza) or 22–36 ft.lb. (Pulsar) and the ball joint-to-tie-rod end locknut to 27–34 ft.lb.

NOTE: *Before finally tightening the tie-rod lock nut or clamp, adjust the toe-in of the vehicle. See section under Front Suspension.*

Power Steering Pump
REMOVAL AND INSTALLATION

1. Remove the hoses at the pump and plug and openings shut to prevent contamination. Position the disconnected lines in a raised attitude to prevent leakage.

2. Loosen the power steering pump drive belt adjuster and the drive belt.

3. Loosen the retaining bolts, then remove the braces and the pump from the vehicle.

4. To install, reverse the removal procedures. Adjust the belt tension and bleed the power steering system.

BLEEDING THE POWER STEERING SYSTEM

1. Fill the pump reservoir and allow to remain undisturbed for a few minutes.

2. Raise the car until the front wheels are clear of the ground.

3. With the engine off, quickly turn the

wheels right and left several times, lightly contacting the stops.

4. Add fluid if necessary.

5. Start the engine and let it idle until it reaches operating temperatures.

6. Repeat Steps 3 and 4 with the engine idling.

NOTE: *Do not allow the steering linkage to contact the stops for any longer than 15 seconds, with the engine running.*

7. Stop the engine, lower the car until the wheels just touch the ground. Start the engine, allow it to idle and turn the wheels back and forth several times. Check the fluid level and refill if necessary.

Manual Steering Gear

REMOVAL AND INSTALLATION

F10 and 310

1. Raise and support the car on jackstands.
2. Remove the steering joint cover and re-

move the steering column-to-lower joint bolts.

3. Remove the lower joint-to-steering pinion gear bolt and disconnect the joint from the gear.

4. Remove the tie-rod ball stud nuts.

5. Using the Ball Joint Remover tool HT72520000, remove the tie-rod ball studs.

6. Unclamp and remove the steering gear.

7. To install, reverse the removal procedures. Torque the tie-rod-to-knuckle arm nut to 40–47 ft.lb., the steering gear-to-frame clamp bolts to 16–25 ft.lb., the lower joint-to-pinion gear bolt to 17–22 ft.lb. and the lower joint-to-steering column bolt to 17–22 ft.lb.

8. Check the wheel alignment.

Pulsar and Stanza

1. Raise and support the car on jackstands.
2. Using the Ball Joint Remover tool HT72520000, remove the tie-rod from the knuckle.
3. Loosen, but do not remove, the steering gear mounting bolts.

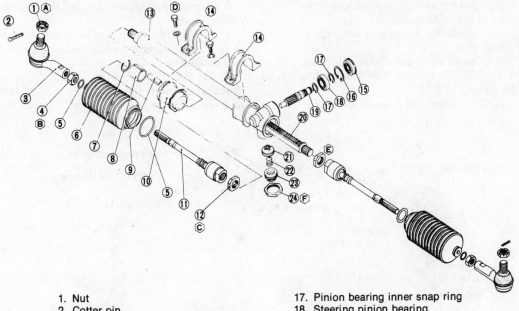

1. Nut	17. Pinion bearing inner snap ring
2. Cotter pin	18. Steering pinion bearing
3. Side rod outer socket assembly	19. Steering gear pinion
4. Lock nut	20. Steering rack gear
5. Boot clamp	21. Retainer
6. Boot	22. Retainer spring
7. Snap ring	23. Adjust screw
8. Steering rack bushing	24. Adjust screw lock nut
9. Plate	Tightening torque:N-m (kg-m, ft-lb)
10. Steering gear mount	Ⓐ 54-64 (5.5-6.5, 40-47)
11. Side rod inner socket assembly	Ⓑ 37-46 (3.8-4.7, 27-34)
12. Lock nut	Ⓒ 78-98 (8-10, 58-72)
13. Steering gear housing assembly	Ⓓ 22-33 (2.2-3.4, 16-25)
14. Steering clamp	Ⓔ 78-98 (8-10, 58-72)
15. Oil seal	Ⓕ 39-59 (4-6, 29-43)
16. Pinion bearing outer snap ring	

F10 and 310 manual steering gear

4. Remove the steering column lower joint.

5. Unbolt and remove the gear.

6. To install, reverse the removal procedures. Torque the tie-rod-to-steering knuckle nut to 22–29 ft.lb. (Stanza) or 26–35 ft.lb. (Pulsar), the steering gear-to-frame clamp bolts to 43–58 ft.lb., the lower joint-to-pinion gear bolt to 23–31 ft.lb. (Stanza) or 22–29 ft.lb. (Pulsar) and the lower joint-to-steering column bolt to 23–31 ft.lb. (Stanza) or 22–29 ft.lb. (Pulsar).

NOTE: *When installing the lower steering joint to the steering gear, make sure that the wheels are aligned with the vehicle and the steering joint slot is aligned with the steering gear cap or spacer mark.*

Power Steering Gear
REMOVAL AND INSTALLATION
310

1. Raise and support the front of the car on jackstands.

2. Remove the lower joint cover and loosen, but do not remove the bolts attaching the lower joint at the column.

3. Unbolt the lower joint from the steering pinion gear.

4. Using the Ball Joint Remover tool HT72520000, remove the tie-rod from the knuckle.

5. Disconnect the hoses at the gear.

6. Unbolt and remove the gear linkage.

7. To install, reverse the removal procedures, then bleed the power steering system and check the wheel alignment. Torque the side rod-to-knuckle arm nut to 40–47 ft.lb., the steering gear clamp bolts to 16–25 ft.lb., the steering gear-to-sub frame bolts to 16–25 ft.lb., the lower joint-to-pinion gear bolt to 17–22 ft.lb., the lower joint-to-steering column bolt to 17–22 ft.lb. and the power steering hoses-to-steering gear to 36–51 ft.lb.

Pulsar

1. Raise and support the car on jackstands.

2. Disconnect the hose clamp and hose at the steering gear. Disconnect the flare nut and the tube at the steering gear, then drain the fluid from the gear.

3. Using the Ball Joint Remover tool HT72520000, remove the tie-rod from the knuckle.

4. Place a floor jack under the transaxle and support it.

5. Remove the exhaust tube and the the rear engine mount.

6. Remove the steering column lower joint.

7. Unbolt and remove the steering gear unit and the linkage.

8. To install, reverse the removal procedures, then bleed the power steering system and check the wheel alignment. Torque the

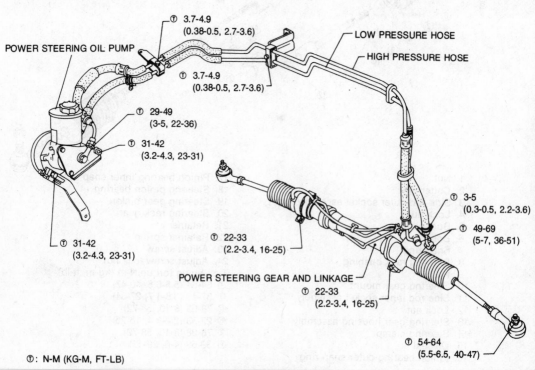

POWER STEERING OIL PUMP

Ⓣ 3.7-4.9
(0.38-0.5, 2.7-3.6)

Ⓣ 3.7-4.9
(0.38-0.5, 2.7-3.6)

Ⓣ 29-49
(3-5, 22-36)

Ⓣ 31-42
(3.2-4.3, 23-31)

Ⓣ 31-42
(3.2-4.3, 23-31)

LOW PRESSURE HOSE

HIGH PRESSURE HOSE

Ⓣ 3-5
(0.3-0.5, 2.2-3.6)

Ⓣ 49-69
(5-7, 36-51)

Ⓣ 22-33
(2.2-3.4, 16-25)

POWER STEERING GEAR AND LINKAGE
Ⓣ 22-33
(2.2-3.4, 16-25)

Ⓣ 54-64
(5.5-6.5, 40-47)

Ⓣ: N-M (KG-M, FT-LB)

310 power steering gear

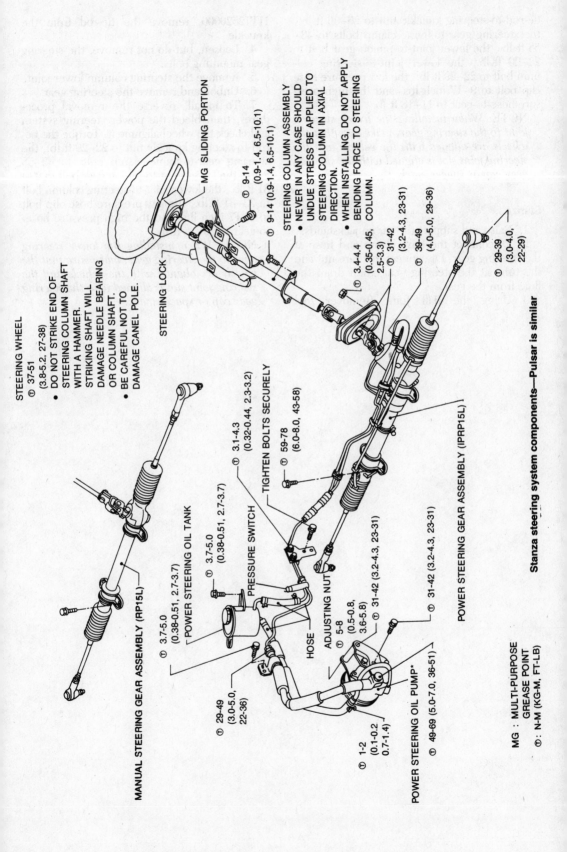

STEERING WHEEL
Ⓣ 37-51
(3.8-5.2, 27-38)
• DO NOT STRIKE END OF
STEERING COLUMN SHAFT
WITH A HAMMER.
STRIKING SHAFT WILL
DAMAGE NEEDLE BEARING
OR COLUMN SHAFT.
• BE CAREFUL NOT TO
DAMAGE CANEL POLE.

MG SLIDING PORTION

Ⓣ 9-14
(0.9-1.4, 6.5-10.1)

Ⓣ 9-14 (0.9-1.4, 6.5-10.1)

STEERING LOCK

STEERING COLUMN ASSEMBLY
• NEVER IN ANY CASE SHOULD
UNDUE STRESS BE APPLIED TO
STEERING COLUMN IN AXIAL
DIRECTION.
• WHEN INSTALLING, DO NOT APPLY
BENDING FORCE TO STEERING
COLUMN.

Ⓣ 3.4-4.4
(0.35-0.45,
2.5-3.3)

31-42
(3.2-4.3, 23-31)

39-49
(4.0-5.0, 29-36)

Ⓣ 29-39
(3.0-4.0,
22-29)

Ⓣ 3.1-4.3
(0.32-0.44, 2.3-3.2)

Ⓣ 59-78
(6.0-8.0, 43-58)

TIGHTEN BOLTS SECURELY

PRESSURE SWITCH

Ⓣ 3.7-5.0
(0.38-0.51, 2.7-3.7)

POWER STEERING OIL TANK

Ⓣ 3.7-5.0
(0.38-0.51, 2.7-3.7)

MANUAL STEERING GEAR ASSEMBLY (RP15L)

Ⓣ 29-49
(3.0-5.0,
22-36)

HOSE

ADJUSTING NUT

Ⓣ 5-8
(0.5-0.8,
3.6-5.8)

Ⓣ 1-2
(0.1-0.2
0.7-1.4)

POWER STEERING OIL PUMP*

Ⓣ 49-69 (5.0-7.0, 36-51)

Ⓣ 31-42 (3.2-4.3, 23-31)

Ⓣ 31-42 (3.2-4.3, 23-31)

POWER STEERING GEAR ASSEMBLY (IPRP15L)

MG : MULTI-PURPOSE
GREASE POINT
Ⓣ : N-M (KG-M, FT-LB)

Stanza steering system components—Pulsar is similar

tie-rod-to-steering knuckle nut to 26–36 ft.lb., the steering gear-to-frame clamp bolts to 43–58 ft.lb., the lower joint-to-pinion gear bolt to 22–29 ft.lb., the lower joint-to-steering column bolt to 22–29 ft.lb., the low pressure hose clip bolt to 9–17 inch lbs. and the high pressure hose-to-gear to 11–18 ft.lb.

NOTE: *When installing the lower steering joint to the steering gear, make sure that the wheels are aligned with the vehicle and the steering joint slot is aligned with the steering gear cap or spacer mark.*

Stanza

1. Raise and support the car on jackstands.
2. Disconnect the hose clamp and hose at the steering gear. Disconnect the flare nut and the tube at the steering gear, then drain the fluid from the gear.
3. Using the Ball Joint Remover tool HT72520000, remove the tie-rod from the knuckle.
4. Loosen, but do not remove, the steering gear mounting bolts.
5. Remove the steering column lower joint.
6. Unbolt and remove the steering gear.
7. To install, reverse the removal procedures, then bleed the power steering system and check the wheel alignment. Torque the tie-rod-to-steering knuckle nut to 22–29 ft.lb., the steering gear-to-frame clamp bolts to 43–58 ft.lb., the lower joint-to-pinion gear bolt to 23–31 ft.lb., the lower joint-to-steering column bolt to 23–31 ft.lb., the low pressure hose clip bolt to 9–17 inch lbs. and the high pressure hose-to-gear to 29–36 ft.lb.

NOTE: *When installing the lower steering joint to the steering gear, make sure that the wheels are aligned with the vehicle and the steering joint slot is aligned with the steering gear cap or spacer mark.*

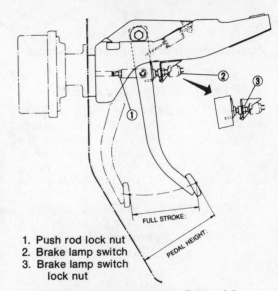

BRAKE SYSTEM

Adjustments

TOOTHED ADJUSTING NUT

1. Raise and support the rear of the vehicle on jackstands.

2. Remove the rubber cover from the backing plate.

3. Insert a brake adjusting tool through the hole in the brake backing plate. Turn the toothed adjusting nut to spread the brake shoes, making contact with the brake drum.

NOTE: *When adjusting the brake shoes, turn the wheel until considerable drag is felt. If necessary, rap the brake drum with a rubber hammer to align the shoes with the drum.*

4. When considerable drag is felt, back off the adjusting nut a few notches, so that the correct clearance is maintained between the brake drum and the brake shoes. Make sure that the wheel rotates freely.

1. Push rod lock nut
2. Brake lamp switch
3. Brake lamp switch lock nut

Typical brake pedal adjustment—F10 model

AUTOMATIC ADJUSTERS

No manual adjustment is necessary. The self adjuster operates whenever the hand or foot brake brakes (on some models) are used.

After Adjustment—All Models

After adjusting the brakes, make sure that there is no rear wheel drag with the hand-brake released. Loosen the hand-brake adjustment, if necessary.

BRAKE PEDAL HEIGHT ADJUSTMENT

Before adjusting the pedal, make sure that the wheel-brakes are correctly adjusted. Adjust the pedal height with the input rod, attached to the top of the brake pedal. Pedal height (floorboard to pedal pad) should be 7 in. (F10), 7¼ in. (301), 6 in. (Stanza) and 7⅞ in. (Pulsar).

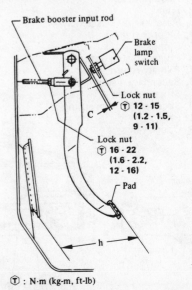

ⓣ : N·m (kg-m, ft-lb)

Pedal adjustments for the Pulsar (1983–84)—310 and Stanza are similar

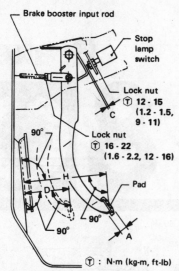

Pedal adjustments for the Pulsar (1985 and later)

STOP LIGHT SWITCH ADJUSTMENT

Adjust the clearance between the brake pedal and the stop lamp switch or the ASCD switch, by loosening the locknut and adjusting the switch. The clearance should be approximately 0.04–0.20 in. for 310, 0–0.04 in. for Pulsar and Stanza (1982–84) or 0.012–0.039 in. for Stanza (1985 and later).

NOTE: *On the F10 models, the stop light switch is adjusted so that the switch is not activated when the brake pedal is relaxed.*

HYDRAULIC SYSTEM

Master Cylinder

REMOVAL AND INSTALLATION

1. Clean the outside of the master cylinder thoroughly, particularly around the cap and fluid lines. Disconnect the fluid lines and cap them to exclude dirt.

2. If equipped with a fluid level sensor, disconnect the wiring harness from the master cylinder.

3. Disconnect the brake fluid tubes, then plug the openings to prevent dirt from entering the system.

4. Remove the mounting bolts at the firewall or the brake booster (if equipped) and remove the master cylinder from the vehicle.

5. To install, reverse the removal procedures. Refill the reservoir with brake fluid and bleed the system.

NOTE: *Ordinary brake fluid will boil and cause brake failure under the high temperatures developed in disc brake systems; use DOT 3 brake fluid in the brake systems.*

OVERHAUL

CAUTION: *Master cylinders are supplied to the manufacturer by two suppliers: Nabco and Tokico. Parts between these manufacturers are not interchangeable. Be sure you obtain the correct rebuilding kit for your master cylinder.*

1. Reservoir cap
2. Filter
3. Reservoir tank assembly
4. Stopper ring
5. Stopper
6. Primary piston assembly
7. Primary return spring
8. Secondary piston assembly
9. Stopper screw
10. Secondary return spring
11. Plug
12. Check valve

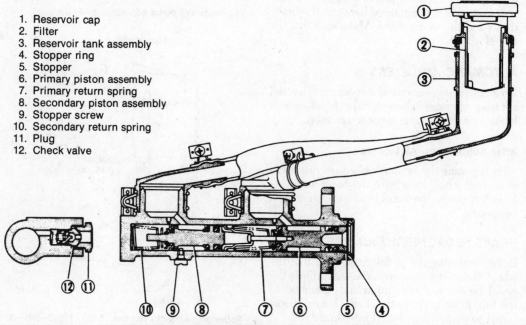

F10 master cylinder

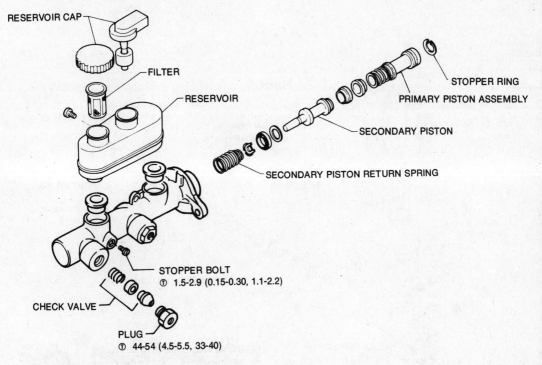

RESERVOIR CAP

FILTER

RESERVOIR

STOPPER RING

PRIMARY PISTON ASSEMBLY

SECONDARY PISTON

SECONDARY PISTON RETURN SPRING

STOPPER BOLT
Ⓣ 1.5-2.9 (0.15-0.30, 1.1-2.2)

CHECK VALVE

PLUG
Ⓣ 44-54 (4.5-5.5, 33-40)

Ⓣ: N-M (KG-M, FI-LB)

310 master cylinder

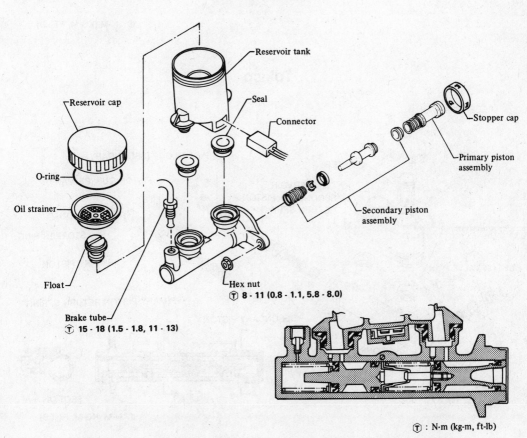

Reservoir tank

Reservoir cap

Seal

Connector

Stopper cap

O-ring

Primary piston
assembly

Oil strainer

Secondary piston
assembly

Float

Hex nut
Ⓣ 8 - 11 (0.8 - 1.1, 5.8 - 8.0)

Brake tube
Ⓣ 15 - 18 (1.5 - 1.8, 11 - 13)

Ⓣ : N·m (kg-m, ft-lb)

Exploded view of master cylinder used on Stanza (1984 and later) and Pulsar

Nabco

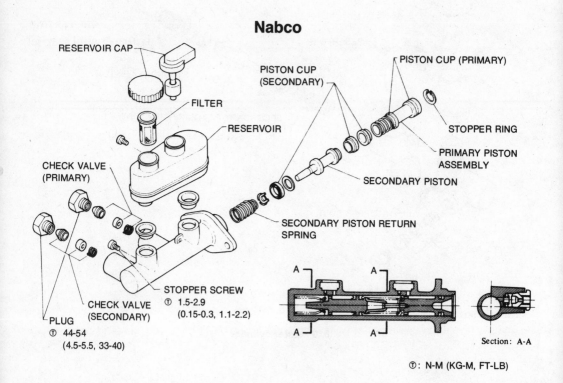

Tokico

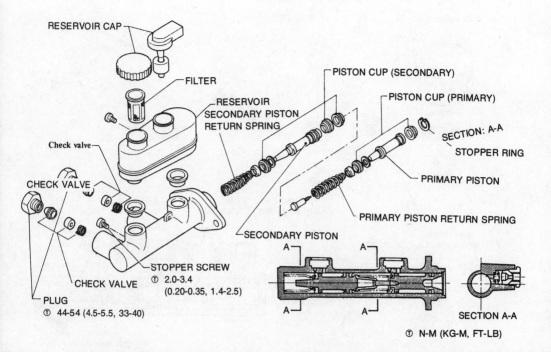

Exploded view of the master cylinders—Stanza (1982–83) and Pulsar (1983–84)

The master cylinder can be disassembled using the illustrations as a guide. Clean all of the parts in clean brake fluid. Replace the cylinder or piston (as necessary), if the clearance between the two exceeds 0.006 in. Lubricate all of the parts with clean brake fluid on assembly.

NOTE: *Master cylinder rebuilding kits, containing all the wearing parts, are available to simplify the overhaul.*

Power Booster
REMOVAL AND INSTALLATION

1. Remove the master cylinder mounting nuts and pull the master cylinder assembly (brake lines connected) away from the power booster.
2. Detach the vacuum lines from the booster.
3. Detach the booster pushrod at the pedal clevis.
4. Unbolt the booster from under the dash and lift it out of the engine compartment.
5. Installation is the reverse of removal. Adjust the length of the pushrod so that the distance between the pushrod clevis hole and the rear face of the booster is 5.12 in. (310 and Stanza) or 5.91 in. (Pulsar). On the F10 models, measure the length of the push rod at the front of the power booster; the distance between the front of the power booster and the master cylinder is 0.38–0.39. Torque the master cylinder to-booster nuts to 6–8 ft.lb.; the booster-to-firewall nuts to 6–8 ft.lb.

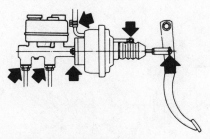

Power booster attaching points

Brake Proportioning Valve

All models covered in this guide are equipped with brake proportioning valves of several different types. The valves all do the same job, which is to separate the front and rear brake lines, allowing them to function independently and preventing the rear brakes from locking before the front brakes. Damage, such as brake line leakage, in either the front or the rear brake system will not affect the normal operation of the unaffected system. If, in the event of a panic stop, the rear brakes lock up before the front brakes, it could mean the proportioning valve is defective. In that case, replace the entire proportioning valve.

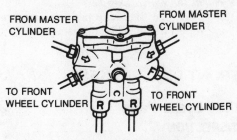

Proportioning valve—310, Stanza and Pulsar

REMOVAL AND INSTALLATION

1. Remove the brake line tubes from the proportioning valve, then plug the openings to prevent dirt from entering the system.
2. Remove the mounting bolt(s) and the valve from the vehicle.
3. To install, reverse the removal procedures. Refill the master cylinder reservoir and bleed the brake system.

System Bleeding

Bleeding is required whenever air in the hydraulic fluid causes a spongy feeling pedal and sluggish response. This is almost always the case after some part of the hydraulic system has been repaired or replaced.

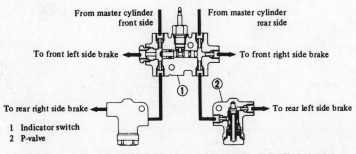

Cut-away view of the proportioning valve used on the F10 model

1. Fill the master cylinder reservoir with DOT 3 brake fluid.

2. The usual procedure is to bleed at the points farthest from the master cylinder first.

3. Fit a rubber hose over the bleeder screw. Submerge the other end of the hole in clean brake fluid in a clear glass container. Loosen the bleeder screw.

4. Slowly pump the brake pedal several times until fluid free of bubbles is discharged. An assistant is required to pump the pedal.

5. On the last pumping stroke, hold the pedal down and tighten the bleeder screw. Check the fluid level periodically during the bleeding operation.

NOTE: *Bleed the front brakes in the same way as the rear brakes.*

6. Check that the brake pedal is now firm. If not, repeat the bleeding operation.

FRONT DISC BRAKES

Disc Brake Pads

INSPECTION

You should be able to check the pad lining thickness without removing the pads. Check the Brake Specifications Chart at the end of this chapter to find the manufacturer's pad wear limit. However, this measurement may disagree with your state inspection laws. When replacing pads, always check the surface of the

rotors for scoring or wear. The rotors should be removed for resurfacing if badly scored.

REMOVAL AND INSTALLATION

F10 and 310

1. Raise and support the front of the vehicle on jackstands, then remove the wheel/tire assemblies.

2. Remove the clip, pull out the pins and remove the pad springs.

3. Remove the pads by pulling them out with pliers.

4. To install, first lightly coat the yoke groove and the end surface of the piston with grease. Do not allow grease to contact the pads or rotor.

5. Open the bleeder screw slightly and push the outer piston into the cylinder until its end aligns with the end of the boot retaining ring. Do not push too far, which will require disassembly of the caliper to correct it. Install the inner pad.

6. Pull the yoke toward the outside of the car to push the inner piston into place. Install the outer pad.

7. Apply the brakes a few times to seat the pads. Check the master cylinder and add fluid if necessary. Bleed the brakes, if necessary.

Stanza and Pulsar

1. Raise and support the front of the vehicle on jackstands, then remove the wheel/tire assemblies.

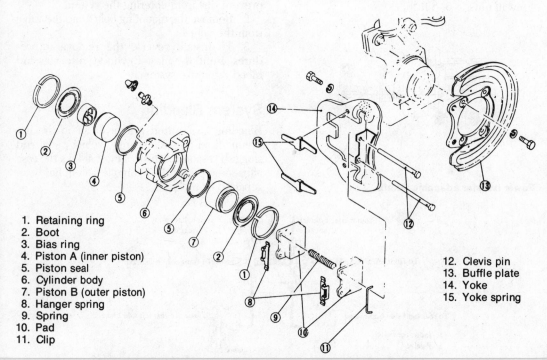

1. Retaining ring
2. Boot
3. Bias ring
4. Piston A (inner piston)
5. Piston seal
6. Cylinder body
7. Piston B (outer piston)
8. Hanger spring
9. Spring
10. Pad
11. Clip

12. Clevis pin
13. Buffle plate
14. Yoke
15. Yoke spring

Exploded view of the 310 front disc brakes—F10 is similar

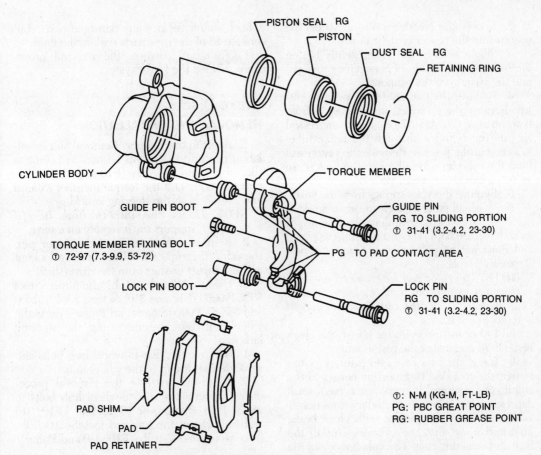

PISTON SEAL RG
PISTON
DUST SEAL RG
RETAINING RING
CYLINDER BODY
TORQUE MEMBER
GUIDE PIN BOOT
GUIDE PIN
RG TO SLIDING PORTION
Ⓣ 31-41 (3.2-4.2, 23-30)
TORQUE MEMBER FIXING BOLT
Ⓣ 72-97 (7.3-9.9, 53-72)
PG TO PAD CONTACT AREA
LOCK PIN BOOT
LOCK PIN
RG TO SLIDING PORTION
Ⓣ 31-41 (3.2-4.2, 23-30)
PAD SHIM
PAD
PAD RETAINER

Ⓣ: N-M (KG-M, FT-LB)
PG: PBC GREAT POINT
RG: RUBBER GREASE POINT

Exploded view of the Stanza front brakes—Pulsar is similar

2. Remove the bottom guide pin (Stanza) or the lock pin (Pulsar) from the caliper and swing the caliper cylinder body upward.

3. Remove the brake pad retainers and the pads.

4. To install, reverse the removal procedures. Torque the guide pin to 23–30 ft.lb.

Calipers

REMOVAL AND INSTALLATION

F10

1. Refer to the Disc Brake Pads, Removal and Installation procedures, in this section and remove the brake pads.

2. Disconnect and plug the brake tube from the caliper assembly.

3. Remove the caliper-to-steering knuckle mounting bolts, then remove the caliper from the vehicle.

4. To install, reverse the removal procedures. Bleed the brake system.

310

1. Refer to the Disc Brake Pads, Removal and Installation procedures, in this section and remove the brake pads.

2. Disconnect and plug the brake tube from the caliper assembly.

3. Remove the steering knuckle arm-to-strut assembly nut(s) and separate the assembly.

4. Remove the caliper-to-steering knuckle spindle mounting bolts, then remove the caliper from the strut.

5. To install, reverse the removal procedures. Bleed the brake system.

Stanza and Pulsar

1. Raise and support the vehicle on jackstands, then remove the wheel/tire assemblies.

2. Disconnect and plug the brake tube at the brake hose connection.

3. Remove the torque member-to-steering knuckle mounting bolts, then remove the caliper assembly from the vehicle.

4. To install, reverse the removal procedures. Bleed the brake system.

OVERHAUL

F10 and 310

1. Refer to the Caliper, Removal and Installation procedures, in this section and remove the cylinder body from the caliper assembly.

2. Loosen the bleeder screw and press the pistons into the center of their bores.

3. While holding the yoke, gently tap on the inboard piston side of the caliper to separate the yoke from the caliper.

4. Remove the bias ring from primary piston. Remove the retaining rings and boots from both pistons. GRADUALLY, feed compressed air into the cylinder (through the brake tube) to force out the pistons. Remove the piston seal from the cylinder carefully with the fingers, so as not to mar the cylinder wall.

5. Remove the yoke springs from the yoke.

6. Wash all parts with clean brake fluid.

7. If the piston or cylinder is badly worn or scored, replace both. The piston surface is plated and must not be polished with emery paper. Replace all seals.

NOTE: *The rotor can be removed and machined if scored, but final thickness must be at least 0.331 in. Runout must not exceed 0.001 in.*

8. Lubricate the cylinder bore with clean brake fluid and install the piston seal.

9. Insert the bias ring into primary piston so that the rounded ring portion comes to the bottom of the piston. Primary piston has a small depression inside, while secondary does not.

10. Lubricate the pistons with clean brake fluid and insert into the cylinder. Install the boot and retaining ring. The yoke groove of the bias ring of primary piston must align with the yoke groove of the cylinder.

11. Install the yoke springs to the yoke so the projecting portion faces to the disc (rotor).

12. Lubricate the sliding portion of the cylinder and yoke. Assemble the cylinder and yoke by tapping the yoke lightly.

13. Replace the caliper assembly and pads. Torque the caliper mounting bolts to 40–47 ft.lb., the disc rotor bolts to 18–25 ft.lb. and the strut bolt torque is 33–44 ft.lb. Bleed the system of air.

Stanza and Pulsar

1. Refer to the Caliper, Removal and Installation procedures, in this section and remove the cylinder body and the torque member from the steering knuckle.

2. Remove the brake tube from the cylinder body.

3. Using compressed air, GRADUALLY, force the piston and the dust seal out of the cylinder body.

CAUTION: *Place a piece of wood in the jaws of the caliper to catch the piston, in case it leaves the caliper too fast.*

4. Remove the piston seal.

5. Clean all of the parts in clean brake fluid.

Check and/or replace any damaged parts. Lubricate all of the new parts with brake fluid.

6. To install, reverse the removal procedures. Bleed the brake system.

Brake Disc
REMOVAL AND INSTALLATION

1. Refer to the Caliper, Removal and Installation procedures, in this section and remove the caliper and the yoke (F10 and 310) or the cylinder body and the torque member (Stanza and Pulsar) from the steering knuckle.

NOTE: *Do not disconnect the brake tube (if possible), support the assembly on a wire.*

2. Remove the grease cap, the cotter pin, the adjusting cap, the wheel bearing locknut and the thrust washer from the drive shaft.

3. Using Wheel Hub Remover tool ST35100000 (F10 and 310) or tools KV40101000 and ST36230000 (Stanza and Pulsar), press the wheel hub/disc assembly from the steering knuckle.

4. Remove the disc-to-wheel hub bolts and separate the disc from the wheel hub.

5. To install, reverse the removal procedures. Torque the disc-to-wheel hub bolts to 28–38 ft.lb. (Stanza) or 18–25 ft.lb. (F10, 310 and Pulsar) and the hub nut to 145–203 ft.lb. (Stanza) or 87–145 ft.lb. (F10, 310 and Pulsar).

INSPECTION

1. Check the disc for cracks and/or chips, if necessary, replace the disc.

2. Using a dial indicator, check the runout of the disc, it should be less than 0.0059 in. (F10), 0.005 in. (310), 0.003 in. (Stanza and Pulsar); if greater than the maximum, replace the disc.

3. Using a dial indicator, check the parallelism of the disc, it should be less than 0.0012 in., if greater than the maximum, replace the disc.

4. Using a micrometer, check the thickness of the disc; it should be greater than 0.339 in. (F10 and 310), 0.63 in. (Stanza) or 0.39 in. (Pulsar), if not, replace the disc.

Wheel Bearings
REMOVAL AND INSTALLATION
Stanza and Pulsar

1. Refer to the Caliper, Removal and Installation procedures, in this section and remove the caliper and the yoke (F10 and 310) or the cylinder body and the torque member (Stanza and Pulsar) from the steering knuckle.

2. Remove the grease cap, the cotter pin and the adjusting cap, then loosen the hub nut.

3. Using the Ball Joint Remover tool HT72520000, remove the tie-rod from steering knuckle; if necessary, use the same tool to separate the control arm ball joint from the steering knuckle.

4. Remove the ball joint-to-lower control arm mounting bolts and separate the ball joint from the control arm.

5. Drain the fluid from the transaxle. Remove the axleshaft from the transaxle and insert a tool to prevent the side gear from dropping into the case.

NOTE: *When the drive shaft is removed from the transaxle, replace the transaxle oil seal and the circlip on the end of the axleshaft.*

6. Remove the strut-to-steering knuckle assembly and the assembly from the vehicle.

7. Connect the Wheel Hub Remover tool ST35100000 (F10 and 310) or tools KV40101000 and ST36230000 (Stanza and Pulsar), then press the wheel hub assembly from the axleshaft.

8. Using a wheel puller, press the outer wheel bearing from the wheel hub. The inner wheel bearing can be removed after removing the grease seal from the steering knuckle.

9. If necessary to remove the wheel bearing races from the steering knuckle, use an internal wheel puller to extract them.

10. Clean all of the parts in cleaning solvent and blow dry with compressed air. Check for damaged parts and replace as necessary.

11. Using a brass drift, drive the new wheel bearing races into the steering knuckle, until they seat against the housing.

12. Using the palm of the hand, force multi-purpose grease into the bearings. Install a new grease seal onto the wheel hub, then press the outer bearing onto the wheel hub until it seats against the shoulder. Install the inner bearing in the steering knuckle, followed by a new grease seal.

NOTE: *To determine the spacer thickness (between the wheel bearings), measure the distance between the outer races (installed in the steering knuckle) and substract 0.0209 in. from that dimension, then insert a spacer of that size.*

13. Place the axleshaft into the steering knuckle, fit the wheel hub onto the axleshaft serrations and torque the assembly together.

14. To complete the installation, reverse the removal procedures.

REAR DRUM BRAKES

Brake Drum

REMOVAL AND INSTALLATION

1. Raise the rear of the vehicle and support it on jackstands.

2. Remove the wheels/tire assemblies.

3. Release the parking brake.

4. Remove the grease cap, the cotter pin and

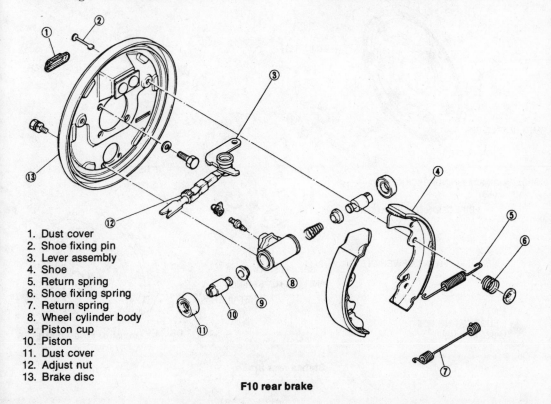

1. Dust cover
2. Shoe fixing pin
3. Lever assembly
4. Shoe
5. Return spring
6. Shoe fixing spring
7. Return spring
8. Wheel cylinder body
9. Piston cup
10. Piston
11. Dust cover
12. Adjust nut
13. Brake disc

F10 rear brake

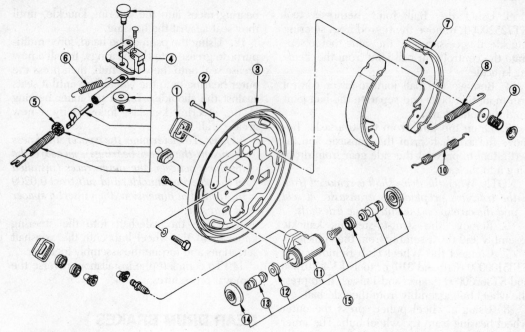

1. Dust cover
2. Shoe fixing pin
3. Back plate
4. Adjuster assembly
5. Adjusting nut
6. Spring
7. Shoe
8. Return spring
9. Shoe fixing spring
10. Return spring
11. Wheel cylinder body
12. Piston cup
13. Piston
14. Dust cover
15. Wheel cylinder assembly

310 rear brake

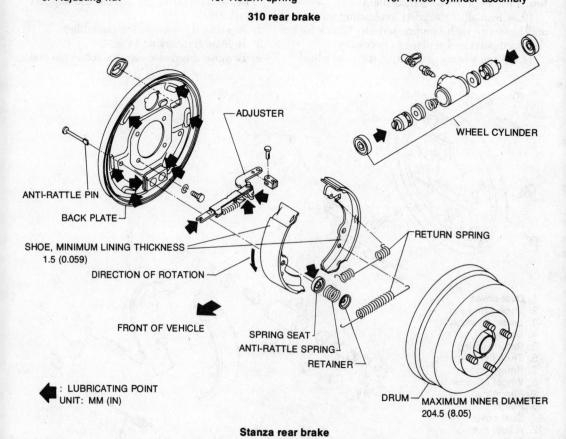

ADJUSTER

WHEEL CYLINDER

ANTI-RATTLE PIN

BACK PLATE

SHOE, MINIMUM LINING THICKNESS
1.5 (0.059)

DIRECTION OF ROTATION

RETURN SPRING

FRONT OF VEHICLE

SPRING SEAT
ANTI-RATTLE SPRING
RETAINER

DRUM — MAXIMUM INNER DIAMETER
204.5 (8.05)

◀ : LUBRICATING POINT
UNIT: MM (IN)

Stanza rear brake

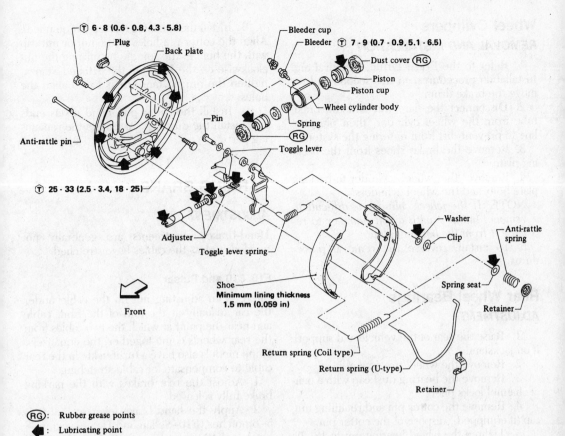

6 - 8 (0.6 - 0.8, 4.3 - 5.8) ⊤
Plug
Back plate
Anti-rattle pin
25 - 33 (2.5 - 3.4, 18 - 25) ⊤

Pin

Bleeder cup
Bleeder ⊤ 7 - 9 (0.7 - 0.9, 5.1 - 6.5)
Dust cover (RG)
Piston
Piston cup
Wheel cylinder body
Spring (RG)
Toggle lever

Adjuster
Toggle lever spring

Shoe
Minimum lining thickness
1.5 mm (0.059 in)

Front

Washer
Clip
Anti-rattle spring
Spring seat
Retainer

Return spring (Coil type)
Return spring (U-type)
Retainer

(RG): Rubber grease points
◄ : Lubricating point
⊤ : N·m (kg-m, ft-lb)

Exploded view of the Pulsar rear brake assembly

the wheel bearing castle nut (F10 and 310) or the adjusting cap and the wheel bearing nut (Pulsar and Stanza).

5. Pull off the drum, taking care not to drop the tapered bearing.

6. To install, reverse the removal procedures. Adjust the wheel bearing. Torque the nut to 30 ft.lb.

INSPECTION

After removing the brake drum, wipe out the accumulated dust with a damp cloth.

CAUTION: *DO NOT blow the brake dust out of the drums with compressed air or lung power. Brake linings contain asbestos, a known cancer causing substance. Dispose of the cloth after use.*

Inspect the drum for cracks, deep grooves, roughness, scoring or out-of-roundness. Replace any brake drum which is cracked.

Smooth any slight scores by polishing the friction surface with the fine emery cloth. Heavy or extensive scoring will cause excessive brake lining wear and should be removed from the brake drum through resurfacing.

Brake Shoes
REMOVAL AND INSTALLATION

1. Refer to the Brake Drum, Removal and Installation procedures, in this section and remove the brake drum.

2. Release the parking brake lever, then remove the anti-rattle spring and the pin from the brake shoes.

NOTE: *To remove the anti-rattle spring and pin, push the spring/pin assembly into the brake shoe, turn it 90° and release it; the retainer cap, spring, washer and pin will separate.*

3. Supporting the brake shoe assembly, remove the return springs and brake shoes.

NOTE: *If the brake shoes are difficult to remove, loosen the brake adjusters. Place a heavy rubber band around the cylinder to prevent the piston from coming out.*

4. Clean the backing plate and check the wheel cylinder for leaks.

5. To install, lubricate the backing plate pads and the screw adjusters with lithium base grease, then reverse the removal procedures.

Wheel Cylinders
REMOVAL AND INSTALLATION

1. Refer to the Brake Drum, Removal and Installation procedures, in this section and remove the brake drum.
2. Disconnect the flare nut and the brake tube from the wheel cylinder, then plug the line to prevent dirt from entering the system.
3. Remove the brake shoes from the backing plate.
4. Remove the wheel cylinder-to-backing plate bolts and the wheel cylinders.
NOTE: *If the wheel cylinder is difficult to remove, bump it with a soft hammer to release it from the backing plate.*
5. To install, reverse the removal procedures.

Rear Wheel Bearings
ADJUSTMENT

1. Raise the rear of the vehicle and support it on jackstands.
2. Remove the wheel/tire assembly.
3. Remove the bearing dust cap with a pair of channel locks pliers.
4. Remove the cotter pin and retaining nut cap (if equipped), dispose of the cotter pin.
5. Tighten the wheel bearing nut to 18–22 ft.lb. (F10) or to 29–33 ft.lb. (all other models).
6. Rotate the drum back and forth a few revolutions to snug down the bearing.
7. On the F10, loosen the nut until it can be turned by hand, then tighten it with a hand held socket as far as it will go.
8. On the 310, and Stanza, after turning the wheel, recheck the torque of the nut, then loosen it 90° from its position.

9. Install the retaining nut cap (if equipped). Align the cotter pin holes in the nut or nut cap with the hole in the spindle by turning the nut clockwise on the F10. On the 310 and Stanza, tighten the nut no more than 15° to align the holes.
10. Install the cotter pin, bend up its ends and install the dust cap. Assemble the remaining parts.

PARKING BRAKE

ADJUSTMENT

Hand-brake adjustments are generally not needed, unless the cables have stretched.

F10, 310 and Pulsar

There is an adjusting nut on the cable under the car, usually at the end of the front cable and near the point at which the two cables from the rear wheels come together (the equalizer). Some models also have a turnbuckle in the rear cable to compensate for cable stretching.
1. Adjust the rear brakes with the parking brake fully released.
2. Apply the hand brake lever so that it is 5–6 notches (F10–Sedan and Hatchback), 6–8 notches (F10–Sport Wagon), 7–8 notches (310) or 6–7 notches (Pulsar) from its fully released position.
3. Adjust the parking brake turnbuckle, locknuts or equalizer so that the rear brakes are locked.
4. Release the parking brake. The wheels should turn freely. If not, loosen the parking brake adjuster until the wheels turn with no drag.

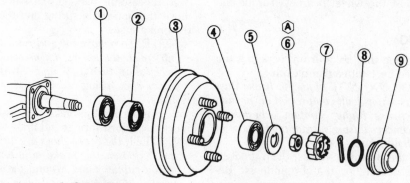

1. Grease seal
2. Inner wheel bearing
3. Brake drum
4. Outer wheel bearing
5. Wheel bearing washer
6. Wheel bearing nut
7. Adjusting cap
8. O-ring
9. Hub cap
Tightening torque
Ⓐ: 39-44 N-m
(4.0-4.5 kg-m, 29-33 ft-lb)

F10, 310 rear hub and bearing

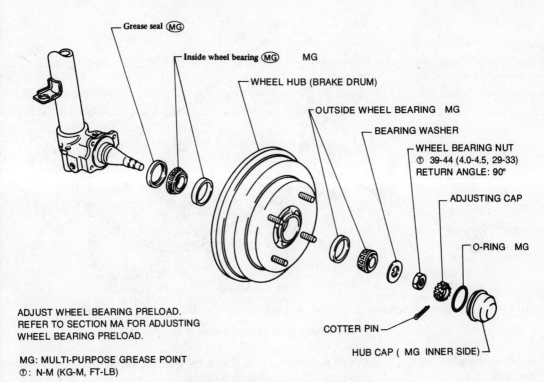

Pulsar and Stanza rear hub and bearing

ADJUST WHEEL BEARING PRELOAD.
REFER TO SECTION MA FOR ADJUSTING
WHEEL BEARING PRELOAD.

MG: MULTI-PURPOSE GREASE POINT
①: N-M (KG-M, FT-LB)

Stanza

1. Make sure that the rear brakes are in good condition.

2. Carefully remove the dust boot from around the parking brake lever.

3. The adjustment is made by determining the amount of force needed to pull up on the lever. A force of 44 lbs. should be needed to raise the lever 7–8 notches or clicks.

4. To adjust the pull, raise and support the vehicle on jackstands. There are two nuts on the hand-brake clevis rod. Loosen the locknut

1. Warning lamp switch
2. Hand brake lever
3. Front cable
4. Cable supporter
5. Lock nut
6. Clevis
7. Adjuster
8. Return spring
9. Equalizer
10. Rear cable

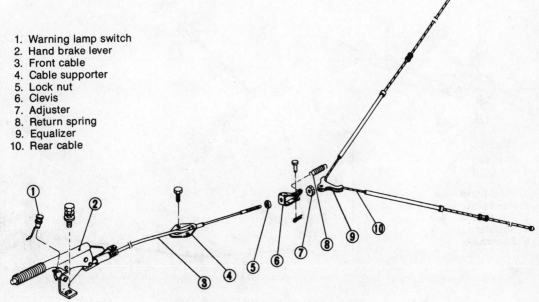

F10 sedan and hatchback parking brake

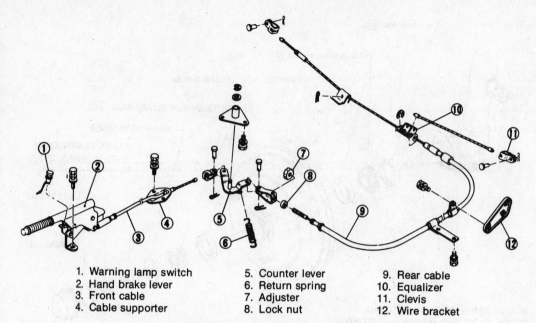

1. Warning lamp switch
2. Hand brake lever
3. Front cable
4. Cable supporter
5. Counter lever
6. Return spring
7. Adjuster
8. Lock nut
9. Rear cable
10. Equalizer
11. Clevis
12. Wire bracket

F10 station wagon parking brake

and turn the adjusting nut to establish the correct pull.

5. Tighten the adjuster locknut.

REMOVAL AND INSTALLATION

Rear Cable

F10 AND 310

1. Raise and support the rear of the vehicle on jackstands.

2. Place the parking brake lever in the released position.

3. Loosen the adjuster locknut and separate the rear cable from the adjuster.

4. Remove the parking brake clevis pin (at each rear wheel) from the rear end of the rear cable.

5. Remove the lock plate and the clamps retaining the rear cable to the vehicle, then remove the rear cable.

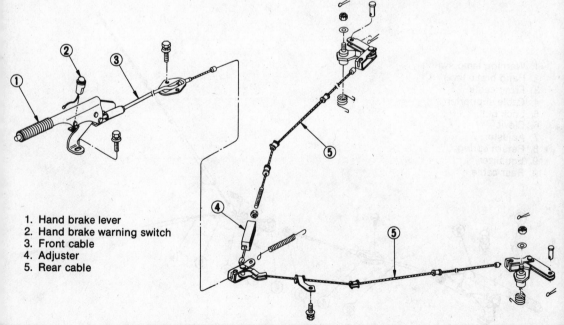

1. Hand brake lever
2. Hand brake warning switch
3. Front cable
4. Adjuster
5. Rear cable

310 parking brake

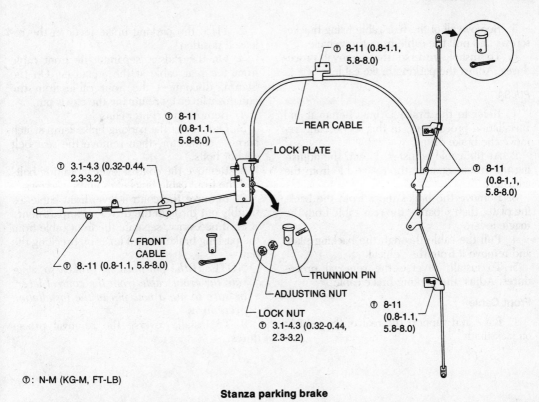

⊤ 8-11 (0.8-1.1, 5.8-8.0)

REAR CABLE

LOCK PLATE

⊤ 8-11 (0.8-1.1, 5.8-8.0)

⊤ 3.1-4.3 (0.32-0.44, 2.3-3.2)

⊤ 8-11 (0.8-1.1, 5.8-8.0)

FRONT CABLE

⊤ 8.-11 (0.8-1.1, 5.8-8.0)

TRUNNION PIN

ADJUSTING NUT

LOCK NUT
⊤ 3.1-4.3 (0.32-0.44, 2.3-3.2)

⊤ 8-11 (0.8-1.1, 5.8-8.0)

⊤: N-M (KG-M, FT-LB)

Stanza parking brake

6. To install, reverse the removal procedures. Adjust the parking brake cable.

STANZA

1. Raise and support the rear of the vehicle on jackstands.

2. Place the parking brake lever in the released position.

3. At the equalizer, loosen the adjusting nut, then remove the locking plate and the rear cable from it.

4. At both rear wheels, disconnect the rear cable clevis pin from the toggle lever.

Brake Specifications

All measurements given are in inches unless noted

Year	Model	Lug Nut Torque (ft. lbs.)	Master Cylinder Bore	Brake Disc		Drum		Minimum Lining Thickness	
				Minimum Thickness	Maximum Run-Out	Diameter	Max. Wear Limit	Front	Rear
1977–78	F-10	58–65	0.750	0.339	0.0059	8.000	8.050	0.063	0.039
1979–82	310	58–72	0.8125	0.339	0.0047	8.000	8.050	0.079	0.059
1982	Stanza	58–72	0.8125	0.630	0.0059	8.000	8.050	0.080	0.059
1983–86	Stanza	58–72	0.8125	0.630	0.0028	8.000	8.050	0.079	0.059
1983	Pulsar	58–72	①	0.394	0.0028	7.090	7.130	0.079	0.059
1984	Pulsar	58–72	②	0.394	0.0028	8.000	8.050	0.079	0.059
1985–86	Pulsar	58–72	①	0.394	0.0028	8.000	8.050	0.079	0.059

NOTE: Minimum lining thickness is as recommended by the manufacturer. Due to variation in state inspection regulations, the minimum allowable thickness may be different than recommended by the manufacturer.
① Small: 0.750
  Large: 0.9375
② Non Turbo; Small: 0.750
        Large: 0.9375
  Turbo; Small: 0.8125
        Large: 1.000

5. Remove all of the rear cable fixing bracket screws and pull the cable from the vehicle.

6. To install, reverse the removal procedures. Adjust the parking brake cable.

PULSAR

1. Refer to the Brake Drum, Removal and Installation procedures, in this section and remove the brake drum.

2. At the cable adjuster, loosen the adjusting nut, then separate the rear cable from the adjuster.

3. Remove the brake shoes from the backing plate, then separate the rear cable from the toggle lever.

4. Pull the cable through the backing plate and remove it from the vehicle.

5. To install, reverse the removal procedures. Adjust the parking brake cable.

Front Cable

1. Raise and support the rear of the vehicle on jackstands.

2. Place the parking brake lever in the released position.

3. On the Pulsar, separate the front cable from the rear cable at the equalizer. On the Stanza, disconnect the front cable from the equalizer lever by removing the clevis pin.

4. Remove the center console.

5. Disconnect the parking brake lamp switch harness connector, then remove the seat belt anchor bolts.

6. Remove the control lever mounting bolts and the front cable bracket mounting screws.

7. Remove the control lever/front cable assembly out through the driver's compartment.

8. If necessary, separate the front cable from the parking brake control lever by breaking the pin.

NOTE: *If the pin must be broken to separate the front cable from the control lever, be sure to use a new pin in the installation procedures.*

9. To install, reverse the removal procedures.

Troubleshooting

9

This section is designed to aid in the quick, accurate diagnosis of automotive problems. While automotive repairs can be made by many people, accurate troubleshooting is a rare skill for the amateur and professional alike.

In its simplest state, troubleshooting is an exercise in logic. It is essential to realize that an automobile is really composed of a series of systems. Some of these systems are interrelated; others are not. Automobiles operate within a framework of logical rules and physical laws, and the key to troubleshooting is a good understanding of all the automotive systems.

This section breaks the car or truck down into its component systems, allowing the problem to be isolated. The charts and diagnostic road maps list the most common problems and the most probable causes of trouble. Obviously it would be impossible to list every possible problem that could happen along with every possible cause, but it will locate MOST problems and eliminate a lot of unnecessary guesswork. The systematic format will locate problems within a given system, but, because many automotive systems are interrelated, the solution to your particular problem may be found in a number of systems on the car or truck.

USING THE TROUBLESHOOTING CHARTS

This book contains all of the specific information that the average do-it-yourself mechanic needs to repair and maintain his or her car or truck. The troubleshooting charts are designed to be used in conjunction with the specific procedures and information in the text. For instance, troubleshooting a point-type ignition system is fairly standard for all models, but you may be directed to the text to find procedures for troubleshooting an individual type of electronic ignition. You will also have to refer to the specification charts throughout the book for specifications applicable to your car or truck.

TOOLS AND EQUIPMENT

The tools illustrated in Chapter 1 (plus two more diagnostic pieces) will be adequate to troubleshoot most problems. The two other tools needed are a voltmeter and an ohmmeter. These can be purchased separately or in combination, known as a VOM meter.

In the event that other tools are required, they will be noted in the procedures.

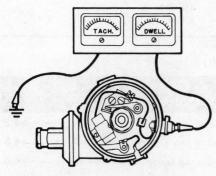

Tach-dwell hooked-up to distributor

Troubleshooting Engine Problems

See Chapters 2, 3, 4 for more information and service procedures.

Index to Systems

System	To Test	Group
Battery	Engine need not be running	1
Starting system	Engine need not be running	2
Primary electrical system	Engine need not be running	3
Secondary electrical system	Engine need not be running	4
Fuel system	Engine need not be running	5
Engine compression	Engine need not be running	6
Engine vacuum	Engine must be running	7
Secondary electrical system	Engine must be running	8
Valve train	Engine must be running	9
Exhaust system	Engine must be running	10
Cooling system	Engine must be running	11
Engine lubrication	Engine must be running	12

Index to Problems

Problem: Symptom	Begin at Specific Diagnosis, Number ___
Engine Won't Start:	
Starter doesn't turn	1.1, 2.1
Starter turns, engine doesn't	2.1
Starter turns engine very slowly	1.1, 2.4
Starter turns engine normally	3.1, 4.1
Starter turns engine very quickly	6.1
Engine fires intermittently	4.1
Engine fires consistently	5.1, 6.1
Engine Runs Poorly:	
Hard starting	3.1, 4.1, 5.1, 8.1
Rough idle	4.1, 5.1, 8.1
Stalling	3.1, 4.1, 5.1, 8.1
Engine dies at high speeds	4.1, 5.1
Hesitation (on acceleration from standing stop)	5.1, 8.1
Poor pickup	4.1, 5.1, 8.1
Lack of power	3.1, 4.1, 5.1, 8.1
Backfire through the carburetor	4.1, 8.1, 9.1
Backfire through the exhaust	4.1, 8.1, 9.1
Blue exhaust gases	6.1, 7.1
Black exhaust gases	5.1
Running on (after the ignition is shut off)	3.1, 8.1
Susceptible to moisture	4.1
Engine misfires under load	4.1, 7.1, 8.4, 9.1
Engine misfires at speed	4.1, 8.4
Engine misfires at idle	3.1, 4.1, 5.1, 7.1, 8.4

Sample Section

Test and Procedure	Results and Indications	Proceed to
4.1—Check for spark: Hold each spark plug wire approximately ¼″ from ground with gloves or a heavy, dry rag. Crank the engine and observe the spark.	→ If no spark is evident:	→ **4.2**
	→ If spark is good in some cases:	→ **4.3**
	→ If spark is good in all cases:	→ **4.6**

Specific Diagnosis

This section is arranged so that following each test, instructions are given to proceed to another, until a problem is diagnosed.

Section 1—Battery

Test and Procedure	Results and Indications	Proceed to
1.1—Inspect the battery visually for case condition (corrosion, cracks) and water level. 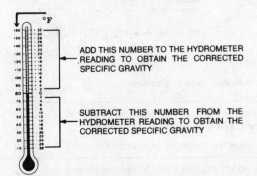 DIRT ON TOP OF BATTERY, PLUGGED VENT, CORROSION, LOOSE CABLE OR POSTS, CRACKS, LOW WATER LEVEL **Inspect the battery case**	If case is cracked, replace battery: If the case is intact, remove corrosion with a solution of baking soda and water (**CAUTION**: *do not get the solution into the battery*), and fill with water:	**1.4** **1.2**
1.2—Check the battery cable connections: Insert a screwdriver between the battery post and the cable clamp. Turn the headlights on high beam, and observe them as the screwdriver is gently twisted to ensure good metal to metal contact. TESTING BATTERY CABLE CONNECTIONS USING A SCREWDRIVER	If the lights brighten, remove and clean the clamp and post; coat the post with petroleum jelly, install and tighten the clamp: If no improvement is noted:	**1.4** **1.3**
1.3—Test the state of charge of the battery using an individual cell tester or hydrometer.	If indicated, charge the battery. **NOTE:** *If no obvious reason exists for the low state of charge (i.e., battery age, prolonged storage), proceed to:*	**1.4**

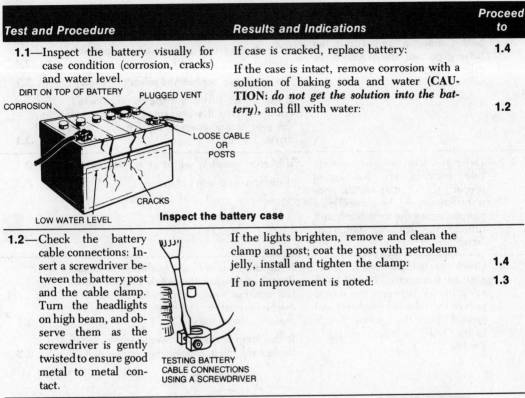

ADD THIS NUMBER TO THE HYDROMETER READING TO OBTAIN THE CORRECTED SPECIFIC GRAVITY

SUBTRACT THIS NUMBER FROM THE HYDROMETER READING TO OBTAIN THE CORRECTED SPECIFIC GRAVITY

Specific Gravity (@ 80° F.)

Minimum	Battery Charge
1.260	100% Charged
1.230	75% Charged
1.200	50% Charged
1.170	25% Charged
1.140	Very Little Power Left
1.110	Completely Discharged

The effects of temperature on battery specific gravity (left) and amount of battery charge in relation to specific gravity (right)

Test and Procedure	Results and Indications	Proceed to
1.4—Visually inspect battery cables for cracking, bad connection to ground, or bad connection to starter.	If necessary, tighten connections or replace the cables:	**2.1**

Section 2—Starting System
See Chapter 3 for service procedures

Test and Procedure	Results and Indications	Proceed to
Note: Tests in Group 2 are performed with coil high tension lead disconnected to prevent accidental starting.		
2.1—Test the starter motor and solenoid: Connect a jumper from the battery post of the solenoid (or relay) to the starter post of the solenoid (or relay).	If starter turns the engine normally:	2.2
	If the starter buzzes, or turns the engine very slowly:	2.4
	If no response, replace the solenoid (or relay).	3.1
	If the starter turns, but the engine doesn't, ensure that the flywheel ring gear is intact. If the gear is undamaged, replace the starter drive.	3.1
2.2—Determine whether ignition override switches are functioning properly (clutch start switch, neutral safety switch), by connecting a jumper across the switch(es), and turning the ignition switch to "start".	If starter operates, adjust or replace switch:	3.1
	If the starter doesn't operate:	2.3
2.3—Check the ignition switch "start" position: Connect a 12V test lamp or voltmeter between the starter post of the solenoid (or relay) and ground. Turn the ignition switch to the "start" position, and jiggle the key.	If the lamp doesn't light or the meter needle doesn't move when the switch is turned, check the ignition switch for loose connections, cracked insulation, or broken wires. Repair or replace as necessary:	3.1
	If the lamp flickers or needle moves when the key is jiggled, replace the ignition switch.	3.3

Checking the ignition switch "start" position

STARTER RELAY
(IF EQUIPPED)

2.4—Remove and bench test the starter, according to specifications in the engine electrical section.	If the starter does not meet specifications, repair or replace as needed:	3.1
	If the starter is operating properly:	2.5
2.5—Determine whether the engine can turn freely: Remove the spark plugs, and check for water in the cylinders. Check for water on the dipstick, or oil in the radiator. Attempt to turn the engine using an 18″ flex drive and socket on the crankshaft pulley nut or bolt.	If the engine will turn freely only with the spark plugs out, and hydrostatic lock (water in the cylinders) is ruled out, check valve timing:	9.2
	If engine will not turn freely, and it is known that the clutch and transmission are free, the engine must be disassembled for further evaluation:	Chapter 3

Section 3—Primary Electrical System

Test and Procedure	Results and Indications	Proceed to
3.1—Check the ignition switch "on" position: Connect a jumper wire between the distributor side of the coil and ground, and a 12V test lamp between the switch side of the coil and ground. Remove the high tension lead from the coil. Turn the ignition switch on and jiggle the key.	If the lamp lights:	3.2
	If the lamp flickers when the key is jiggled, replace the ignition switch:	3.3
	If the lamp doesn't light, check for loose or open connections. If none are found, remove the ignition switch and check for continuity. If the switch is faulty, replace it:	3.3

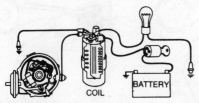

Checking the ignition switch "on" position

3.2—Check the ballast resistor or resistance wire for an open circuit, using an ohmmeter. See Chapter 3 for specific tests.	Replace the resistor or resistance wire if the resistance is zero. **NOTE:** *Some ignition systems have no ballast resistor.*	3.3

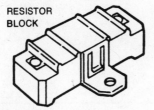

Two types of resistors

3.3—On point-type ignition systems, visually inspect the breaker points for burning, pitting or excessive wear. Gray coloring of the point contact surfaces is normal. Rotate the crankshaft until the contact heel rests on a high point of the distributor cam and adjust the point gap to specifications. On electronic ignition models, remove the distributor cap and visually inspect the armature. Ensure that the armature pin is in place, and that the armature is on tight and rotates when the engine is cranked. Make sure there are no cracks, chips or rounded edges on the armature.	If the breaker points are intact, clean the contact surfaces with fine emery cloth, and adjust the point gap to specifications. If the points are worn, replace them. On electronic systems, replace any parts which appear defective. If condition persists:	3.4

Test and Procedure	Results and Indications	Proceed to
3.4—On point-type ignition systems, connect a dwell-meter between the distributor primary lead and ground. Crank the engine and observe the point dwell angle. On electronic ignition systems, conduct a stator (magnetic pickup assembly) test. See Chapter 3.	On point-type systems, adjust the dwell angle if necessary. **NOTE:** *Increasing the point gap decreases the dwell angle and vice-versa.*	**3.6**
	If the dwell meter shows little or no reading;	**3.5**
	On electronic ignition systems, if the stator is bad, replace the stator. If the stator is good, proceed to the other tests in Chapter 3.	

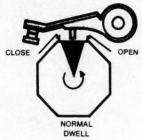 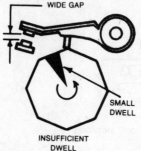 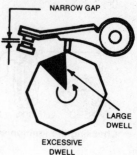

Dwell is a function of point gap

3.5—On the point-type ignition systems, check the condenser for short: connect an ohmeter across the condenser body and the pigtail lead.	If any reading other than infinite is noted, replace the condenser	**3.6**

Checking the condenser for short

3.6—Test the coil primary resistance: On point-type ignition systems, connect an ohmmeter across the coil primary terminals, and read the resistance on the low scale. Note whether an external ballast resistor or resistance wire is used. On electronic ignition systems, test the coil primary resistance as in Chapter 3.	Point-type ignition coils utilizing ballast resistors or resistance wires should have approximately 1.0 ohms resistance. Coils with internal resistors should have approximately 4.0 ohms resistance. If values far from the above are noted, replace the coil.	**4.1**

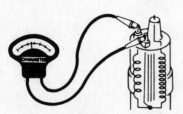

Check the coil primary resistance

Section 4—Secondary Electrical System
See Chapters 2–3 for service procedures

Test and Procedure	Results and Indications	Proceed to
4.1—Check for spark: Hold each spark plug wire approximately ¼″ from ground with gloves or a heavy, dry rag. Crank the engine, and observe the spark.	If no spark is evident:	**4.2**
	If spark is good in some cylinders:	**4.3**
	If spark is good in all cylinders:	**4.6**

Check for spark at the plugs

4.2—Check for spark at the coil high tension lead: Remove the coil high tension lead from the distributor and position it approximately ¼″ from ground. Crank the engine and observe spark. **CAUTION: *This test should not be performed on engines equipped with electronic ignition.***	If the spark is good and consistent:	**4.3**
	If the spark is good but intermittent, test the primary electrical system starting at 3.3:	**3.3**
	If the spark is weak or non-existent, replace the coil high tension lead, clean and tighten all connections and retest. If no improvement is noted:	**4.4**
4.3—Visually inspect the distributor cap and rotor for burned or corroded contacts, cracks, carbon tracks, or moisture. Also check the fit of the rotor on the distributor shaft (where applicable).	If moisture is present, dry thoroughly, and retest per 4.1:	**4.1**
	If burned or excessively corroded contacts, cracks, or carbon tracks are noted, replace the defective part(s) and retest per 4.1:	**4.1**
	If the rotor and cap appear intact, or are only slightly corroded, clean the contacts thoroughly (including the cap towers and spark plug wire ends) and retest per 4.1:	
	If the spark is good in all cases:	**4.6**
	If the spark is poor in all cases:	**4.5**

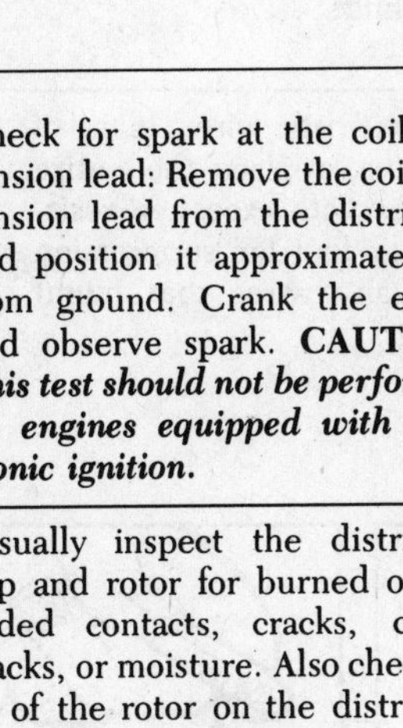

CORRODED OR LOOSE WIRE

EXCESSIVE WEAR OF BUTTON

HIGH RESISTANCE CARBON

ROTOR TIP BURNED AWAY

Inspect the distributor cap and rotor

Test and Procedure	Results and Indications	Proceed to
4.4—Check the coil secondary resistance: On point-type systems connect an ohmmeter across the distributor side of the coil and the coil tower. Read the resistance on the high scale of the ohmmeter. On electronic ignition systems, see Chapter 3 for specific tests.	The resistance of a satisfactory coil should be between 4,000 and 10,000 ohms. If resistance is considerably higher (i.e., 40,000 ohms) replace the coil and retest per 4.1. **NOTE:** *This does not apply to high performance coils.*	

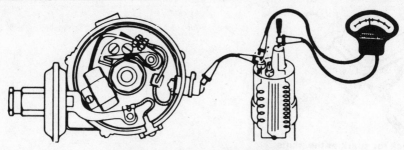

Testing the coil secondary resistance

Test and Procedure	Results and Indications	Proceed to
4.5—Visually inspect the spark plug wires for cracking or brittleness. Ensure that no two wires are positioned so as to cause induction firing (adjacent and parallel). Remove each wire, one by one, and check resistance with an ohmmeter.	Replace any cracked or brittle wires. If any of the wires are defective, replace the entire set. Replace any wires with excessive resistance (over $8000\,\Omega$ per foot for suppression wire), and separate any wires that might cause induction firing.	4.6

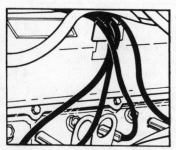

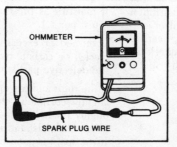

Misfiring can be the result of spark plug leads to adjacent, consecutively firing cylinders running parallel and too close together

On point-type ignition systems, check the spark plug wires as shown. On electronic ignitions, do not remove the wire from the distributor cap terminal; instead, test through the cap

Spark plug wires can be checked visually by bending them in a loop over your finger. This will reveal any cracks, burned or broken insulation. Any wire with cracked insulation should be replaced

Test and Procedure	Results and Indications	Proceed to
4.6—Remove the spark plugs, noting the cylinders from which they were removed, and evaluate according to the color photos in the middle of this book.	See following.	**See following.**

CHILTON'S
AUTO BODY REPAIR TIPS

Tools and Materials • Step-by-Step Illustrated Procedures
How To Repair Dents, Scratches and Rust Holes
Spray Painting and Refinishing Tips

With a little practice, basic body repair procedures can be mastered by any do-it-yourself mechanic. The step-by-step repairs shown here can be applied to almost any type of auto body repair.

TOOLS & MATERIALS

You may already have basic tools, such as hammers and electric drills. Other tools unique to body repair — body hammers, grinding attachments, sanding blocks, dent puller, half-round plastic file and plastic spreaders — are relatively inexpensive and can be obtained wherever auto parts or auto body repair parts are sold. Portable air compressors and paint spray guns can be purchased or rented.

Auto Body Repair Kits

The best and most often used products are available to the do-it-yourselfer in kit form, from major manufacturers of auto body repair products. The same manufacturers also merchandise the individual products for use by pros.

Kits are available to make a wide variety of repairs, including holes, dents and scratches and fiberglass, and offer the advantage of buying the materials you'll need for the job. There is little waste or chance of materials going bad from not being used. Many kits may also contain basic body-working tools such as body files, sanding blocks and spreaders. Check the contents of the kit before buying your tools.

BODY REPAIR TIPS

Safety

Many of the products associated with auto body repair and refinishing contain toxic chemicals. Read all labels before opening containers and store them in a safe place and manner.

• Wear eye protection (safety goggles) when using power tools or when performing any operation that involves

the removal of any type of material.

• Wear lung protection (disposable mask or respirator) when grinding, sanding or painting.

Sanding

1 Sand off paint before using a dent puller. When using a non-adhesive sanding disc, cover the back of the disc with an overlapping layer or two of masking tape and trim the edges. The disc will last considerably longer.

2 Use the circular motion of the sanding disc to grind *into* the edge of the repair. Grinding or sanding away from the jagged edge will only tear the sandpaper.

3 Use the palm of your hand flat on the panel to detect high and low spots. Do not use your fingertips. Slide your hand slowly back and forth.

WORKING WITH BODY FILLER

Mixing The Filler

Cleanliness and proper mixing and application are extremely important. Use a clean piece of plastic or glass or a disposable artist's palette to mix body filler.

1 Allow plenty of time and follow directions. No useful purpose will be served by adding more hardener to make it cure (set-up) faster. Less hardener means more curing time, but the mixture dries harder; more hardener means less curing time but a softer mixture.

2 Both the hardener and the filler should be thoroughly kneaded or stirred before mixing. Hardener should be a solid paste and dispense like thin toothpaste. Body filler should be smooth, and free of lumps or thick spots.

Getting the proper amount of hardener in the filler is the trickiest part of preparing the filler. Use the same amount of hardener in cold or warm weather. For contour filler (thick coats), a bead of hardener twice the diameter of the filler is about right. There's about a 15% margin on either side, but, if in doubt use less hardener.

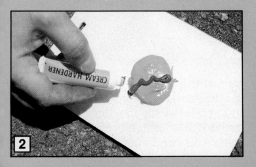

3 Mix the body filler and hardener by wiping across the mixing surface, picking the mixture up and wiping it again. Colder weather requires longer mixing times. Do not mix in a circular motion; this will trap air bubbles which will become holes in the cured filler.

Applying The Filler

1 For best results, filler should not be applied over ¼″ thick.

Apply the filler in several coats. Build it up to above the level of the repair surface so that it can be sanded or grated down.

The first coat of filler must be pressed on with a firm wiping motion.

Apply the filler in one direction only. Working the filler back and forth will either pull it off the metal or trap air bubbles.

REPAIRING DENTS

Before you start, take a few minutes to study the damaged area. Try to visualize the shape of the panel before it was damaged. If the damage is on the left fender, look at the right fender and use it as a guide. If there is access to the panel from behind, you can reshape it with a body hammer. If not, you'll have to use a dent puller. Go slowly and work the metal a little at a time. Get the panel as straight as possible before applying filler.

1 This dent is typical of one that can be pulled out or hammered out from behind. Remove the headlight cover, headlight assembly and turn signal housing.

2 Drill a series of holes ½ the size of the end of the dent puller along the stress line. Make some trial pulls and assess the results. If necessary, drill more holes and try again. Do not hurry.

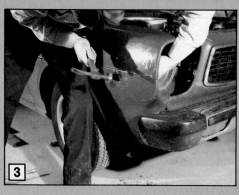

3 If possible, use a body hammer and block to shape the metal back to its original contours. Get the metal back as close to its original shape as possible. Don't depend on body filler to fill dents.

4 Using an 80-grit grinding disc on an electric drill, grind the paint from the surrounding area down to bare metal. Use a new grinding pad to prevent heat buildup that will warp metal.

5 The area should look like this when you're finished grinding. Knock the drill holes in and tape over small openings to keep plastic filler out.

6 Mix the body filler (see Body Repair Tips). Spread the body filler evenly over the entire area (see Body Repair Tips). Be sure to cover the area completely.

7 Let the body filler dry until the surface can just be scratched with your fingernail. Knock the high spots from the body filler with a body file ("Cheesegrater"). Check frequently with the palm of your hand for high and low spots.

8 Check to be sure that trim pieces that will be installed later will fit exactly. Sand the area with 40-grit paper.

9 If you wind up with low spots, you may have to apply another layer of filler.

10 Knock the high spots off with 40-grit paper. When you are satisfied with the contours of the repair, apply a thin coat of filler to cover pin holes and scratches.

11 Block sand the area with 40-grit paper to a smooth finish. Pay particular attention to body lines and ridges that must be well-defined.

12 Sand the area with 400 paper and then finish with a scuff pad. The finished repair is ready for priming and painting (see Painting Tips).

Materials and photos courtesy of Ritt Jones Auto Body, Prospect Park, PA.

REPAIRING RUST HOLES

There are many ways to repair rust holes. The fiberglass cloth kit shown here is one of the most cost efficient for the owner because it provides a strong repair that resists cracking and moisture and is relatively easy to use. It can be used on large and small holes (with or without backing) and can be applied over contoured areas. Remember, however, that short of replacing an entire panel, no repair is a guarantee that the rust will not return.

1 Remove any trim that will be in the way. Clean away all loose debris. Cut away all the rusted metal. But be sure to leave enough metal to retain the contour or body shape.

2 Grind away all traces of rust with a 24-grit grinding disc. Be sure to grind back 3-4 inches from the edge of the hole down to bare metal and be sure all traces of paint, primer and rust are removed.

3 Block sand the area with 80 or 100 grit sandpaper to get a clear, shiny surface and feathered paint edge. Tap the edges of the hole inward with a ball peen hammer.

4 If you are going to use release film, cut a piece about 2-3" larger than the area you have sanded. Place the film over the repair and mark the sanded area on the film. Avoid any unnecessary wrinkling of the film.

5 Cut 2 pieces of fiberglass matte to match the shape of the repair. One piece should be about 1" smaller than the sanded area and the second piece should be 1" smaller than the first. Mix enough filler and hardener to saturate the fiberglass material (see Body Repair Tips).

6 Lay the release sheet on a flat surface and spread an even layer of filler, large enough to cover the repair. Lay the smaller piece of fiberglass cloth in the center of the sheet and spread another layer of filler over the fiberglass cloth. Repeat the operation for the larger piece of cloth.

7 Place the repair material over the repair area, with the release film facing outward. Use a spreader and work from the center outward to smooth the material, following the body contours. Be sure to remove all air bubbles.

8 Wait until the repair has dried tack-free and peel off the release sheet. The ideal working temperature is 60°-90° F. Cooler or warmer temperatures or high humidity may require additional curing time. Wait longer, if in doubt.

9

Sand and feather-edge the entire area. The initial sanding can be done with a sanding disc on an electric drill if care is used. Finish the sanding with a block sander. Low spots can be filled with body filler; this may require several applications.

10 When the filler can just be scratched with a fingernail, knock the high spots down with a body file and smooth the entire area with 80-grit. Feather the filled areas into the surrounding areas.

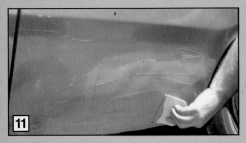

11 When the area is sanded smooth, mix some topcoat and hardener and apply it directly with a spreader. This will give a smooth finish and prevent the glass matte from showing through the paint.

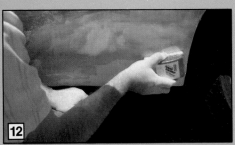

12 Block sand the topcoat smooth with finishing sandpaper (200 grit), and 400 grit. The repair is ready for masking, priming and painting (see Painting Tips).

Materials and photos courtesy Marson Corporation, Chelsea, Massachusetts

PAINTING TIPS

Preparation

1 SANDING — Use a 400 or 600 grit wet or dry sandpaper. Wet-sand the area with a ¼ sheet of sandpaper soaked in clean water. Keep the paper wet while sanding. Sand the area until the repaired area tapers into the original finish.

2 CLEANING — Wash the area to be painted thoroughly with water and a clean rag. Rinse it thoroughly and wipe the surface dry until you're sure it's completely free of dirt, dust, fingerprints, wax, detergent or other foreign matter.

3 MASKING — Protect any areas you don't want to overspray by covering them with masking tape and newspaper. Be careful not get fingerprints on the area to be painted.

4 PRIMING — All exposed metal should be primed before painting. Primer protects the metal and provides an excellent surface for paint adhesion. When the primer is dry, wet-sand the area again with 600 grit wet-sandpaper. Clean the area again after sanding.

Painting Techniques

Paint applied from either a spray gun or a spray can (for small areas) will provide good results. Experiment on an old piece of metal to get the right combination before you begin painting.

SPRAYING VISCOSITY (SPRAY GUN ONLY) — Paint should be thinned to spraying viscosity according to the directions on the can. Use only the recommended thinner or reducer and the same amount of reduction regardless of temperature.

AIR PRESSURE (SPRAY GUN ONLY) — This is extremely important. Be sure you are using the proper recommended pressure.

TEMPERATURE — The surface to be painted should be approximately the same temperature as the surrounding air. Applying warm paint to a cold surface, or vice versa, will completely upset the paint characteristics.

THICKNESS — Spray with smooth strokes. In general, the thicker the coat of paint, the longer the drying time. Apply several thin coats about 30 seconds apart. The paint should remain wet long enough to flow out and no longer; heavier coats will only produce sags or wrinkles. Spray a light (fog) coat, followed by heavier color coats.

DISTANCE — The ideal spraying distance is 8″-12″ from the gun or can to the surface. Shorter distances will produce ripples, while greater distances will result in orange peel, dry film and poor color match and loss of material due to overspray.

OVERLAPPING — The gun or can should be kept at right angles to the surface at all times. Work to a wet edge at an even speed, using a 50% overlap and direct the center of the spray at the lower or nearest edge of the previous stroke.

RUBBING OUT (BLENDING) FRESH PAINT — Let the paint dry thoroughly. Runs or imperfections can be sanded out, primed and repainted.

Don't be in too big a hurry to remove the masking. This only produces paint ridges. When the finish has dried for at least a week, apply a small amount of fine grade rubbing compound with a clean, wet cloth. Use lots of water and blend the new paint with the surrounding area.

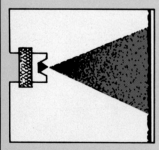

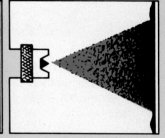

WRONG

Thin coat. Stroke too fast, not enough overlap, gun too far away.

CORRECT

Medium coat. Proper distance, good stroke, proper overlap.

WRONG

Heavy coat. Stroke too slow, too much overlap, gun too close.

Test and Procedure	Results and Indications	Proceed to
4.7—Examine the location of all the plugs.	The following diagrams illustrate some of the conditions that the location of plugs will reveal.	**4.8**

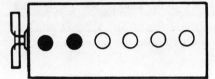

Two adjacent plugs are fouled in a 6-cylinder engine, 4-cylinder engine or either bank of a V-8. This is probably due to a blown head gasket between the two cylinders

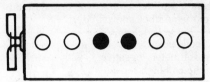

The two center plugs in a 6-cylinder engine are fouled. Raw fuel may be "boiled" out of the carburetor into the intake manifold after the engine is shut-off. Stop-start driving can also foul the center plugs, due to overly rich mixture. Proper float level, a new float needle and seat or use of an insulating spacer may help this problem

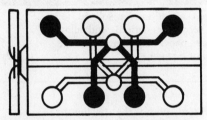

An unbalanced carburetor is indicated. Following the fuel flow on this particular design shows that the cylinders fed by the right-hand barrel are fouled from overly rich mixture, while the cylinders fed by the left-hand barrel are normal

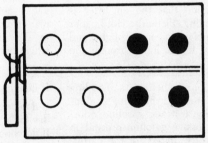

If the four rear plugs are overheated, a cooling system problem is suggested. A thorough cleaning of the cooling system may restore coolant circulation and cure the problem

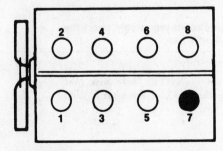

Finding one plug overheated may indicate an intake manifold leak near the affected cylinder. If the overheated plug is the second of two adjacent, consecutively firing plugs, it could be the result of ignition cross-firing. Separating the leads to these two plugs will eliminate cross-fire

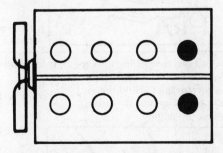

Occasionally, the two rear plugs in large, lightly used V-8's will become oil fouled. High oil consumption and smoky exhaust may also be noticed. It is probably due to plugged oil drain holes in the rear of the cylinder head, causing oil to be sucked in around the valve stems. This usually occurs in the rear cylinders first, because the engine slants that way

Test and Procedure	Results and Indications	Proceed to
4.8—Determine the static ignition timing. Using the crankshaft pulley timing marks as a guide, locate top dead center on the compression stroke of the number one cylinder.	The rotor should be pointing toward the No. 1 tower in the distributor cap, and, on electronic ignitions, the armature spoke for that cylinder should be lined up with the stator.	4.8
4.9—Check coil polarity: Connect a voltmeter negative lead to the coil high tension lead, and the positive lead to ground (**NOTE:** *Reverse the hook-up for positive ground systems*). Crank the engine momentarily. **Checking coil polarity**	If the voltmeter reads up-scale, the polarity is correct: If the voltmeter reads down-scale, reverse the coil polarity (switch the primary leads):	5.1 5.1

Section 5—Fuel System
See Chapter 4 for service procedures

Test and Procedure	Results and Indications	Proceed to
5.1—Determine that the air filter is functioning efficiently: Hold paper elements up to a strong light, and attempt to see light through the filter.	Clean permanent air filters in solvent (or manufacturer's recommendation), and allow to dry. Replace paper elements through which light cannot be seen:	5.2
5.2—Determine whether a flooding condition exists: Flooding is identified by a strong gasoline odor, and excessive gasoline present in the throttle bore(s) of the carburetor. **If the engine floods repeatedly, check the choke butterfly flap**	If flooding is not evident: If flooding is evident, permit the gasoline to dry for a few moments and restart. If flooding doesn't recur: If flooding is persistent:	5.3 5.7 5.5
5.3—Check that fuel is reaching the carburetor: Detach the fuel line at the carburetor inlet. Hold the end of the line in a cup (not styrofoam), and crank the engine. **Check the fuel pump by disconnecting the output line (fuel pump-to-carburetor) at the carburetor and operating the starter briefly**	If fuel flows smoothly: If fuel doesn't flow (**NOTE:** *Make sure that there is fuel in the tank*), or flows erratically:	5.7 5.4

Test and Procedure	Results and Indications	Proceed to
5.4—Test the fuel pump: Disconnect all fuel lines from the fuel pump. Hold a finger over the input fitting, crank the engine (with electric pump, turn the ignition or pump on); and feel for suction.	If suction is evident, blow out the fuel line to the tank with low pressure compressed air until bubbling is heard from the fuel filler neck. Also blow out the carburetor fuel line (both ends disconnected):	5.7
	If no suction is evident, replace or repair the fuel pump: **NOTE:** *Repeated oil fouling of the spark plugs, or a no-start condition, could be the result of a ruptured vacuum booster pump diaphragm, through which oil or gasoline is being drawn into the intake manifold (where applicable).*	5.7
5.5—Occasionally, small specks of dirt will clog the small jets and orifices in the carburetor. With the engine cold, hold a flat piece of wood or similar material over the carburetor, where possible, and crank the engine.	If the engine starts, but runs roughly the engine is probably not run enough. If the engine won't start:	5.9
5.6—Check the needle and seat: Tap the carburetor in the area of the needle and seat.	If flooding stops, a gasoline additive (e.g., Gumout) will often cure the problem:	5.7
	If flooding continues, check the fuel pump for excessive pressure at the carburetor (according to specifications). If the pressure is normal, the needle and seat must be removed and checked, and/or the float level adjusted:	5.7
5.7—Test the accelerator pump by looking into the throttle bores while operating the throttle.	If the accelerator pump appears to be operating normally:	5.8
	If the accelerator pump is not operating, the pump must be reconditioned. Where possible, service the pump with the carburetor(s) installed on the engine. If necessary, remove the carburetor. Prior to removal:	5.8
5.8—Determine whether the carburetor main fuel system is functioning: Spray a commercial starting fluid into the carburetor while attempting to start the engine.	If the engine starts, runs for a few seconds, and dies:	5.9
	If the engine doesn't start:	6.1

Check for gas at the carburetor by looking down the carburetor throat while someone moves the accelerator

Test and Procedure	Results and Indications	Proceed to
5.9—Uncommon fuel system malfunctions: See below:	If the problem is solved: If the problem remains, remove and recondition the carburetor.	**6.1**

Condition	Indication	Test	Prevailing Weather Conditions	Remedy
Vapor lock	Engine will not restart shortly after running.	Cool the components of the fuel system until the engine starts. Vapor lock can be cured faster by draping a wet cloth over a mechanical fuel pump.	Hot to very hot	Ensure that the exhaust manifold heat control valve is operating. Check with the vehicle manufacturer for the recommended solution to vapor lock on the model in question.
Carburetor icing	Engine will not idle, stalls at low speeds.	Visually inspect the throttle plate area of the throttle bores for frost.	High humidity, 32–40° F.	Ensure that the exhaust manifold heat control valve is operating, and that the intake manifold heat riser is not blocked.
Water in the fuel	Engine sputters and stalls; may not start.	Pump a small amount of fuel into a glass jar. Allow to stand, and inspect for droplets or a layer of water.	High humidity, extreme temperature changes.	For droplets, use one or two cans of commercial gas line anti-freeze. For a layer of water, the tank must be drained, and the fuel lines blown out with compressed air.

Section 6—Engine Compression
See Chapter 3 for service procedures

6.1—Test engine compression: Remove all spark plugs. Block the throttle wide open. Insert a compression gauge into a spark plug port, crank the engine to obtain the maximum reading, and record.	If compression is within limits on all cylinders: If gauge reading is extremely low on all cylinders: If gauge reading is low on one or two cylinders: (If gauge readings are identical and low on two or more adjacent cylinders, the head gasket must be replaced.)	**7.1** **6.2** **6.2**

Checking compression

6.2—Test engine compression (wet): Squirt approximately 30 cc. of engine oil into each cylinder, and retest per 6.1.	If the readings improve, worn or cracked rings or broken pistons are indicated: If the readings do not improve, burned or excessively carboned valves or a jumped timing chain are indicated: NOTE: *A jumped timing chain is often indicated by difficult cranking.*	**See Chapter 3** **7.1**

Section 7—Engine Vacuum
See Chapter 3 for service procedures

Test and Procedure	Results and Indications	Proceed to
7.1—Attach a vacuum gauge to the intake manifold beyond the throttle plate. Start the engine, and observe the action of the needle over the range of engine speeds.	See below.	**See below**

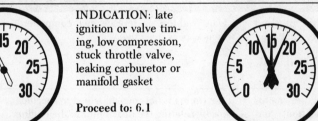

INDICATION: normal engine in good condition

Proceed to: 8.1

INDICATION: sticking valves or ignition miss

Proceed to: 9.1, 8.3

Normal engine
Gauge reading: steady, from 17–22 in./Hg.

Sticking valves
Gauge reading: intermittent fluctuation at idle

 INDICATION: late ignition or valve timing, low compression, stuck throttle valve, leaking carburetor or manifold gasket

Proceed to: 6.1

 INDICATION: improper carburetor adjustment or minor intake leak.

Proceed to: 7.2

Incorrect valve timing
Gauge reading: low (10–15 in./Hg) but steady

Carburetor requires adjustment
Gauge reading: drifting needle

 INDICATION: ignition miss, blown cylinder head gasket, leaking valve or weak valve spring

Proceed to: 8.3, 6.1

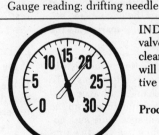 INDICATION: burnt valve or faulty valve clearance. Needle will fall when defective valve operates

Proceed to: 9.1

Blown head gasket
Gauge reading: needle fluctuates as engine speed increases

Burnt or leaking valves
Gauge reading: steady needle, but drops regularly

 INDICATION: choked muffler, excessive back pressure in system

Proceed to: 10.1

 INDICATION: worn valve guides

Proceed to: 9.1

Clogged exhaust system
Gauge reading: gradual drop in reading at idle

Worn valve guides
Gauge reading: needle vibrates excessively at idle, but steadies as engine speed increases

White pointer = steady gauge hand

Black pointer = fluctuating gauge hand

Test and Procedure	Results and Indications	Proceed to
7.2—Attach a vacuum gauge per 7.1, and test for an intake manifold leak. Squirt a small amount of oil around the intake manifold gaskets, carburetor gaskets, plugs and fittings. Observe the action of the vacuum gauge.	If the reading improves, replace the indicated gasket, or seal the indicated fitting or plug: If the reading remains low:	8.1 7.3
7.3—Test all vacuum hoses and accessories for leaks as described in 7.2. Also check the carburetor body (dashpots, automatic choke mechanism, throttle shafts) for leaks in the same manner.	If the reading improves, service or replace the offending part(s): If the reading remains low:	8.1 6.1

Section 8—Secondary Electrical System
See Chapter 2 for service procedures

Test and Procedure	Results and Indications	Proceed to
8.1—Remove the distributor cap and check to make sure that the rotor turns when the engine is cranked. Visually inspect the distributor components.	Clean, tighten or replace any components which appear defective.	8.2
8.2—Connect a timing light (per manufacturer's recommendation) and check the dynamic ignition timing. Disconnect and plug the vacuum hose(s) to the distributor if specified, start the engine, and observe the timing marks at the specified engine speed.	If the timing is not correct, adjust to specifications by rotating the distributor in the engine: (Advance timing by rotating distributor opposite normal direction of rotor rotation, retard timing by rotating distributor in same direction as rotor rotation.)	8.3
8.3—Check the operation of the distributor advance mechanism(s): To test the mechanical advance, disconnect the vacuum lines from the distributor advance unit and observe the timing marks with a timing light as the engine speed is increased from idle. If the mark moves smoothly, without hesitation, it may be assumed that the mechanical advance is functioning properly. To test vacuum advance and/or retard systems, alternately crimp and release the vacuum line, and observe the timing mark for movement. If movement is noted, the system is operating.	If the systems are functioning: If the systems are not functioning, remove the distributor, and test on a distributor tester:	8.4 8.4
8.4—Locate an ignition miss: With the engine running, remove each spark plug wire, one at a time, until one is found that doesn't cause the engine to roughen and slow down.	When the missing cylinder is identified:	4.1

Section 9—Valve Train

See Chapter 3 for service procedures

Test and Procedure	Results and Indications	Proceed to
9.1—Evaluate the valve train: Remove the valve cover, and ensure that the valves are adjusted to specifications. A mechanic's stethoscope may be used to aid in the diagnosis of the valve train. By pushing the probe on or near push rods or rockers, valve noise often can be isolated. A timing light also may be used to diagnose valve problems. Connect the light according to manufacturer's recommendations, and start the engine. Vary the firing moment of the light by increasing the engine speed (and therefore the ignition advance), and moving the trigger from cylinder to cylinder. Observe the movement of each valve.	Sticking valves or erratic valve train motion can be observed with the timing light. The cylinder head must be disassembled for repairs.	**See Chapter 3**
9.2—Check the valve timing: Locate top dead center of the No. 1 piston, and install a degree wheel or tape on the crankshaft pulley or damper with zero corresponding to an index mark on the engine. Rotate the crankshaft in its direction of rotation, and observe the opening of the No. 1 cylinder intake valve. The opening should correspond with the correct mark on the degree wheel according to specifications.	If the timing is not correct, the timing cover must be removed for further investigation.	**See Chapter 3**

Section 10—Exhaust System

Test and Procedure	Results and Indications	Proceed to
10.1—Determine whether the exhaust manifold heat control valve is operating: Operate the valve by hand to determine whether it is free to move. If the valve is free, run the engine to operating temperature and observe the action of the valve, to ensure that it is opening.	If the valve sticks, spray it with a suitable solvent, open and close the valve to free it, and retest. If the valve functions properly: If the valve does not free, or does not operate, replace the valve:	10.2 10.2
10.2—Ensure that there are no exhaust restrictions: Visually inspect the exhaust system for kinks, dents, or crushing. Also note that gases are flowing freely from the tailpipe at all engine speeds, indicating no restriction in the muffler or resonator.	Replace any damaged portion of the system:	11.1

Section 11—Cooling System
See Chapter 3 for service procedures

Test and Procedure	Results and Indications	Proceed to
11.1—Visually inspect the fan belt for glazing, cracks, and fraying, and replace if necessary. Tighten the belt so that the longest span has approximately ½″ play at its midpoint under thumb pressure (see Chapter 1).	Replace or tighten the fan belt as necessary:	**11.2**

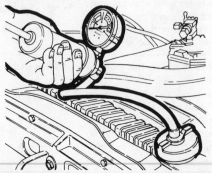

Checking belt tension

Test and Procedure	Results and Indications	Proceed to
11.2—Check the fluid level of the cooling system.	If full or slightly low, fill as necessary:	**11.5**
	If extremely low:	**11.3**
11.3—Visually inspect the external portions of the cooling system (radiator, radiator hoses, thermostat elbow, water pump seals, heater hoses, etc.) for leaks. If none are found, pressurize the cooling system to 14–15 psi.	If cooling system holds the pressure:	**11.5**
	If cooling system loses pressure rapidly, reinspect external parts of the system for leaks under pressure. If none are found, check dipstick for coolant in crankcase. If no coolant is present, but pressure loss continues:	**11.4**
	If coolant is evident in crankcase, remove cylinder head(s), and check gasket(s). If gaskets are intact, block and cylinder head(s) should be checked for cracks or holes.	
	If the gasket(s) is blown, replace, and purge the crankcase of coolant: **NOTE:** *Occasionally, due to atmospheric and driving conditions, condensation of water can occur in the crankcase. This causes the oil to appear milky white. To remedy, run the engine until hot, and change the oil and oil filter.*	**12.6**
11.4—Check for combustion leaks into the cooling system: Pressurize the cooling system as above. Start the engine, and observe the pressure gauge. If the needle fluctuates, remove each spark plug wire, one at a time, noting which cylinder(s) reduce or eliminate the fluctuation.	Cylinders which reduce or eliminate the fluctuation, when the spark plug wire is removed, are leaking into the cooling system. Replace the head gasket on the affected cylinder bank(s).	

Pressurizing the cooling system

Test and Procedure	Results and Indications	Proceed to
11.5—Check the radiator pressure cap: Attach a radiator pressure tester to the radiator cap (wet the seal prior to installation). Quickly pump up the pressure, noting the point at which the cap releases.	If the cap releases within ± 1 psi of the specified rating, it is operating properly:	**11.6**
	If the cap releases at more than ± 1 psi of the specified rating, it should be replaced:	**11.6**

Checking radiator pressure cap

Test and Procedure	Results and Indications	Proceed to
11.6—Test the thermostat: Start the engine cold, remove the radiator cap, and insert a thermometer into the radiator. Allow the engine to idle. After a short while, there will be a sudden, rapid increase in coolant temperature. The temperature at which this sharp rise stops is the thermostat opening temperature.	If the thermostat opens at or about the specified temperature:	**11.7**
	If the temperature doesn't increase: (If the temperature increases slowly and gradually, replace the thermostat.)	**11.7**
11.7—Check the water pump: Remove the thermostat elbow and the thermostat, disconnect the coil high tension lead (to prevent starting), and crank the engine momentarily.	If coolant flows, replace the thermostat and retest per 11.6:	**11.6**
	If coolant doesn't flow, reverse flush the cooling system to alleviate any blockage that might exist. If system is not blocked, and coolant will not flow, replace the water pump.	

Section 12—Lubrication
See Chapter 3 for service procedures

Test and Procedure	Results and Indications	Proceed to
12.1—Check the oil pressure gauge or warning light: If the gauge shows low pressure, or the light is on for no obvious reason, remove the oil pressure sender. Install an accurate oil pressure gauge and run the engine momentarily.	If oil pressure builds normally, run engine for a few moments to determine that it is functioning normally, and replace the sender.	—
	If the pressure remains low:	**12.2**
	If the pressure surges:	**12.3**
	If the oil pressure is zero:	**12.3**
12.2—Visually inspect the oil: If the oil is watery or very thin, milky, or foamy, replace the oil and oil filter.	If the oil is normal:	**12.3**
	If after replacing oil the pressure remains low:	**12.3**
	If after replacing oil the pressure becomes normal:	—

Test and Procedure	Results and Indications	Proceed to
12.3—Inspect the oil pressure relief valve and spring, to ensure that it is not sticking or stuck. Remove and thoroughly clean the valve, spring, and the valve body.	If the oil pressure improves: If no improvement is noted:	— **12.4**
12.4—Check to ensure that the oil pump is not cavitating (sucking air instead of oil): See that the crankcase is neither over nor underfull, and that the pickup in the sump is in the proper position and free from sludge.	Fill or drain the crankcase to the proper capacity, and clean the pickup screen in solvent if necessary. If no improvement is noted:	**12.5**
12.5—Inspect the oil pump drive and the oil pump:	If the pump drive or the oil pump appear to be defective, service as necessary and retest per 12.1: If the pump drive and pump appear to be operating normally, the engine should be disassembled to determine where blockage exists:	**12.1** **See Chapter 3**
12.6—Purge the engine of ethylene glycol coolant: Completely drain the crankcase and the oil filter. Obtain a commercial butyl cellosolve base solvent, designated for this purpose, and follow the instructions precisely. Following this, install a new oil filter and refill the crankcase with the proper weight oil. The next oil and filter change should follow shortly thereafter (1000 miles).		

TROUBLESHOOTING EMISSION CONTROL SYSTEMS

See Chapter 4 for procedures applicable to individual emission control systems used on specific combinations of engine/transmission/model.

TROUBLESHOOTING THE CARBURETOR

See Chapter 4 for service procedures

Carburetor problems cannot be effectively isolated unless all other engine systems (particularly ignition and emission) are functioning properly and the engine is properly tuned.

Condition	Possible Cause
Engine cranks, but does not start	1. Improper starting procedure 2. No fuel in tank 3. Clogged fuel line or filter 4. Defective fuel pump 5. Choke valve not closing properly 6. Engine flooded 7. Choke valve not unloading 8. Throttle linkage not making full travel 9. Stuck needle or float 10. Leaking float needle or seat 11. Improper float adjustment
Engine stalls	1. Improperly adjusted idle speed or mixture **Engine hot** 2. Improperly adjusted dashpot 3. Defective or improperly adjusted solenoid 4. Incorrect fuel level in fuel bowl 5. Fuel pump pressure too high 6. Leaking float needle seat 7. Secondary throttle valve stuck open 8. Air or fuel leaks 9. Idle air bleeds plugged or missing 10. Idle passages plugged **Engine Cold** 11. Incorrectly adjusted choke 12. Improperly adjusted fast idle speed 13. Air leaks 14. Plugged idle or idle air passages 15. Stuck choke valve or binding linkage 16. Stuck secondary throttle valves 17. Engine flooding—high fuel level 18. Leaking or misaligned float
Engine hesitates on acceleration	1. Clogged fuel filter 2. Leaking fuel pump diaphragm 3. Low fuel pump pressure 4. Secondary throttle valves stuck, bent or misadjusted 5. Sticking or binding air valve 6. Defective accelerator pump 7. Vacuum leaks 8. Clogged air filter 9. Incorrect choke adjustment (engine cold)
Engine feels sluggish or flat on acceleration	1. Improperly adjusted idle speed or mixture 2. Clogged fuel filter 3. Defective accelerator pump 4. Dirty, plugged or incorrect main metering jets 5. Bent or sticking main metering rods 6. Sticking throttle valves 7. Stuck heat riser 8. Binding or stuck air valve 9. Dirty, plugged or incorrect secondary jets 10. Bent or sticking secondary metering rods. 11. Throttle body or manifold heat passages plugged 12. Improperly adjusted choke or choke vacuum break.
Carburetor floods	1. Defective fuel pump. Pressure too high. 2. Stuck choke valve 3. Dirty, worn or damaged float or needle valve/seat 4. Incorrect float/fuel level 5. Leaking float bowl

Condition	Possible Cause
Engine idles roughly and stalls	1. Incorrect idle speed 2. Clogged fuel filter 3. Dirt in fuel system or carburetor 4. Loose carburetor screws or attaching bolts 5. Broken carburetor gaskets 6. Air leaks 7. Dirty carburetor 8. Worn idle mixture needles 9. Throttle valves stuck open 10. Incorrectly adjusted float or fuel level 11. Clogged air filter
Engine runs unevenly or surges	1. Defective fuel pump 2. Dirty or clogged fuel filter 3. Plugged, loose or incorrect main metering jets or rods 4. Air leaks 5. Bent or sticking main metering rods 6. Stuck power piston 7. Incorrect float adjustment 8. Incorrect idle speed or mixture 9. Dirty or plugged idle system passages 10. Hard, brittle or broken gaskets 11. Loose attaching or mounting screws 12. Stuck or misaligned secondary throttle valves
Poor fuel economy	1. Poor driving habits 2. Stuck choke valve 3. Binding choke linkage 4. Stuck heat riser 5. Incorrect idle mixture 6. Defective accelerator pump 7. Air leaks 8. Plugged, loose or incorrect main metering jets 9. Improperly adjusted float or fuel level 10. Bent, misaligned or fuel-clogged float 11. Leaking float needle seat 12. Fuel leak 13. Accelerator pump discharge ball not seating properly 14. Incorrect main jets
Engine lacks high speed performance or power	1. Incorrect throttle linkage adjustment 2. Stuck or binding power piston 3. Defective accelerator pump 4. Air leaks 5. Incorrect float setting or fuel level 6. Dirty, plugged, worn or incorrect main metering jets or rods 7. Binding or sticking air valve 8. Brittle or cracked gaskets 9. Bent, incorrect or improperly adjusted secondary metering rods 10. Clogged fuel filter 11. Clogged air filter 12. Defective fuel pump

TROUBLESHOOTING FUEL INJECTION PROBLEMS

Each fuel injection system has its own unique components and test procedures, for which it is impossible to generalize. Refer to Chapter 4 of this Repair & Tune-Up Guide for specific test and repair procedures, if the vehicle is equipped with fuel injection.

TROUBLESHOOTING ELECTRICAL PROBLEMS

See Chapter 5 for service procedures

For any electrical system to operate, it must make a complete circuit. This simply means that the power flow from the battery must make a complete circle. When an electrical component is operating, power flows from the battery to the component, passes through the component causing it to perform its function (lighting a light bulb), and then returns to the battery through the ground of the circuit. This ground is usually (but not always) the metal part of the car or truck on which the electrical component is mounted.

Perhaps the easiest way to visualize this is to think of connecting a light bulb with two wires attached to it to the battery. If one of the two wires attached to the light bulb were attached to the negative post of the battery and the other were attached to the positive post of the battery, you would have a complete circuit. Current from the battery would flow to the light bulb, causing it to light, and return to the negative post of the battery.

The normal automotive circuit differs from this simple example in two ways. First, instead of having a return wire from the bulb to the battery, the light bulb returns the current to the battery through the chassis of the vehicle. Since the negative battery cable is attached to the chassis and the chassis is made of electrically conductive metal, the chassis of the vehicle can serve as a ground wire to complete the circuit. Secondly, most automotive circuits contain switches to turn components on and off as required.

Every complete circuit from a power source must include a component which is using the power from the power source. If you were to disconnect the light bulb from the wires and touch the two wires together (don't do this) the power supply wire to the component would be grounded before the normal ground connection for the circuit.

Because grounding a wire from a power source makes a complete circuit—less the required component to use the power—this phenomenon is called a short circuit. Common causes are: broken insulation (exposing the metal wire to a metal part of the car or truck), or a shorted switch.

Some electrical components which require a large amount of current to operate also have a relay in their circuit. Since these circuits carry a large amount of current, the thickness of the wire in the circuit (gauge size) is also greater. If this large wire were connected from the component to the control switch on the instrument panel, and then back to the component, a voltage drop would occur in the circuit. To prevent this potential drop in voltage, an electromagnetic switch (relay) is used. The large wires in the circuit are connected from the battery to one side of the relay, and from the opposite side of the relay to the component. The relay is normally open, preventing current from passing through the circuit. An additional, smaller, wire is connected from the relay to the control switch for the circuit. When the control switch is turned on, it grounds the smaller wire from the relay and completes the circuit. This closes the relay and allows current to flow from the battery to the component. The horn, headlight, and starter circuits are three which use relays.

It is possible for larger surges of current to pass through the electrical system of your car or truck. If this surge of current were to reach an electrical component, it could burn it out. To prevent this, fuses, circuit breakers or fusible links are connected into the current supply wires of most of the major electrical systems. When an electrical current of excessive power passes through the component's fuse, the fuse blows out and breaks the circuit, saving the component from destruction.

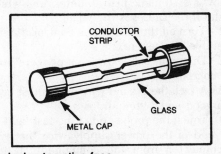

Typical automotive fuse

A circuit breaker is basically a self-repairing fuse. The circuit breaker opens the circuit the same way a fuse does. However, when either the short is removed from the circuit or the surge subsides, the circuit breaker resets itself and does not have to be replaced as a fuse does.

A fuse link is a wire that acts as a fuse. It is normally connected between the starter relay and the main wiring harness. This connection is usually under the hood. The fuse link (if installed) protects all the

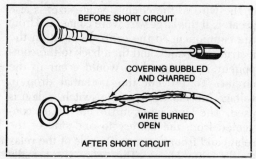

BEFORE SHORT CIRCUIT

COVERING BUBBLED AND CHARRED

WIRE BURNED OPEN

AFTER SHORT CIRCUIT

Most fusible links show a charred, melted insulation when they burn out

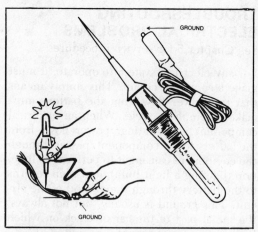

GROUND

GROUND

The test light will show the presence of current when touched to a hot wire and grounded at the other end

chassis electrical components, and is the probable cause of trouble when none of the electrical components function, unless the battery is disconnected or dead.

Electrical problems generally fall into one of three areas:

1. The component that is not functioning is not receiving current.

2. The component itself is not functioning.

3. The component is not properly grounded.

The electrical system can be checked with a test light and a jumper wire. A test light is a device that looks like a pointed screwdriver with a wire attached to it and has a light bulb in its handle. A jumper wire is a piece of insulated wire with an alligator clip attached to each end.

If a component is not working, you must follow a systematic plan to determine which of the three causes is the villain.

1. Turn on the switch that controls the inoperable component.

2. Disconnect the power supply wire from the component.

3. Attach the ground wire on the test light to a good metal ground.

4. Touch the probe end of the test light to the end of the power supply wire that was disconnected from the component. If the component is receiving current, the test light will go on.

NOTE: *Some components work only when the ignition switch is turned on.*

If the test light does not go on, then the problem is in the circuit between the battery and the component. This includes all the switches, fuses, and relays in the system. Follow the wire that runs back to the battery. The problem is an open circuit between the

battery and the component. If the fuse is blown and, when replaced, immediately blows again, there is a short circuit in the system which must be located and repaired. If there is a switch in the system, bypass it with a jumper wire. This is done by connecting one end of the jumper wire to the power supply wire into the switch and the other end of the jumper wire to the wire coming out of the switch. If the test light lights with the jumper wire installed, the switch or whatever was bypassed is defective.

NOTE: *Never substitute the jumper wire for the component, since it is required to use the power from the power source.*

5. If the bulb in the test light goes on, then the current is getting to the component that is not working. This eliminates the first of the three possible causes. Connect the power supply wire and connect a jumper wire from the component to a good metal ground. Do this with the switch which controls the component turned on, and also the ignition switch turned on if it is required for the component to work. If the component works with the jumper wire installed, then it has a bad ground. This is usually caused by the metal area on which the component mounts to the chassis being coated with some type of foreign matter.

6. If neither test located the source of the trouble, then the component itself is defective. Remember that for any electrical system to work, all connections must be clean and tight.

Troubleshooting Basic Turn Signal and Flasher Problems
See Chapter 5 for service procedures

Most problems in the turn signals or flasher system can be reduced to defective flashers or bulbs, which are easily replaced. Occasionally, the turn signal switch will prove defective.

F = Front   R = Rear   ● = Lights off   ○ = Lights on

Condition		Possible Cause
Turn signals light, but do not flash	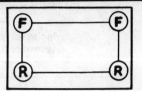	Defective flasher
No turn signals light on either side	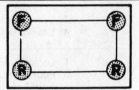	Blown fuse. Replace if defective. Defective flasher. Check by substitution. Open circuit, short circuit or poor ground.
Both turn signals on one side don't work	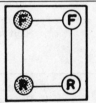	Bad bulbs. Bad ground in both (or either) housings.
One turn signal light on one side doesn't work	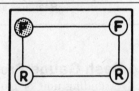	Defective bulb. Corrosion in socket. Clean contacts. Poor ground at socket.
Turn signal flashes too fast or too slowly	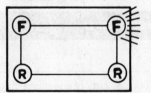	Check any bulb on the side flashing too fast. A heavy-duty bulb is probably installed in place of a regular bulb. Check the bulb flashing too slowly. A standard bulb was probably installed in place of a heavy-duty bulb. Loose connections or corrosion at the bulb socket.
Indicator lights don't work in either direction		Check if the turn signals are working. Check the dash indicator lights. Check the flasher by substitution.
One indicator light doesn't light		On systems with one dash indicator: See if the lights work on the same side. Often the filaments have been reversed in systems combining stoplights with taillights and turn signals. Check the flasher by substitution. On systems with two indicators: Check the bulbs on the same side. Check the indicator light bulb. Check the flasher by substitution.

Troubleshooting Lighting Problems
See Chapter 5 for service procedures

Condition	Possible Cause
One or more lights don't work, but others do	1. Defective bulb(s) 2. Blown fuse(s) 3. Dirty fuse clips or light sockets 4. Poor ground circuit
Lights burn out quickly	1. Incorrect voltage regulator setting or defective regulator 2. Poor battery/alternator connections
Lights go dim	1. Low/discharged battery 2. Alternator not charging 3. Corroded sockets or connections 4. Low voltage output
Lights flicker	1. Loose connection 2. Poor ground. (Run ground wire from light housing to frame) 3. Circuit breaker operating (short circuit)
Lights "flare"—Some flare is normal on acceleration—If excessive, see "Lights Burn Out Quickly"	High voltage setting
Lights glare—approaching drivers are blinded	1. Lights adjusted too high 2. Rear springs or shocks sagging 3. Rear tires soft

Troubleshooting Dash Gauge Problems
Most problems can be traced to a defective sending unit or faulty wiring. Occasionally, the gauge itself is at fault. See Chapter 5 for service procedures.

Condition	Possible Cause
COOLANT TEMPERATURE GAUGE	
Gauge reads erratically or not at all	1. Loose or dirty connections 2. Defective sending unit. 3. Defective gauge. To test a bi-metal gauge, remove the wire from the sending unit. Ground the wire for an instant. If the gauge registers, replace the sending unit. To test a magnetic gauge, disconnect the wire at the sending unit. With ignition ON gauge should register COLD. Ground the wire; gauge should register HOT.
AMMETER GAUGE—TURN HEADLIGHTS ON (DO NOT START ENGINE). NOTE REACTION	
Ammeter shows charge Ammeter shows discharge Ammeter does not move	1. Connections reversed on gauge 2. Ammeter is OK 3. Loose connections or faulty wiring 4. Defective gauge

Condition	Possible Cause

OIL PRESSURE GAUGE

Gauge does not register or is inaccurate	1. On mechanical gauge, Bourdon tube may be bent or kinked. 2. Low oil pressure. Remove sending unit. Idle the engine briefly. If no oil flows from sending unit hole, problem is in engine. 3. Defective gauge. Remove the wire from the sending unit and ground it for an instant with the ignition ON. A good gauge will go to the top of the scale. 4. Defective wiring. Check the wiring to the gauge. If it's OK and the gauge doesn't register when grounded, replace the gauge. 5. Defective sending unit.

ALL GAUGES

All gauges do not operate All gauges read low or erratically All gauges pegged	1. Blown fuse 2. Defective instrument regulator 3. Defective or dirty instrument voltage regulator 4. Loss of ground between instrument voltage regulator and frame 5. Defective instrument regulator

WARNING LIGHTS

Light(s) do not come on when ignition is ON, but engine is not started Light comes on with engine running	1. Defective bulb 2. Defective wire 3. Defective sending unit. Disconnect the wire from the sending unit and ground it. Replace the sending unit if the light comes on with the ignition ON. 4. Problem in individual system 5. Defective sending unit

Troubleshooting Clutch Problems

It is false economy to replace individual clutch components. The pressure plate, clutch plate and throwout bearing should be replaced as a set, and the flywheel face inspected, whenever the clutch is overhauled. See Chapter 6 for service procedures.

Condition	Possible Cause
Clutch chatter	1. Grease on driven plate (disc) facing 2. Binding clutch linkage or cable 3. Loose, damaged facings on driven plate (disc) 4. Engine mounts loose 5. Incorrect height adjustment of pressure plate release levers 6. Clutch housing or housing to transmission adapter misalignment 7. Loose driven plate hub
Clutch grabbing	1. Oil, grease on driven plate (disc) facing 2. Broken pressure plate 3. Warped or binding driven plate. Driven plate binding on clutch shaft
Clutch slips	1. Lack of lubrication in clutch linkage or cable (linkage or cable binds, causes incomplete engagement) 2. Incorrect pedal, or linkage adjustment 3. Broken pressure plate springs 4. Weak pressure plate springs 5. Grease on driven plate facings (disc)

Troubleshooting Clutch Problems (cont.)

Condition	Possible Cause
Incomplete clutch release	1. Incorrect pedal or linkage adjustment or linkage or cable binding 2. Incorrect height adjustment on pressure plate release levers 3. Loose, broken facings on driven plate (disc) 4. Bent, dished, warped driven plate caused by overheating
Grinding, whirring grating noise when pedal is depressed	1. Worn or defective throwout bearing 2. Starter drive teeth contacting flywheel ring gear teeth. Look for milled or polished teeth on ring gear.
Squeal, howl, trumpeting noise when pedal is being released (occurs during first inch to inch and one-half of pedal travel)	Pilot bushing worn or lack of lubricant. If bushing appears OK, polish bushing with emery cloth, soak lube wick in oil, lube bushing with oil, apply film of chassis grease to clutch shaft pilot hub, reassemble. NOTE: Bushing wear may be due to misalignment of clutch housing or housing to transmission adapter
Vibration or clutch pedal pulsation with clutch disengaged (pedal fully depressed)	1. Worn or defective engine transmission mounts 2. Flywheel run out. (Flywheel run out at face not to exceed 0.005″) 3. Damaged or defective clutch components

Troubleshooting Manual Transmission Problems
See Chapter 6 for service procedures

Condition	Possible Cause
Transmission jumps out of gear	1. Misalignment of transmission case or clutch housing. 2. Worn pilot bearing in crankshaft. 3. Bent transmission shaft. 4. Worn high speed sliding gear. 5. Worn teeth or end-play in clutch shaft. 6. Insufficient spring tension on shifter rail plunger. 7. Bent or loose shifter fork. 8. Gears not engaging completely. 9. Loose or worn bearings on clutch shaft or mainshaft. 10. Worn gear teeth. 11. Worn or damaged detent balls.
Transmission sticks in gear	1. Clutch not releasing fully. 2. Burred or battered teeth on clutch shaft, or sliding sleeve. 3. Burred or battered transmission mainshaft. 4. Frozen synchronizing clutch. 5. Stuck shifter rail plunger. 6. Gearshift lever twisting and binding shifter rail. 7. Battered teeth on high speed sliding gear or on sleeve. 8. Improper lubrication, or lack of lubrication. 9. Corroded transmission parts. 10. Defective mainshaft pilot bearing. 11. Locked gear bearings will give same effect as stuck in gear.
Transmission gears will not synchronize	1. Binding pilot bearing on mainshaft, will synchronize in high gear only. 2. Clutch not releasing fully. 3. Detent spring weak or broken. 4. Weak or broken springs under balls in sliding gear sleeve. 5. Binding bearing on clutch shaft, or binding countershaft. 6. Binding pilot bearing in crankshaft. 7. Badly worn gear teeth. 8. Improper lubrication. 9. Constant mesh gear not turning freely on transmission mainshaft. Will synchronize in that gear only.

Condition	Possible Cause
Gears spinning when shifting into gear from neutral	1. Clutch not releasing fully. 2. In some cases an extremely light lubricant in transmission will cause gears to continue to spin for a short time after clutch is released. 3. Binding pilot bearing in crankshaft.
Transmission noisy in all gears	1. Insufficient lubricant, or improper lubricant. 2. Worn countergear bearings. 3. Worn or damaged main drive gear or countergear. 4. Damaged main drive gear or mainshaft bearings. 5. Worn or damaged countergear anti-lash plate.
Transmission noisy in neutral only	1. Damaged main drive gear bearing. 2. Damaged or loose mainshaft pilot bearing. 3. Worn or damaged countergear anti-lash plate. 4. Worn countergear bearings.
Transmission noisy in one gear only	1. Damaged or worn constant mesh gears. 2. Worn or damaged countergear bearings. 3. Damaged or worn synchronizer.
Transmission noisy in reverse only	1. Worn or damaged reverse idler gear or idler bushing. 2. Worn or damaged mainshaft reverse gear. 3. Worn or damaged reverse countergear. 4. Damaged shift mechanism.

TROUBLESHOOTING AUTOMATIC TRANSMISSION PROBLEMS

Keeping alert to changes in the operating characteristics of the transmission (changing shift points, noises, etc.) can prevent small problems from becoming large ones. If the problem cannot be traced to loose bolts, fluid level, misadjusted linkage, clogged filters or similar problems, you should probably seek professional service.

Transmission Fluid Indications

The appearance and odor of the transmission fluid can give valuable clues to the overall condition of the transmission. Always note the appearance of the fluid when you check the fluid level or change the fluid. Rub a small amount of fluid between your fingers to feel for grit and smell the fluid on the dipstick.

If the fluid appears:	It indicates:
Clear and red colored	Normal operation
Discolored (extremely dark red or brownish) or smells burned	Band or clutch pack failure, usually caused by an overheated transmission. Hauling very heavy loads with insufficient power or failure to change the fluid often result in overheating. Do not confuse this appearance with newer fluids that have a darker red color and a strong odor (though not a burned odor).
Foamy or aerated (light in color and full of bubbles)	1. The level is too high (gear train is churning oil) 2. An internal air leak (air is mixing with the fluid). Have the transmission checked professionally.
Solid residue in the fluid	Defective bands, clutch pack or bearings. Bits of band material or metal abrasives are clinging to the dipstick. Have the transmission checked professionally.
Varnish coating on the dipstick	The transmission fluid is overheating

TROUBLESHOOTING DRIVE AXLE PROBLEMS

First, determine when the noise is most noticeable.

Drive Noise: Produced under vehicle acceleration.

Coast Noise: Produced while coasting with a closed throttle.

Float Noise: Occurs while maintaining constant speed (just enough to keep speed constant) on a level road.

External Noise Elimination

It is advisable to make a thorough road test to determine whether the noise originates in the rear axle or whether it originates from the tires, engine, transmission, wheel bearings or road surface. Noise originating from other places cannot be corrected by servicing the rear axle.

ROAD NOISE

Brick or rough surfaced concrete roads produce noises that seem to come from the rear axle. Road noise is usually identical in Drive or Coast and driving on a different type of road will tell whether the road is the problem.

TIRE NOISE

Tire noise can be mistaken as rear axle noise, even though the tires on the front are at fault. Snow tread and mud tread tires or tires worn unevenly will frequently cause vibrations which seem to originate elsewhere; *temporarily, and for test purposes only,* inflate the tires to 40–50 lbs. This will significantly alter the noise produced by the tires, but will not alter noise from the rear axle. Noises from the rear axle will normally cease at speeds below 30 mph on coast, while tire noise will continue at lower tone as speed is decreased. The rear axle noise will usually change from drive conditions to coast conditions, while tire noise will not. Do not forget to lower the tire pressure to normal after the test is complete.

ENGINE/TRANSMISSION NOISE

Determine at what speed the noise is most pronounced, then stop in a quiet place. With the transmission in Neutral, run the engine through speeds corresponding to road speeds where the noise was noticed. Noises produced with the vehicle standing still are coming from the engine or transmission.

FRONT WHEEL BEARINGS

Front wheel bearing noises, sometimes confused with rear axle noises, will not change when comparing drive and coast conditions. While holding the speed steady, lightly apply the footbrake. This will often cause wheel bearing noise to lessen, as some of the weight is taken off the bearing. Front wheel bearings are easily checked by jacking up the wheels and spinning the wheels. Shaking the wheels will also determine if the wheel bearings are excessively loose.

REAR AXLE NOISES

Eliminating other possible sources can narrow the cause to the rear axle, which normally produces noise from worn gears or bearings. Gear noises tend to peak in a narrow speed range, while bearing noises will usually vary in pitch with engine speeds.

Noise Diagnosis

The Noise Is:	Most Probably Produced By:
1. Identical under Drive or Coast	Road surface, tires or front wheel bearings
2. Different depending on road surface	Road surface or tires
3. Lower as speed is lowered	Tires
4. Similar when standing or moving	Engine or transmission
5. A vibration	Unbalanced tires, rear wheel bearing, unbalanced driveshaft or worn U-joint
6. A knock or click about every two tire revolutions	Rear wheel bearing
7. Most pronounced on turns	Damaged differential gears
8. A steady low-pitched whirring or scraping, starting at low speeds	Damaged or worn pinion bearing
9. A chattering vibration on turns	Wrong differential lubricant or worn clutch plates (limited slip rear axle)
10. Noticed only in Drive, Coast or Float conditions	Worn ring gear and/or pinion gear

Troubleshooting Steering & Suspension Problems

Condition	Possible Cause
Hard steering (wheel is hard to turn)	1. Improper tire pressure 2. Loose or glazed pump drive belt 3. Low or incorrect fluid 4. Loose, bent or poorly lubricated front end parts 5. Improper front end alignment (excessive caster) 6. Bind in steering column or linkage 7. Kinked hydraulic hose 8. Air in hydraulic system 9. Low pump output or leaks in system 10. Obstruction in lines 11. Pump valves sticking or out of adjustment 12. Incorrect wheel alignment
Loose steering (too much play in steering wheel)	1. Loose wheel bearings 2. Faulty shocks 3. Worn linkage or suspension components 4. Loose steering gear mounting or linkage points 5. Steering mechanism worn or improperly adjusted 6. Valve spool improperly adjusted 7. Worn ball joints, tie-rod ends, etc.
Veers or wanders (pulls to one side with hands off steering wheel)	1. Improper tire pressure 2. Improper front end alignment 3. Dragging or improperly adjusted brakes 4. Bent frame 5. Improper rear end alignment 6. Faulty shocks or springs 7. Loose or bent front end components 8. Play in Pitman arm 9. Steering gear mountings loose 10. Loose wheel bearings 11. Binding Pitman arm 12. Spool valve sticking or improperly adjusted 13. Worn ball joints
Wheel oscillation or vibration transmitted through steering wheel	1. Low or uneven tire pressure 2. Loose wheel bearings 3. Improper front end alignment 4. Bent spindle 5. Worn, bent or broken front end components 6. Tires out of round or out of balance 7. Excessive lateral runout in disc brake rotor 8. Loose or bent shock absorber or strut
Noises (see also "Troubleshooting Drive Axle Problems")	1. Loose belts 2. Low fluid, air in system 3. Foreign matter in system 4. Improper lubrication 5. Interference or chafing in linkage 6. Steering gear mountings loose 7. Incorrect adjustment or wear in gear box 8. Faulty valves or wear in pump 9. Kinked hydraulic lines 10. Worn wheel bearings
Poor return of steering	1. Over-inflated tires 2. Improperly aligned front end (excessive caster) 3. Binding in steering column 4. No lubrication in front end 5. Steering gear adjusted too tight
Uneven tire wear (see "How To Read Tire Wear")	1. Incorrect tire pressure 2. Improperly aligned front end 3. Tires out-of-balance 4. Bent or worn suspension parts

HOW TO READ TIRE WEAR

The way your tires wear is a good indicator of other parts of the suspension. Abnormal wear patterns are often caused by the need for simple tire maintenance, or for front end alignment.

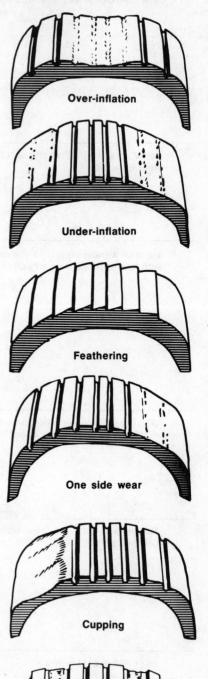

Excessive wear at the center of the tread indicates that the air pressure in the tire is consistently too high. The tire is riding on the center of the tread and wearing it prematurely. Occasionally, this wear pattern can result from outrageously wide tires on narrow rims. The cure for this is to replace either the tires or the wheels.

Over-inflation

This type of wear usually results from consistent under-inflation. When a tire is under-inflated, there is too much contact with the road by the outer treads, which wear prematurely. When this type of wear occurs, and the tire pressure is known to be consistently correct, a bent or worn steering component or the need for wheel alignment could be indicated.

Under-inflation

Feathering is a condition when the edge of each tread rib develops a slightly rounded edge on one side and a sharp edge on the other. By running your hand over the tire, you can usually feel the sharper edges before you'll be able to see them. The most common causes of feathering are incorrect toe-in setting or deteriorated bushings in the front suspension.

Feathering

When an inner or outer rib wears faster than the rest of the tire, the need for wheel alignment is indicated. There is excessive camber in the front suspension, causing the wheel to lean too much putting excessive load on one side of the tire. Misalignment could also be due to sagging springs, worn ball joints, or worn control arm bushings. Be sure the vehicle is loaded the way it's normally driven when you have the wheels aligned.

One side wear

Cups or scalloped dips appearing around the edge of the tread almost always indicate worn (sometimes bent) suspension parts. Adjustment of wheel alignment alone will seldom cure the problem. Any worn component that connects the wheel to the suspension can cause this type of wear. Occasionally, wheels that are out of balance will wear like this, but wheel imbalance usually shows up as bald spots between the outside edges and center of the tread.

Cupping

Second-rib wear is usually found only in radial tires, and appears where the steel belts end in relation to the tread. It can be kept to a minimum by paying careful attention to tire pressure and frequently rotating the tires. This is often considered normal wear but excessive amounts indicate that the tires are too wide for the wheels.

Second-rib wear

Troubleshooting Disc Brake Problems

Condition	Possible Cause
Noise—groan—brake noise emanating when slowly releasing brakes (creep-groan)	Not detrimental to function of disc brakes—no corrective action required. (This noise may be eliminated by slightly increasing or decreasing brake pedal efforts.)
Rattle—brake noise or rattle emanating at low speeds on rough roads, (front wheels only).	1. Shoe anti-rattle spring missing or not properly positioned. 2. Excessive clearance between shoe and caliper. 3. Soft or broken caliper seals. 4. Deformed or misaligned disc. 5. Loose caliper.
Scraping	1. Mounting bolts too long. 2. Loose wheel bearings. 3. Bent, loose, or misaligned splash shield.
Front brakes heat up during driving and fail to release	1. Operator riding brake pedal. 2. Stop light switch improperly adjusted. 3. Sticking pedal linkage. 4. Frozen or seized piston. 5. Residual pressure valve in master cylinder. 6. Power brake malfunction. 7. Proportioning valve malfunction.
Leaky brake caliper	1. Damaged or worn caliper piston seal. 2. Scores or corrosion on surface of cylinder bore.
Grabbing or uneven brake action— Brakes pull to one side	1. Causes listed under ''Brakes Pull''. 2. Power brake malfunction. 3. Low fluid level in master cylinder. 4. Air in hydraulic system. 5. Brake fluid, oil or grease on linings. 6. Unmatched linings. 7. Distorted brake pads. 8. Frozen or seized pistons. 9. Incorrect tire pressure. 10. Front end out of alignment. 11. Broken rear spring. 12. Brake caliper pistons sticking. 13. Restricted hose or line. 14. Caliper not in proper alignment to braking disc. 15. Stuck or malfunctioning metering valve. 16. Soft or broken caliper seals. 17. Loose caliper.
Brake pedal can be depressed without braking effect	1. Air in hydraulic system or improper bleeding procedure. 2. Leak past primary cup in master cylinder. 3. Leak in system. 4. Rear brakes out of adjustment. 5. Bleeder screw open.
Excessive pedal travel	1. Air, leak, or insufficient fluid in system or caliper. 2. Warped or excessively tapered shoe and lining assembly. 3. Excessive disc runout. 4. Rear brake adjustment required. 5. Loose wheel bearing adjustment. 6. Damaged caliper piston seal. 7. Improper brake fluid (boil). 8. Power brake malfunction. 9. Weak or soft hoses.

Troubleshooting Disc Brake Problems (cont.)

Condition	Possible Cause
Brake roughness or chatter (pedal pumping)	1. Excessive thickness variation of braking disc. 2. Excessive lateral runout of braking disc. 3. Rear brake drums out-of-round. 4. Excessive front bearing clearance.
Excessive pedal effort	1. Brake fluid, oil or grease on linings. 2. Incorrect lining. 3. Frozen or seized pistons. 4. Power brake malfunction. 5. Kinked or collapsed hose or line. 6. Stuck metering valve. 7. Scored caliper or master cylinder bore. 8. Seized caliper pistons.
Brake pedal fades (pedal travel increases with foot on brake)	1. Rough master cylinder or caliper bore. 2. Loose or broken hydraulic lines/connections. 3. Air in hydraulic system. 4. Fluid level low. 5. Weak or soft hoses. 6. Inferior quality brake shoes or fluid. 7. Worn master cylinder piston cups or seals.

Troubleshooting Drum Brakes

Condition	Possible Cause
Pedal goes to floor	1. Fluid low in reservoir. 2. Air in hydraulic system. 3. Improperly adjusted brake. 4. Leaking wheel cylinders. 5. Loose or broken brake lines. 6. Leaking or worn master cylinder. 7. Excessively worn brake lining.
Spongy brake pedal	1. Air in hydraulic system. 2. Improper brake fluid (low boiling point). 3. Excessively worn or cracked brake drums. 4. Broken pedal pivot bushing.
Brakes pulling	1. Contaminated lining. 2. Front end out of alignment. 3. Incorrect brake adjustment. 4. Unmatched brake lining. 5. Brake drums out of round. 6. Brake shoes distorted. 7. Restricted brake hose or line. 8. Broken rear spring. 9. Worn brake linings. 10. Uneven lining wear. 11. Glazed brake lining. 12. Excessive brake lining dust. 13. Heat spotted brake drums. 14. Weak brake return springs. 15. Faulty automatic adjusters. 16. Low or incorrect tire pressure.

Condition	Possible Cause
Squealing brakes	1. Glazed brake lining. 2. Saturated brake lining. 3. Weak or broken brake shoe retaining spring. 4. Broken or weak brake shoe return spring. 5. Incorrect brake lining. 6. Distorted brake shoes. 7. Bent support plate. 8. Dust in brakes or scored brake drums. 9. Linings worn below limit. 10. Uneven brake lining wear. 11. Heat spotted brake drums.
Chirping brakes	1. Out of round drum or eccentric axle flange pilot.
Dragging brakes	1. Incorrect wheel or parking brake adjustment. 2. Parking brakes engaged or improperly adjusted. 3. Weak or broken brake shoe return spring. 4. Brake pedal binding. 5. Master cylinder cup sticking. 6. Obstructed master cylinder relief port. 7. Saturated brake lining. 8. Bent or out of round brake drum. 9. Contaminated or improper brake fluid. 10. Sticking wheel cylinder pistons. 11. Driver riding brake pedal. 12. Defective proportioning valve. 13. Insufficient brake shoe lubricant.
Hard pedal	1. Brake booster inoperative. 2. Incorrect brake lining. 3. Restricted brake line or hose. 4. Frozen brake pedal linkage. 5. Stuck wheel cylinder. 6. Binding pedal linkage. 7. Faulty proportioning valve.
Wheel locks	1. Contaminated brake lining. 2. Loose or torn brake lining. 3. Wheel cylinder cups sticking. 4. Incorrect wheel bearing adjustment. 5. Faulty proportioning valve.
Brakes fade (high speed)	1. Incorrect lining. 2. Overheated brake drums. 3. Incorrect brake fluid (low boiling temperature). 4. Saturated brake lining. 5. Leak in hydraulic system. 6. Faulty automatic adjusters.
Pedal pulsates	1. Bent or out of round brake drum.
Brake chatter and shoe knock	1. Out of round brake drum. 2. Loose support plate. 3. Bent support plate. 4. Distorted brake shoes. 5. Machine grooves in contact face of brake drum (Shoe Knock). 6. Contaminated brake lining. 7. Missing or loose components. 8. Incorrect lining material. 9. Out-of-round brake drums. 10. Heat spotted or scored brake drums. 11. Out-of-balance wheels.

Troubleshooting Drum Brakes (cont.)

Condition	Possible Cause
Brakes do not self adjust	1. Adjuster screw frozen in thread. 2. Adjuster screw corroded at thrust washer. 3. Adjuster lever does not engage star wheel. 4. Adjuster installed on wrong wheel.
Brake light glows	1. Leak in the hydraulic system. 2. Air in the system. 3. Improperly adjusted master cylinder pushrod. 4. Uneven lining wear. 5. Failure to center combination valve or proportioning valve.

Mechanic's Data

General Conversion Table

Multiply By	To Convert	To	
LENGTH			
2.54	Inches	Centimeters	.3937
25.4	Inches	Millimeters	.03937
30.48	Feet	Centimeters	.0328
.304	Feet	Meters	3.28
.914	Yards	Meters	1.094
1.609	Miles	Kilometers	.621
VOLUME			
.473	Pints	Liters	2.11
.946	Quarts	Liters	1.06
3.785	Gallons	Liters	.264
.016	Cubic inches	Liters	61.02
16.39	Cubic inches	Cubic cms.	.061
28.3	Cubic feet	Liters	.0353
MASS (Weight)			
28.35	Ounces	Grams	.035
.4536	Pounds	Kilograms	2.20
—	To obtain	From	Multiply by

Multiply By	To Convert	To	
AREA			
.645	Square inches	Square cms.	.155
.836	Square yds.	Square meters	1.196
FORCE			
4.448	Pounds	Newtons	.225
.138	Ft./lbs.	Kilogram/meters	7.23
1.36	Ft./lbs.	Newton-meters	.737
.112	In./lbs.	Newton-meters	8.844
PRESSURE			
.068	Psi	Atmospheres	14.7
6.89	Psi	Kilopascals	.145
OTHER			
1.104	Horsepower (DIN)	Horsepower (SAE)	.9861
.746	Horsepower (SAE)	Kilowatts (KW)	1.34
1.60	Mph	Km/h	.625
.425	Mpg	Km/1	2.35
—	To obtain	From	Multiply by

Tap Drill Sizes

National Coarse or U.S.S.

Screw & Tap Size	Threads Per Inch	Use Drill Number
No. 5	40	.39
No. 6	32	.36
No. 8	32	.29
No. 10	24	.25
No. 12	24	.17
1/4	20	8
5/16	18	F
3/8	16	5/16
7/16	14	U
1/2	13	27/64
9/16	12	31/64
5/8	11	17/32
3/4	10	21/32
7/8	9	49/64

National Coarse or U.S.S.

Screw & Tap Size	Threads Per Inch	Use Drill Number
1	8	7/8
1 1/8	7	63/64
1 1/4	7	1 7/64
1 1/2	6	1 11/32

National Fine or S.A.E.

Screw & Tap Size	Threads Per Inch	Use Drill Number
No. 5	44	.37
No. 6	40	.33
No. 8	36	.29
No. 10	32	.21

National Fine or S.A.E.

Screw & Tap Size	Threads Per Inch	Use Drill Number
No. 12	28	15
1/4	28	3
6/16	24	1
3/8	24	Q
7/16	20	W
1/2	20	29/64
9/16	18	33/64
5/8	18	37/64
3/4	16	11/16
7/8	14	13/16
1 1/8	12	13/64
1 1/4	12	1 11/64
1 1/2	12	1 27/64

Index

Chilton's Repair & Tune-Up Guides

The Complete line covers domestic cars, imports, trucks, vans, RV's and 4-wheel drive vehicles.

RTUG Title	Part No.
AMC 1975-82	7199
Covers all U.S. and Canadian models	
Aspen/Volare 1976-80	6637
Covers all U.S. and Canadian models	
Audi 1970-73	5902
Covers all U.S. and Canadian models.	
Audi 4000/5000 1978-81	7028
Covers all U.S. and Canadian models including turbocharged and diesel engines	
Barracuda/Challenger 1965-72	5807
Covers all U.S. and Canadian models	
Blazer/Jimmy 1969-82	6931
Covers all U.S. and Canadian 2- and 4-wheel drive models, including diesel engines	
BMW 1970-82	6844
Covers U.S. and Canadian models	
Buick/Olds/Pontiac 1975-85	7308
Covers all U.S. and Canadian full size rear wheel drive models	
Cadillac 1967-84	7462
Covers all U.S. and Canadian rear wheel drive models	
Camaro 1967-81	6735
Covers all U.S. and Canadian models	
Camaro 1982-85	7317
Covers all U.S. and Canadian models	
Capri 1970-77	6695
Covers all U.S. and Canadian models	
Caravan/Voyager 1984-85	7482
Covers all U.S. and Canadian models	
Century/Regal 1975-85	7307
Covers all U.S. and Canadian rear wheel drive models, including turbocharged engines	
Champ/Arrow/Sapporo 1978-83	7041
Covers all U.S. and Canadian models	
Chevette/1000 1976-86	6836
Covers all U.S. and Canadian models	
Chevrolet 1968-85	7135
Covers all U.S. and Canadian models	
Chevrolet 1968-79 Spanish	7082
Chevrolet/GMC Pick-Ups 1970-82 Spanish	7468
Chevrolet/GMC Pick-Ups and Suburban 1970-86	6936
Covers all U.S. and Canadian 1/2, 3/4 and 1 ton models, including 4-wheel drive and diesel engines	
Chevrolet LUV 1972-81	6815
Covers all U.S. and Canadian models	
Chevrolet Mid-Size 1964-86	6840
Covers all U.S. and Canadian models of 1964-77 Chevelle, Malibu and Malibu SS; 1974-77 Laguna; 1978-85 Malibu; 1970-86 Monte Carlo; 1964-84 El Camino, including diesel engines	
Chevrolet Nova 1986	7658
Covers all U.S. and Canadian models	
Chevy/GMC Vans 1967-84	6930
Covers all U.S. and Canadian models of 1/2, 3/4, and 1 ton vans, cutaways, and motor home chassis, including diesel engines	
Chevy S-10 Blazer/GMC S-15 Jimmy 1982-85	7383
Covers all U.S. and Canadian models	
Chevy S-10/GMC S-15 Pick-Ups 1982-85	7310
Covers all U.S. and Canadian models	
Chevy II/Nova 1962-79	6841
Covers all U.S. and Canadian models	
Chrysler K- and E-Car 1981-85	7163
Covers all U.S. and Canadian front wheel drive models	
Colt/Challenger/Vista/Conquest 1971-85	7037
Covers all U.S. and Canadian models	
Corolla/Carina/Tercel/Starlet 1970-85	7036
Covers all U.S. and Canadian models	
Corona/Cressida/Crown/Mk.II/Camry/Van 1970-84	7044
Covers all U.S. and Canadian models	

RTUG Title	Part No.
Corvair 1960-69	6691
Covers all U.S. and Canadian models	
Corvette 1953-62	6576
Covers all U.S. and Canadian models	
Corvette 1963-84	6843
Covers all U.S. and Canadian models	
Cutlass 1970-85	6933
Covers all U.S. and Canadian models	
Dart/Demon 1968-76	6324
Covers all U.S. and Canadian models	
Datsun 1961-72	5790
Covers all U.S. and Canadian models of Nissan Patrol; 1500, 1600 and 2000 sports cars; Pick-Ups; 410, 411, 510, 1200 and 240Z	
Datsun 1973-80 Spanish	7083
Datsun/Nissan F-10, 310, Stanza, Pulsar 1977-86	7196
Covers all U.S. and Canadian models	
Datsun/Nissan Pick-Ups 1970-84	6816
Covers all U.S and Canadian models	
Datsun/Nissan Z & ZX 1970-86	6932
Covers all U.S. and Canadian models	
Datsun/Nissan 1200, 210, Sentra 1973-86	7197
Covers all U.S. and Canadian models	
Datsun/Nissan 200SX, 510, 610, 710, 810, Maxima 1973-84	7170
Covers all U.S. and Canadian models	
Dodge 1968-77	6554
Covers all U.S. and Canadian models	
Dodge Charger 1967-70	6486
Covers all U.S. and Canadian models	
Dodge/Plymouth Trucks 1967-84	7459
Covers all 1/2, 3/4, and 1 ton 2- and 4-wheel drive U.S. and Canadian models, including diesel engines	
Dodge/Plymouth Vans 1967-84	6934
Covers all 1/2, 3/4, and 1 ton U.S. and Canadian models of vans, cutaways and motor home chassis	
D-50/Arrow Pick-Up 1979-81	7032
Covers all U.S. and Canadian models	
Fairlane/Torino 1962-75	6320
Covers all U.S. and Canadian models	
Fairmont/Zephyr 1978-83	6965
Covers all U.S. and Canadian models	
Fiat 1969-81	7042
Covers all U.S. and Canadian models	
Fiesta 1978-80	6846
Covers all U.S. and Canadian models	
Firebird 1967-81	5996
Covers all U.S. and Canadian models	
Firebird 1982-85	7345
Covers all U.S. and Canadian models	
Ford 1968-79 Spanish	7084
Ford Bronco 1966-83	7140
Covers all U.S. and Canadian models	
Ford Bronco II 1984	7408
Covers all U.S. and Canadian models	
Ford Courier 1972-82	6983
Covers all U.S. and Canadian models	
Ford/Mercury Front Wheel Drive 1981-85	7055
Covers all U.S. and Canadian models Escort, EXP, Tempo, Lynx, LN-7 and Topaz	
Ford/Mercury/Lincoln 1968-85	6842
Covers all U.S. and Canadian models of FORD Country Sedan, Country Squire, Crown Victoria, Custom, Custom 500, Galaxie 500, LTD through 1982, Ranch Wagon, and XL; MERCURY Colony Park, Commuter, Marquis through 1982, Gran Marquis, Monterey and Park Lane; LINCOLN Continental and Towne Car	
Ford/Mercury/Lincoln Mid-Size 1971-85	6696
Covers all U.S. and Canadian models of FORD Elite, 1983-85 LTD, 1977-79 LTD II, Ranchero, Torino, Gran Torino, 1977-85 Thunderbird; MERCURY 1972-85 Cougar,	

continued on next page

RTUG Title	Part No.	RTUG Title	Part No.
1983-85 Marquis, Montego, 1980-85 XR-7; LINCOLN 1982-85 Continental, 1984-85 Mark VII, 1978-80 Versailles		Mercedes-Benz 1974-84 Covers all U.S. and Canadian models	6809
Ford Pick-Ups 1965-86 Covers all ½, ¾ and 1 ton, 2- and 4-wheel drive U.S. and Canadian pick-up, chassis cab and camper models, including diesel engines	6913	**Mitsubishi, Cordia, Tredia, Starion, Galant 1983-85** Covers all U.S. and Canadian models **MG 1961-81** Covers all U.S. and Canadian models	7583 6780
Ford Pick-Ups 1965-82 Spanish	7469	**Mustang/Capri/Merkur 1979-85** Covers all U.S. and Canadian models	6963
Ford Ranger 1983-84 Covers all U.S. and Canadian models	7338	**Mustang/Cougar 1965-73** Covers all U.S. and Canadian models	6542
Ford Vans 1961-86 Covers all U.S. and Canadian ½, ¾ and 1 ton van and cutaway chassis models, including diesel engines	6849	**Mustang II 1974-78** Covers all U.S. and Canadian models	6812
GM A-Body 1982-85 Covers all front wheel drive U.S. and Canadian models of BUICK Century, CHEVROLET Celebrity, OLDSMOBILE Cutlass Ciera and PONTIAC 6000	7309	**Omni/Horizon/Rampage 1978-84** Covers all U.S. and Canadian models of DODGE omni, Miser, 024, Charger 2.2; PLYMOUTH Horizon, Miser, TC3, TC3 Tourismo; Rampage	6845
GM C-Body 1985 Covers all front wheel drive U.S. and Canadian models of BUICK Electra Park Avenue and Electra T-Type, CADILLAC Fleetwood and deVille, OLDSMOBILE 98 Regency and Regency Brougham	7587	**Opel 1971-75** Covers all U.S. and Canadian models **Peugeot 1970-74** Covers all U.S. and Canadian models **Pinto/Bobcat 1971-80** Covers all U.S. and Canadian models	6575 5982 7027
GM J-Car 1982-85 Covers all U.S. and Canadian models of BUICK Skyhawk, CHEVROLET Cavalier, CADILLAC Cimarron, OLDSMOBILE Firenza and PONTIAC 2000 and Sunbird	7059	**Plymouth 1968-76** Covers all U.S. and Canadian models **Pontiac Fiero 1984-85** Covers all U.S. and Canadian models	6552 7571
GM N-Body 1985-86 Covers all U.S. and Canadian models of front wheel drive BUICK Somerset and Skylark, OLDSMOBILE Calais, and PONTIAC Grand Am	7657	**Pontiac Mid-Size 1974-83** Covers all U.S. and Canadian models of Ventura, Grand Am, LeMans, Grand LeMans, GTO, Phoenix, and Grand Prix	7346
GM X-Body 1980-85 Covers all U.S. and Canadian models of BUICK Skylark, CHEVROLET Citation, OLDSMOBILE Omega and PONTIAC Phoenix	7049	**Porsche 924/928 1976-81** Covers all U.S. and Canadian models **Renault 1975-85** Covers all U.S. and Canadian models	7048 7165
GM Subcompact 1971-80 Covers all U.S. and Canadian models of BUICK Skyhawk (1975-80), CHEVROLET Vega and Monza, OLDSMOBILE Starfire, and PONTIAC Astre and 1975-80 Sunbird	6935	**Roadrunner/Satellite/Belvedere/GTX 1968-73** Covers all U.S. and Canadian models **RX-7 1979-81** Covers all U.S. and Canadian models **SAAB 99 1969-75** Covers all U.S. and Canadian models	5821 7031 5988
Granada/Monarch 1975-82 Covers all U.S. and Canadian models	6937	**SAAB 900 1979-85** Covers all U.S. and Canadian models	7572
Honda 1973-84 Covers all U.S. and Canadian models	6980	**Snowmobiles 1976-80** Covers Arctic Cat, John Deere, Kawasaki, Polaris, Ski-Doo and Yamaha	6978
International Scout 1967-73 Covers all U.S. and Canadian models	5912	**Subaru 1970-84** Covers all U.S. and Canadian models	6982
Jeep 1945-87 Covers all U.S. and Canadian CJ-2A, CJ-3A, CJ-3B, CJ-5, CJ-6, CJ-7, Scrambler and Wrangler models	6817	**Tempest/GTO/LeMans 1968-73** Covers all U.S. and Canadian models **Toyota 1966-70** Covers all U.S. and Canadian models of Corona, MkII, Corolla, Crown, Land Cruiser, Stout and Hi-Lux	5905 5795
Jeep Wagoneer, Commando, Cherokee, Truck 1957-86 Covers all U.S. and Canadian models of Wagoneer, Cherokee, Grand Wagoneer, Jeepster, Jeepster Commando, J-100, J-200, J-300, J-10, J20, FC-150 and FC-170	6739	**Toyota 1970-79 Spanish**	7467
		Toyota Celica/Supra 1971-85 Covers all U.S. and Canadian models	7043
Laser/Daytona 1984-85 Covers all U.S. and Canadian models	7563	**Toyota Trucks 1970-85** Covers all U.S. and Canadian models of pick-ups, Land Cruiser and 4Runner	7035
Maverick/Comet 1970-77 Covers all U.S. and Canadian models	6634	**Valiant/Duster 1968-76** Covers all U.S. and Canadian models	6326
Mazda 1971-84 Covers all U.S. and Canadian models of RX-2, RX-3, RX-4, 808, 1300, 1600, Cosmo, GLC and 626	6981	**Volvo 1956-69** Covers all U.S. and Canadian models **Volvo 1970-83** Covers all U.S. and Canadian models	6529 7040
Mazda Pick-Ups 1972-86 Covers all U.S. and Canadian models	7659	**VW Front Wheel Drive 1974-85** Covers all U.S. and Canadian models	6962
Mercedes-Benz 1959-70 Covers all U.S. and Canadian models	6065	**VW 1949-71** Covers all U.S. and Canadian models	5796
Mereceds-Benz 1968-73 Covers all U.S. and Canadian models	5907	**VW 1970-79 Spanish** **VW 1970-81** Covers all U.S. and Canadian Beetles, Karmann Ghia, Fastback, Squareback, Vans, 411 and 412	7081 6837

Chilton's Repair & Tune-Up Guides are available at your local retailer or by mailing a check or money order for **$13.95** plus **$3.25** to cover postage and handling to:

Chilton Book Company
Dept. DM
Radnor, PA 19089

NOTE: When ordering be sure to include your name & address, book part No. & title.